Exceptional Language
and Linguistics

This is a volume in

PERSPECTIVES IN
NEUROLINGUISTICS, NEUROPSYCHOLOGY, AND PSYCHO-
  LINGUISTICS

A Series of Monographs and Treatises

A complete list of titles in this series appears at the end of this volume.

Exceptional Language and Linguistics

Edited by

Loraine K. Obler
Lise Menn

Department of Neurology
Boston Veterans Administration Medical Center
and
Aphasia Research Center
Boston University School of Medicine
Boston, Massachusetts

1982

ACADEMIC PRESS

A Subsidiary of Harcourt Brace Jovanovich, Publishers

New York   London
Paris   San Diego   San Francisco   São Paulo   Sydney   Tokyo   Toronto

The extract on page 143 is a quotation from Geoffrey Hill's
"History as Poetry" from *King Log*, copyright 1968 by Geoffrey
Hill and *Somewhere Is Such A Kingdom*, copyright 1975 by
Geoffrey Hill, and is reprinted by permission of Andre Deutsch
Limited and the Houghton Mifflin Company.

The extract on page 145 is a quotation from Wallace Stevens's
"Notes Toward a Supreme Fiction" from *The Collected Poems
of Wallace Stevens* copyright 1954 by Wallace Stevens and
The Palm at the End of the Mind, copyright 1967, 1969, 1971
by Holly Stevens and is used by permission of Alfred A. Knopf, Inc.

ACADEMIC PRESS, INC.
111 Fifth Avenue, New York, New York 10003

United Kingdom Edition published by
ACADEMIC PRESS, INC. (LONDON) LTD.
24/28 Oval Road, London NW1 7DX

Library of Congress Cataloging in Publication Data
Main entry under title:

Exceptional language and linguistics.

(Perspectives in neurolinguistics, neuropsychology,
and psycholinguistics)
Includes bibliographies and index.
1. Linguistics. 2. Psycholinguistics. I. Obler,
Loraine K. II. Menn, Lise. III. Series.
P123.E95   401   82-6815
ISBN 0-12-523680-8   AACR2

PRINTED IN THE UNITED STATES OF AMERICA

82 83 84 85   9 8 7 6 5 4 3 2 1

To Margaret S. Fearey
and my other exceptional friends

LKO

And to mine:
Ronnie B. Wilbur and Christine Tanz

LM

Contents

Part II

Part III

16 Formulas in First and Second Language Acquisition   261

MARILYN MAY VIHMAN

17 Developmental Dissociation of Language and Cognition   285

SUSAN CURTISS

18 Signed Language and Linguistic Theory   313

PATRICIA SIPLE

19 The Parsimonious Bilingual   339

LORAINE K. OBLER

20 Converging Evidence for Linguistic Theory from the Study of Aphasia and Child Language   347

JEAN BERKO GLEASON

Contributors

Numbers in parentheses indicate the pages on which the authors' contributions begin.

DEREK BICKERTON (15), Department of Linguistics, University of Hawaii at Manoa, Honolulu, Hawaii 96822

SHEILA E. BLUMSTEIN (203), Department of Linguistics, Brown University, Providence, Rhode Island 02912

VEDA R. CHARROW (81), Document Design Center, American Institute for Research, Washington, D.C. 20007

EDNA AMIR COFFIN (103), Near East Department, University of Michigan, Ann Arbor, Michigan 48104

SUSAN CURTISS (285), Department of Linguistics, University of California, Los Angeles, Los Angeles, California 90024

NANCY C. DORIAN (31), Department of German, Bryn Mawr College, Bryn Mawr, Pennsylvania 19010

CHARLES A. FERGUSON (49), Department of Linguistics, Stanford University, Stanford, California 94305

JEAN BERKO GLEASON (347), Department of Psychology, Boston University, Boston, Massachusetts 02215

GALIT HASAN-ROKEM (169), Department of Hebrew Literature, Hebrew University, Jerusalem, Israel

ROBERT K. HERBERT (217), Linguistics Program, State University of New York at Binghamton, Binghamton, New York 13901

ADRIENNE LEHRER (67), Department of Linguistics, University of Arizona, Tucson, Arizona 85721

LISE MENN (3, 247), Department of Neurology, Boston Veterans Administration Medical Center, and Aphasia Research Center, Boston University School of Medicine, Boston, Massachusetts 02130

M. P. O'CONNOR (143), Ann Arbor, Michigan 48104

LORAINE K. OBLER (3, 339), Department of Neurology, Boston Veterans Administration Medical Center, and Aphasia Research Center, Boston University School of Medicine, Boston, Massachusetts 02130

STEFANIE SHATTUCK-HUFNAGEL (133), Research Laboratory of Electronics, Massachusetts Institute of Technology, Cambridge, Massachusetts 02139

JOEL SHERZER (175), Department of Anthropology, University of Texas at Austin, Austin, Texas 78712

PATRICIA SIPLE (313), Department of Psychology, Wayne State University, Detroit, Michigan 48202

MARILYN MAY VIHMAN (261), Department of Linguistics, Stanford University, Stanford, California 94305

KAREN Z. WALTENSPERGER (217), Southwest Detroit, Community Mental Health Service, Inc., Detroit, Michigan 48216

ARNOLD M. ZWICKY (115), Department of Linguistics, Ohio State University, Columbus, Ohio 43210

Preface

Linguists working with aphasic patients have long assumed that the study of language disturbance contributes to linguistic theory. Likewise, linguists concerned with children's acquisition of first, and more recently, second languages take it for granted that a proper theory of synchronic linguistics must account for the development of language over time in the child (as well as in the history of the language). Similar assertions can be defended for any of the numerous fields where speaker-hearers are not "ideal" monolingual adults: Study focused on how their data differ from those we consider "normal" will illuminate linguistic theory.

In some instances—with children or aphasics or speakers of pidgins, for example—it is the putative simplicity of the speech which makes it seem likely to reveal linguistic truths. In other instances—in literary or ritual languages or speech addressed to foreigners—it is special conditions for using language which are presumed to highlight linguistic facts. Special events in the course of the speech of normal adults such as speech errors or malapropisms are also considered valuable sources for betraying linguistic regularities. Likewise, special events in the course of a language, such as its birth from a creole or its death through diminution of the native-speaker population are assumed to give us insight into the complexities of language structures and processes in the ideal speaker-hearer.

Yet what often happens to those of us who choose to work in the peripheral fields, the ones we term *exceptional* as opposed to *core*, is that for a variety of reasons we are concerned with issues quite distinct from those of core theory. C. J. Bailey (1981) likens static-discrete grammarians "to color-blind individuals who cannot understand the joys of color." Those who are used to seeing the world in color (developmentalists in Bailey's argument, more generally students of exceptional language data in ours) "could never be convinced of the advantages of going back to the black-and-white world of the other; for that would be a retrograde step from the point of view of both the pleasure and the validity of doing linguistics." So in the symposium that gave rise to this book, the mandate to contributors was to examine the claim that work in their field offered insights useful or crucial to linguistic theory and to document how this work did and could enhance linguistic theory.

At the Winter LSA meeting in 1980 we were able to cover only six exceptional subfields: aphasic language, language in senile dementia, child acquisition of phonology, language death, second language acquisition, and pidgins and creoles. In this volume we have expanded our collection to cover more areas of exceptional language study. As the book has taken shape we have realized that the exceptional fields we study cluster according to the criteria which make them exceptional. Thus we have represented *language in special populations* such as aphasics (Blumstein), schizophrenics (Herbert and Waltensperger), language-advanced and language-delayed children (Curtiss), healthy children (Vihman, Menn), and bilinguals (Obler). We also have *language in special situations* such as rituals and language games (Scherzer), therapy and wine tasting (Lehrer), speaking to children or foreigners (Ferguson), learning a second language in childhood (Vihman), translation (Coffin), and bureaucratese and legalese (Redish). A third cluster of exceptional language data consists of observations on *language change*. Indeed, given the strong synchronic basis of current linguistic theory, even historical linguistics might be considered as "exceptional" with regard to synchronic "core" linguistics. In this book we have discussion of two critical periods in the course of language development: The language birth of pidgins (Bickerton) and language death (Dorian). *Deliberately creative language use* constitutes a fourth category, including literary language (O'Connor), proverbs (Hasan-Rokem), and language games (Sherzer). We also consider the *unintentional creativity* of normals' speech errors (Shattuck-Hufnagel) and of malapropisms (Zwicky). *Special language modalities* such as sign language (Siple) constitute the final category. Certain topics, of course, are susceptible to listing in more than one of our categories. Translation, for example, is not only language in a special situation; it also is practiced by a special population, and often demands creative language use. To represent the cross-fertilization of the exceptional fields we have Berko Gleason's article on convergence of evidence from aphasia and from child language.

As this book has evolved, we have observed that two sorts of demonstration have been prominent in discussing the relationship of exceptional language data to linguistic theory. In one, authors document the psychological reality of units or constructs already suggested by core theory. In the second, they argue for expansion of the realm of generalizations covered by theory in order to account for "deviant" yet systematic patterns of language behavior in the exceptional fields. In regrettably few instances have data from exceptional fields been invoked to discriminate or even motivate a choice between alternative theoretical systems. (Harry Whitaker, 1972, and Foss and Fay, 1979, are notable exceptions.) The reader will find that these issues comprise the bulk of topics covered by our authors in this book.

Questions also arose for us about the status of so-called performance data for linguistic theory, and, related to this, about the status of linguistics as a science and more specifically as an empirical science, topics referred to in the introductory chapter. Our focus, however, is not primarily on these issues, since we found that those of us already working in the exceptional fields take for granted the necessity of accounting for exceptional data within linguistic theory. Also unexplored at this stage, but worthy of at least another symposium, was the converse to the relationship we were exploring—namely, how our training in linguistic theory has informed our approach to data in the exceptional fields. Certainly outside the bounds of the task we set ourselves was the task of answering the question (which we recommend to psychologists and sociologists of science) of why certain of us get involved in exceptional linguistics while others of us turn to core questions. Also remaining for further study are the questions of how the methodologies suggested or demanded by working in exceptional fields influence the research questions we ask, the methodologies we employ, and the answers we get. So we see this book as an exploratory piece, bringing together a set of fields which share only the assumption that they *should* be pertinent to linguistic theory, and bringing together a set of authors who share a linguistic orientation to examine the ways in which their fields *are* pertinent to linguistic theory. We have learned a great deal from studying their papers, and we wish our readers the same pleasure.

Numerous people and institutions are to be thanked for their support in producing the book and the symposium which was its precursor. Jean Berko Gleason has been enthusiastically involved throughout the planning stages as well as in her capacity as discussant and contributor. Charles Ferguson is also to be thanked for his suggestions about topics and individuals to be included. We appreciate the support of the program committee of the Linguistics Society of America and Bernard Spolsky, in particular, and their suggestions for strengthening the program. Without the help of Margaret Reynolds of the Linguistics Society, the conference itself could not have been so smoothly carried off. William Labov, James McCawley, and Gillian Sankoff are to be thanked for their contributions to that symposium. We express our gratitude to Paul Chapin and the National Science Foundation for support of the symposium and the production of this book which grew from it. And we acknowledge Victoria Fromkin's vital encouragement above and beyond her role as symposium discussant. We consider ourselves most fortunate in Harry Whitaker's early encouragement to realize *Exceptional Language and Linguistics* as a book. Marj Nicolas's assistance in the final stages of production has been most valuable.

References

Bailey, C.-J. (1981) Theory, description and differences among linguists (or what keeps linguistics from becoming a science?). *Language and communication, 1981, 1,* 39–66.

Foss, D. & Fay, D. (1979) Linguistic theory and performance models. In D. Cohen & J. Wirth, (Eds.), *Testing linguistic hypotheses.* New York: Halsted Press (John Wiley). Pp. 65–89.

Whitaker, Harry (1972) Unsolicited nominalizations by aphasics: The plausibility of the lexicalist model. *Linguistics, 78,* 62–71.

Part I

1

LISE MENN

LORAINE K. OBLER

Exceptional Language Data as Linguistic Evidence: An Introduction

Scientists studying planets to learn about Earth
Newsweek, Sept. 10, 1979

We see three general reasons for linguistic theory to pay attention to exceptional types of language or language use. Each chapter of this book presents explicit or implicit instances of those reasons, which we will label (*a*) grounding explanations (*b*) testing connections (*c*) highlighting. These terms are short for the following respective considerations:

1) Explanation of linguistic phenomena must ultimately lie outside linguistics. We look especially to neurolinguistics (via psycholinguistics) to account for what messages and codes the mind can deal with, and to social communication studies to account for the messages which we need to send and receive. Similar dependencies are found in all the biological sciences; for example, the eventual explanation of genetic phenomena lies in the substratum of molecular biology on the one hand, and in the ecology of replication and survival on the other.

2) Separating the essential properties of language from those which are matters of historical accident cannot be carried out by examining language as a static system. Only by observing how parts of a language cohere as perturbations are introduced—say by language contact, artificial experiment, or accident to the brain—can we tell whether apparent linkages are real; we may also discover links which were not previously apparent. As Kiparsky (1973) put it, "Changes in phonological systems may reveal ordinarily hidden structure, as a tiger lurking on the edge of a jungle, his stripes blending in with the background, becomes visible the moment he begins to move [cited in Bailey 1981, p. 49]."

3

3) Language in exceptional settings may display particular aspects more prominently; once they have been studied in these cases, they can be traced back into the language of ordinary speaker–hearers. Exceptional language studies frequently use this third reason as their claim to theoretical relevance, and some very interesting phenomena in this volume are best discussed under this rubric. However, the "tracing back" process is not always easy to carry out properly. Our final concern in this chapter will be to remind the reader of some problems with the validity of certain claims about linguistic theory that have been based on observations in exceptional areas.

Let us consider each of these topics in some detail.

Grounding Explanations

An extended family of linguists is familiar with a parable about "explanation," the story (said to be about the philosopher William James) with which J.R. Ross started off his dissertation. In the story, a naive character remarks to James that the world rests on a huge turtle; when he asks her what that turtle stands on, she replies that "it's turtles all the way down!"

In linguistics, there are two senses of the word "explanation" which are used and quarrelled over; one of the most delicious of the polemic pieces is Givón 1979. In one sense, we "explain" a fact of language by showing that it fits in with a more general class of linguistic phenomena: New verbs are coined with a certain ending "because" that is the productive one; relativization of a certain noun in a certain sentence is not possible "because" it is dominated by an S-node. But as Givón points out, such explanations are very limited. They are essentially just generalizations, and they can be seen as no more than economical restatements of the phenomena observed. This becomes apparent when we ask "How do you know that this is a productive verb ending?" Answer: "Because new verbs are formed with it." "How do you know that an S-node dominates this noun?" Answer: "Because in this construction and in a set of similar constructions, certain movement rules and/or deletion rules do not produce grammatical sentences."

What one eventually wants, however, is to determine why these generalizations are true and others are not. Why are there only a few productive verb-making endings in languages which may have many unproductive ones? Why should there be something like an A-over-A principle?

In short, we want to get to the next turtle down—to be able to say that a particular structure results from the nature of the human signal processor, the message content, and the channels available. This goal has been formulated in various programmatic statements about linguistics, but it is not uniformly espoused. It has remained a popular goal only in one area, articulatory–acoustic phonetics. There, we can use physics to deal with reasonable models of the resonances of the vocal tract, and to some extent with vocal fold vibrations; cineradiography and other techniques give information about the articulatory configuration.

But no other link in the 'speech chain' is so observable. In syntax and semantics, lack of sufficient information about the brain's resources and mechanisms and about the speaker's communicative goals has virtually forced us to abandon this level of explanation. Early attempts have proven premature, as Bailey (1981) points out, and the intermediate goal of simulation of human performance has been substituted by some recent researchers.

Performance simulation is certainly an important avenue of approach, but it cannot get us off the present turtle. To do that, we still need experimental and observational psycho- and neurolinguistics, as the chapters by Shattuck-Hufnagel and Blumstein (this volume) indicate. Work by Whitaker (1970) and his students Buckingham (1978) and Schnitzer (1975) and by Caplan (1980), and Zurif and Caramazza (1976), to list a few examples, also promises advances in this direction. The study of simplified and other special registers should be helpful in moving in the other explanatory direction, the "ecological" consideration of communicative needs. For example, it is suggested that certain linguistic devices, such as the contrastive structure of phonemic oppositions, the postponement of heavy noun phrases until the end of a sentence, or the placement of bound morphemes in highly constrained orders, facilitate the decoding of a message. Such devices should then be exaggerated in some settings where the hearer has decoding problems, and be relaxed in some cases when the hearer's burden is light.

We argue, then, that the study of exceptional speakers and language under exceptional conditions is essential to constructing the notions we will need to explain linguistic phenomena in terms of the nature of the speaker and the speaker's goals.

Testing Connections: Essence and Accident

Linguistic theory traditionally attempts to determine which of the patterns that appear in languages are "real" and which are "accidental." The search for language universals is one approach to this problem, but it has inherent limitations. The most serious of them is the fact that a correlation between two phenomena can do no more than suggest a linkage. It tells nothing about which causes the other, or whether a third factor causes both. Historical linguistics offers one approach to the question of which linguistic phenomena are causally connected and which merely co-occur, but exceptional language studies are also rich sources of such information, and many of them have already been recognized as such (Slobin 1977).

In order to test the notion that a configuration of phenomena is not a mere accident, one must perturb it in some way (or look for a naturally occurring perturbation), and then see how the ripples propagate. The classic experiment of this type in morphophonology was Berko's (1958) introduction of nonsense words and her observation of how children used them when derivational and inflectional affixes were called for; the corresponding "experiment of nature" occurs when a loanword is brought into a language, or when a poet like Lewis Carroll creates *Jabberwocky*.

Indeed, hypotheses in any science can be cast in terms of connections or interactions among observed phenomena. The hypothesis that children learn to use inflectional morphemes productively is a claim that a particular connection exists between all the instances of a morpheme. The claim that sound-symbolism plays a role in the meanings of deictic words (Cooper & Ross 1975, Tanz 1971) is obviously a claim that certain aspects of sound and meaning are connected. The claim that output constraints should be represented in a model of a speaker's knowledge can be restated as a claim that resemblance between the outputs of different derivations are not accidental (Kisseberth 1970; Menn this volume). Martinet's hypotheses that sound-shifts form 'push-chains' or 'drag-chains' are again transparently claims about connections.

This list could be extended indefinitely. One would ideally hope to find, for each case, some artificial or natural perturbation experiment that would support the claimed connection. Unfortunately, the perfect experiment can seldom be devised or found. While efforts to work in this direction are very important, it seems equally productive to take natural experiments in which the speaker or hearer's resources have been impaired, enhanced, or skewed, and search for issues which they might illuminate. In this sense, we may consider the fields of experimental psycholinguistics and exceptional language study as complementary. In exceptional psycholinguistics one starts from a question and devises an experiment to answer it, while in the study of exceptional language, one starts with a natural experiment, and, by working out its correct characterization, deduces the questions as well as the answers. (Note that this conception of "natural experiment" is broad enough to include the artifice, deliberate or unconscious, of poets and other players of language games.)

Highlighting Particular Aspects of Linguistic Structure

In many exceptional settings, particular aspects of language become more apparent. For example, the relaxation of time constraints for composition and comprehension in written language allows the transmission of exceptionally complex messages; in these, we can see an enhancement of some of the parallel, allusive channels available to speakers and hearers—channels whose messages qualify and give context to the denotative, core "meaning" of its words. The notion of parallel channel is also applicable to delivery (e.g., sarcasm), levels of diction, and choices of metaphor that project a particular subculture (e.g., class, ethnos, profession, or sexual orientation).

Numerous other examples of highlighting can be found in this book. The fact that writers get less feedback than speakers about the incomprehensibility of their utterances permits the linguist to see the ways in which the sentence construction mechanism can run on, producing the multiply ambiguous and even undecodable sentences of bureaucratese (Charrow this volume).

Again, the study of critical communication, as Lehrer indicates (this volume), leads us back to two aspects of "core" language: the making of names, and the study of ordinary discourse in which nonconventionalized meaning travels along with the conventional, thereby eluding word-based semantics.

Ferguson's chapter points out that "marginal" phones (such as the glottal stop in English), are highlighted in special registers, specifically in talk to babies. Once they have been brought so sharply to our attention, we are obliged to extend phonological theory to deal with them. This extension will also connect with the phonology of language games and poetics, for Sherzer (this volume) and O'Connor (this volume) both note that creative resources are restricted to the use of phonological patterns which are distinct from the meaning-encoding repertoire of the language.

Formulaic aspects of language, overlaid in sentence-based grammar, are revealed under a suggestive variety of exceptional circumstances. In language acquisition—most especially in "natural" (immersion) second language acquisition by younger children; in rituals of law and religion, in the speech of aphasic and dementing patients, and in traditional oral literature. The existence of formulaic utterances highlighted in these fields of exceptional language reminds us that linguistic theory must deal with language as a continuum from the most creative to the most stereotypic communication.

The field of natural experiments which stand to highlight linguistic essence is not exhausted in this book. Among the variations which have been partially explored elsewhere, we may list:

1. Language acquisition in hearing children of deaf parents— imperfect information about the target language, impoverished grammar input (Sachs *et al.* 1981).
2. Oral traditional literature—competing cognitive load on the speaker, listeners with much shared experience (Lord 1965).
3. Language in dementing patients—speaker–hearers with limited cognitive resources (Obler forthcoming).
4. Language of conference participants—heavy competing cognitive load (Maclay & Osgood 1959).
5. Language in theatre, including puppetry—conversation honed to an artistic edge (Proschan 1980).
6. Language marking of real or assumed sexual, ethnic, professional, age cohort, or other social identity (Labov 1972).
7. Language to computers—as hearers with highly constrained, rule-governed, and limited auditory and cognitive resources (Lea, Ed. 1980).

Caution: The Art of Reasoning from Exceptional Language Data

Since we are advocating the use of data from exceptional language as a tool for linguistic theory, we must, in conscience, point out that it is a slippery tool. Some types of flawed arguments are especially frequent in the study of exceptional linguistics—indeed, we as well as others have occasionally been guilty of these errors and may very well stumble into them again.

The first type of flaw arises from the assumption that similar units of analysis are appropriate for all areas of linguistics. This is not true in general, and the applicability of analytic units or other concepts must be treated as a hypothesis to be demonstrated in each area. Indeed, it is precisely by observing how traditional units of analysis may fail to be appropriate for the exceptional fields that we should be able to advance linguistic theory.

In cross-linguistic studies, this problem already occurs to some extent; consider the debates on the universality of units like Verb Phrase or the comparability of "case endings" in agglutinative versus inflectional languages. But the difficulty seems to be intensified in exceptional language areas: the usual notions of "phoneme," for example, are inadequate to handle some phenomena of early child phonology (Menn in press), Obler's paper in this volume suggests that these notions do not fit the bilingual's phonological structure either, and description of aphasic segmental errors in terms of any school's categories of phonemic versus phonetic is also very difficult.

To take another example, the notion of "rule" in child phonology is known to be rather more like the notion in historical linguistics—a relation between surface forms—than it is like the generative notion of rule, in spite of shared notations. On the other hand, rules written for children's syntax are conceptually like rules in generative grammar. Yet perhaps they ought not to be, given the heavy formulaic component of children's output; consider the evidence for children "performing without competence" in various constructions (see Berko Gleason's chapter this volume).

The possible nonequivalence of similarly named notions is especially treacherous when we try to strengthen linguistic arguments by what is often called "triangulation": calling on data from several different areas to support an argument (e.g., Jakobson 1941, Carroll 1972). This can be a very valuable way of avoiding the errors likely to arise from relying on any single method of investigation, but great care is required in making sure that the same phenomenon is really what is under discussion in each of the areas. To pick perhaps the most famous example, Jakobson (1941) assumed that the presence or absence of phonemic contrasts in child language, aphasic language, and "normal" adult language were comparable phenomena. However, as we claimed earlier in this section, this is not the case. Many similar examples of non-comparability are examined in Caramazza and Zurif's (1978) collection of papers, *Language Acquisition and Language Breakdown: Parallels and Divergencies.*

The second type of flaw appears all too frequently in arguments for the "psychological reality" of one or another linguistic construct. It consists of the assumption that if a certain construct has been employed in the description of a phenomenon of exceptional language, then that construct has psychological reality. Let us consider a hypothetical argument, from the field of language breakdown, where the literature contains valid as well as fallacious arguments for "psychological reality."

With a little effort, one can employ a large number of linguistic concepts in describing the anomalous character of a single sentence used by a dementing patient in recounting a familiar story: "The wolf took a liking to Red Riding Hood's basket."

There is a peculiar lexical selection here. The patient, we might guess, failed to retrieve a lexical item or phrase appropriate to interest in inanimate objects, such as *be attracted to* or *want*, and could only find *take a liking to*, from the same semantic field. We therefore might argue that the odd word choice supports the reality of the notion of semantic field. Also, *take a liking to* might be considered wrong because the register is slightly inappropriate for story telling, thus providing putative evidence for discourse analysis and register. Since the error involves the breaking of the lexical cooccurrence constraint that *take a liking to* requires an animate object, we might say that semantic features, animateness in particular, and lexical cooccurrence constraints are validated as psychologically real by the fact that this sentence was produced. Moreover, the fact that the error *take a liking to* occurred in the middle of the sentence might be taken to support yet other theoretical notions, namely, 'lexical insertion,' 'target meaning,' and 'syntactic frame,' since one way to describe the commission of this error would be to say that the patient made a mistake in lexical selection after the target meaning had been generated and the syntactic frame had been generated. Which, if any, of these inferences is justified? They all begin to look suspect when they are lined up side by side!

The question has two kinds of answers. Let us consider the patient's utterance again. To begin with, it has two important properties:

1. It is anomalous.
2. It was really spoken by a patient with a degenerative brain disease who probably did not intend it to be anomalous.

Now, we know that all of the hypothetical linguistic constructs listed—semantic fields, animacy, register, etc.,—are of value in explaining what is anomalous about the sentence. In this sense, the fact that we judge the sentence anomalous supports the "reality" of the concepts.

But that also would have been the case if the sentence were merely a starred example created by a linguist. What additional evidential weight does this sentence gain from having been spoken by a dementing patient? Some reflection is required to answer this question. Consider: we are looking for evidence that the speaker or hearer is using some computational entity which corresponds well to a linguistic notion. In the present case of *take a liking to,* the patient's choice was neither correct nor random. Instead, some sense of semantic nearness seems to have constrained his response. From this example and others like it, we obtain evidence for what the psychological measures of semantic distance might be, and we hope eventually to judge whether semantic fields, semantic features, prototypicality structures, or some other construct gives the best fit to this kind of performance.

Note that if the speaker had not made a semantic error, we would have been given no opportunity to look for evidence of semantic structure. From a correct performance, we learn nothing that description of normals has not already given us, and from absence of response or error along some other dimension we learn nothing about semantics. The crucial cases for the study of any linguistic structure are those in which an error of substitution has been made, and in which that substitution appears to have been constrained by that linguistic structure.

This is not to say that such structures are necessarily used in sentence formulation by intact speakers—they may have other routes to speech production—but it is to say that such information is or can be made available to the speaker. (We do make the assumption that brain damage does not enhance one's language knowledge. There is a possibility that the brain-damaged speaker may find novel channels of access to information. If this turns out to be true, it will require eventual modification of this assumption.)

So far, then, we have argued that the psychological reality of a notion is supported if a speaker commits an error and yet appears to be obeying the constraints specified by that notion. On the other hand, if the constraints associated with some linguistic notion are violated, we cannot draw any conclusion about the reality of those violated constraints. In the present case, the patient could have violated the animacy and co-occurrence constraints either because their presumed psychological counterparts have been impaired, or because those counterparts never existed in the first place. To establish psychological reality for, say, animacy, we need to look for other exceptional speakers (among whom we include normals making slips of the tongue or perturbed by psycholinguistic experiments) who happen to show performance errors of the relevant kind—in this case, errors constrained by animacy in some way.

One more kind of information is available, however, from the present patient's behavior. His disregard of register and co-occurrence in the face of preservation of semantic field, gender, number, and syntax suggests that the latter several constructs are independent of the first two.

The reasoning here is, as we have indicated, applicable to all fields in which some deficit with respect to normal abilities may be assumed. The instructive cases are neither those in which a patient performs normally nor those in which he or she is unable to perform at all, but rather those in which some partial performance is evident. Patterns of partial preservation provide additional psychological evidence for the constructs that appear to be preserved and for the separation of those respected from those violated. But we learn nothing about the internal structures of areas which are wholly preserved or wholly destroyed (see also Wilbur 1980).

Similar reasoning can be applied to areas of increased language facility, especially to cases of the intentional manipulation of language by the poet, the translator, the propagandist–advertiser, the actor, or the player of language games. These activities, although carried on as metalinguistic and optional performances, are no less valuable as experiments of nature. The observing linguist must now ask: What is the speaker or writer capable of manipulating? To what manipulations can the hearer respond, and what sorts of responses are they? We maintain that in these fields, exaggerations of certain linguistic phenomena serve much the same function as selective deficits do in the study of brain-damaged patients.

In summary, then: Exceptional language offers rich matter for linguistic theory. We have argued, first, that it provides needed links to study of the brain and of social communication—the fields from which explanations of the form of language must ultimately come. Second, the diverse exceptional circumstances represent experiments of nature, which allow us to see how linguistic phenomena are linked into functioning systems. And third, under these circumstances particular properties of language may be highlighted. Exceptional language use, as compared with the idealized core use, typically involves "performance" differences, but these performances are of theoretical interest whenever they are sensitive to linguistically-defined categories. However, data from exceptional fields must be used with particular care, for some constructs do not map smoothly from the core to exceptional areas.

Finally, claims for "psychological reality" of linguistic constructs must be based on cases in which those constructs appear to constrain linguistic behavior which is nonetheless aberrant in some way. The mere fact that a term is useful in describing why we find an exceptional speaker's utterance strange gives it no more (and no less) validity than the fact of its being useful in describing why a hypothetical utterance is ungrammatical or unacceptable.

References

Bailey, C.J. (1981) Theory, description and differences among linguists (or what keeps linguistics from becoming a science). *Language and communication, 1,* 39–66.

Berko, J. (1958) The child's learning of English morphology. *Word 14,* 150–157. [Reprinted in A. Bar-Adon & W. Leopold (Eds.), *Child language: A book of readings.* Englewood Cliffs, N.J.: Prentice-Hall, 1971. Pp. 153–167.]

Buckingham, H.L. (1978) What aphasia tells us about normal language. Paper presented at winter LSA meeting, Boston.

Caplan, D. (1980) *Biological studies of mental processing.* Cambridge, Mass.: MIT Press.

Caramazza, A., & Zurif, E. (Eds.) (1978) *Language acquisition and language breakdown: Parallels and divergences.* Baltimore: Johns Hopkins University Press.

Carroll, J. (1972) Language acquisition, bilingualism, and language change. In S. Saporta (Ed.), *Psycholinguistics: A book of readings.* New York: Holt, Rinehart, and Winston. Pp. 744–752.

Cooper, W.E., & Ross, J.R. (1975) World order. In R.E. Grossman, San, J.L. and Vance, T.J. (Eds.), *Papers from the parasession on functionalism.* Chicago: Chicago Linguistic Society. Pp. 63–111.

Givón, T. (1979) *On understanding grammar.* New York: Academic Press.

Gleason, J.B. (this volume) Converging evidence for linguistic theory from the study of aphasia and child language.

Jakobson, R. (1968) *Child language, aphasia, and phonological universals.* Translated by A. Keiler. Mouton: The Hague. (originally published in 1941).

Kiparsky, P. (1973) Phonological representations I: How abstract is phonology? In O. Fujimura (Ed.), *Three dimensions of linguistic theory.* Tokyo: T.E.L. Company, Ltd., for Tokyo Institute of Advanced Studies of Language. Pp. 5–56.

Kisseberth, C.W. (1970) On the functional unity of phonological rules. *Linguistic inquiry, 1* 291–306.

Labov, W. (1972) *Sociolinguistic patterns.* Philadelphia: University of Pennsylvania Press.

Lea, W.A. (Ed.), (1980) *Trends in speech recognition.* Englewood Cliffs: Prentice Hall.

Lord, A.B. (1965) *The singer of tales.* New York: Atheneum.

Maclay, H. & Osgood, C.E. (1959) Hesitation phenomena in spontaneous English speech. *Word, 15* 19–44. [Reprinted in L.A. Jakobowits & M.S. Miron (Eds.) (1965) *Readings in the psychology of language.* Englewood Cliffs, N.J.: Prentice-Hall.]

Menn, L. (in press) Development of articulatory, phonetic, and phonological capabilities. In B. Butterworth (Ed.), *Language production,* Vol. II. London: Academic Press.

Obler, L., (forthcoming) Language and brain dysfunction in dementia. In S. Segalowitz (Ed.), *Language functions and brain organization.* New York: Academic Press.

Proschan, F. (1980) Of puppet voices and interlocutors: Exposing essences of puppetry and speech. *Sociolinguistic working paper number 79.* Southwest Educational Development Laboratory, Austin, Texas.

Ross, J.R. (1967) Constraints on variables in syntax. Unpublished doctoral dissertation, Massachusetts Institute of Technology, Cambridge, Massachusetts.

Sachs, J.S., Bard, B., & Johnson, M.L. (1981) Language learning with restricted input: Case studies of two hearing children of deaf parents. *Applied psycholinguistics, 2,* 33–54.

Slobin, D.I. (1977) Language change in childhood and history. In J. Macnamara (Ed.), *Language learning and thought.* New York: Academic Press. Pp. 185–214.

Schnitzer, M. (1975) Aphasiological evidence for five linguistic hypotheses. *Language, 50,* 300–315.

Tanz, C. (1971) Sound symbolism in words relating to proximity and distance. *Language and speech, 14,* 266–276.

Whitaker, H. (1970) Linguistic competence: Evidence from aphasia, *Glossa, 4,* 46–53.

Wilbur, R.B. (1980) Theoretical phonology and child phonology: Argumentation and implications. In D. Goyvaerts (Ed.), *Phonology in the 1980's.* Ghent: Story-Scientia.

Zurif, E., & Caramazza, A. (1976) Psycholinguistic structures in aphasia: Studies in syntax and semantics. In H. and H. Whitaker (Eds.), *Studies in neurolinguistics,* Vol. I. New York: Academic Press.

2 DEREK BICKERTON

Learning without Experience the Creole Way[1]

The problems which creole languages pose for general linguistics have not yet begun to be understood, let alone faced, and are yet further from being answered by the vast majority of linguists. I am not referring to issues such as the existence of "mixed languages," problems posed for *Stammbaum* theories, questions of "simplification" or other matters that have on occasion tempted core linguists to paddle in the seemingly pellucid yet treacherous waters of creole studies. A single quotation will be enough to show that the first sentence of this article is not an exaggeration.

Speaking of child language acquisition, Snow (1979) remarked that

> Chomsky's position regarding the unimportance of the linguistic input was unproven, since ALL CHILDREN, IN ADDITION TO POSSESSING AN INNATE LINGUISTIC ABILITY, ALSO RECEIVE A SIMPLIFIED, WELL-FORMED AND REDUNDANT CORPUS. . . . The prediction was made that children without access to such a simplified, redundant corpus would be unsuccessful or retarded in learning language. If such could be proven to be the case, then it could indeed be concluded that an innate, species-specific language component was relatively less important than Chomsky had hypothesized [p. 367, emphasis added].

Snow's statement epitomizes a trend in acquisition studies over the last fifteen years, in which an uncritical acceptance of Chomskyan innateness has given way to a profound suspicion of all proposals regard-

[1] The research on which this chapter is based was carried out under National Science Foundation Grants GS-39748 and SOC75-14481, for which grateful acknowledgment is hereby made.

ing innateness, a belief that prelinguistic communication and extralinguistic knowledge contribute massively to the learning of language, and a belief that language learning is "massively dependent" upon both linguistic and paralinguistic interaction between caretaker and child— "Mothers TEACH their children to speak," as Bruner (1979) puts it.

Unfortunately for the current paradigm in acquisition, and for orthodox generativists, the emphasized statement in the Snow quotation is, quite simply, false. It is not correct to assume that all children receive a simplified, well-formed, and redundant corpus. This statement, which most students of acquisition, and many general linguists, would today accept without question, cannot be true of at least two sets of human children, neither of which has been any the worse for the experience—quite the reverse. I refer to those children born in the generation(s) in which language first developed on earth, and those children who formed the first locally born generation in communities which spoke an early-stage pidgin language.

I shall not discuss the original development of human language here, although it is highly relevant to the creole situation. (Bickerton 1981 Chap. 4).[2] I shall discuss the achievements of children born at a time and in a place where no adequate language model existed, who could not have been taught by mother, since mother herself did not know the language that her children would acquire.

It may be objected that the situation I am talking about is extremely rare, that it can happen only once in the history of a language, and that in the history of most languages it never happens at all. I am prepared to concede that it may have happened no more than 15 or 20 times in the history of the world. Its frequency is of course quite irrelevant. If it had happened only once, that would be all the proof we would need that it could happen. The fact that it did happen, and presumably not as a result of some idiosyncracy of the group it happened in, suggests that the properties which enabled it to happen are general properties of the species which may make themselves known whenever the situation calls for them, and which indeed may play a crucial role in "normal" language acquisition.

Further, it may be objected that I have misrepresented the relationship between pidgins and creoles. While introductions to the field (e.g., Hall 1966; Todd 1974) claim that a creole "expands" the pidgin that

---

[2] This claim has been specifically denied by at least one writer (Sankoff 1979), according to whom the study of pidginization and creolization "has no bearing on the question of the origin of language as it first evolved as a human capacity two or three million years ago." Since no evidence whatsoever is advanced for this statement—it is presumably presumed to be self-evident—we can disregard it.

preceded it—although without speculating as to how such "expansion" might be achieved—recent empirical studies of Tok Pisin (the pidgin/ creole of New Guinea) by Sankoff and her associates (Sankoff & Brown 1976; Sankoff & Laberge 1974) have shown that, in the case of that language, most structural features were developed by adult, nonnative (i.e., pidgin) speakers, and that the recent appearance of native (creole) speakers was accompanied by little more than the few cosmetic changes required to facilitate discourse processes.

Unfortunately, many scholars (e.g., Clark & Clark 1977) have taken the Tok Pisin case as paradigmatic of the pidgin-to-creole transition. In fact, Tok Pisin existed as a pidgin, nonnative language for at least 80 years (from 1870 to 1950) and perhaps considerably longer, before it acquired native speakers, giving ample time for gradual stabilization and elaboration. However, extensive evidence, linguistic as well as historical, shows that creole languages from Surinam to Mauritius came into being within half a century or less (Chaudenson 1977; Rens 1953), whereas a reconstruction of the process from the outputs of living speakers (Bickerton 1977; Bickerton & Givón 1976; Bickerton & Odo 1976) shows that, in Hawaii, the transition from pidgin to creole was accomplished in a single generation. In none of these cases can there have been time for a stable, expanded contact language to come into being before the birth of a substantial body of native speakers. In any case, we have abundant empirical evidence that no stable, expanded contact language arose in Hawaii prior to creolization.

Many languages have been called creoles—even English—but I am concerned here only with a particular set of creole languages (although, hereafter, the term **creole** will be understood as applying to just that set). These languages arose when a tropical island or remote stretch of tropical littoral was colonized by Europeans and labor was brought in from a wide variety of language groups, either by force (as under slavery) or cajolement (under the indenture system). Perhaps a majority of such areas are found in and around the Caribbean, although they also exist off the African coast, in the Indian Ocean, and at one or two other sites, such as Hawaii. In these areas, speakers of the dominant (European) language were in a minority of as little as 10% or less, while the highly-stratified nature of these societies barred the access of the majority of the population to even the few native-speaker models that were available. As that majority might be split between a dozen, or even several dozen different language groups, some kind of impromptu mode of communication had to be devised, using mainly (though not exclusively) words from the dominant language which were common (or at least, equally foreign) to members of all groups.

No adequate record—in many cases, no record at all—has survived of any of these pre-creole pidgins, except in the case of Hawaii, where there still survived, at the beginning of the last decade, many veterans of the pidgin era. However, what little evidence is available suggests that such pidgins were probably no different from that of Hawaii.

Hawaiian Pidgin English was both highly restricted and highly variable. Variability is due in the main to heavy first-language influence on phonology, syntax, and lexicon, which create strikingly different versions of Hawaiian Pidgin English for different ethnic groups, as well as considerable variation in proficiency. However, for the most proficient of its speakers, Hawaiian Pidgin English still lacked many of the features which are found in all natural languages, such as sentential complements, relative clauses, movement rules, or a system of tense, aspect, and modality. Were speakers of Hawaiian Pidgin English equipped to provide a "simplified, well-formed, and redundant corpus" to their children? Simplified it may have been—oversimplified would be a better word. Redundant it most certainly was—pidgin speakers were used to having to say things two or three times over, in different ways, before they could make themselves properly understood. "Well-formed" it could not have been by the stretch of the most lenient imagination; the two largest immigrant groups, Japanese and Filipinos, could not even agree on word-order, with the former producing a majority of OV sentences, while the latter produced a considerable proportion of VS sentences (Bickerton & Givón 1976).

If language learning proceeded as the "motherese" experts assure us that it does, or even if a generativist LAD (Language Acquisition Device) formed hypotheses on the basis of its *faculté de language* and tested them against input data, then the first native generation would have either learned the native languages of their parents (which, in fact, most of them did not) or would simply have reproduced the chaotic and functionally inadequate pidgin of their parents, perhaps levelling some of its more striking inconsistencies. In fact, they produced a creole language, Hawaiian Creole English, which included a wide range of rules and features which Hawaiian Pidgin English lacked.

The fact that they produced a viable human language where none was previously present might appear striking enough, but this fact alone by no means exhausts the interest of their creation. The rules and features they created were strikingly similar to the rules and features created by other first creole generations in areas separated from them by centuries and thousands of miles—areas, too, where very different sets of languages were in contact (in Hawaii the major languages in contact were English, Hawaiian, Chinese, Japanese, Ilocano and Tagalog; in Surinam, English, Portuguese and Kwa and Northern Bantu languages;

in the Indian Ocean, French, Malagasy, Eastern Bantu and Indian languages). This fact renders it improbable that creole rules could have
somehow been derived, not from the pidgin, but directly from the substratum languages; indeed, Hawaiian Pidgin English shows far heavier
substratum influence than Hawaiian Creole English, and extensive research has indicated that none of the latter's innovations could plausibly
have been derived from features of the substratum languages, or from
English.

In order to show the nature of Hawaiian Creole English innovations, I
shall examine three of them, comparing the Hawaiian Pidgin English
input with the Hawaiian Creole English output, and then comparing
the latter with other creole languages. I shall discuss, first, the marking
of nonspecific reference in the article system; second, the creation of a
nonpunctual aspect marker from a locative verb; and third, the development of distinct complementizers for realized and nonrealized complements.

Articles were not unknown in Hawaiian Pidgin English, but their
distribution was random and quite unpredictable, varying markedly
from group to group. Many Japanese immigrants hardly used articles at
all; indefinites were even rarer than definites, and definites would only
occur, especially among the earlier arrivals, in about one out of ten
environments in which English would require them. Filipino immigrants, who also tended to underuse indefinites, overgeneralized the
definite article to include many cases which would not have been thus
marked in English—perhaps confusing it with some kind of topic
marker. It follows that, while many NP appear without an article, the
fact that a given NP lacks an article does not correlate with any particular
quality of that NP, which could be old or new information, specific or
nonspecific in reference, in or out of the scope of negation, etc.

In Hawaiian Creole English, the picture is entirely different. Definite
articles are allotted only to NPs of specific reference when the referent is
assumed to be known to the hearer, and indefinite NPs are allotted only
to NPs of specific reference when the referent is assumed to be unknown
to the hearer. However, all such cases are obligatorily marked with
either definite or indefinite. Zero is reserved for all nonspecifics,
whether they be generics:

(1)   *dag smat.*
        'The dog is smart.'
        (in answer to question, *Which is smarter, **the horse** or **the dog?**).

or NP in the scope of negation:

(2)   *poho ai neva bai **big wan.***
        'It's a pity I didn't buy a big one'.

or cases where the referent is hypothetical:

(3)   *hu go daun frs iz* **luza.**
        'The one who goes down first is the loser'.

or where the referent is an unspecified group of uncertain membership:

(4)   *as tu bin get had taim reizing* **dag.**
        'The two of us used to have a hard time raising dogs'.

While any of the italicized NPs might have occurred with zero article in Hawaiian Pidgin English, it is equally true to say that any of them might have occurred WITH an article, whereas zero would certainly not have been restricted to the types of environment illustrated. But if the rule allotting zero only to nonspecific NPs could not have been learned from Hawaiian Pidgin English, neither could it have been learned from English, as the substantive differences between Hawaiian Creole English and English rules illustrated in (1)–(4) show. Neither could it have been acquired from any of the substratum languages, many of which do not have articles. Hawaiian and Portuguese (two that do) although permitting zero forms of nondefinites in object position [as in (4)], have obligatory definite marking of subject generics [in contrast with (1)]. In other words, none of the languages in contact in Hawaii had a rule which singled out NPs of nonspecific reference for identical treatment. Yet all Hawaiian Creole English speakers acquired a specific-nonspecific distinction and allotted zero marking to all nonspecific NPs.

Stei did occur preverbally in the speech of a very few Hawaiian Pidgin English speakers—seven times in many hours of recording, as opposed to hundreds of times in Hawaiian Creole English recordings of comparable length—but the uses of the form were so confusing and ambiguous that, even if such uses had occurred in pre-creole speech, no child could possibly have induced the meaning arrived at by the first Hawaiian Creole English generation (for a full analysis of these examples, see Bickerton 1981, Chap. 1). Moreover, there is a high probability that even these uses of *stei* by Hawaiian Pidgin English speakers—recorded in the early 1970s, at least 50 years after creolization took place—were in fact learned (quite inadequately) by pidgin speakers from younger creole speakers, and thus could not have formed part of the childrens' input.

Among Hawaiian Creole English speakers, *stei* + V may express present continuous:

(5)   *ai no kea hu* **stei hant** *insai dea, ai gon hant.*
        'I don't care who's hunting in there, I'm going to hunt'.

past continuous:

(6)   *wail wi* **stei paedl,** *jan* **stei put** *wata insai da kanu—hei, da san av a gan haed sink!*
'While we were paddling, John was letting water into the canoe—hey, the son-of-a-gun sunk it!'

present habitual:

(7)   *yu no waet dei* **stei kawl** *mi, dakain—kawl mi gad.*
'You know what they call me, that bunch? They call me God'.

and past habitual:

(8)   *ai* **stei kam** *ap hia evri dei las yia.*
'I used to come up here every day last year'.

In other words, Hawaiian Creole English *stei* is neutral to the English past–nonpast distinction. *Stei* never occurs with stative verbs, although it can and does combine with other auxiliaries such as *go* and *bin/wen.*

Clearly, *stei* is distinct in form and meaning from anything in English grammar, but it is also markedly different from anything in the substratum languages. Perhaps the closest thing to *stei*, from a semantic viewpoint, is Japanese *-te iru/-te ita;* here, however, nonpunctuality is conveyed by the morphemes *te i, ru* and *ta* being suffixes which express present and past tense respectively, and, moreover, all the Japanese forms are postverbal affixes as opposed to preverbal free morphemes.

However, we find once again that structures that have no parallel in the contact languages of Hawaii's plantation period are exactly replicated across a wide range of creole languages. Examples (5) through (8) have Guyanese Creole equivalents with *a + V* instead of *stei + V:*

(9)   *mi* **a kom** *bak haptanum.*
'I'm coming back in the afternoon' (present continuous).

(10)   *di kuliman bin prapa fraikn di blakman—evribadi* **a wach aut de an nait.**
'The Indians were really afraid of the black people—everybody was watching out day and night' (past continuous).

(11)   *evri de mi* **a ron** *a raisfiil.*
'Every day I run to the ricefield' (present habitual).

(12)   *evribadi bin gatu wach aut an evribadi* **a de** *aal abaut.*
'Everyone had to watch out and everybody used to be all over the place' (past habitual).

The preceding structures and semantic range are not limited to creoles with an English vocabulary, as is shown by the following examples from Haitian Creole, which uses *ap(e)* + V with the same distribution:

(13)   *papa, mê mwê fè mwê mal, m-**ap-lagé** kò mwê*
        daddy hand my do me bad, I-ASP-*leave body my*
        'Daddy, my hand hurts me, I'm letting go'   (present continuous).

(14)   *li fè-l kône jâ l-apé-mouri pou-fiy-a*
        he make-him know manner he-ASP-die for-girl-the
        'He showed him how he was dying for the girl'   (past continuous).

(15)   *tout moun sou-latè ap-chaché pou-yo viv avek êtélijâs*
        all person on-earth ASP-seek for-they live with intelligence
        'Everyone on earth tries to live intelligently'   (present habitual)

(16)   *sa k-**ap-fè** mâjé, **ap-fè** mâje pou-apézé lwa-yo*
        that which-ASP-make eat, ASP-make eat for-appease *loa* PL
        'Whatever they used to give it to eat, they gave it to eat to appease the African gods'   (past habitual).

Once again, we have a rule which Hawaiian Creole English speakers could not have induced from Hawaiian Pidgin English input, or from any of the languages with which they were in contact, but which is identical with a rule which was, somehow, derived by other creole speakers in far-distant corners of the world.

   Finally, in the case of complement structures, we have what is perhaps an even clearer and more striking case of parallel innovation. In the first case examined, although there was no article system in Hawaiian Pidgin English, there were some articles which could have provided the surface forms, if not the underlying semantic structures, involved in the Hawaiian Creole English rule. Similarly, although there was no auxiliary system in Hawaiian Pidgin English, there were scattered occasions in which verbs might be used in an auxiliarylike way. In the third area, however, there were no forerunners whatsoever of the structures Hawaiian Creole English "invented". Hawaiian Pidgin English had no complementizers and no sentential complements at all.

   The two forms used by Hawaiian Creole English as complementizers are *fo* and *go*. *Fo*, derived presumably from English *for*, occurs very occasionally in Hawaiian Pidgin English as a preposition introducing an NP, but has no other use. *Go* occurs frequently in Hawaiian Pidgin English, but its functions are limited to those of a main verb and of a preverbal marker of very uncertain meaning. In the latter function it commonly precedes imperatives, and perhaps derives ultimately from English structures such as *go (and) do X*. Such uses can occur in a series of imperatives, such as:

(17)   *go tek tu fala go **hapai** dis wan.*
         go take two men go carry this one
         'Take two men and take this away'.

They can also occur in quoted imperatives:

(18)   *ai no tel yu palas, go join pentikosta.*
         'I'm not telling you guys, "Join the Penticostal Church" '.

Although such sentences contain neither complementizers nor complements, it is not inconceivable that creole speakers might reinterpret them as *take two men **to** carry this away* or *I'm not telling you guys **to** join the Penticostal Church*—provided that they already had some idea of what complement sentences were like! [When we analyze (17) and (18) in this way, we are doing so only by virtue of our knowledge of English complement structures.] But it is unlikely that they would have had much opportunity for such reanalyses, since sentences such as (17) and (18) are extremely rare; these were practically the only examples we found in many hours of recordings. Moreover, in the case of *fo*, there were NO comparable sentences from which complement structures might have been induced by reanalysis.

However, in Hawaiian Creole English we find sentences like the following with *go:*

(19)   *dei wen go ap dea erli in da mawning **go** plaen.*
         'They went up there early in the morning to plant'.

(20)   *so ai go daun kiapu **go** push.*
         'So I went down to Kiapu to push' (clear land with a bulldozer)

(21)   *ai gata **go** haia wan kapinta **go** fiks da fom.*
         'I had to hire a carpenter to fix the form'.

All these sentences have in common the fact that the actions described in the complements actually took place. We find, also, sentences like the following with *fo:*

(22)   *aen dei figa, get sambadi **fo** push dem.*
         'And they figured, there'd be someone to encourage them' (but there wasn't).

(23)   *mo beta a bin go hanalulu fo bai maiself.*
         'It would have been better if I'd gone to Honolulu to buy it
         myself' (but of course I didn't).

(24)   *hau yu ekspek a gai fo mek pau hiz haus?*
         'How do you expect a guy to complete his house?' (under those
         conditions).

All these sentences have in common the fact that the actions described
in the complements did not take place. In other words, Hawaiian Creole
English formally and systematically marks the distinction between
realized and unrealized complements. This is something that is not
done in English (compare *I managed to escape* with *I failed to escape*), or
in any of the substratum languages, so there is no possibility of
Hawaiian Creole English speakers having derived the marking of the
distinction from any other language, even by the most circuitous of
routes.

However, the same distinction is marked in other creoles. Roberts
(1975) reports the following contrast from Jamaican Creole:

(25)   *im gaan fi bied, bot im duon bied.*
         'He went to wash, but he didn't wash'.

(26)   **im gaan go bied, bot im duon bied.*

The complementizer *fi*, like Hawaiian Creole English *fo*, will take a
negative conjunct, because the complement it introduces does not
necessarily have a realized action as its referent, but the complementizer
go will not take a negative conjunct, since the complement it introduces
must have as its referent an action which actually took place.

Jansen, Koopman, & Muysken (1978) independently report the same
contrast for Sranan:

(27)   *a teki a nefi foe koti a brede, ma no koti en.*
         'He took the knife to cut the bread, but didn't cut it'.

(28)   **a teki a nefi Ø koti a brede, ma no koti en.*

Here, a zero complementizer in (28) takes the place of *go*, but the principle involved is an identical one—realized and unrealized complements
are systematically distinguished by means of complementizers.

Again, an example can be found in a creole which is unrelated to
English (and also unrelated to Sranan and Jamaican Creole, naturally).
In the texts of Mauritian Creole given by Baker (1972), we find the
following sentence:

(29)   *li desid **al** met posoh ladah*
         she decide go put fish in-it
         'She decided to put a fish in (the pool)'.

Al—the realized complementizer which is the equivalent of *go* in English creoles—is used here because, as the story subsequently indicates,
the woman DID put a fish in the pool. However, in another story, we
find:

(30)   *li ti pu ale aswar **pu al** bril lakaz sa garsoh-la,*
         he TNS MOD go evening for go burn house that boy-the
         me lor sime ban dayin fin atake li
         but on path PL witch ASP attack him
         'He would have gone that evening to burn the boy's house, but
         on the way he was attacked by witches'.

Here *pu,* derived from French *pour* 'for', is used together with *al* to
indicate an intended action which was not, in fact, carried out (a combination of *fo* and *go* in Hawaiian Creole English can be used for a
similar purpose).

   Here again we have a case in which a rule not found in Hawaiian
Pidgin English, English, or any of the contact languages (and which is
indeed quite rare in languages generally) is acquired by Hawaiian
Creole English speakers and by speakers of other creole languages. The
three cases chosen here are far from unique: Bickerton (1981) lists many
other areas of the grammar in which similarities among creoles, fully as
striking and as widespread as these, are to be found. However, they
should suffice to give the reader some conception of the kinds of processes set in motion when a pidgin is "expanded" to become a creole.

   How can we account for such processes? Note that there are two quite
distinct phenomena to be accounted for. First, we have to explain how
children in Hawaii were able to learn things that neither their mothers
nor anyone else could have taught them. Second, we have to explain
why the result of this type of learning whenever and wherever it occurs,
should show such striking similarities.

   The first phenomenon shows that language learning can be carried
out without any of the hypothesis-forming, hypothesis-testing apparatus which is currently accepted by generativist and "motheresian"
alike. The only difference between the two schools on this point is that
the generativist believes that the child analyzes degenerate data with
the help of a language-specific acquisition device while the "motheresian" believes that the child analyzes preadapted data with the help
of a general problem-solving device. Both schools have stubbornly re-

fused to consider situations in which there was simply not enough (or the right kind of) data to give satisfactory results, no matter what kind of device for processing input the child possessed.

We might hypothesize that in cases where input is deficient to this extent, some kind of general cognitive apparatus comes into action and "invents" those devices necessary for language to fulfil all its required human functions. Such a view could, one might think, draw support from the fact that such "inventions" are found in relatively few natural languages, and are not, therefore, linguistic universals in the sense in which that term is generally used.[3] It would not, however, explain the second phenomenon. If creole "inventions" are the work of some general problem-solving device, one would expect—given that human languages have many different ways of solving problems such as these—that those "inventions" would differ significantly from one creole to another. For, if they did not, we would have to conclude that the "general problem-solving device" was capable of coming up with only one solution out of the wide range of theoretically-possible solutions—in which case, the difference between that device and a language-specific device would be one of name only.

But the orthodox generativist fares no better than the empiricist when confronted with these phenomena. Since language acquisition devices, as generally conceived, are only restricted by certain universal constraints that limit the forms of human languages, all that the orthodox generativist could predict about a creole would be that it would not violate any of those constraints. Within the limits imposed by those constraints, it could take any form possible for a natural language. The generativist prediction would therefore gravely underspecify the nature of creole languages.

There is only one hypothesis that will account for both phenomena: the hypothesis of an innate bioprogram for language, which, instead of imposing outer limits on possible forms of language, specifies a set of

---

[3] Hitherto it has been assumed (and assumed to be self-evident) that universals are things that are in every language, as well as being contained (in some sense) in the innate language capacity of each individual in the species. The possibility that there may be features in the innate language capacity that do not necessarily surface in all human languages—as illustrated in this chapter—has simply never been considered by generativists. I can see no a priori reason against such a proposal, but I can see that the resolutely adynamic, antiprocessual stance of generative theory (an accidental, rather than a necessary stance, incidentally) would make such a proposal exceedingly difficult to comprehend (a recent affirmation of this stance is Chomsky's claim, backed by no shred of conjecture, much less evidence, that primitive man spoke languages much like ours, Chomsky 1979, p. 55). The position argued here merely defends the capacity of cultural evolution to modify the products of biological evolution, a position that surely ought to be noncontroversial, although I am sure it is not.

highly particularized, substantive structures which are accessible to the child in the event that linguistic input should be too limited and/or too unstable for an adequate human language system to be derived from it.

If this is the case, it is somewhat misleading to talk about first-generation creole children "learning" language. No doubt their mothers "taught" them as diligently as other mothers; the only trouble was that, by the time the children were about 2 or 2½, the mothers must have run out of things to teach. From that point on, the children had to rely on the hypothesized "bioprogram" to build a language adequate for their needs.

However, if such a bioprogram forms part of the genetic equipment of our species, it would follow that it must be activated, not merely when input is inadequate, but also when it is adequate, or has hitherto been regarded as adequate. For one would hardly expect a species, even one as advanced as our own, to come equipped with not one, but two distinct and differently-operating language acquisition devices: one that worked by traditional learning methods and was used in "normal" acquisition, and a second, emergency device that "cut in," so to speak, when "triggered" by defective input, and that provided ready-made the minimum structures necessary for a first language to function as such. Thus, if we say that creole children do not "learn," we have to say that children everywhere do not learn, either, at least in the earlier part of the acquisition process. They simply have their bioprogram activated by linguistic input of any kind, and that bioprogram—which probably replicates the phylogeny of human language, (cf. Lamendella 1976; Bickerton 1981, Chap. 4)—proceeds to unfold until the child is, say, 4 years of age or so. Of course, the bioprogram does not immunize the child against the strenuous efforts of Mother to teach him English, or German, or Swahili, or whatever. On the contrary, if it were not for the biopro-gram, it is probable that Mother could not have taught him English—indeed, that Mother could never have learned enough English to teach it, or even, if one pushes things back far enough, that there would not have been any such thing as English to teach. Fodor (1975) has produced a simple and elegant proof of the claim that one cannot learn a language unless he already knows a language,[4] which is precisely what the pres-ent paper (on totally different grounds from Fodor's) also claims. What

[4] Marshall (1979) points out that nobody has refuted Fodor's argument, although everyone ignores it. The parallel between the reception afforded Fodor's work and the systematic turning of the blind eye to evidence of the kind presented here should not be allowed to go unnoticed. With this negative gambit, all defenders of outdated Kuhnian paradigms attempt to prolong the lives of their doomed artifacts. Alas, students can read, and delight in finding the Achilles' heels of their teachers. It would appear that knowledge can advance only along such crooked paths.

in fact happens in the acquisition process is that, thanks to the efforts of mothers and other caregivers, the child is able to modify and adapt the bioprogram language to such an extent that, by age ten or so, it has become a respectable simulacrum of modern adult English (or whatever other language the target might happen to be).

There is not space here to review the substantial evidence from previous acquisition studies that supports the view of acquisition expressed here. The reader is referred to Bickerton (1981, Chap. 3,) where several aspects of acquisition, previously unclear, are shown to follow naturally from the bioprogram hypothesis. But those whose training and beliefs would lead them instinctively to reject such a hypothesis should note that, even if that particular hypothesis were to be proven false, the problem which gave rise to it would still remain, and would have to be accounted for by any adequate theory of language. To date, as I have shown, no previously existing theory even begins to approach a solution. To this extent, the origin of creoles presents a challenge to general linguistics which the latter cannot answer without re-examining some of its most basic concepts.

References

Baker, P. (1972) *Kreol: A description of Mauritian Creole*. London: C. Hurst.

Bickerton, D. (1977) *Change and variation in Hawaiian English*, Vol 2: *Creole syntax*. Final report on NSF Grant No. GS-39748, University of Hawaii. Mimeo.

Bickerton, D. (1981) *Roots of language*, Ann Arbor: Karoma.

Bickerton, D., & Odo C. (1976) *Change and variation in Hawaiian English*, Vol. 1: *General phonology and Pidgin syntax*. Final Report on NSF Grant No. GS-39748, University of Hawaii. Mimeo.

Bickerton, D., & Givón, T. (1976) Pidginization and syntactic change: From SXV and VSX to SVX. *Papers from the parasession on diachronic syntax*. Chicago: Chicago Linguistic Society.

Bruner, L. (1979) Learning how to do things with words. In D. Aaronson & R.W. Rieber (Eds.), *Psycholonguistic research: Implications and applications*. New York: Wiley.

Clark, H.H., & Clark, E.V. (1977) *Psychology and language*. New York: Harcourt.

Chaudenson, R. (1977) Toward the reconstruction of the social matrix of creole language. In A. Valdman (Ed.), *Pidgin and creole linguistics*. Bloomington: Indiana University Press.

Chomsky, N. (1979) *Language and responsibility*. New York: Pantheon Books.

Fodor, J. (1975) *The language of thought*. New York: Crowell.

Hall, R.A. Jr. (1966) *Pidgin and creole languages*. Ithaca: Cornell University Press.

Jansen, B., Koopman, H., & Muysken, P. (1978) Serial verbs in the creole languages, *Amsterdam Creole Studies*, Vol. II. Universiteit van Amsterdam.

Lamendella, J. (1976) Relations between the ontogeny and phylogeny of language: A neo-recapitulationist view. In S.R. Harnad *et al.* (Eds.), *Origins and evolution of language and speech*. Annals of the New York Academy of Science No. 280.

Marshall, J.C. (1979) Language acquisition in a biological frame of reference. In P. Fletcher & M. Garman (Eds.), *Language acquisition.* Cambridge: Cambridge University Press.

Rens, L.E. (1953) *The historical and social background of Surinam's Negro English,* Amsterdam: North-Holland.

Roberts, P.A. (1975) The adequacy of certain linguistic theories for showing important relationships in a creole language. Paper presented at the International Conference on Pidgins and Creoles, Honolulu, Hawaii.

Sankoff, G. (1979) The genesis of a language. *The genesis of language.* K. Hill (Ed.); Ann Arbor: Karoma.

Sankoff, G., & Brown, P. (1976) The origins of syntax in discourse, *Language 52,* 631–666.

Sankoff, G., & Laberge, S. (1974) On the acquisition of native speakers by a language. In D. DeCamp & I.A. Hancock (Eds.), *Pidgins and creoles: Current trends and prospects.* Washington, D.C.: Georgetown University Press.

Snow, C.E. (1979) Conversations with children. In P. Fletcher & M. Garman (Eds.), *Language acquisition.* Cambridge: Cambridge University Press.

Todd, L. (1974) *Pidgins and creoles.* London: Routledge & Kegan Paul.

3 NANCY C. DORIAN

Linguistic Models and Language Death Evidence

It is not a necessary feature of linguistic extinction that a dying language be structurally "exceptional." In a particularly famous case of linguistic extinction, Ishi, the last of the Yahi Indians of California, died in what was taken to be "flawless command of his own language [Swadesh 1948, p. 228]." This presumably means that there was nothing unusual, in terms of the linguistic structure of Yahi, in Yahi utterances produced by Ishi up to the time of his death. The extinction of Yahi was atypical, however, in that its last speakers remained throughout their lives either monolingual in Yahi or at least clearly Yahi-dominant.

The more usual pattern in the extinction of a language, in our own time at any rate, is a gradual shift within a speech community to the use of another language. Under these circumstances the last speakers of a given language are bilingual, and are generally more proficient in a language other than the dying language. In cases such as this, the dying language is likely to show marked differences, both in form and in function, between its last stages and the earlier stages when it was still spoken by monolinguals. Most of the differences will be in the direction of contraction and reduction, as speakers who increasingly make use of another language show less command of the dying language than their parents and grandparents did. It is this feature of the reduced or incompletely developed linguistic system that the dying language shares with the speech of aphasics, young children, and pidgin users.

As with all of these forms of speech, the questions raised for linguistic theory by the peculiar characteristics of the dying language are numer-

EXCEPTIONAL LANGUAGE AND LINGUISTICS

ous. My initial remarks are prompted by a persuasive statement by
Hymes: "A general theory of the interaction of language and social life
must encompass THE MULTIPLE RELATIONS BETWEEN LINGUISTIC MEANS
AND SOCIAL MEANING [1974, p. 31; emphasis added]." For the last speakers of a dying language, the linguistic means are typically reduced, at
least as far as that language is concerned. This raises the question of the
expression of social meaning. Since these speakers are normally bilingual, with superior skills in another language, they can make use of that
other language for many purposes. But insofar as they still interact via
the dying language, they must either settle for constricted social meaning to suit their linguistic means, or extend their linguistic means in
various ways to compensate for the reductions.

I call these last, imperfect speakers of a dying language **semispeakers.**
They represent the youngest age group in the community to make use of
the dying language (see Dorian 1973, p. 417 for the initial use of the
term). They can be distinguished at the lower levels of skill from people
who know only words and a few fixed phrases by their ability to MANIP-
ULATE words and form sentences. They can be distinguished at the
upper levels of skill from the youngest of the fully fluent speakers by the
presence of deviations in their dialect which are generally recognized by
the rest of the community as "mistakes." (The younger fluent speakers
also deviate fairly sharply from conservative norms, but in more subtle
ways and/or to a lesser degree; almost none of their deviations are
noticed by the community at large.)

One of the ways in which semispeakers compensate for their incomplete control of the language is to make full use of their superb PASSIVE
bilingualism. The Scottish Gaelic and Pennsylvania Dutch semispeakers
of my acquaintance have a very partial command of the productive skills
required to speak the dying language, but they have almost perfect
command of the receptive skills required to understand it. It is an easy
matter for the visiting linguist to outstrip the semispeaker in the ability
to produce correct sentences in the dying language, or even in the ability
to converse, but it is unlikely that he or she will ever even come close to
the semispeaker's ability to understand rapid-fire banter, puns, teasing,
or conversations carried on under conditions of high noise.

Despite the asymmetry of semispeakers' skills in East Sutherland
Gaelic (the dying language I have studied longest and most fully and
hence will draw upon most frequently for this discussion), these speakers are able to participate successfully in Gaelic as members of the
speech community in East Sutherland. This has some significance for
attempts to define the speech community, a concept often under discussion in recent years (e.g., Fishman 1971; Gumperz 1968; Hymes 1974;

Labov 1966). The two most notable contributions of sociolinguistics to the discussion, perhaps, have dispelled the notions that the speech community is simply coterminous with a language (see especially Bloomfield 1933) or that it rests primarily on shared grammatical usage or even grammatical knowledge (see especially Chomsky 1965). Gumperz (1968) effectively combats the former notion and Hymes (1974) the latter. Labov (1966, 1972) has contributed the insight that people's shared evaluation of language usages, rather than any sharing of speech patterns as such, can be criterial for the speech community. With the exception of Hymes, however, and to a lesser extent Fishman, linguists who have discussed the speech community have thought in terms of norms and patterns which concern the structure of language, or with the evaluation of that structure. Hymes, on the other hand, has pointed out repeatedly (e.g., 1964a, 1964b, 1967, 1971, 1974) that much more is involved in communicative competence than knowing how to produce and understand an utterance or evaluate the social meaning of its linguistic form. One must also know when to say something (as opposed to keeping silent), whether to phrase it as a statement or a question, to whom one dare say it, and so forth. If we now ask which of these various competences is most basic to membership in a speech community, the position of the East Sutherland Gaelic semispeakers offers us reason to believe that Hymes' view of the speech community has a necessary breadth which the others lack.

At the lower levels of semispeaker proficiency there are some individuals who actually say very little yet continue to interact in a highly successful fashion with fluent speakers. Thanks to their superb passive bilingualism they follow all verbal interactions without any difficulty, and by limiting their own contributions to very short phrases made up of high-frequency vocabulary in the simplest structures, they can participate for years in a linguistic network without anyone paying much attention to the asymmetrical nature of their interactions, or even to their flawed productions. This situation is aided by the fact that these speakers are always younger than the fully fluent ones and are not necessarily expected to take a prominent part in their elders' conversations. But such an unremarkable interaction is possible only because the semispeakers know such things as that last fact (that is, that younger people may appropriately say little in the presence of their elders), and many others besides; for example, when a phrase of thanks must be produced, when assent must be voiced rather than just nodded, when a few words of confirmation are expected, and so forth. Contrast with this the all-too-familiar phenomenon of the fluent foreign LEARNER of a language who constantly betrays his nonmembership in the speech community by social failures in the use of the language: speaking when he should be silent, asking "rude" questions, failing to recognize a situation in which greetings are obligatory, and the like.

While investigating a particularly low-proficiency semispeaker, I unintentionally exposed her severe lack of productive skills in East Sutherland Gaelic by testing her Gaelic in the presence of an older kinswoman. Both she and her extremely fluent kinswoman were surprised and distressed when it became evident how many things she was unable to say in acceptable East Sutherland Gaelic (or even, in some cases, at all). They lived next door to one another and had been interacting partly in Gaelic for years on end without either of them noticing the largely passive role of the younger woman. Essential to this woman's success as a Gaelic participant in the speech community was not only her ability to understand everything said to her in Gaelic, but also her knowledge of when and how to use the meager productive skills she did possess in an unremarkable fashion. Thus, the broader view of communicative competence taken by Hymes seems necessary to account for the structure of the speech community which exists in Gaelic-speaking East Sutherland.[1]

Another aspect of the relationship between linguistic means and social meaning may be revealed when the semispeakers do choose to speak in their less developed language. By definition, they do not control the full grammatical (nor, usually, phonological) resources of that language. What features of the language survive the incomplete acquisitional histories and functionally restricted performances of the semispeakers? Can we assume that there is something more basic or simple about the features or structures controlled by ALL speakers of a language, including semispeakers, than there is about the features or struc-

---

[1] Judgments of what another person does or does not understand may seem particularly fallible. However, my role as a participant–observer in the East Sutherland Gaelic speech community over a 16-year period permits me to say with confidence that the semispeakers reported on here have a native speaker's ability in decoding messages in East Sutherland Gaelic. I have seen them react to jokes and teasing, pick up whispers, follow minute instructions, and participate effortlessly in group interactions where fluent speakers were using Gaelic to such different purposes as drafting a shopping list or planning attendance at a funeral. It occasionally happened that I missed some rapid or poorly enunciated communication in Gaelic, only to have a semispeaker friend supply me with an English translation of it. It was precisely by measuring my own frequent failures in comprehension against the perfect ease of the semispeakers' comprehension of any given Gaelic message that I became acutely aware of the fact that the foreign learner can speak a significantly more grammatical and fluent East Sutherland Gaelic than any semispeaker, as I do, without coming close to their degree of receptive bilingualism. Furthermore, both East Sutherland Gaelic and Pennsylvania Dutch semispeakers explicitly STATE that they understand everything said in their presence, and give this as a reason for their comfortable sense of inclusion in gatherings of fluent speakers.

tures controlled only by fluent speakers, or by fluent speakers always and by semispeakers only rarely or sporadically? These questions are of course akin to the questions raised by research on child language and pidgins. And since one can also refer, when looking at dying languages diachronically, to features and structures "lost" with declining proficiency, questions related to those raised by research on aphasia also arise: Does loss of features and structures follow a recognizable pattern according to the complexity or frequency of the item? Does the pattern of loss in any way parallel the pattern of acquisition?

These are very complex questions, and certainly the first response from the student of language death would have to be that not nearly enough data are in to attempt firm answers. The body of data on linguistic (as opposed to sociohistorical and sociolinguistic) aspects of language death is still quite small, not in any way comparable to the body of data on child language, pidgins and creoles, or aphasia, for example. Several papers appear on the historical and political causes of linguistic extinction, and on the interrelationships between social structure and language choice in terminal speech communities, for every one paper which deals with changes in the structure of the language as it dies. Nonetheless, there have been a number of contributions over the last decade which deal with or touch on the linguistic structure of dying languages (Dorian 1973, 1977, 1978b; Dressler 1972, 1977; Hill 1973; Kieffer 1977; Rankin 1978; Trudgill 1976–1977; Voegelin and Voegelin 1977), and it seems likely that increased interest in the subject will soon give rise to a more adequate data base for generalization on such topics. For the present, however, it is probably important to state explicitly that the remarks which follow on linguistic change in language death are based on data that are scanty indeed when compared with those from the relatively abundant studies of linguistic aspects of children's acquisition of language or of pidgin formation.

One of the questions which has preoccupied investigators of the "exceptional" language systems is whether there is a linguistic PROFILE characteristic of the entire group of speakers, or of identifiable subgroups within the larger group of speakers. If a profile emerges, it indicates at the very least that the group deserves to be considered linguistically (that is, as opposed to socially or sociolinguistically distinctive); and it may indicate more interesting things, such as the possible existence of some linguistic universal(s). Thus a good deal of attention has been paid to the establishment of a regular order of acquisition for certain grammatical morphemes and allomorphs of English in both child-language studies (Brown 1973; de Villiers and de Villiers 1973) and second-language learning studies (Bailey et al. 1974; Dulay and Burt

1974; Larsen-Freeman 1976) in the hope that such an order, if discovered, would make it possible to discover what constraints operate to produce the order, and whether any of these constraints operate over all languages, or over all languages of a given type.

Once a particular profile, or partial profile, seems established for users of one of the "exceptional" language systems, a further question arises regarding possible similarities among the "exceptional" language systems themselves. Because of the shared feature of incomplete elaboration (a reduced structure compared to ordinary speech in healthy adult monolinguals), researchers sometimes look for a shared deficit or shared scale of incompleteness. Hence the investigation of retention of grammatical morphemes and allomorphs in English-speaking aphasics, explicitly linked to the investigation of acquisition of the same items by English-speaking children (de Villiers 1978; Gleason 1978).

In view of the potential interest of language death studies for language acquisition studies, pidgin and creole studies, and aphasia studies, it is unfortunate that few if any languages which are now dying have been used for acquisition or aphasia studies in their earlier, more intact stages, or have served as the basis for any pidgin or creole recorded in some form. Consequently, direct comparison of dissolution or reduction with acquisition is difficult or impossible, but the potential parallels are being raised with increasing frequency. Trudgill (1976–1977) titled his paper on the decay of Arvanitika, the Albanian spoken in Greece, "Creolization in reverse," and Voegelin & Voegelin (1977) asked in the title of their paper on dying Tübatulabal "Is Tübatulabal de-acquisition relevant to theories of language acquisition?" My own expectation is that at least some modest parallels will appear—perhaps some of them already within the studies of this present volume; but at the same time, it is surely premature to expect definitive conclusions regarding the strictly linguistic aspects of language death when the data are as yet so meager.

More modest objectives seem appropriate for the moment, and I would now like to consider some data from dying East Sutherland Gaelic in order to determine whether semispeaker ability to control various grammatical devices is in line with general notions of linguistic simplicity, and whether their limited control of such devices is part of a reliable linguistic profile for East Sutherland Gaelic semispeakers as a group. The data to be discussed were gathered by direct testing over a 4-year period from six semispeakers (five in East Sutherland and one in London). For comparison with the semispeakers' test results, responses to the same tests were gathered from eight fully fluent speakers of the same dialect, four older fluent speakers representing the most conservative norm available in the 1970s and four younger fluent speakers representing a form of the dialect noticeably less conservative in some respects to the linguist, but not perceived as different from older fluent speakers' usage within the community. That is, the distinction between **older fluent speaker** and **younger fluent speaker** is an artifact of the linguistic analysis, whereas the distinction between **fluent speaker** and **semispeaker** is generally recognized within the community (although those terms are not used).

Testing was used to elicit data because it would not otherwise have been possible to obtain either a sufficient quantity of Gaelic speech from some of the semispeakers or a broad enough range of grammatical structures from most of the semispeakers. The tests consisted of approximately 265 English sentences presented for translation into Gaelic. The strain and artificiality of the task were reduced to a considerable extent by the following facts:

1. Most of the sentences were deliberately kept relatively simple in lexicon and grammar.
2. Translation in both directions (Gaelic–English, English–Gaelic) is a common phenomenon in the dialect because of kinship networks comprising both bilinguals and monolinguals.
3. The testing was spaced over well-separated intervals.
4. I had worked in the community intermittently for 11 years before undertaking any of these tests, and was known to all of the speakers, and very well acquainted with the great majority.
5. The setting for the tests was always the speaker's own home, and a great deal of encouragement and appreciation was expressed for his or her efforts throughout the task.

The test results of interest here involve semispeaker control of three word-bounded grammatical categories (the past, future, and conditional tenses in the verb[2]) and three clause-bounded syntactic structures (the relativization of subject and object NPs, *that*-subordination, and *if*-subordination[3]). The three tense structures involve morphological or morphophonological modifications of the verbal root. The three subordination structures involve embedding (for present purposes, a syntactic model in which embedding is taken to represent a degree of syntactic

---

[2] There is no distinct present tense in Gaelic except for the verb *to be;* the future is used to express some present-tense senses, and the progressive verb phrase built on *to be* to express others.

[3] All of these structures are considered only in their positive form. The corresponding negative forms show considerable differences and, in any case, occurred too rarely in the tests to be useful.

complexity is accepted) plus several additional complex choices: selection of a conjunction or particle, selection of one of at least two roots of any irregular verb, the overriding of tense-governed morphophonology by conjunction- or particle-governed morphophonology, and tense-formation within the embedded sentence. More will be said about the formation of these structures in the following discussion of results.

Note that in scoring embeddings as correct or incorrect, correctness of tense in the finite verb was not counted; otherwise the embedding task would have been at the same time a tense-assignment task. Correctness was scored on other grounds, such as the presence of an obligatory particle or conjunction, the use of an obligatory dependent form of the verb, the presence of an obligatory initial consonant mutation appropriate to the clause-introducer. Where the item in question was NOT obligatory by older fluent speaker standards (e.g., the relative particle is deletable after vowel-final antecedents), the INSTANCE was discounted (i.e., instances of the relative after vowel-final antecedents were not included in the count).

Semispeaker test results for tense and embedding are shown in Table 3.1.

It is evident from Table 3.1 that the prediction of greater semispeaker success with tense than with embedding is confirmed in general. For three of the six semispeakers the greater success with tense is very marked, and for two others it is still considerable. The weakest of the semispeakers controls two of the tenses in part, but none of the embeddings at all. For only one semispeaker is embedding controlled better than tense, and then the difference is small (2%). The past tense is quite well controlled by all the semispeakers, and the future tense fairly well controlled by half of them. The conditional is well controlled by only one semispeaker, however, a fact which again may reflect relative degree of difficulty. The regular past tense in Gaelic is formed solely by an initial consonant mutation of the root, the regular future tense solely by a suffix. The regular conditional tense requires BOTH initial consonant mutation of the root and ALSO a suffix; that is, its formation is more complex than either of the other tenses. (The corresponding three tenses for irregular verbs show roughly the same difference in complexity; the future loses its suffix, but the very fact of having to remember NOT to suffix in the irregular future is a complexity in itself, and indeed some semispeakers make precisely the mistake of adding a suffix to the future of irregular verbs.)

However, while relative complexity may account for the poor showing of the conditional tense as compared with the past and future tenses, it certainly does not explain the better control of *that-* and *if-*

TABLE 3.1
Control of Tense and Embedding by Six Scottish Gaelic Semispeakers

	Tense									Embedding								
	Past			Future			Conditional			Relative			that			if		
	No.	cor-rect	(%)	No.	cor-rect	(%)	No.	cor-rect	(%)	No.	cor-rect	(%)	No.	cor-rect	(%)	No.	cor-rect	(%)
JR	24	24	100	18	15	83	11	6	54.5	8	3	37.5	9	8	89	5	4	80
WR	23	23	100	17	15	88	10	8	80	8	6	75	9	1	11	5	4	80
CM	24	23	96	18	15	83	9	3	33	7	5	71.5	10	8	80	5	0	0
JM	22	20	91	16	2	12.5	9	0	0	7	0	0	10	0	0	5	0	0
IF	24	20	83	18	6	33	9	1	11	8	1	12.5	9	0	0	5	1	20
IH	20	15	75	17	5	29	6	0	0	8	4	50	10	6	60	5	0	0
Average for structure			90.8			54.8			29.8			41.1			40			30

	Individual average for tense percentages	Individual average for embedding percentages	Difference between averages
JR	79.2	68.8	10.4
WR	89.3	55.3	34
CM	70.7	57.2	13.5
JM	34.5	0	34.5
IF	42.3	10.8	31.5
IH	34.7	36.7	2.

subordination as compared with the conditional. Relativization of subject and object NPs is actually quite uncomplicated in Gaelic; the greater part of the semispeaker mistakes with that structure consisted of deleting the relative particle where deletion was not permissable. On the other hand, *that-* and *if*-subordination are highly complex and require the correct choice of conjunction,[4] root form (independent or dependent), and initial consonant mutation (lenition or nasalization) versus unmutated root. The rather surprising level of failure with the conditional tense as compared with the embeddings may in part be due to the kind of use to which the conditional is put in East Sutherland Gaelic. One of its commonest meanings is 'used to', and it is a tense heavily used among older people who are recalling their earlier days. It may be that the semispeakers, who are relatively young by East Sutherland Gaelic standards, simply have a much lower frequency of contexts which would call for the conditional in their speech. Certainly it is generally characteristic of East Sutherland Gaelic semispeakers as a group, speaking in terms of a total sample twice the size of the sample reported on here, to control the conditional poorly or not at all. On the other hand, semispeaker comprehension of the conditional is workable in that they respond meaningfully to questions in the conditional.[5]

Generally speaking, apart from the lesser degree of failure with subordination than with the conditional, the results of the subordination testing are in line with the findings of language-death researchers elsewhere. One of the few grammatical phenomena independently reported for more than one dying language is that subordination structures become either less frequent or less well-formed, or both. Hill (1973) reports this for dying Cupeño and Luiseño, and Voegelin & Voegelin (1977) for dying Tübatulabal. The data for East Sutherland Gaelic conform to this general pattern in that the three subordination structures all showed a success rate of 40% or less.

---

[4] The choice of a conjunction is a less simple matter in Gaelic than in English, since many conjunctions (including *that* and *if*) have distinct positive and negative forms (e.g., /kən/, 'that', /nax/, 'that not'). Thus the speaker has to distinguish each conjunction from its own paired alternative as well as from all other (pairs of) conjunctions.

[5] East Sutherland Gaelic has no words for 'yes' or 'no', and uses verb phrases to give yes-or-no responses to questions. By preparing personalized sets of interview questions couched in the conditional, and requiring semispeakers to answer 'yes' or 'no' before giving a fuller answer, I was able to determine which semispeakers had no active control of the conditional and yet understood it. For example, asked whether they would move to the city if her husband were to get a good job there, a semispeaker might be unable to frame the answer 'no' correctly (that is 'would not move') and yet go on to explain sensibly and appropriately why they would in fact not make such a move if the opportunity offered.

The results of the tense and embedding tests also provide an answer to the question of whether there is a linguistic profile characteristic of the entire group of East Sutherland Gaelic semispeakers. Apart from the fact that all of the semispeakers have better control over the past tense than the other six structures tested, there are few identical orderings. JR controls *that*-subordination better than her sister WR does, and WR, in turn, controls the conditional much better than JR. IH can produce some correct *that*-subordinates, while her cousin IF produced none; on the other hand, IF produced one correct conditional and one correct *if*-subordinate, while IH produced none. But this internal variation in the level of control of the six structures within the semispeaker group is much less important than the contrast between the "typical" semispeaker performance and the performance of a FLUENT East Sutherland Gaelic speaker.

As it happens, the semispeaker JR has a brother only 1 year older than she who is a fluent speaker, and this brother served as the youngest of the fluent speakers in the translation tests. Not only is the brother, AR, a scant 1 year older than JR, but they are both unmarried and live in the same household, headed by their older-fluent-speaker mother. If there is a semispeaker linguistic profile, then it should be reflected in a clear difference between AR's performance on these tests and JR's. Also, JR's results should be more like those of other semispeakers than like AR's. Table 3.2 makes this comparison possible by giving the percentage of control of each of the structures for AR and for the six semispeakers.

AR's only aberrant form in all of the tests of the six structures was a lone future formed on the dependent instead of the independent root of an irregular verb. Otherwise, despite his relative youth and the fact that there are certainly East Sutherland Gaelic structures in the formation of

TABLE 3.2
Comparison of Control of the Six Structures, Six Semispeakers versus the Youngest of the Fluent Speakers (AR)

	AR	JR	WR	CM	JM	IF	IH
Past	100%	100%	100%	96%	91%	83%	75%
Future	94.5	83	88	83	12.5	33	29
Relative	100	37.5	75	71.5	0	12.5	50
that	100	89	11	80	0	0	60
if	100	80	80	0	0	20	0
Conditional	100	54.5	80	33	0	11	0
Average	99.1	74	72.3	60.6	17.3	26.6	35.7

which he is NOT conservative (see Dorian 1973, where AR appears as E19), he produces only correct forms. This performance testifies to the fact that the six structures reported on here are structures which show little decay in fluent-speaker East Sutherland Gaelic; one must be a semispeaker to form them incorrectly to any great degree.

JR is in fact the best of the semispeakers, yet there is a 25-point percentage gap between her averaged success rate and her brother's. Her performance is much more like that of her sister WR, 4 years younger than she, than like that of her brother AR, 1 year older. CM's rather middling performance is also less distant in terms of percentage average than AR's. The six semispeakers fall into two groups, roughly: JR, WR, and CM are moderately competent speakers where tenses and embeddings are concerned, whereas IH, IF, and especially JM are considerably weaker. I might add that these test results also correspond well to what I know of the respective speakers' grammatical abilities in general conversation, except that I have no basis for comparison in the case of IH, who does not voluntarily SPEAK Gaelic at all and only undertook the tests as a personal favor.

It should also be noted that the drop in semispeaker grammatical control, as compared with fluent speaker control, appears without regard to acquisitional history. Of the six semispeakers reported on here, at least one was a fluent child-speaker of Gaelic, and Gaelic-dominant up to school entrance at the age of 5 or 6. A second semispeaker (a same-age relative who lived in the same household for some years) most probably had the same acquisitional history. The other four have never spoken a grammatically "normal" East Sutherland Gaelic at any age. Ironically, the one semispeaker of whom it is certain that she was fully fluent at age 5 or 6 is the one who now performs least well, JM. This is not the result of having emotionally distanced herself, or physically withdrawn herself, from the Gaelic speech community, as she is also the semispeaker mentioned previously who used her excellent passive bilingualism so successfully in Gaelic interactions with her nextdoor kinswoman and other older speakers.

It is clear from Table 3.2 that changes have appeared in semispeaker East Sutherland Gaelic as compared with fluent-speaker East Sutherland Gaelic. Let me now present further evidence of the degree of grammatical variation in East Sutherland Gaelic in the form of a table showing the differential preservation of the nominal and verbal categories of the dialect. The semispeaker percentages in Table 3.3 represent the results of the tests for all semispeakers available to me, not only the six discussed previously. In the figures shown for tense, only the major distinguishing feature was considered in judging the correctness of semispeaker

TABLE 3.3

Summary of Retention and Failure of Occurrence for Nominal and Verbal
Categories in East Sutherland Gaelic by Speaker Group

Category	Percentage of Retention			Some Failure of Occurrence		
	OFS	YFS	SS	OFS	YFS	SS
Nominal						
Gender						
Fem. pron. replacement	66.5	29	0		×	×
Gender-accurate diminutive	97	94	64			
Gender-accurate noun mut.	100	94	65			
Gender-accurate adj. len.	42.5	33	−4	×[a]		×
Case						
Genitive singular	44	19	12	×	×	×
Distinction nom./acc. vs. dat.	98	—	56 (Brora, Golspie)			
	77	46	32 (Embo)			
Vocative sing. and plural	95	75	26			×
Number						
Plural noun	100	100	92			
Verbal						
Tense						
Past tense lenition	100	100	90			
Future suffix	100	100	57			×
Conditional suffix	100	100	46			×
Number						
Imperative plural	73	43	0		×	×
First person sing. cond.	92	83	5			×
Voice						
Recognizable passives	100	100	37			×

Abbreviations: OFS = older fluent speakers; YFS = younger fluent speakers; SS = semi-speakers;
fem. = feminine; pron. = pronoun; adj. = adjective; len. = lenition; nom. = nominative; acc. = accusative; dat. = dative; sing. = singular; cond. = conditional; mut. = mutation.

[a] One OFS idiosyncratically lenites ALL attributive adjectives, regardless of the gender of the
noun.

versions (initial mutation for the past tense, and the respective conservative suffixes for the future and the conditional). The conservative norm
adopted in evaluating retention among fluent speakers was the usage of
the most proficieint and conservative fluent speakers available to me in
the early 1960s, when I began my work on the grammar of East Sutherland Gaelic.

Table 3.3 indicates that grammatical change is very broadly characteristic of East Sutherland Gaelic, not just characteristic of the speech of
semispeakers as compared with fluent speakers. In most categories the
older fluent speakers themselves show some movement away from the

conservative norm; verbal voice, which looks intact in this table (and is, in the sense of being recognizably present as such in every instance), actually shows movement toward the convergence of two different passive structures (see Dorian 1973), so that only nominal number and verbal tense are produced in perfect conformity with the most conservative norm. Flux is apparent not only across speaker groups (with the percentage of retention falling consistently from left to right), but within individual categories for a single speaker group; thus the various signals of gender are differentially preserved, and likewise the various cases.

The kind of controlled translation testing across a full range of age groups that yielded these results for East Sutherland Gaelic could conceivably also be tried in a stable bilingual setting, and especially if one of the languages involved were an unwritten dialect, like East Sutherland Gaelic, the results might indicate whether a dying language is particularly likely to show a very high rate of change in basic grammatical categories. It seems unlikely that the amount of flux in the basic grammatical categories of noun and verb would be so great in a stable "healthy" language—unless of course the language in question were undergoing major phonological change, like the stress reassignment which brought about such restructuring of morphology in the Germanic branch of the Indo-European family. But phonological change is not a significant factor in the grammatical changes of East Sutherland Gaelic nominal and verbal morphology; except for loss of consonant length, which accounted for 4.6% of the noun-plural failures among semispeakers, no other phonological developments came into play at all.

Full and accurate assessments of the amount of change in the grammars of other dying languages will be needed before we can determine whether the amount of change present in East Sutherland Gaelic is characteristic of dying languages. But with just the facts for East Sutherland Gaelic in hand, some of our commonest theories regarding large-scale systematic change are challenged. I have already mentioned the absence of significant phonological change which could leave such pervasive grammatical change in its wake. Neither can language contact account for the scope of the changes revealed in Table 3.3. Although the absence of gender-marking in pronoun replacement for inanimates in English may well encourage the loss of gender-marked pronoun replacement for inanimates in East Sutherland Gaelic, or the small amount of number-marking in the English verb encourage the decline of number-marking in Gaelic verbs, English influence can scarcely lead to the loss of tense markings in semispeakers' verbs and verb phrases. And since English has a formally marked genitive but no formally marked vocative, English influence is unlikely to have produced the uniformly higher preservation of the vocative case than the genitive case in the Gaelic of all speaker-groups. The passives of Gaelic and English are quite dissimilar, to take another example, and in any case the changes in the East Sutherland Gaelic fluent-speaker passive are explainable strictly in terms of competing structures internal to Gaelic.

Two social factors invoked to account for the spread of structural change are likewise inadequate to serve as explanations for the high degree of grammatical change in East Sutherland Gaelic. This change certainly shows strong generational organization; indeed, age is the chief dimension along which it has been possible to demonstrate systematic change. But it is characteristic of the last generation in terminal speech communities that communication in the dying language is largely vertical rather than horizontal, so that there are not sharp generational breaks in the communication network. On the contrary, semispeakers very frequently acquired their Gaelic primarily from a grandparent rather than from a parent, and they universally did and still do use their Gaelic for verbal interaction with their elders rather than with their peers (as do semispeakers of Pennsylvania Dutch). Thus it is certainly not generational divisions in any simple sense which account for the degree of change.

Finally, and most importantly, given the attention paid in recent years to a highly differentiated social structure as a major factor in organizing the inherent variability of any language in such a way as to promote change (e.g., Fasold 1972; Labov 1963, 1966; Trudgill 1974), there is a marked absence of rich internal differentiation in the East Sutherland Gaelic speech community, despite the large amount of systematic grammatical change apparent. Ethnicity is uniform; all speakers of East Sutherland Gaelic are of the fisherfolk, this being a major ethnic identity in East Sutherland. Socioeconomically, any differences in wealth are quite recent, and there are no significant differences in education. The fisherfolk were a stigmatized group; all were poor, and none who remained in the community had more than the legal minimum of education. The degree of consanguinity is ferociously high, and the size of the population quite small (about 200 speakers in 1964, about 100 in 1978). Geographical division into ghettos attached to three separate villages has produced a good deal of systematic phonological differentiation and a small amount of lexical differentiation (Dorian 1978a Pp. 151–158), but it played a role in only one of the grammatical changes of Table 3.3 (the Gaelic of the southernmost village retained the distinction between nominative–accusative case and dative case less well than the Gaelic of the other two villages, across all age groups). The male–female division does not seem to correlate with patterns of change at all.

The steadily decreasing use of Gaelic might be invoked to explain the amount of change, and clearly it is a major factor in the differences between semispeaker grammar and fluent-speaker grammar. Where there is sharp discontinuity between semispeaker performance and fluent-speaker performance (as in verbal tense, the ability to express the passive, two of the gender signals, and number in the 1st person conditional), the key factor must be the lesser use of Gaelic, which resulted initially in incomplete acquisition, and is currently reflected in rather extreme functional specialization. On the other hand, where there is a regular, progressive decline across speaker groups (as in all of the cases, number in the imperative plural, and two others of the gender signals), matters cannot be quite so simple, since there is no sharp falling-off in the use of Gaelic among younger fluent speakers as compared with the older fluent speakers. Likewise, the merger of the two passive structures among younger fluent speakers (reported in Dorian 1973) cannot be attributed simply to a lesser use of Gaelic. Both groups use Gaelic as the habitual home language; by accident of personal circumstances, the younger fluent speakers in my sample use if anything rather *more* Gaelic in their home lives than the older fluent speakers who were tested. Most of the fluent speakers of both groups are clearly Gaelic-dominant (i.e., more comfortable in Gaelic, inclined to use Gaelic in excitement or anger, etc.) but three of the four younger fluent speakers in the sample live in "intact" Gaelic-speaking households with other fluent speakers present, whereas only two of the older fluent speakers had other fluent speakers available in their households. Only one older fluent speaker had another fluent speaker of the same age and proficiency in her household.

Quite possibly there are conditions characteristic of language death which help to account for the rather high degree of change among even fully fluent language-loyal speakers of a threatened language. For example, self-appointed monitors of grammatical norms may become increasingly rare in dying language communities. I heard of old men who had scolded and corrected today's fluent speakers, in their youth, for departing from grammatical and lexical norms. But even at my arrival in the community 16 years ago there were no notable grammatical purists left, and I heard just a little mockery of aberrant lexical choices and of one aberrant morphological choice. When other dying languages are fully studied, this relaxation of internal grammatical monitoring may well turn out to be widespread among the last fluent generations. Until it is clearer what features East Sutherland Gaelic shares with other dying languages, it is hard to know which features of the linguistic and sociolinguistic profile of East Sutherland Gaelic are significant.

This chapter has dwelt on the manifestations of a single dying language; this is more a matter of necessity than of choice. The most useful outcome of this chapter would not be to make an important statement about what the study of dying languages has contributed to linguistic theory, but to stimulate enough interest in what it MIGHT contribute to send more linguists out to gather the basic data on which that contribution will have to be based.

References

Bailey, N., Madden, C., & Krashen, S. (1974) Is there a "natural sequence" in adult second language learning? *Language learning, 24,* 235–44.

Bloomfield, L. (1933) *Language.* New York: Henry Holt and Company.

Brown, R. (1973) *A first language.* Cambridge, Mass.: Harvard University Press.

Chomsky, N. (1965) *Aspects of the theory of syntax.* Cambridge, Mass.: M.I.T. Press.

de Villiers, J. (1978) Fourteen grammatical morphemes in acquisition and aphasia. In Caramazza, Alfonso, & E.B. Zurif (Eds.), *Language acquisition and language breakdown: Parallels and divergencies.* Baltimore: The Johns Hopkins University Press.

de Villiers, J., & de Villiers, P. (1973) A cross-sectional study of the acquisition of grammatical morphemes in child speech. *Journal of psycholinguistic research, 2,* 267–278.

Dulay, H., & Burt, M. (1974) Natural sequences in child second language acquisition. *Language learning, 24,* 37–53.

Dorian, N.C. (1973) Grammatical change in a dying dialect. *Language, 49,* 414–438.

Dorian, N.C. (1977) The problem of the semi-speaker in language death. *International journal of the sociology of language, 12,* 23–32.

Dorian, N.C. (1978a) *East Sutherland Gaelic: The dialect of the Brora, Golspie, and Embo fishing communities.* Dublin: Dublin Institute for Advanced Studies.

Dorian, N.C. (1978b) The fate of morphological complexity in language death: Evidence from East Sutherland Gaelic. *Language, 54,* 590–609.

Dressler, W. (1972) On the phonology of language death. *Papers of the Chicago Linguistic Society, 8,* 448–457.

Dressler, W. (1977) Wortbildung bei Sprachverfall. In H.E. Brekle, & D. Kastovsky (Eds.), *Perspektiven der Wortbildungsforschung.* Bonn: Bouvier Verlag Herbert Grundmann.

Fasold, R.W. (1972) *Tense marking in Black English.* Arlington, Virginia: Center for Applied Linguistics.

Fishman, J.A. (1971) The sociology of language. In: Fishman, Joshua A. (Ed.), *Advances in the sociology of language,* Vol. I. The Hague: Mouton.

Gleason, J.B. (1978) The acquisition and dissolution of the English inflectional system. In Caramazza, Alfonso, & E.B. Zurif (Eds.) *Language acquisition and language breakdown: Parallels and divergencies.* Baltimore: The Johns Hopkins University Press.

Gumperz, J.J. (1968) The speech community. In: D.L. Sills (Ed.), *International encyclopedia of the social sciences,* Vol. 9. New York: Crowell Collier and Macmillan. Pp. 381–386.

Hill, J.H. (1973) Subordinate clause density and language function. In C. Corum, T.C. Smith-Stark, & A. Weiser (Eds.); *You take the high node and I'll take the low node: Papers from the Comparative Syntax Festival.* Chicago: Chicago Linguistics Society.

Hymes, D. (1964a) Introduction: Toward ethnographies of communication. In J.J. Gumperz, & D. Hymes (Eds.), *The ethnography of communication. (American anthropologist special publication*, Vol. 66, No. 6, Part 2) Menasha, Wisconsin: American Anthropological Association. Pp. 1–34.

Hymes, D. (1964b) Directions in (ethno-)linguistic theory. In A.K. Romney, & R.G. D'Andrade (Eds.), *Transcultural studies in cognition*. (*American anthropologist special publication*, Vol. 66, No. 3, Part 2) Menasha, Wisconsin: American Anthropological Association. Pp. 6–56.

Hymes, D. (1967) Models of the interaction of language and social setting. *Journal of social issues, 23*, 8–28.

Hymes, D. (1971) Sociolinguistics and the ethnography of speaking. In E. Ardener (Ed.), *Social anthropology and language*. (A.S.A. Monographs 10) London: Tavistock Publications.

Hymes, D. (1974) *Foundations in sociolinguistics*. Philadelphia: University of Pennsylvania Press.

Kieffer, C. (1977) The approaching end of the relict Southeast Iranian languages Ōrmuri and Parāči. *International journal of the sociology of language, 12*, 71–100.

Labov, W. (1963) The social motivation of a sound change. *Word, 19*, 273–309.

Labov, W. (1966) *The social stratification of English in New York City*. Washington, D.C.: Center for Applied Linguistics.

Labov, W. (1972) The study of language in its social context. In W. Labov, *Sociolinguistic patterns*. Philadelphia: University of Pennsylvania Press.

Larsen-Freeman, D. (1976) An explanation for the morpheme accuracy order of learners of English as a second language. *Language learning, 26*, 125–135.

Rankin, R.L. (1978) The unmarking of Quapaw phonology: A study of language death. *Kansas working papers in linguistics, 3*, 45–52.

Swadesh, M. (1948) Sociologic notes on obsolescent languages. *International journal of American linguistics, 14*, 226–35.

Trudgill, P. (1974) *The social differentiation of English in Norwich*. Cambridge: Cambridge University Press.

Trudgill, P. (1976–1977) Creolization in reverse: Reduction and simplification in the Albanian dialects of Greece. *Transactions of the Philological Society, 1976–1977*, 32–50.

Voegelin, C.F., & Voegelin, F.M. (1977) Is Tübatulabal de-acquisition relevant to theories of language acquisition? *International journal of American linguistics, 43*, 333–338.

4
CHARLES A. FERGUSON

Simplified Registers and Linguistic Theory[1]

The term **simplified register** was suggested by Ferguson (1971) as the name for modified varieties of speech typically addressed to listeners not believed to be fully competent in the language, such as young children, foreigners, deaf people, or retarded individuals. Such speech varieties were held to be relatively conventionalized, identifiable parts of the total verbal repertoire of a speech community, interesting for what they show about the nature of functional variation in language. Although such simplified registers were acknowledged to be marginal to language structure as traditionally studied by linguists, they seemed to be widespread (possibly universal?) and could provide valuable data on the nature of linguistic systems. In particular, baby talk and foreigner talk registers were identified, and subsequent work on these by scholars representing different research perspectives has led to a substantial body of descriptive material as well as some theoretical discussions and a growing literature reporting experimental investigation of particular hypotheses. My own attempts to summarize and draw conclusions from the descriptive work appear in Ferguson (1977; 1978) and Ferguson (1981). A large part of the work on baby talk, however, has been concerned with its role in the development of the child's communicative competence and with other issues not directly related to linguistic

[1] Parts of this chapter are nearly identical with sections of a lecture on the same topic given at the Seventh Annual Minnesota Regional Conference on Language and Linguistics, in Minneapolis, May 1981.

theory as usually conceived. Much of this work has had little or no connection with register-oriented research, and no attempt will be made to review it here (cf. Gleason & Weintraub 1978; Snow 1979). Similarly, a large part of the work on foreigner talk has been concerned with the relation of foreigner talk to language learning and pidginization (e.g., Ferguson & DeBose 1977; review of the field, Long 1981) rather than its relation to linguistic theory. A representative collection of current foreigner talk studies appears in Clyne (1981).

In this chapter I discuss simplified registers in relation to linguistic theory—or, more broadly, theory about language—under three headings: marginality, register variation, and the notion of simplification.

Marginality

The first item that directed my attention to marginal systems in language was the Moroccan Arabic baby talk word [bap:a] 'bread, food.' This well-attested lexical item was pronounced by my informants with an unmistakably voiceless labial stop medially, yet Moroccan Arabic, like many other varieties of Arabic, has no /p/ in its phonemic inventory. Moroccans, like other Arabs, tend to have trouble with p's when learning other languages, either substituting voiced b's for them or hypercorrectly using p's where they do not belong. Speakers of Moroccan Arabic are constrained by the nature of their phonological system to find p difficult to perceive and produce appropriately, yet they produce it easily (and presumably perceive it correctly) in this marginal word used primarily in talking to very young children. Essentially the same phenomenon of phonological marginality appears in the use of glottal stop by speakers of American English. These speakers produce glottal stops regularly and easily in such expressions as *uh-oh* or *oh-oh*, a mild exclamation of unpleasant surprise, *uh-uh* [ʔʌ̃ʔʌ̃] or [ʔm̩ʔm̩], an informal negative response, or [ʔæʔæ] an expression of warning or disapproval to young children. In all these items they may even lengthen or geminate the glottal stop to be more emphatic. Yet when they are faced with the problem of using [ʔ] as a full-fledged consonant in the phonology of another language (e.g., in learning Syrian Arabic) they are unable to perceive or produce it appropriately, or to geminate it when required, without great practice.[2]

---

[2] A different but related transfer phenomenon is the boundary use of glottal stop in English corresponding to the consonantal glottal stop of Syrian Arabic. English speakers can be led to say /biʔul/ 'he says' quite satisfactorily by telling them to regard it as a two-word expression pronounced emphatically *be + ool*, but when they speed up their

Most linguistic work during the structuralist and generative periods has assumed that a language or language variety has a homogeneous, unified structure in which everything has its place (*où tout se tient*). Such a view of language leaves no room for *p*'s that occur only in baby talk or glottal stops that occur only in marginal (but frequently used) exclamations, if these phenomena cannot be integrated into the rule system of the language.[3] One of the most convincing arguments for the psychological validity of the phonological system constructed by linguists is the way it serves as a filter when a speaker of the language acquires another language, yet these marginal cases, though clearly part of the total linguistic repertoires of the respective speech communities, do not serve as filters in the usual way and seem partly in and partly out of the system.

All the simplified registers so far described include material which is marginal in this sense. Examples just as clearcut as the Moroccan Arabic baby talk *p* can be found in many aspects of language, including intonation, phoneme inventory, pronoun use, genitive constructions, and basic word order. All these phenomena raise two familiar questions of theory:

1. What is the object of linguistic description, i.e., just what is a linguist's grammar intended to generate or explicate?
2. What is the "psychological reality" of a linguistic analysis, that is, to what extent does a linguist's grammar (or a general theory of language) reflect the human speaker–hearer's actual processing of language?

The characteristics of simplified registers, as of many other marginal phenomena in language, suggest a model of the linguistic repertoire of either an individual or a social group that is somewhere between the two extremes of order and chaos, neither a unified system in which everything fits into an intricate network, nor a congeries of disparate elements in crisscrossing and contradictory relationships. Simplified registers tend to function as restricted subsystems within a major core system but they may involve systematic shifts or structural transforms and they may also include material that lies outside any such core system. Thus, an important area of investigation for students of simplified

---

speaking rate they drop the [?] as they would in English, giving an unsatisfactory pronunciation [biju:l]. For the relation between transfer and "developmental" errors in phonology (cf. Macken & Ferguson 1981).

[3] Praguian structuralists have been more concerned than American linguists about marginal phenomena, especially in phonology, and they generally operate with the distinction between center and periphery in the system (cf. Vachek 1966; Uspensky & Zhivov 1977) although not explicitly in a framework of register variation.

registers is the nature of their marginality: in what ways the matrix
system may be restricted, modified, or transcended.

As an example, let us examine the phenomenon of pronoun shift that
occurs in many simplified registers. **Pronoun shift** means the use of a
noun or a different pronoun in place of an expected pronoun or the
complete absence of the pronoun (Wills 1977). In the simplified registers
of many languages, pronouns are frequently replaced by proper names
or kinterms, as in English baby talk: *Baby's hungry? Mommy will get your
bottle.* ('Are you hungry? I'll get your bottle'.) In the simplified registers
of English and other languages addressed to hearers being tended or
cared for, the pronoun shift of first person plural for second person
singular is well attested. *Are we ready for our nap? Let's not throw our
toys out of the playpen. Shall we sit up for our dinner today?* In the baby
talk of Japanese and possibly other East Asian languages, a different
kind of pronoun shift occurs, the use of the first person singular pronoun in place of the second person, the pronoun selected being the one
that would be appropriate for the addressee to use in self-reference.
Boku mo iku? ('Are you (lit. 'I' masculine, informal) coming along?') said
to a young boy. Some seekers of language universals have claimed that
pronoun shift is a universal feature of simplified registers or at least of
baby talk (Rūķe-Draviņa, 1976; Ferguson 1978).

As suggested previously, simplified register pronoun systems may be
restricted versions of the core system (e.g., *I, me, my* reduced to *me* in
some styles of English foreigner talk, *Sie* and *du* reduced to *du* in some
styles of German foreigner talk). They may involve categorial shift (e.g.,
we for *you, boku* for *anata, mommy* for *I*), and they may involve pronominal elements not present at all in the core system (e.g., extreme English
baby talk *ums* 'you'). The pronoun shift found in simplified registers is a
marginal phenomenon traditionally ignored in standard treatments of
syntax, semantics, and discourse analysis, yet it immediately raises
questions as to the nature and extent of categorial shifting possible in a
language to mark changes in situational context or in interactants' purposes, attitudes, or communicative strategies. In particular, it raises the
question of the special susceptibility of pronoun systems to registral
and stylistic shifting, an aspect of language structure and use which
should be covered both in general linguistic theory and in the grammars
of languages. Some of the pronoun shifts that occur in simplified registers are closely related to the pronoun shifts of deference systems, politeness strategies, and the like (cf. Head 1978; Brown & Levinson 1978).
An examination of all this marginal material taken together would lead
to a better understanding of the nature of pronoun systems.

The restricted nature of some of the simplified register phenomena can be interpreted as simplification (cf. page 58), which we can hypothesize may aid in communication by making the perception–comprehension task of the hearer easier, or may aid in acquisition by making the input to the learner simpler and more orderly. It is very difficult to obtain convincing evidence that this is the case, but the hypothesis remains plausible and investigation of the hypothesis continues. It is less inherently plausible, however, to hypothesize that the shifted or added material helps in perception–comprehension. Accordingly, it is interesting to look for instances where these apparently unhelpful distortions of the core system play a facilitative role for acquisition, in addition to the expressive or other communicative function they may serve. Let us look at examples from phoneme inventory and pronoun shift, since we have already referred to these phenomena.

In Arabic baby talk the frequency of emphatic labials /ḅ ṃ/ and pharyngeal spirants /ħ ʕ/ is much greater than one would expect, given the relative rarity of the former in normal adult Arabic and the highly 'marked' nature of the latter in universal phonetic terms. The baby talk expressions /b̄āḅa/ 'daddy' and /māṃa/ 'mommy' are the chief instances of emphatic labial in native adult Arabic, in which they are reciprocal terms of affective address between parent and son or daughter, although some dialects have a few other common words containing an emphatic labial (e.g., Syrian Arabic /ṃayye/ 'water'). It is plausible that the early use of /ḅāḅa/ and /ṃāṃa/ serves as a foundation for the mastery of the phonetic feature of emphasis (tafx̄im), distinctive for a whole series of consonants in Arabic. The phenomenon has the appearance of a device evolved over a long period of time, both to help in the acquisition of phonology and to foster affective communication between child and parent. This explanation remains speculative until evidence accumulates from Arabic language development studies, but it is a testable hypothesis. In a somewhat different way, the appearance of the pharyngeal spirants in Arabic baby talk may be related to the stability and high frequency of these sounds in adult Arabic, in spite of their relative rarity in the world's languages. What little evidence there is suggests that these sounds are indeed acquired early rather than later by children, counter to commonly held expectations about order of acquisition of phonological contrasts.

In the case of pronoun shift, the use of proper names and namelike nouns for the second person pronoun represents a reduction of the adult system and postpones the problem of shifting the semantic value of *I* and *you*. Thus, as a simplification it is readily interpreted as facilitating acquisition, and there is a little evidence to suggest that it functions in that way (e.g., Cruttenden 1977). The striking case of the Japanese pronoun substitution, however, is not obviously simplification, and a facilitative function is correspondingly less plausible. Yet even here it seems likely that the pronoun shift contributes to the early acquisition of *I* in Japanese, and establishes the sex-linking of pronouns and other grammatical forms which is so pervasive in the language.

But let us return to our main concern, the marginality of simplified register phenomena in the linguistic repertoire of the speaker. How can we fit these systematic restrictions, modifications, and additions into the structuralist–generative unified system? In an earlier paper I suggested that the easiest way to conceive of these modifications was as a supplementary set of rules applied after all the normal rules. Now I prefer, however, the metaphor of plugging in a supplementary system which ordinarily remains unplugged and does not affect the working of the system unless plugged in. The supplementary unit may be a minor attachment which affects only a small part of the total system or may be a much more substantial unit or complete system that rivals the primary system or serves as an alternative to it.

One of the closest analogies to this kind of phenomenon is the use of secret languages such as English Pig Latin or the Spanish insertion of *-po-*. The "grammars" of these "languages" consist typically of one rule or a handful of rules which modify normal speech. Halle (1962), in one of the early articles about generative phonology, used Pig Latin as an argument for the rule nature of phonological systems. In that article Halle failed to mention three important characteristics of play language rules.

1. The rules are of the types which almost never occur in normal phonologies. There is no natural language in which for some normal grammatical or lexical purpose the speakers move the initial consonant of a word to the end of the word and add a vowel, or in which they insert a syllable like *-po-* between every two syllables of the word. The application of a play language rule must, after all, produce an utterance that does not sound like normal language and in fact disguises the meaning of the utterance.
2. The rules are learned later, in most speech communities by early teenagers, and are mastered quite variably by different individuals, some being able to use Pig Latin or *popo* talk in Spanish quite fluently and others only with difficulty and many errors.
3. The rules are applied for social and psychological purposes, such as group identification and the prevention of understanding by certain hearers, which occur elsewhere in human language use but are not characteristic of phonological rules in general. The linguis-

tic literature on play languages treats these and other characteristics in detail (reviewed in Sherzer 1976; Ferguson & Macken 1981).

What interests us here, however, is the resemblance between the rules of play languages and those of simplified registers. Both seem to be plug-ins that change the normal rules for special purposes, but they differ in formal characteristics and functions. The comparison of these two types of extrasystemic rules would be an intriguing area for psycholinguistic research to discover secrets of human language processing.

Register Variation

In the mid 1950s T.B.W. Reid (1956) suggested the term **register** to refer to a variety of a language appropriate for particular situations, and the term has been used by a number of researchers in the succeeding decades, chiefly at first by British linguists but more frequently in recent years by others. Many language researchers have investigated the phenomena for which the term was suggested, but have refrained from using the word itself—because of a preference for another term, doubts about the discreteness of registers and the validity of register boundaries, or out of appreciation for the complexity of language variation phenomena. No one doubts the reality of the phenomenon of register variation itself and its universality in human language. "It often takes less than a sentence of speech to decide whether we are hearing a news broadcast, commercial message, 'soap opera', campaign speech, or sermon. In other societies a tape recording might just as readily be identified as adolescent instruction, recitation of a myth, joking between uncle and nephew, or spirit possession [Ferguson 1977 Pp. 211–212]." The problem is how to incorporate this variation into our grammars and theory of language.

Three models have been offered for handling register variation. The first, involving the use of **variable rules,** was originally proposed by Labov (1969) and further developed by Labov and others in the following years (cf., e.g., Cedergren & Sankoff 1974). The variable rule model has proved to be of great value in identifying the linguistic and social conditioning factors involved in certain kinds of variation and has contributed greatly to our understanding of certain aspects of language change. It is singularly inappropriate, however, for the description of register variation, because of its fundamentally atomistic nature and its special appropriateness for phonological characteristics. The primary focus of register analysis is the co-occurrence of variation patterns across a number of linguistic features, in relation to particular sets of situations—lexical and collocational variation is critically important. Also, variable rules represent generalizations about so-called "free variation," that is, alternative ways of saying the same thing, whereas register variation is concerned with saying somewhat different things in different situations (cf. Lavandera 1978, for a cogent discussion of aspects of this problem). It may be possible to develop statistical techniques for comparing variables and for representing situationally conditioned variation in something like variable rule format, but this has not yet been seriously attempted.

The second model is that of the **implicational hierarchy,** first presented as a type of sociolinguistic analysis by DeCamp (1971) and utilized subsequently by many sociolinguists, especially by creolists (cf., e.g., Bickerton 1973). The implicational scale model has proved to be a valuable tool for discovering and presenting linguistic variation which fits a single-dimension linear scale. As such it has been used to good purpose in studies of child language development, in creole continua, and in certain phenomena of language change; understandably it has been pushed to a central position by variationists interested in a "developmental linguistics" which ties language diachrony and acquisition together at the core of language theory. This model, however, is not readily applicable to multidimensional variation, and the focus of register analysis is on the multidimensional variation that distinguishes the language of public worship from that of sports news, classroom teacher talk from the language of the lawyer's brief, the register of mother talking to infant from that of the writing of business correspondence.

The third model, and the only one directly concerned with register variation, is that of **variety grammar** as outlined in Klein (1974). This model, which has been applied chiefly to the language spoken to and by foreign workers in Germany (Dittmar & Klein 1979), recognizes the inadequacies of the other two models as well as the unsuitability of any model that takes a single variety as norm and all others as derivatives. The model proposes simultaneously constructing a set of grammars of different varieties; the grammars are then related to one another by the assignment of probabilities, much in the manner of variable rules. The variety grammar was designed to be applicable to variation that represents successive stages in acquisition, to regional and social dialect variation, and to register variation within a single dialect or period of time. This model seems more promising than the others but its application still remains quite problematic. Its proponents have been more concerned with the formal elaboration of its probability-assigning mechanisms than with the two serious conceptual problems it raises for the register analyst. One problem is that of the discreteness and identifiability of varieties. Register boundaries tend to be relatively "soft" and even fairly clearcut registers tend to show internal variation, especially along a single dimension of intensity (e.g., degree of "babyishness" in baby talk). The other problem concerns the combination of registers, that is, in the terms of our earlier metaphor, just where a given register "plugs in" to another, the extent to which it neatly replaces sectors of other registers, restructures parts of them, or actually adds to the total linguistic spectrum of the other registers.

In the present state of inadequate models for register analysis (perhaps not so different from other kinds of linguistic analysis), the most constructive approach may well be to do our best to DESCRIBE particular registers or aspects of register variation with careful attention to both linguistic structure and situational use, drawing on whatever models may seem helpful, in the hope that more comprehensive models may gradually emerge. At this point I would like to state the basic working assumptions of register variation that I think should be made by analysts; they are essentially restatements of the relevant sections of Ferguson (1978) and (1981).

1. REGISTER VARIATION IS UNIVERSAL. All languages (better, all speech communities) show register variation, that is, variation in structure (e.g., phonological, grammatical, lexical, discoursal) depending on use, including alternatives of addressee, topic, occasion, "situation," etc. In some speech communities, register variation may even include the use of completely different languages.

2. REGISTERS EXIST. Although register variation is universal, establishing the existence of discrete, uniquely characterized registers is more problematic. Still, at times, there are sufficiently delimited sets of correlated language characteristics (both structural and situational) to justify the recognition of particular registers.

3. REGISTER SYSTEMS DIFFER CROSS-LINGUISTICALLY AND CHANGE DIACHRONICALLY. Since part of the language structure or of the linguistic repertoire of a speech community consists of a system of register variation, such systems may be compared between different languages, communities, and time periods, in order to discover typological patterns and principles of change.

4. A GIVEN REGISTER IS VARIABLE IN THE DEGREE OF ITS DISTINCTIVENESS. The structural and situational boundaries of a register are often blurred, and the degree of its implementation may vary. This variation in degree of distinctiveness (from other registers or an unmarked, "neu-

tral" variety) may itself be used as a marker of adjustment and eventually become conventionalized.

5. COMPETENCE IN REGISTER VARIATION IS ACQUIRED AS PART OF LANGUAGE DEVELOPMENT. Register variation is not something added on to the grammar or a way of using the grammar which is acquired separately; it is an integral part of language and is acquired simultaneously. Some registers may be acquired late in life, but register variation as such begins as soon as the child produces recognizable language.

I would like to conclude this section with an extension of assumption (5), offered as an hypothesis to be borne in mind as we continue to study the acquisition of communicative competence, and as we try to relate our findings to the understanding of the nature of human language and the construction of a general theory of language. If register variation is the tying of linguistic form to situational context, it may well be the case that human infants exhibit register variation even before they produce vocalizations recognizable as the beginnings of language. One aspect of language development, supported in studies of phonology, syntax, semantics, and lexicon, is the movement from situationally bound elements (e.g., words, sound complexes, formulaic routines) to decontextualized words, sounds, constructions, or forms of discourse that can be applied productively in new contexts (cf. Chaps. 16–18 in Lock 1978). In an important sense, then, register variation may be seen not as a refinement in the use of language but as a principal source of language structure itself.

Simplification

The notions of "simplicity" and "simplification" are among the most elusive concepts used in the characterization of language, and it may have caused more confusion than clarity to designate baby talk, foreigner talk, etc. as "simplified" registers. Yet, focussing on the evident simplification of such registers, in contrast to other language varieties, has the important consequence of relating these instances of linguistic simplification to other not obviously related instances.

Before proceeding to a discussion of simplification as such, two observations must be made. First, all simplified registers show differences from other registers (or from some hypothesized neutral, registrally unmarked variety) that are not simplifications. These other differences reflect such dimensions as expressivity or register identification (Ferguson 1977) and also deserve investigation, but they will be disregarded here.

Second, linguistic simplification may vary greatly in the functions or purposes it serves. A given linguistic subsystem, or even a whole variety, may be simplified from a corresponding subsystem or variety in order to facilitate acquisition, to reduce cognitive load, to save time and effort in communication, to give an appearance of ignorance, or to accommodate an interlocutor, to mention only a few purposes. The simplification may be done by language learner or language teacher, by note-taker or headline writer, by child acquiring mother tongue or adult speaking to foreigner. These different functions and occasions of simplification deserve extensive empirical investigation, but here they will be treated only marginally.[4]

Perhaps the most surprising fact about linguistic simplification—given the different definitions and theoretical perspectives of researchers and the widespread view that it is difficult to determine or measure simplicity either in language or in linguists' grammars of languages—is the general consensus regarding what in fact constitutes simplification. There is agreement, for example, that the characteristics shown in Table 4.1 represent simplification, either in the sense that B has been simplified from A, or at least in the sense that B is simpler than A.

Of the many authors who have made lists of the sort shown in Table 4.1, some have attempted to find common characterizations to subsume all the features listed. These are generally translatable into (a) reduction of inventory (linguistic form), semantic range, or language functions, and (b) regularization, that is, the elimination of alternative structures at certain levels (Mühlhäusler 1974). Simplification phenomena appear in forms of language other than simplified registers as defined here. For example, they appear in register variation that is not correlated with expectations of the hearer's inadequate linguistic competence.

Other examples include so-called "mother-in-law registers" (cf. Dixon 1971; Haviland 1979), which are used in the presence of certain in-laws before whom it is not appropriate to speak in unrestricted language, or note-taking (Janda forthcoming), in which the writer produces an abbreviated form of a lecture or other text for later use as a reminder or record of its content. Perhaps the term **simplified register** could be extended to such registers.

More importantly, simplification phenomena appear in instances other than register variation. Pidgins are typically simpler than their source language(s). The grammars of young children are typically sim-

---

[4] In particular we ignore here the question of whether fully competent speakers who "simplify" their speech are doing something cognitively more complex than using their normal, unsimplified language. Various types and functions of simplification are considered by the papers in Corder & Roulet (1977).

TABLE 4.1

A (More complex or unsimplified linguistic structure, as source or target)	B (Simpler or simplified linguistic structure)
Lexicon	
Larger vocabulary in a given semantic area or overall.	Smaller vocabulary, generic terms rather than specific.
Compounds and morphologically complex words.	Monomorphemic words, paraphrases of complex words.
Syntax	
Sentences with subordinate clauses.	No subordinate clauses, parataxis.
Variable word order conditioned by syntax (e.g., inversions, negative placement).	Invariant word order.
Presence of copula, pronouns, function words.	Absence of copula, pronouns, function words.
Morphology	
Extensive inflectional systems.	No inflections.
Allomorphy of stems.	Invariant stems (e.g., full forms as opposed to contractions).
Phonology	
Consonant clusters. Polysyllabic words.	CV monosyllables and CVCV disyllables.

pler than the grammars of the older children and adults whose language they are acquiring. The interlanguages of second-language learners are typically simpler than their target languages. The linguistic structure of a language which is being replaced by another language and is dying out is often simpler than the structure of the language when it was the principal language of its speech community. Often a language at one period in its history is simpler in many respects than the same language at another period either earlier or later. And there are many other instances. It is tempting to make the double hypothesis that these forms of simplification and their corresponding forms of elaboration or complexification represent similar linguistic or cognitive processes, and are elicited (triggered or caused) by similar communicative needs or conditions.

It is my conviction, however, that the greatest progress in this area will come from detailed empirical studies of DIFFERENCES in the synchronic patterns of simplification and diachronic paths to simplification in selected instances, and their relation to DIFFERENCES in occasions of occurrence and apparent functions. Two examples of this kind of research are (a) the simplification of consonant clusters in L_1 and L_2 acquisition and in language change (Macken & Ferguson 1981; Vihman 1980), and (b) the simplification of negative placement in L_1 and L_2 acquisition and pidginization (Meisel 1980; Wode 1976).

The first type of research has shown that cluster simplification may have similar outcomes in language acquisition and change, but that the paths followed, i.e., the intermediate steps between A and B, are considerably different. Also, the simplification in L_1 acquisition differs in many respects from that in L_2 acquisition: L_1 acquisition exhibits simplification processes such as consonant harmony and reduplication which are rare or nonexistent in L_2, and L_2 acquisition may involve interference or negative transfer from L_1, which does not occur in L_1 acquisition.

The second has shown that a general simplifying tendency to place the negative element immediately before the constituent to be negated frequently overrides other factors such as different patterns of negative placement, either in the source language or the target language. Meisel (1980) shows that the very same simplification pattern may be, in one speaker, part of a transitory grammar which is a prelude to further development (**elaborative simplification**) and in another speaker may be a kind of "taking it easy" when he or she knows better (**restrictive simplification**).

These two examples of research, though very limited in scope, have provided rich results and could possibly be extended to related patterns and occasions of simplification. Simplified registers would be an obvious field for extending the research. Some observations have been made about consonant clusters and negative placement in baby talk and foreigner talk, but they have lacked the precision of longitudinal case studies and quantitative comparisons found in the research cited.

At this point I would like to state and comment on three basic working assumptions of linguistic simplification that are widely followed by linguists.

1. All human languages are of EQUAL COMPLEXITY in their semantic–morphosyntactic–phonological systems and are acquired equally readily by children as their first language.
2. Human beings acquire their first language in accordance with a UNIVERSAL ORDER OF ACQUISITION going from simple to complex.
3. Human beings have an INNATE CAPACITY to recognize linguistic manifestations of a cognitive dimension of simple to complex.

The equal complexity assumption probably arose as a corrective to ethnocentric notions about the inadequacy of so-called "primitive languages" and to traditional views of the superiority of languages that have extensive and varied literature and documented histories. As such, it has played a useful role, but we must now acknowledge that, like any other proposed general principle, it requires empirical verification. Languages obviously differ in the simplicity of subsystems such as inflectional apparatus, and children take longer to acquire the more complex systems.[5] There is no convincing evidence that complexity in inflection in a language entails complementary simplicity in some other aspect of a language.[6] It also seems unlikely that all languages are acquired equally rapidly by L_1 learners, and linguistic simplicity is very likely one of the factors involved. Certainly the standard arguments for equal complexity do not withstand close scrutiny. For example, if all languages are equally complex because they are acquired at roughly the same age, how do we account for the fact that a child may acquire two or even three languages by that age? Are two languages taken together no more complex than a single language? Or, if pidgins are less complex than full natural languages and become normal languages by acquiring native speakers, how about the transition period? Does an incipient creole immediately snap into the position of equal complexity with all other languages? A few linguists have begun to discuss the sensitive issue of language inequality (Ferguson 1968; Hymes 1974; Hudson 1980), but serious cross-language study of linguistic simplicity–complexity has not even begun.

The universal order assumption was first enunciated by Jakobson (1968) for phonological development and later extended by psycholinguists to syntax and other aspects of language development. This assumption proved a valuable corrective to such concepts of language development as the notions of random error, the principle of least effort, and later to behaviorist models of development; it inspired a large number of empirical studies and has been one of the basic assumptions of psycholinguistic research. This body of research, however, led to increasing disillusionment as findings of individual differences, alternate routes of development, and various anomalies accumulated. The need for more complex models became evident as factors such as input, interactive patterns, cognitive strategies, and cultural differences in language socialization were recognized. It is only very recently that new, more cautious and heavily qualified formulations of universal order have begun to reappear (for phonology see Leonard *et al.*, 1980; for

---

[5] Slobin and his colleagues have repeatedly made this point in their cross-linguistic studies of language acquisition (e.g., Johnston & Slobin 1977).

[6] Even the widely held view that greater complexity in case morphology implies greater freedom in word order, turns out not to be valid in any simple, direct way (Steele 1978).

syntax see Meisel 1980) in which the authors provide for interaction of universal hierarchies of complexity with other kinds of factors.

The innate capacity assumption, at least in its modern version, began with Chomsky's rationalist outlook in linguistics which emphasized the innate, biologically given component in language acquisition, and a universal human capacity for language. This assumption served as a useful corrective to previous emphases on the environmentally given component in acquisition and the great structural diversity in human languages. This assumption, like the other two, has also had to withstand counterarguments and discrepant empirical findings, but instead of being abandoned it has been watered down to the assumption of a less linguistically specific capacity. The wording I have offered here is a modified version which includes linguistic simplicity (and its recognition by human language users) in a larger cognitive framework. The wording is suggested by Meisel's (1980) paper and the substance derives from the approach in Ferguson (1971). In any case, an hypothesized innate capacity to judge relative cognitive simplicity in language structure can be investigated by experimental psycholinguistic techniques, and simplified registers constitute an excellent field for such investigation. Even with the complications of overriding conventionalization of simplified register features, and the different purposes for which they are created and utilized, it is still possible to examine simplified registers for indications of the nature and applicability of human abilities to recognize linguistic–cognitive hierarchies of complexity.

Conclusion

Let me conclude by saying that the significance of the study of simplified registers is that it has much to teach us about the human processing of marginal systems in language, about the fundamental role of situational variation in the characterization of language structure, and about the elusive family of notions called simplicity which enter into many crucial areas of language change, acquisition, and loss. All three of these areas touch on fundamental issues of language theory, and simplified registers offer a unique resource for their investigation.

References

Bickerton, D. (1973) The nature of a creole continuum. *Language, 49,* 640–669.
Brown, P., & Levinson, S. (1978) Universals in language usage: politeness phenomena. In E. Goody (Ed.), *Questions and politeness: Strategies in social interaction.* Cambridge: Cambridge University Press. Pp. 56–289, esp. 183–209.

Cedergren, H., & Sankoff, D. (1974) Variable rules: Performance as a statistical reflection of competence. *Language, 50,* 333–355.

Clyne, M.G., (Ed.) (1981) *Foreigner talk (International journal of the sociology of language 28).* The Hague: Mouton.

Corder, S.P., & Roulet, E., (Eds.) (1977) *The Notions of simplification interlanguages and pidgins and their relations to second language pedagogy.* Neuchâtel, Switzerland: Université Neuchâtel Faculté des lettres.

Cruttenden, A. (1977) The acquisition of personal pronouns and language "simplification." *Language and speech, 20,* 191–197.

DeCamp, D. (1971) Toward a generative analysis of a post-creole continuum. In D. Hymes (Ed.), *Pidginization and creolization of language.* Cambridge: Cambridge University Press. Pp. 349–370.

Dittmar, N., & Klein, W. (1979) *Developing grammars: The acquisition of German syntax by foreign workers.* Berlin: Springer-Verlag.

Dixon, R.M.W. (1971) A method of semantic description. In D.D. Steinberg & L.A. Jakobovits (Eds.), *Semantics: An interdisciplinary reader in philosophy, linguistics, and psychology.* Cambridge: Cambridge University Press. Pp. 436–471.

Ferguson, C.A. (1968) Language development. In J.A. Fishman *et al.* (Eds.), *Language problems of developing nations.* New York: Holt, Rinehart & Winston. Pp. 27–35. [Also in A.S. Dil (Ed.) (1971) *Language structure and language use.* Stanford, CA: Stanford University Press.]

Ferguson, C.A. (1971) Absence of copula and the notion of simplicity: A study of normal speech, baby talk, foreigner talk and pidgins. In D. Hymes (Ed.), *Pidginization and creolization of language.* Cambridge: Cambridge University Press. Pp. 141–150.

Ferguson, C.A. (1977) Baby talk as a simplified register. In C.E. Snow & C.A. Ferguson (Eds.), *Talking to children: Language input and acquisition.* Cambridge: Cambridge University Press. Pp. 209–235.

Ferguson, C.A. (1978) Talking to children: A search for universals. In J.H. Greenberg *et al.* (Eds.), *Universals of human language,* Vol. 1. Stanford, CA: Stanford University Press. Pp. 203–224.

Ferguson, C.A. (1981) "Foreigner talk" as the name of a simplified register. *International journal of the sociology of language, 28,* 9–18.

Ferguson, C.A., & DeBose, C.E. (1977) Simplified registers, broken language, and pidginization. In A. Valdman (Ed.), *Pidgin and creole linguistics.* Bloomington, IN: Indiana University Press. Pp. 99–125.

Ferguson, C.A., & Macken, M.A. (1981) Phonological development in children: Play and cognition. In K.E. Nelson (Ed.), *Children's language,* Vol. 4. New York: Gardner Press.

Gleason, J.B., & Weintraub, S. (1978) Input language and the acquisition of communicative competence. In K.E. Nelson (Ed.), *Children's language,* Vol. 1. New York: Gardner Press. Pp. 171–222.

Halle, M. (1962) Phonology in generative grammar. *Word, 18,* 54–72.

Haviland, J.B. (1979) How to talk to your brother-in-law in Guugu Yimidhirr. In T. Shopen (Ed.), *Languages and their speakers.* Cambridge, MA: Winthrop Publishers. Pp. 161–239.

Head, B.F. (1978) Respect degrees in pronominal reference. In J.H. Greenberg *et al.* (Eds.), *Universals of human language,* Vol. 3. Stanford, CA: Stanford University Press. Pp. 151–211.

Hudson, R.A. (1980) Linguistic and social inequality. In *Sociolinguistics.* Cambridge: Cambridge University Press. Pp. 191–230.

Hymes, D. (1974) Speech and language: On the origins and foundations of inequality among speakers. In M. Bloomfield & E. Haugen (Eds.), *Language as a human problem.* New York: Norton. Pp. 45–71.

Jakobson, R. (1968) *Child language, aphasia, and phonological universals.* The Hague: Mouton. (Tr. of original edition in German 1941).

Janda, R.D. (forthcoming) The language of note-taking as a simplified register. To appear in *Discourse Processes.*

Johnston, J.R., & Slobin, D.I. (1977) The development of locative expressions in English, Italian, Serbo-Croatian, and Turkish. *Papers and reports in child language development,* 13, 134–147.

Klein, W. (1974) *Variation in der Sprache; ein Verfahren zu ihrer Beschreibung.* Kronberg Ts.: Scriptor Verlag.

Labov, W. (1969) Contraction, deletion, and inherent variability of the English copula. *Language, 45,* 715–762.

Lavandera, B. (1978) When does the sociolinguistic variable stop? *Language in Society, 7,* 171–182.

Leonard, L.B., Newhoff, M., & Mesalam, L. (1980) Individual differences in early child phonology. *Journal of applied psycholinguistics, 1,* 7–30.

Lock, A. (Ed.) (1978) *Action, gesture and symbol: the emergence of language.* London: Academic Press.

Long, M.H. (1981) Input, interaction, and second language acquisition. Paper presented at the New York Academy of Sciences Conference on Native Language and Foreign Language Acquisition. To appear in *The Annals of the New York Academy of Sciences.*

Macken, M.A., & Ferguson, C.A. (1981) Phonological universals in language acquisition. Paper presented at the New York Academy of Sciences Conference on Native Language and Foreign Language Acquisition. To appear in *The Annals of the New York Academy of Sciences.*

Meisel, J.M. (1980) Strategies of second language acquisition, more than one kind of simplification. Unpublished paper, University of Hamburg.

Mühlhäusler, P. (1974) *Pidginization and simplification of language.* (*Pacific linguistics,* series B, Monograph No. 26.) Canberra: Department of Linguistics, Research School of Pacific Studies, Australian National University.

Reid, T.B.W. (1956) Linguistics, structuralism and philology. *Archivum Linguisticum, 8,* 28–37.

Rūķe-Draviņa, V. (1976) Gibt es Universalien in der Ammensprache? *Salzburger Beiträge zur Linguistik, 2,* 3–16.

Sherzer, J. (1976) Play languages: implications for (socio-)linguistics. In B. Kirschenblatt-Gimblett (Ed.), *Speech play.* Philadelphia: University of Pennsylvania Press. Pp. 19–36.

Snow, C.E. (1979) Conversations with children. In P. Fletcher & M. Garman (Eds.), *Language acquisition.* Cambridge: Cambridge University Press. Pp. 363–375.

Steele, S. (1978) Word order variation: A typological study. In J.H. Greenberg *et al.* (Eds.), *Universals of human language,* Vol. 4. Stanford, CA: Stanford University Press. Pp. 585–623.

Uspensky, B.A., & Zhivov, V.M. (1977) Center–periphery opposition and language universals. *Linguistics,* 196, Pp. 5–24.

Vachek, J. (Ed.) (1966) *Les problèmes du centre et de la périphérie du système de la langue.* (*Travaux linguistiques de Prague 2*) Prague: Academia and University, AL: University of Alabama Press.

Vihman, M.M. (1980) Sound change and child language. In E.C. Traugott *et al.* (Eds.), *Papers from the Fourth International Conference on Historical Linguistics*. Amsterdam: John Benjamins. Pp. 303–320.

Wills, D.D. (1977) Participant deixis in English and baby talk. In C.E. Snow & C.A. Ferguson (Eds.), *Talking to children: Language input and acquisition*. Cambridge: Cambridge University Press. Pp. 271–295.

Wode, H. (1976) Developmental sequences in naturalistic L_2 acquisition. *Working Papers on Bilingualism, 11*, 1–31.

5
ADRIENNE LEHRER

Critical Communication: Wine and Therapy

When considering syntax and phonology, we have some notion of how an ideal speaker might behave. Such a speaker would not make grammatical mistakes even when very drunk and tired, could handle sentences with multiple embedding, would always finish sentences, would never dangle participles, and would always make the verbs agree with the subject. When we turn to semantics, however, it is not so clear how an ideal speaker would behave. Presumably he or she would have a huge vocabulary. Such a speaker of English would know the whole of *Webster's Third*, the *Oxford English Dictionary*, the *Dictionary of American Slang*, and *Roget's Thesaurus*. Beyond that, would such an ideal speaker always speak literally, or would he or she also be a poet and use rich imagery and novel metaphors? The vocabularies of languages continue to grow not only because of new inventions and processes, but also because speakers discover new ways of talking about things that they had not before known how to talk about. Would our ideal speaker be so creative that nothing was ineffable?

Real speakers do not, of course, have the total resources of the vocabulary available to them. Moreover, the meaning of many words is fluid and vague. The vocabulary is finite, but the number of situations, things, and facts is infinite, and real speakers must therefore make do with what they have. In addition, there are areas of experience in which many speakers acknowledge lexical gaps, either on their own part or on the part of the language, yet they are areas of experience that people want to talk about. One such domain is sensation.

EXCEPTIONAL LANGUAGE AND LINGUISTICS

Finding words to describe perceptions and sensations often strikes people as a hard task. When I tell others that I have been working on the vocabulary of wine tasting, a common response is, "That must be difficult. English has so few words for tastes." And Langer (1957) writes, "Everybody knows that language is a very poor medium for expressing our emotional nature. It merely names certain vaguely and crudely conceived states, but fails miserably in any attempt to convey the ever moving patterns, the ambivalence and intricacies of inner experience. . . . [p. 100]." Yet people do manage, somehow, to find words for their sensations and feelings.

In this chapter I will look at conversations involving these two topics, drawing on the notion of "critical communication," a term introduced by Isenberg (1954) to analyze aesthetics discourse. In this kind of discourse, language is used in novel and nonstereotypical ways; moreover, the words are very loosely linked to their referents and denotata. Later I will contrast critical communication with scientific discourse. Isenberg is concerned with the function of criticism.

> It seems that the critic's *meaning* is 'filled in', 'rounded out', or 'completed' by the act of perception, which is performed not to judge the truth of his description but in a certain sense to *understand* it. And if *communication* is a process by which a mental content is transmitted by symbols from one person to another, then we can say that it is a function of criticism to bring about communication at the level of the senses; that is, to induce a sameness of vision, of experienced content. If this is accomplished, it may or may not be followed by agreement, or what is called 'communion'—a community of feeling which expresses itself in identical value judgments [pp. 137–138].

The critic, in other words, tries to get others to perceive some nonobvious property or quality in a work of art, literature, or a piece of music— that is, to see or hear or feel what the critic has seen, heard, or felt. The reader of such criticism, in order to benefit, must have the aesthetic object present or with "direct recollect." The communication is successful if the individual who hears or reads the criticism is able to pick out the property or quality described.

If two conversational participants are looking at a painting, for example, one speaker could simply point to a part of the painting and say, *Look at this here.* But a deictic like *this* might be insufficient, since a painting can be enjoyed or studied at many levels. Does the speaker wish to call attention to the color, the lines, the forms, or something more abstract like balance, excitement, or originality? The speaker could more precisely convey specific intentions with, *Notice the tension pro-*

duced in this corner—the bright red pulls your eye in one direction, while the bright blue over here pulls it away.

Case I: Wine Conversation

Wine shares some characteristics with natural substances (like sucrose or olive oil) but also some characteristics with aesthetic objects. People often discuss wine, and my original interest in wine conversation grew out of observing people talk about wine, seemingly enjoying the conversation as much as the wine. It is in the setting of two or more people drinking and discussing wine together that critical communication occurs. Because wines are complex objects, and because there is a great variety among the wines available, wine conversation often consists of one conversational participant pointing out some subtle property in a particular wine to others in this setting, and it is necessary to use language. It is of little help to point physically. It is not even clear what to point at—the glass of wine or the wine drinker's tongue.

I have studied wine discussions for the past several years and have conducted experiments to elicit such talk. One set of experiments was done in as naturalistic a setting as possible, by holding wine parties at my home (see Lehrer 1978a). The conversations were recorded, and the discussions were similar to spontaneous ones I have observed at dinner parties or in wine tasting rooms.

Although my subjects (at least those who considered themselves nonexpert, ordinary wine drinkers) would frequently apologize by saying that they did not know many wine words, when they actually began to describe wines, they managed to find lots of words. Consider the discussion of two wines which were served to a group of subjects meeting for the first time. Three wines were served at this session. Subjects were provided with a list of wine descriptors which they could use to describe each wine. Afterward the group described the three wines. Excerpts from the conversations follow.

Adrienne: *Why don't we start with [wine] B?*
 L: *There's something funny in the smell of that, I can't quite get hold of—Strange.*
 N: *Rich or something.*
 C: *Smell is okay in the beginning.*
 L: *The other two are a little—*
 O: *Fat.*
Adrienne: *The wine instructor we had in California described this as the **furry – vegy** smell.*

L: *Vegetable.*
H: *It smells like a chemical used.*
L: *It's interesting; I don't get that in the bouquet any more, but I get it in the taste.*
H: *Like Mazola?*
L: *I think I'd describe it as **fruity**, but not vegetable.*
B: *It's acidic, so dry, I couldn't get any other taste.*
L: *Pretty acidic. There's something about B, because it didn't drink well, which acidic wines usually do.*
K: *Age in the glass.*
B: *Very young.*
L: *You tolerated it better as you went on.*
K: *But after a rinse of water, it was like starting fresh again. Let it sit on your tongue and it hit you again.*
Adrienne: *How about wine V?*
L: *I did **oaky** because it's related to **vegetable**, though it isn't technical because it's not characteristic of oak. It reminds me of wood.*
C: *I just put down **insipid**—that's the only word.*
M: ***Ordinary.** I put that down.*
O: *I thought it was pretty rugged.*
H: *Yeah, rugged . . . almost chewy.*
K: *You can almost chew on it.*
R: *Yeah, that's very good. That tastes like mutton.*
H: *Tastes like lamb, especially if you're fond of lamb.*
R: *It tastes like the kind of wine you drink with good food.*
L: *Strong flavor.*
R: *I don't know, it just reminded me of mutton.*

I had provided subjects with a list of common wine descriptors so that they would not feel tongue-tied by not knowing any wine words, but the list in no way constrained the subjects, who freely used other words, for example, *vegetable, chewy, taste of mutton, chemical.*

In the discussion of wine B, subjects noticed something salient in the smell and attempted to more precisely characterize what it was. In the case of wine V, the description of chewy, and the comparison with lamb or mutton succeeded, at least with some of the wine drinkers, in getting others to perceive a quality or property.

At a session 2 weeks later with the same subjects, three white wines were served.

Adrienne: *Why don't we start with wine Q, because that seems to be the driest.*
C: *It smells like roast nuts.*
Adrienne: *It smells like what?*
C: *Roast nuts.*
H: *Like something burnt.*

L: *Burnt rubber, chemical, medicinal.*
C: *No.*
L: *No?*
M: *Half medicinal.*
Adrienne: *I gather that you people didn't like Q.*
M: *I put **withered.***
G: *Austere.*
B: *I like the sort of sour taste on my tongue, but then it turned very sweet.*
Adrienne: *You get a sweet aftertaste?*
M: *I get a medicinal aftertaste.*
L: *I get that in wine P, but you got that in Q?*
B: *I got that in Q.*
H: *Sweet aftertaste?*
B: *Well, maybe it's sour and then right afterwards it's sweet. But then it wasn't all that unpleasant. I thought that it was interesting.*
Adrienne: *What other terms were selected?*
M: *I put **alcoholic.** It smells like something I met up with in lab.*
N: *You don't have **vinegary** on your list. That struck me as vinegary.*
R: *A little bit too pungent for vinegar. You know, it's almost autumnal.*
G: *Like burning leaves in New England?*
P: *Yeah.*
G: *Like burning leaves.*

The description of wine Q provides an especially good example of critical communication. This wine apparently had two properties. One was something unusual in the aftertaste, and was described as *medicinal* or *sweet*. The other had to do with the smell that was described in terms of words related to burnt—burnt rubber, burning leaves in New England, or roast nuts. Such descriptions get other tasters to focus on properties of the wine and to try to find some quality that fits the description. Characterization like *autumnal* or *burning leaves in New England* may be rather far-fetched, but these phrases were apparently successful for subjects H and R. "Success" here means that the intentions of the speaker were correctly recognized by the hearer.

We might ask whether wine Q really had the aroma of roast nuts. But is this a legitimate question to ask in the context of critical communication? Suppose that two individuals—A and B—are drinking a wine together, and A says to B, *Notice the earthy quality on the back of the tongue in the aftertaste.* If B then notices a property of the wine, the communication has succeeded, even if the most distinguished wine experts would deny that this wine had any earthiness about it. And suppose that two different individuals—C and D—are drinking the same wine, but C describes this very same property as *chalky*. If D notices this property as a result of what C says, then their communication has succeeded as well. In both of these cases, the communication was successful—that is, the hearers correctly apprehended the speakers intentions, although the words used—*earthy* in one case and *chalky* in the other—were different. But since the words are not synonyms, from a normative or scientific point of view, both cannot be correct, and in fact both could be incorrect. From the point of view of critical communication it does not matter, since the question of correctness is irrelevant.

In critical communication, truth plays a secondary role. Isenberg (1954) remarks that these utterances look like other kinds of statements, and have thus misled philosophers into trying to analyze them like other kinds of statements, using a truth-conditional analysis, for example. The function of an utterance like *some chalkiness on the back of the tongue,* is according to Isenberg, not to state a truth but to point out a quality. The statement serves merely to get the hearer to notice something.

But, one may ask, how do we know that they are referring to the same property? Suppose that the wine in question has two subtle properties. Speaker A refers to one of them by describing it as *earthy,* but Speaker B picks out the other property. In this case, the communication could not be called successful, although neither conversational participant would know that. Yet speaker B's experience might have been enhanced anyway.

I will give one more example of wine discourse. At one session three tasters were describing three different wines for a matching experiment. The other subjects would later be served the same three wines, and they would have to match these wines with the descriptions offered by the first three.

F: *I think this wine is spicy with dill or something.* (To V) *You don't get the dill?*
V: *Un-un.*
E: *Smell is sort of dill.*
V: *I agree on the spicy, but*
P: *Not **dill**. Hm.*
O: *This one* [O] *is just sort of spicy and tangy, and this one* [F] *is really pungent.*
F: *Not dill. Huh. Some vegetable, though.*
E: *Spicy, dill, what else? Grass? That's ambiguous. Grain.*
V: *It doesn't taste citrusy to you? It kind of tastes—quininish or something.*
F: *Quinine. I don't know quinine as a taste, so—oh, the quinine water. Well, now I wouldn't have said dill the first time when I tasted it, but when I got it fresh—*
D: *I was thinking rooty—sort of rooty.*
E: *It's interesting—**charcoal** is a word that—charcoal is a common flavor. It seems to me to fit food because we're used to eating charcoaled food.*

The characterization that was finally agreed on was "spicy bouquet, spicy on the palate, tangy, intermediate in flavor and body, good character."

The group of three was finally satisfied with its description, and the members felt that it succeeded in its critical communication—at least with respect to noticing certain aromas and flavors. There may have been less satisfaction, however, in naming these properties. During the experiment, when the rest of the subjects were presented with three wines and three descriptions, some subjects failed to match correctly. A discussion later revealed some of the linguistic problems.

I: *I had trouble with the word* **spicy.** *How do people usually use that? I don't think of oregano.*

F: *How would* **dill** *have been? Would that have been helpful?*

P: *That would have been much better.* **Spicy** *I think of maybe cinnamon.*

I: *When I think of* **spicy,** *I think of the sweet side—I think of spice cake rather than garlic pizza.*

F: *What do you think about* **spicy?**

O: *Think same things, spice cake.*

F: *Yeah, I thought* **dill** *or* **oregano**—*in that direction.*

B: *Would* **herbal** *have been better?*

F: **Herbal.** *That would have been better.*

I: *Yeah.*

Notice the differences between these two tasting circumstances. In the presession, the speakers knew that they were drinking the same wines, and so their problem was to try to find appropriate words to describe it. They assumed that they were noticing the same properties for each of the wines. And if that were so, their critical communication was successful. During the matching experiment, the task was quite different, and the choice of one word—*spicy*—rather than a different word which would have designated a slightly different property—*herbal*—led to a communication failure on the part of some subjects.

When speakers can agree on a wine description, they are often very pleased at having done so. I have noticed throughout my wine research the great satisfaction experienced by wine drinkers when they could find appropriate words for the wines they were drinking.

Case II: Psychotherapeutic Discourse

The therapeutic situation has some of the properties of discourse which we have called critical communication. The client or patient and the therapist talk to each other about the client's feelings, motives, and problems. There are additional problems besides that of finding the right words. The client may, according to some theories, be trying to repress or suppress feelings rather than express them. The therapist, too, has a problem, since he or she must present an interpretation to the client which is acceptable. However, the therapeutic case *is* like critical communication in that communication is successful if the speaker can somehow convey to the hearer feelings, beliefs, or interpretation of those feelings and beliefs, using whatever linguistic or other means are available. The language used may be personal, idiosyncratic, and un-conventional, as is often found in aesthetic language.

As Labov and Fanshel (1977) point out, the therapeutic literature takes for granted the texts of patients' discourse. Only a few writers discuss the difficulties involved in using language. Greenson (1967) writes:

> Skill in imparting insight to a patient depends upon one's ability to put into words the thoughts, fantasies, and feelings which the patient is not fully aware of and to present them in such a way that the patient can accept them as his own. One must translate from one's own vocabulary into the living language of the patient at the moment [p. 385].

Sullivan (1954) discusses the linguistic limitations which some patients have.

> Sometimes the patient's use of words is extraordinary. He is apparently depending on a word to communicate something to you which it doesn't communicate at all, and you realize that he is still quite autistic in his verbal thinking and that there has been a very serious impairment of this extremely important aspect of his socialization [p. 152].

Rogers (1961, 1965) presents many lengthy quotations from clients trying to describe their feelings. One can see in these texts a creative and original as well as a personal use of language. One example is from the notes of Miss Cam, who kept a diary of her feelings.

> It took four hours to write that page and a half—four hours of sinking down—no, it's not sinking down, it's more like expanding, as if bonds were loosened, and an homogeneous design got larger and larger, until you could see that what looked like continuous lines were really composed of rows of separate points, and as the design spreads out, the points get farther apart, until finally the connections become so tenuous that it snaps, and the pattern collapses into a wild jumble of unrelated bits and pieces [Rogers 1965 p. 95].

Miss Cam combines movement and design images to convey her feelings. Other descriptions reported in Rogers compare the feelings of the patient to a dam or an animal.

> It suddenly became clear that loving and hating, for example, are neither right nor wrong, they just are. After this, the wall seemed to disappear but beyond it, I discovered a dam holding back violent, churning waters. I felt as if I were holding back the force of these waters and if I opened even a tiny hole, I and all about me would be destroyed in the ensuing torrent of feelings represented by the water [Rogers 1965 p. 169].

> I have felt it . . . inside as though it were a little animal coming out of a case—just a defenseless animal, who has been unmercifully defeated, horribly lacerated and bleeding. . . . Now I don't feel any longer as though I see him. I feel as though I *am* that little animal, whipped and helpless and terribly wounded [Rogers 1965 p. 124].

This last description is interesting in several respects. First, the patient had to imagine and project what a beaten and wounded animal must feel like. Then, in comparing herself to this animal, she must assume that the therapist would also be able to imagine and project the same thing.

The responses by the therapists to the descriptions of feelings by the patients are not given, so that we do not know whether such descriptions were successful—or at least whether the therapists thought they understood what feeling was being discussed.

One very interesting case is discussed by Labov and Fanshel (1977). The patient, Rhoda, could not admit that she felt anger toward her mother and aunt and would only admit to feeling *bothered* or *annoyed*.

> *Therapist:* So-then-and for some reason you feel they're angry because you're so underweight, or because they think you're underweight.
> *Rhoda:* I don't—I dunno, I don't—I don't—I never felt like that—it's just that . . . no I never thought if I like that and I don't I don't think I feel anger because I mean I just get annoyed, like I'm not—I don't say I get—angry, but it just gets annoying, to hear the same thing.
> (Later in the interview)
> *Therapist:* So there's a lot of anger passing back and forth.
> (This remark is followed by a long silence.)
> *Rhoda:* Yeh.   [Labov & Fanshel, 1977 Pp. 318–320]

The case with Rhoda illustrates the need for each pair in the therapeutic session to work out a satisfactory vocabulary. The therapist and Labov and Fanshel describe Rhoda's feeling as *anger,* a feeling which she cannot admit at this state of treatment. So Rhoda's own description of her feelings as *bothered* is inaccurate. It is possible that a therapist might want to say something like, *See here, Rhoda, you're mad as hell. Why don't you admit that?* However, such a strategy would be used only for therapeutic purposes—because the therapist thought it would influence the course of treatment in a constructive way—not for the purposes of scientific accuracy.

Sullivan (1954) comments on the use of theoretical terms in therapy interviews: " 'Mother-fixation' may be a beautiful, abstract idea, useful for the psychiatrist's private ruminations, but to the person who suffers the 'mother-fixation', the term is as nearly devoid of meaning, as near to being claptrap, as anything I can think of [p. 36]." Whatever the merits of theoretical terms for scientific purposes, they may be ineffective or detrimental in the therapeutic context. Stephen Shanfield (personal communication) points out that a therapist will discourage the use of these technical terms so that the patients will not immediately intellectualize their feelings.

What are the features of critical communication in the therapeutic situation? First of all, assuming that the patient is not trying to deceive himself or the therapist, he is trying to convey his feelings using descriptive words, if such words are available to him, or metaphors, comparisons, or images that might evoke "a sameness of vision, or experienced content" (Isenberg 1954 p. 138). Second, we see the conversation must be meaningful and appropriate to the participants. Scientific accuracy, as determined by an authoritative body of psychological experts, is simply irrelevant.

Critical Communication and Theories of Meaning

There has been a tendency in philosophy to regard scientific language as the ideal form of language. This can be seen in the writing of the logical positivists, such as Carnap (1937), and more recently in the works of Putnam (1975), in which we are told to ask experts in a field about how to use words properly and to give us the correct meaning. The communicative needs of a scientific community, however, are different from those of participants engaging in critical communication. A scientific community disseminates information for the most part by written means—books and journals—to members throughout the world. Moreover, most members do not know personally all of the other members of this community. Under these conditions, it is not possible for each member to learn about the idiosyncratic word usages of the others. In addition, one goal of scientific discourse is to communicate truth statements, not to induce a sameness of vision or to enhance an experience.

The problem of **theory-laden description** has been discussed by Hanson (1958) and Kuhn (1962). They argue that simple observations are not purely objective and free of bias. Indeed, one's observations are often influenced by one's beliefs, expectations, and previous experiences. But even if members of a scientific community (or subcommunity, if you like) share a theoretical perspective, can we be sure that they describe and report observations in the same way?

In certain physical sciences, physics and chemistry for example, descriptive statements involving perceptual terms like *blue* or *hot* have been replaced by a different set of concepts—color by wave length, heat by molecular motion, and substances like water by molecular formulae, where descriptions can be stated in terms of instrumental measurements. Practitioners in the social sciences have not yet achieved this degree of precision, and it is not clear that they ever will. One concern in the social sciences is to study the ways people perceive, think, and categorize. Therefore, scientists cannot IN PRINCIPLE replace statements of perception and judgment with mechanical or instrumental measurements unless a one-to-one correlation between the judgments and the measurements can be proved. But this kind of correlation is often not found. One of the major results of the acoustic studies of speech is that a perceived sound cannot be placed in a one-to-one correspondence with its physical signal.

Many social scientists are acutely aware of the problems of standardizing observational language and of training the young scientists to learn and use this vocabulary properly—that is, consensually. Scientists involved in the emerging science of enology—the study of wine—have described the training procedures for teaching people to use a descriptive vocabulary. (See Amerine, Panghorn, & Roessler 1965, and Williams 1975, for a procedure for investigating sensory judgments of ciders.)

Many studies of psychiatric diagnosis have shown that diagnoses are not sufficiently reliable. As a result, recent researchers, as those involved in the World Health Organization Report of the International Pilot Study of Schizophrenia (1973); went to great lengths to standardize the use of terms among clinicians participating in the study, to train those clinicians using videotapes, to check diagnoses with other clinicians, and to assess the reliability of the whole study.

An enologist who writes that a wine is earthy, or a clinician who writes that a patient has simple schizophrenia, or a phonetician who writes that a language has breathy vowels, hopes that the audience will understand the words in the same way—that the observational language is truly conventionalized, not only in terms of the definitions, which show intralinguist relationships, (synonymy, antonymy, hyponymy, incompatibility, etc.), but also in the denotations—and in the same way that members of that community apply words to things and properties.

This situation and its communicative needs are special, and they arise under certain conditions. There is no reason to hold up scientific language as a model for all language use. The critical communication situation is completely different. There, the participants talk to each other directly, generally in the presence of a stimulus, such as a bottle of wine or a work of art. A set of conventionalized descriptors may not exist, or if they do, the participants may not know them.

Even outside of scientific discourse, theories of meaning have tended to assume that words have relatively fixed meanings, though these meanings may change over time through standard processes of semantic change, such as widening, and metaphorical transfer. The bulk of work in psycholinguistics with which I am familiar has focused on the stereotypical aspects of meaning. There is nothing wrong with this as a start, since to appreciate novel and creative word uses one must set them against a background of ordinary and mundane word uses.

Moreover, the nature of creativity and novelty is such that scientists cannot predict what will occur or when. However, linguists can pay more attention to work done by their colleagues in stylistics and literary analysis, and psycholinguists can try to set up experiments to elicit creativity and imagination. A very nice study which describes and explains creativity after the facts is by Clark and Clark (1978), who analyze expressions such as *He houdinied his way out of the closet.* They examine a variety of pragmatic strategies available to speakers for turning nouns into verbs. Semantic field theories also provide a basis for explaining and, to a limited extent, predicting how word meanings can be expanded and transferred to account for new meanings (see Kittay & Lehrer 1981; Lehrer 1978b; forthcoming). These linguistic studies, however, focus on intralinguistic relationships—the connections between linguistic items—which must be combined with reference and denotation to provide a complete theory of meaning.

The theories of meaning most able to handle critical communication would be intention-based theories, such as those advocated by Bach and Harnish (1979), Grice (1957), and Schiffer (1973). The hearer must figure out the intentions of the speaker on the basis of what the speaker says in that context, and on the basis of what he/she knows about the speaker and his or her idiolect. Conventional meaning may exist but is not required in this analysis.

Theories of meaning in which reference, denotation, and truth play a major role, have a much more limited role in critical communication.

Truth conditional theories of semantics equate meaning with truth conditions, so that to know the meaning of a sentence is to know the conditions under which a sentence would be true. Speakers might be genuinely perplexed if they were required to decide under what conditions sentences such as *This wine is autumnal* might be true. However, such an utterance might spark recognition and joy in the hearer. In critical communication, if a speaker says that a wine has an earthy taste, and if the hearer picks out that property, then it does not matter whether experts would identify that property as earthy or as something else.

Summary

I have argued that scientific discourse and truth conditional theories of meaning are limited in their scope and applicability. The need for precise, conventionalized, and standardized description arises out of special needs—namely, to do science. I have presented material from two domains—describing wines and describing feelings—where participants want to communicate but in which either no precise descriptors exist, or where the participants do not know them. However, they have at their disposal linguistic means to communicate anyway, and one can observe a great deal of creativity, inventiveness, and imagination in their use of language. If the hearers succeed in understanding, that is, apprehending the intentions of the speakers, and in picking out the properties referred to, then the communication is successful. Although original and novel word and sentence uses cannot be predicted, the devices and strategies available to speakers can be studied and described, enabling us to at least predict the kinds of creativity that are likely to occur.

References

Amerine, M., Panghorn, R.M., & Roessler, E. (1965) *Principles of sensory evaluation of food.* New York: Academic Press.

Bach, K. & Harnish, R.M. (1979) *Linguistic communication and speech acts.* Cambridge, MA: MIT Press.

Carnap, R. (1937) *Logical syntax of language.* New York: Harcourt, Brace & Co.

Clark, E. & Clark, H. (1978) When nouns surface as verbs. *Language, 55,* 767–811.

Greenson, R. (1967) *The technique and practice of psychoanalysis, I.* New York: International University Press.

Grice, H.P. (1957) Meaning. *Philosophical review, 66,* 377–88.

Hanson, N.R. (1958) *Patterns of discovery.* Cambridge: Cambridge University Press.

Isenberg, A. (1954) Critical communication. In W. Elton (Ed.), *Aesthetics and language.* New York: Philosophical Library. Pp. 114–30.

Kittay, E. & Lehrer, A. (1981) Semantic fields and the structure of metaphor. *Studies in language 5*, 31–63.

Kuhn, T. (1962) *The structure of scientific revolution.* Chicago: University of Chicago Press.

Labov, W., & Fanshel, D. (1977) *Therapeutic discourse.* New York: Academic Press.

Langer, S.K. (1957) *Philosophy in a new key.* Cambridge, MA: Harvard University Press.

Lehrer, A. (1978a) We drank wine, we talked, and a good time was had by all. *Semiotica, 23*, 243–78.

Lehrer, A. (1978b) Structures of the lexicon and transfer of meaning. *Lingua, 45*, 95–123.

Lehrer, A. (in press) *Wine and Conversation.* Bloomington: Indiana University Press.

Putnam, H. (1975) The meaning of meaning. K. Gunderson (Ed.) In *Language, mind, and knowledge. Minnesota studies in the philosophy of science,* VII. Minneapolis: University of Minnesota Press.

Rogers, C.R. (1961) *On becoming a person.* Boston: Houghton Mifflin.

Rogers, C.R. (1965) *Client-centered therapy.* Boston: Houghton Mifflin.

Schiffer, S. (1973) *Meaning.* Oxford: Oxford University Press.

Sullivan, H.S. (1954) *The psychiatric interview.* New York: Norton.

Williams, A.A. (1975) The development of a vocabulary and profile assessment method for evaluating the flavor contribution of cider and perry aroma constituents. *Journal of the science of food and agriculture, 26*, 567–82.

World Health Organization (1973) *Report of the international pilot study of schizophrenia,* Vol 1, Geneva.

6 VEDA R. CHARROW

Linguistic Theory and the Study of Legal and Bureaucratic Language

The purpose of this chapter is to examine some aspects of linguistic theory in light of the real-world phenomena of legal and bureaucratic language. It is, on the one hand, an attempt to characterize briefly legal and bureaucratic language from a linguistic point of view. It is also an attempt to characterize what it is that linguists know about language that would allow them to analyze, describe, and explain legal and bureaucratic language and other exceptional varieties of language. But, more importantly, it is an attempt to find the gaps in the linguist's metalinguistic competence and performance—areas where the science of linguistics lacks the pieces of theory that would allow us to better understand these varieties of language, or where we as linguists have not traditionally had the interest or impetus to study real-world language use. It is an attempt to demonstrate how an understanding of legal and bureaucratic language can contribute to building theory in historical linguistics, grammar, sociolinguistics, and linguistic metatheory.

I will first discuss the work of linguists and other social scientists in the area of legal and bureaucratic language. On the basis of studies and linguists' experiences in working with legal and bureaucratic language, I will provide a brief description of these varieties of English. I will then point out how various aspects of linguistic theory—historical linguistics, theories of grammar, sociolinguistic theories, and theories of language competence and performance—have contributed to our understanding of language use in the real world of law and government. I will also point out gaps in our theoretical knowledge—areas where linguistic

81

theory has not offered anything useful to the investigator of real-world language use, and areas that theoretical linguists have not yet tackled. I will attempt to point out areas where the study of real-world language can be used to find gaps and flaws in linguistic theory, and a few areas where an understanding of legal and bureaucratic language is potentially useful as a metric for choosing among competing theories of grammar.

An Introduction to Legal and Bureaucratic Language

Legal language, ("legalese"), as I use the term in this chapter, is the variety of English[1] used by lawyers, judges, and other members of the legal community in the course of their work. It is primarily a WRITTEN code, although there are specific instances of spoken legalese—particularly in court proceedings. Legalese is used in all types of legal documents—wills, leases, contracts, loan forms, briefs, memoranda, statutes, laws—as well as in legal opinions, law school textbooks, and casebooks. The following is an example of typical legalese:

> *You are hereby commanded to take Larry Litigant if he shall be found in your bailiwick, and keep him safe so that you have his body before the Circuit Court of this County now holding at the town of Upper Marlboro, in this County, immediately to answer unto the plaintiff on her petition and rule to seek alimony and support payments and bond in the amount of _____ dollars ($___) pursuant to the provisions of the law of the State of Maryland. Fail not at your peril, and have you then and there this Writ.*

As I have explained in greater detail in previous descriptions of legal language (Charrow & Crandall 1978; Charrow, Crandall, & Charrow in press), it is unclear how best to characterize legalese: it is not a register, as only a small proportion of the population controls it, and it is acquired only through a very special type of schooling. It also differs significantly from normal usage. It is more than a professional jargon, as it contains its own peculiar syntactic constructions. However, it may not actually qualify as a dialect of English, because most of its odd syntactic structures are not productive, and because it is not acquired in a "natural" manner.

Bureaucratic language, as I and others have characterized it elsewhere (Charrow in press; Redish in press), is similar to legal language—in fact, it is based on legal language. It is the variety of English which is found

---

[1] Other languages have legalese, as well. However, for the purposes of this chapter, I am limiting my discussion to English legalese.

in the documents (and less often the oral pronouncements) which emanate from government agencies, and which has the force of federal and state statutes behind it. Bureaucratese (also known as gobbledygook) is used in regulations and their associated documents, in government forms (for Medicaid, education grants, Social Security, housing, small businesses, etc.) and in guidelines, brochures, and other explanatory material put out by government agencies. The following is an example of bureaucratese from an immigration form:

> *If you are the spouse or unmarried minor child of a person who has been granted preference classification by the Immigration and Naturalization Service or has applied for preference classification, and you are claiming the same preference classification, or if you are claiming special immigrant classification as the spouse or unmarried child of a minister of religion who has been accorded or is seeking classification as a special immigrant, submit the following . . . [INS Form I-485].*

Bureaucratese shares many of the basic characteristics of legalese, but it also contains features of its own that make it identifiable as a "subvariety" of legalese—notably, a specialized lexicon and a few characteristic grammatical constructions. It is also possible that some examples of bureaucratese are actually hypercorrected legalese; they may be the pieces that end up being ridiculed by "guardians of the public tongue" such as Edwin Newman and William Safire.

Figure 6.1 schematizes the possible relationship between legal and bureaucratic language and between bureaucratese and the various technical vocabularies it borrows from time to time (in regulations affecting specific industries, etc.):

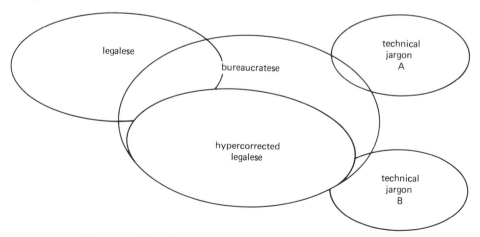

Figure 6.1. The relationship between legalese and bureaucratese.

Both legal and bureaucratic language appear to span continua—from almost "normal" formal usage to highly complex varieties that differ substantially from normal formal usage.

The Formal Study of Legal and Bureaucratic Language

Nonlawyers have been criticizing legal language for hundreds of years. But lawyers were the first to examine their sublanguage critically and objectively. Mellinkoff (1978), to give the best example, describes legal language, traces its development, explains how it differs from ordinary usage, and describes some of the problems it creates. Nonetheless, like others who attempt to describe varieties of language but who lack specific training in linguistics, the legal scholars who have described legal language lack both the vocabulary and the specialized knowledge to present a thorough and fully explanatory analysis of legalese. Mellinkoff, for example, has identified nine characteristics of legal language:

1. Frequent use of common words with uncommon meanings (using *action* for *lawsuit, of course* for *as a matter of right,* etc.)
2. Frequent use of Old and Middle English words once in use but now rare (*aforesaid, whereas, said* and *such* as adjectives, etc.)
3. Frequent use of Latin words and phrases (*in propria persona, amicus curiae, mens rea,* etc.)
4. Use of French words not in the general vocabulary (*lien, easement, tort,* etc.)
5. Use of terms of art—or what we'd call jargon (*month-to-month tenancy, negotiable instrument, eminent domain,* etc.)
6. Use of argot—ingroup communication or "professional language" (*pierce the corporate veil, damages, due care*)
7. Frequent use of formal words (*Oyez, oyez, oyez,* which is used in convening the Supreme Court; *I do solemnly swear;* and *the truth, the whole truth, and nothing but the truth, so help you God*)
8. Deliberate use of words and expressions with flexible meanings (*extraordinary compensation, reasonable man, undue influence*)
9. Attempts at extreme precision (consider the following formbook general release):

   Know ye that I, _____ , of _____ , for and in consideration of _____ dollars, to me in hand paid by _____ , do by these presents for myself, my heirs, executors, and administrators, remise, release, and forever discharge, _____ of _____ , his heirs, executors, and administrators, of and from any and all manner of action or actions, cause and causes of action, suits, debts, dues, sums of money, accounts, reckonings, bonds, bills, specialties, covenants, contracts, controversies, agreements, promises, trepasses, damages, judgments, executions, claims, and demands whatsoever, . . . [pp. 11–23]

This classification of the features of legal language, although revealing, is hardly complete; it does not cover legal sentence structure or discourse structure. It is also not systematic from a linguistic point of view: semantic, syntactic, and sociolinguistic categories overlap and are considered in the same light.

Most other descriptions of legal language by lawyers are not even as sophisticated as Mellinkoff's. Rodell for example, calls legal language "high class mumbo jumbo" and elaborates on this by saying merely that there are only two things wrong with most legal writing: style and content (cited in Goldfarb 1978). Humorous, perhaps, but hardly an objective, systematic analysis.

Linguists and other scientists have become interested in legal language only in the last few years. They have conducted systematic studies of various aspects of legal language, and the language used in legal situations, which have yielded useful information about the characteristics and functions of legal and bureaucratic language.

Kroll (1975) applied sociolinguistic principles and theories of speech acts to an instance of cross-examination in the courtroom. She analyzed the testimony of a witness (an undercover policewoman) from the point of view of Robin Lakoff's "contextual change," and other theories of denotation and connotation. Courtroom language is again special; it consists of some utterances that are in typical legalese and others that appear to be in ordinary English. However, Kroll pointed out that courtroom language does not follow the rules of ordinary conversation.

Williams (1976) examined how lawyers and judges in conspiracy trials treat opaque contexts. He noted that linguistic theory can be extremely useful for solving legal problems involving language.[2]

Labov (1976) actually applied linguistics to a real-world problem involving legal language. At the request of a lawyer for a group of steelworkers, he investigated the relative comprehensibility and coerciveness of a cover letter and a consent agreement that the management of the steel industry had sent to steelworkers as the result of a class action suit.

[2] Heath (1979) has reported on other linguistic studies involving legal language.

In general, however, there have been very few empirical studies of legal language by linguists. The first such study was Charrow & Charrow's (1978; 1979; 1980) study of the comprehensibility of standard jury instructions. Using a psycholinguistic methodology and discourse analysis, the investigators not only demonstrated that legal language, as embodied in standard jury instructions, was difficult for lay people (jurors) to understand, but they isolated the syntactic, lexical, and discourse features that appeared to obstruct comprehension. Charrow and Charrow also demonstrated that if the jury instructions were rewritten using principles derived from linguistic theories of syntax and discourse structure, speech acts, and conversational rules, comprehension could be increased dramatically.

As linguists' interest in legal and bureaucratic language was slowly growing, other social scientists were finding legal language a fertile area for investigation and theory building.

Experimental psychologists such as Harris (1975) and Loftus (1975; Loftus & Palmer 1974) have empirically examined aspects of legal language involving presuppositions and inferences (e.g., leading questions, eyewitness testimony).

Anthropologists, notably O'Barr et al. (1975), O'Barr & Conley (1976), have conducted a series of studies of speech styles in the courtroom, which showed, among other things, that witnesses' speech styles manifesting indices of "powerlessness" (hedging; hypercorrected legalese, etc.) tended to be regarded as less credible than more "powerful" speech styles.

Sociologists—Danet (1980a); Danet et al. (1980)—have studied sociological aspects of legal language, such as lawyers' questioning styles in the courtroom, and the differences in the use of certain crucial descriptions by the prosecution as opposed to the defense. These and other studies have fed into a growing theory of the social role of the law and legal language (Danet 1980b).

In the area of bureaucratic language, there have been a very few descriptive studies (Charrow in press; Charrow & Redish 1980) and a few empirical studies of one or two features of it (e.g., Holland 1981; Holland & Rose 1980; Redish, Felker, & Rose in press; Rose & Cox 1980; Swarts et al. 1980).

Characteristics of Legal and Bureaucratic Language

The various studies of legal language by linguists and other social scientists yield an interesting if incomplete description of legal language. From these studies, it appears that legal language is marked by the following features:

At the Discourse Level

At the discourse level, legal and bureaucratic language appear to violate many rules of ordinary usage. As Danet (1980b) notes, legal documents often avoid pronouns, resulting in violations of linguistic rules of anaphora both within and between sentences. In leases, contracts, and insurance policies, clauses are set out in numbered lists which do not indicate the relative importance or logical sequence of the ideas (Shuy & Larkin 1978; Charrow, in press; Redish, in press).

In addition, bureaucratic documents, in particular, often lack a context—information that would allow readers to relate the information in the document to their own experience, or alert them to the fact that what they are about to read is not connected to any of their pre-existing notions.

Some instances of legalese—jury instructions are a good example— contain the same information repeated in different sentence structures and words. Charrow & Charrow (1979) found that when subject–jurors were not alerted to the fact that they were hearing the same information twice, they thought the repeated information was saying something different, even contradicting the original statement. In short, legal language, at the discourse level, appears to often violate Grice's (1975) Maxim of Quantity.

Charrow (in press) has pointed out that bureaucratic discourse is often structured very differently from everyday discourse, resulting in documents that do not meet the needs of their audiences. Writers of regulations and other legal–bureaucratic documents often organize these documents from the point-of-view of the writer, making them illogical from the point-of-view of the reader. Thus, regulations which should be reference documents for the reader are often written as historical documents, memorializing the policy decisions and procedures of the government agency.

At the Syntactic Level

Results of the various studies referred to previously indicate that bureaucratic and legal written and oral language share many unusual grammatical and syntactic features. Charrow and Charrow (1979) found that standard jury instructions contain what appear to be an abnormally large number of passives, truncated passives, past participial phrases, nominalizations, multiple negatives, misplaced or intrusive phrases, parallel structures, unusually long sentences, and unusual and complex embeddings.[3]

In addition, bureaucratic language—especially in forms and regulations—appears to have an unusually large number of complex and ambiguous conditions (Charrow in press; Charrow & Redish 1980; Holland 1981). For example (from an IRS form),

> *Did you pay more than half the cost of keeping up a home in the U.S. in which you lived and which for the entire year (except for temporary absences for vacation, school, etc.) was also the home of (1) your child who was under 19 years of age or a full-time student, OR (2) your dependent child who is disabled (see pages 7 and 8)?*

Some quasi-syntactic features of legal and bureaucratic language (constructions larger than a single word, but smaller than a clause) include **doublets** such as:

> *any and all*
> *cease and desist*
> *false and untrue;*

word lists such as:

> *A witness who has special **knowledge, skill, experience, training, or education** in a particular **science, profession or occupation;***

and **unusual prepositional phrases** (and clauses), such as those beginning with *absent, as to, in the event of,* or *until such time as.*

Bureaucratic language also contains large numbers of long and complex noun strings, which often serve as the names of programs or institutions (Charrow, in press; Charrow & Redish 1980). Examples are *health maintenance organization, Federal Emergency Management Agency (FEMA).* Other bureaucratic noun strings, however, are not names of organizations or programs; they simply appear in the text as though they were completely transparent constructions. For example:

> *label accuracy*
> *health services utilization*
> *young driver risk-taking research*

---

[3] Danet (1980) reports that Crystal and Davy (1969), Gustafsson (1975), Sales *et al.* (1977), and Shuy and Larkin (1978), among others, have also found these features in their examinations of legal language.

prototype crisis shelter development plans
the FEMA-sponsored host area crisis shelter production planning work-
book

At the Lexical Level

Many of Mellinkoff's categories (see pages 84–85) were noted by re-searchers in their studies of legal language—particularly words of French, Latin, and Old English origin, common terms with uncommon meanings (e.g., *consideration, assign*), and technical terms—what law-yers call "terms of art" (e.g., *eminent domain, trespass, indenture de-benture*).

Bureaucratic language creates or adopts lexical items that come to be the earmarks of bureaucratic jargon (e.g., *prioritize* and *impact (on)* used as a verb).

In addition, both legal and bureaucratic language use words to achieve either vagueness (e.g., *all the rights and remedies; as soon as is practicable*) or extreme precision (e.g., *no animal of the dog kind; release and forever discharge* _____, *his heirs, executors and administrators, of and from any and all manner of action or actions, cause and causes of action, suits, debts, dues, sums of money, accounts, reckonings, bonds, bills, specialties, . . .*)

How Legal and Bureaucratic Language Can Contribute to Four Areas of Linguistic Theory

What is it, one may ask, that linguists know (metalinguistic compe-tence, if you will) that makes it possible for us to study, understand, and describe legal and bureaucratic language? What kinds of theories do we bring to bear when investigating these varieties of exceptional lan-guage? On the other hand, how can the study of legal and bureaucratic language highlight the gaps in these theories and help fill them in?

There are four main areas of linguistic theory that relate to, and that, in turn, can benefit from, a study of legal and bureaucratic language:

I. Historical linguistics—theories of how languages develop and change.
II. Grammatical theories—theories of the structure of discourse; grammatical "rules."
III. Sociolinguistic theories—theories of language use for different societal purposes.

IV. Linguistic metatheory—philosophical theories of why human be-
    ings develop language, theories of linguistic competence and per-
    formance, and theoretical principles of human communication.

In this section, I will briefly discuss some of the ways in which each
of these areas of linguistic theory relates to legal and bureaucratic language. I will also bring up as yet unanswered questions about these
varieties of English which theoreticians might be interested in investigating.

Historical Linguistics

To understand how legal language got to be the way it is, it is necessary to understand normal processes of development and change in
language. It is also useful to understand the types of grammatical and
lexical changes and pidginization processes that languages can undergo
over time or as a result of historical accidents. It is useful to know these
things in order to be able to trace the (rather well-documented) development of legal language through the centuries. In doing so, one finds
that the factors that influenced the evolution of legal language into the
unique variety of English that it is are somewhat different from (or
perhaps more specific than) the factors that cause ordinary language to
evolve.

As my colleagues and I have discussed elsewhere (Charrow, Crandall,
& Charrow 1981, in press), legal language has had its own historical
development, which has paralleled, but has often been independent of,
the historical development of the rest of the English language. Legal
language has its own subprocesses of change and growth—legal–
historical, political, and jurisprudential. Thus, for example, while languages change lexically—through normal social processes—by dropping
archaic terms, developing new meanings and losing the old meanings of
words, the legal sublanguage develops and changes lexical meaning
through legislation and judicial decisions, and because of socio-legal
factors (e.g., the use of ritualized language to convey the power of the
law; the conservatism of the legal profession, etc.). Whereas ordinary
English has replaced older vocabulary items with newer ones, legal
language does not usually replace its older forms. Rather, it simply adds
the new terms to previously used terms, creating doublets or strings of
largely synonymous words. For example;

> *cease and desist*
> *remise, release, and forever discharge*

As French gave way to English in the courts (which happened much later than it did for ordinary usage), an English word was often added to the French predecessor, producing:

new and novel
false and untrue

Although this process parallelled the fashion, in ordinary usage, of using strings of synonyms for ornament (Mellinkoff 1978, p. 121), there were different historical reasons for the use of doublets and word strings in legal language—for example, the apparent need to preserve legal force by preserving the legal words that carry the force of the law; the legal need for speakers of both official languages to, at least in theory, understand the language of the law. Thus the use of doublets and word strings has died out in ordinary usage, but it persists in legal language to this day.

Similarly, legal language retains many French, Latin, and archaic English words, such as *voir dire, lien,* and *tort* (French); *prima facie* and *habeas corpus* (Latin); and *writ* and *aforethought* (archaic English). Such terms, it should be noted, are partially Anglicized in their pronunciation, more than other nonlegal borrowings from the French and Latin such as *ancien regime.* So the term spelled *pur* [sic] *autre vie,* for example, is pronounced /pur otr vi/, and law students who attempt a more French pronunciation are laughed into "correct" pronunciation. Certain grammatical constructions in legal language are likewise retained. Some are "frozen" forms, which come from grammatical constructions that were either borrowed from French or Latin, or that were brought forward from archaic English. For example:

malice aforethought
fee simple
revoking all wills and codicils by me made

Other constructions, such as the extensive use of the passive voice and multiple negatives, the use of nominalizations rather than clauses, the use of complex conditionals and multiple embeddings, appear to be the result of various legal–historical processes, as well as legal conservatism, tradition, and time constraints, that legitimized the copying of model forms and "boilerplate."

A great deal still remains to be explained regarding the historical development of legal language. It may be worth comparing the changes in legal language to those in ordinary English over several centuries. Was legal language ever closer to ordinary usage, or has it always been just as inaccessible to the lay person? If, at times, legal language was more similar to ordinary usage, in what ways was it more similar, and what were the factors that contributed to this? What factors caused it to move away from ordinary English? Is legal language currently chang- ing? What effect, if any, is the current movement toward simplifying legal documents having on legal language? What are the features of legal language that are the most impervious to change, and why?

Regarding bureaucratic language, when, for instance, did it arise? How has it developed and changed? Have noun strings, for example, always been an earmark of bureaucratese?

Once we have answers to some of these questions, it would be time to look at theories of language change, to see how well (if at all) they accommodate the development of exceptional varieties of language. It would be worth knowing whether theories of language change can take into account ANY varieties of language that are controlled by institutions (e.g., advertising language), and whether there is any place in the theory for semantic change—or the lack of it—occasioned by judicial or gov- ernmental fiat.

Historical linguistics ought to be able to account for lack of change as well. Study of the broad linguistic conservatism in special subvarieties of language should shed light on the formation and preservation of conservative islands within ordinary language and help us understand why some idioms endure and others are ephemeral.

Grammatical Theory

It is not, of course, a direct connection that links grammatical theories with the study of legal and bureaucratic language, since theories of grammar are based on competence, not performance. Nonetheless, grammatical theories and rules can be helpful to those who study legal and bureaucratic language by pointing to particularly interesting con- structions or potential trouble spots in these varieties of English. And whatever school of linguistic theory (or whatever linguistic heresy) one chooses to follow, it is necessary to know about linguistic rules such as passivization and nominalization in order to be able to adequately de- scribe what is going on in legal and bureaucratic language. It is neces- sary to be able to identify and explain such constructions to lawyers and bureaucrats, in order to counter their tendency to use those construc- tions to the exclusion of all others.

An understanding of legal and bureaucratic language can be useful for choosing between competing linguistic theories. For example, Ross's (1973) argument for a continuum—"squishy boundaries"—between nouns and sentences is a far more useful explanation of the phenomenon of nominalization in legal and bureaucratic language than Chomsky's lexical treatment of derived nominals. Lawyers and bureaucrats do, in fact, change the verbs in subordinate clauses into static, nominal phrases, to make a sentence more remote and abstract, and to avoid placing or taking responsibility. And while linguistic theory does not routinely take into account what people actually DO, it probably should start doing so, if only to avoid the embarrassment of a possible "phlogiston theory" in linguistics.[4] In any case, no matter which theory ultimately prevailed (cf. Newmeyer 1980, p. 91, p. 159), Ross's explanation is far more intuitively satisfying and far more useful than Chomsky's for explaining what really is going on in legalese and bureaucratese. The best theory, after all, will be more than an account of the formal links between structures; it will also account for why people might choose to use one structure rather than another. Thus, although case grammar has been dormant for many years (cf. Fillmore 1968) a case grammar approach can explain certain phenomena in legal and bureaucratic language better than transformational grammar: It is particularly useful, for example, for convincing bureaucrats and lawyers that their truncated passives lack important information—namely the identity of the AGENT or the INSTRUMENT.

For psycholinguistic researchers, legal and bureaucratic language provide potential areas for empirical research and model building. Empirical research, in turn, helps to confirm (or disconfirm) the psychological validity of some theoretical constructs. Empirical studies could help to explain how legal and bureaucratic language differ from ordinary usage, and to predict where lay persons will have difficulties in processing these varieties; but few psycholinguistic studies of legal language and none of bureaucratic language have been performed.

The psycholinguistic research that has been done has focused on grammatical constructions that happen also to be features of legal and bureaucratic language (cf. Just & Carpenter 1971; Just & Clark 1973; Wason 1962, on negatives and multiple negatives). In attempting to discover the linguistic features of jury instructions that caused subject–jurors difficulty in paraphrasing the instructions, Charrow and Charrow (1979) followed clues from psycholinguistic studies of individual constructions, which ultimately led to their isolating nine linguistic con-

---

[4] A case in point is Miller's (1962) report of Mehler's psycholinguistic experiment confirming the relative complexity of Negative, Passive and Question transformations. The experiment could not be successfully replicated, and subsequently—although not consequently, we are assured—the theory itself and transformational rules underwent radical change.

structions typical of legal language which appeared to have the most
deleterious effects on comprehension.

Theoreticians should deal with the possibility that grammatical well-
formedness may be a matter of degree—that the length, awkwardness,
or unusualness of a construction may affect our judgements of the well-
formedness of the construction. For example, in the following sentence
from a USDA regulation, where does length and awkwardness end and
ungrammaticality begin?

> **Order.** (a) No handler shall ship any container of papayas (except
> immature papayas handled pursuant to Section 928.152 of this part):
>
> (1) During the period January 1 through April 15, 1980, to any destina-
> tion within the production area unless said papayas grade at least
> Hawaii No. 1, except that allowable tolerances for defects may total 10
> percent: **Provided,** That not more than 5 percent shall be for serious
> damage, not more than 1 percent for immature fruit, and not more than
> 1 percent for decay: **Provided further,** such papayas shall individually
> weigh not less than 11 ounces each.

Sociolinguistics

Sociolinguistics is particularly relevant to the study of legal and bureaucratic language, since legal language, especially, embodies and reflects the power of law over society. Some of this function is reflected in
the use of performatives in legalese; some is reflected in the ritualistic
quality of much legalese—the use of rhythm, of parallel structures, or
archaic incantations. For example:

> Failure of recollection is a common experience, and innocent misrecollec-
> tion is not uncommon. [From California Jury Instructions—Civil—Book
> of Approved Jury Instructions]

or

> Oyez, oyez, oyez! Court is now in session!

or

> Do you solemnly swear to tell the truth, the whole truth, and nothing
> but the truth, so help you God?

In fact, as has been noted elsewhere (Charrow & Crandall 1978; Charrow, Crandall, & Charrow 1981, in press; Danet 1980b) legal language is
very much like religious language in certain specific situations, and it
serves a similar function: to impress ordinary people with the power,

importance, and seriousness of the law. In a way, the performative function of legal language is also a MAGICAL function: by using the proper legal formula under the right set of circumstances, saying something is so makes it so:

> *By the power invested in me, (under* _____ *),*
> *I now pronounce you husband and wife.*
>
> *I hereby give, devise, and bequeath . . .*

As Charrow, Crandall, & Charrow noted, it is not necessary for the lay person to understand, or even know about, a given law in order to be governed by it. The legal maxim, "Ignorance of the law is no excuse" makes it quite clear that it is the EXISTENCE of a law—the fact that it has been proclaimed or written somewhere, and not repealed—that gives it its force.

Legal language serves other sociolinguistic functions. As Crandall and I have explained (Charrow & Crandall 1978), legalese serves to establish and maintain solidarity among its users, and to keep out outsiders. It is also a prestigious variety of English. Those who are fluent in it—certain lawyers and judges—have a great deal of power and influence, and (generally) command respect. In fact, we have argued that legalese is more like a dialect than a jargon, in that its history, its structure, its social functions, and its method of acquisition are far more complex than those of jargons and more like those of dialects.

Many of the sociolinguistic properties and processes of legal language also apply to bureaucratic language. Bureaucratic language does not have as much magic as legal language, and hence lacks some of the rhythmic and ritualistic features of legalese. However, it does share much of the power of legal language. Government regulations are meant to be followed; there are often severe penalties for not doing so. Furthermore, as Charrow (in press) has explained, because the government bureaucracy has great power over large numbers of people, bureaucrats usually do not have to listen to nonbureaucrats at all. Outsiders must deal with the government on the government's terms. This creates a closed communication system, with strange usages that may be unconstrained by normal rules of conversation, discourse structure, or even grammar (e.g., *This impacts* [on] *the program in the following way.*). Thus, it may be that the separating function of bureaucratic language (i.e., keeping outsiders out) is more important than its unifying function. This would be ironic, indeed, in that if people cannot understand bureaucratese, they will not be able to comply with what the bureaucracy wants. And since most people do not have the same respect for the government as they do for the law, they will probably be less likely to try to comply.

In spite of negative feelings on the part of many people about the bureaucracy and bureaucratic language, bureaucratic language is still a prestige variety of English. Many people do consider it valuable, and worth emulating. As Charrow (in press) points out, the news media often latch onto bureaucratic jargon and use it as their own, and this contributes to its spread and further enhances its prestige.

Aside from these observations, there have been relatively few sociolinguistic studies of legal or bureaucratic language, and sociolinguistic theories do not deal very well with phenomena such as legal and bureaucratic language. For example, sociolinguistic categories exist that take into account registers, jargons, and dialects. But none of these categories adequately describes legal language. Charrow & Crandall (1978) make a case for legalese as a dialect of English, but only by stretching somewhat the accepted sociolinguistic definitions of dialect. Likewise, the sociolinguistic concept of continuum along which the registers or the varieties of a language fall is potentially useful for explaining the variations in legal language, but it cannot be used "as is." Danet (1980b), for instance, has created a matrix—a "typology of situations in which Legal English is used, by style and mode," which ranges from "frozen" forms used in certain legal documents to casual forms used in lawyer–lawyer conversations.

Heath (personal communication, 1981) has looked at legalese and other professional sublanguages from a somewhat broader sociolinguistic perspective. She has postulated that there are sociolinguistic processes of "complexification" and "simplification," and that professional languages are manifestations of a universal tendency toward complexification in languages (which is sometimes offset by an opposing tendency toward simplification). Redish (personal communication) has suggested that the situation is more complex than Heath has postulated); that there are ordinary complexification processes that create formal registers, but that there are other processes above and beyond these that lead to the creation of legal language (and perhaps, to a lesser extent, to other professional jargons). This is supported by the fact that many well-educated people who command the formal registers of English do not have a productive or receptive command of legalese.

There are still sociolinguistic aspects of legal and bureaucratic language that remain to be discovered and explained. Danet (1980b) touches on some of these in her excellent article. For example, how do lawyers learn to become competent in legal language? How do bureaucrats become competent in bureaucratic language? In what order are different features of legalese acquired? Which aspects are easier or more difficult to acquire, and why? What are the significant differences between legal language and religious language?

Once we have some of the answers to these questions, we will clearly need more theoretical work and more theory building in sociolinguistics to take these forms of exceptional language into account.

Linguistic Metatheory

In order to understand the phenomena of legal and bureaucratic language, and some of the problems they cause for nonlawyers, it is useful to have some understanding of linguistic metatheories. And it may turn out to be equally useful to linguistic metatheory to understand the phenomena of legal and bureaucratic language. Although Chomsky (1959) probably did not intend the concept of the Language Acquisition Device to apply to anything but an abstract device (in infants) for acquiring a first language, one could argue that the theory should be expanded to cover language acquisition throughout life. Looking at legal and bureaucratic language, and their acquisition processes, there certainly appears to be evidence that, as human beings, we cannot help but create sublanguages. Even once we have acquired our native language(s), the mechanism does not entirely shut off. We go on creating and acquiring dialects, jargons, registers, and other subsystems well into maturity (and perhaps senility).

We can also argue for the value of the distinction between "competence" and "performance," difficult as these have been to define. It is our linguistic competence that allows us, given infinite time and patience, to make sense of the very complex structures of legalese. On the other hand, it is certainly plausible that only performance constraints make legal and bureaucratic language difficult for many people to deal with. Aside from law students, attorneys, and judges, who have been specifically trained in legalese, who are constantly exposed to it, and who depend upon it for their livelihoods, most people do not have the time, patience, memory capacity, or specific vocabulary to tease out the meaning from legal documents or spoken legal pronouncements. In building any theory of performance, it would be important not to ignore legal and bureaucratic language.

Speech act theory (Austin 1962) is particularly useful for describing the power of legal language and the use of language as a tool by the legal profession. Many legal pronouncements are **performatives:** When a judge pronounces a defendant guilty, he IS guilty—whether or not he actually committed the crime. Written or spoken words within the cor-

rect context are used to create contracts—performance obligations—
between people. A marriage license—a written legal formula—and certain oral pronouncements made with the proper legal authority join two
people in marriage. If a legal notice is published where a fairly large
number of people can be assumed to see it, there is, in certain circumstances, a presumption under the law that all people have been notified.
This is despite the fact that most people do not read legal notices, and
probably would not understand them if they did read them. Most
egregiously, in many jurisdictions, if a person is missing for a certain
number of years, a court can pronounce him or her DEAD, whether or not
that is the case. For many purposes, a legally dead person is indeed
dead. It is no wonder that lawyers refer to their documents as legal
instruments. But speech act theorists have not, in fact, looked at legal
language as a whole. And so the theory does not take into account the
existence of a variety of language that contains an extraordinary proportion of performatives.

Grice's cooperative principle appears to be useful in explaining why
legal language often does not work as communication. Because of other
overriding functions of legal language, such as the performative function and the various social functions that it serves, legal language often
does not follow Grice's maxims of Quantity and Manner. It is sometimes
necessary for legal language to be more or less informative than is required for ordinary communication purposes, and it is sometimes either
useful or customary for legal language to embrace obscurity of expression, to be prolix, and to deliberately abuse order (e.g., questions on
cross-examination are often presented in a random order to confuse the
witness). As a result, legal language at times fails as communication for
certain audiences.

But should these be considered VIOLATIONS of the Cooperative Principle? Or are they rather a manifestation of a different type of principle
of conversation, governing types of situations that Grice never took into
account? Perhaps there exists, for some aspects of legal language, what
Rosenbaum (personal communication, 1981) has suggested be termed
an **Uncooperative Principle:** the use of language to CONSTRAIN others
from doing certain things, to PROTECT people, information, or things,
and to PENALIZE others for violating those constraints and protections.
Cross-examination appears to fit the Uncooperative Principle very well.

Legal language (and to some extent bureaucratic language) certainly
does have additional conversational rules of its own which govern lay
persons as well as lawyers. In some cases, the lay person is ignorant of
these rules, and lawyers and judges are aware of this ignorance. In other
cases, courts (lawyers, judges) simply assume—for convenience's

sake—that lay people know the "conversational rules" of the court when in fact they do not know them, and no allowance is made for this. Thus, if jurors do not understand a jury instruction, they often ask for it to be repeated, in the mistaken belief that the judge will then EXPLAIN the instruction. In fact, following the legal rule of conversation that governs this situation, the judge will merely repeat the instruction.

Rules for turn-taking are different in courtroom "conversation" than in ordinary conversation. And even if witnesses are aware of the existence of different rules, they do not usually know what those rules are, and are either penalized or left at a disadvantage. Linguistic theory as it currently stands cannot account for these rules. Nor can it explain the conversational structure when two different sets of rules meet and conflict—as they do when a lawyer and a nonlawyer converse.

Summary

I have presented only some of the areas in which linguistic theories and legal and bureaucratic language intersect, and only a few of the many questions that remain unanswered. A fair amount is known, but there is much more to be investigated, and more to be learned—both about legal and bureaucratic language, and about what theoretical linguists can derive from the study of these varieties of exceptional language. As I have suggested, at least four areas of linguistic theory—historical linguistics, grammatical theory, sociolinguistics, and linguistic metatheory—could benefit from the study of legal and bureaucratic language. Here is an opportunity for theoreticians to look beyond the standard language, and their own intuitions, in order to construct theories that more accurately reflect the real workings of language.

References

Austin, J.L. (1962) *How to do things with words.* Cambridge, MA: Harvard University Press.

California jury instructions, Civil, Book of approved jury instructions (1969) (5th Ed.) St. Paul, Minn.: West Publishing Co.

Charrow, V. (In press) Language in the bureaucracy. *Proceedings of the Delaware symposium II on language studies.*

Charrow, V. & Charrow, R. (1978) *The comprehension of standard jury instructions* (working paper). Arlington, Va.: Center for Applied Linguistics.

Charrow, R. & Charrow, V. (1979) Making legal language understandable: A psycholinguistic study of jury instructions. *Columbia law review, 79,* Pp. 1306–1374.

Charrow, V. & Charrow, R. (1980) Lawyers' views of the comprehensibility of legal language. In R. Shuy & A. Shnukal (Eds.), *Language use and the uses of language*. Washington, D.C.: Georgetown University Press.

Charrow, V. & Crandall, J. (1978) *Legal language: What is it and what can we do about it?* Paper presented at the American Dialect Society Conference/Georgetown NWAVE Conference, Washington, D.C., October.

Charrow, V., Crandall, J. & Charrow, R. (In press) Characteristics and functions of legal language. In R. Kittredge & J. Lehrberger (Eds.), *Sublanguage: Studies of language in restricted semantic domains*. Berlin: Walter de Gruyter.

Charrow, V. & Redish, J. (1980) *Finding the problems in bureaucratic documents*. Paper presented at the Symposium on Writing and Designing Documents: Research and Practical Solutions. Carnegie Mellon University, Pittsburgh, Pa., October.

Chomsky, N. (1959) Review of Skinner's "Verbal behavior." *Language, 35*, 26–58.

Crystal, D. & Davy, D. (1969) *Investigating English style*. London: Longman.

Danet, B. (1980a) Language in the courtroom. In H. Giles, P. Smith, & P. Robinson (Eds.), *Social psychology and language: Proceedings of an international conference*. Oxford: Pergamon.

Danet, B. (1980b) Language in the legal process. *Law & society review, 14*, 445–564.

Danet, B., Hoffman, K.B., Kermish, N.E., Rafn, J., & Stayman, D.G. (1980) An ethnography of questioning. In R. Shuy & A. Shnukal (Eds.), *Language use and the uses of language*. Washington, D.C.: Georgetown University Press.

Fillmore, C. (1968) The case for case. In E. Bach & R. Harms (Eds.), *Universals in linguistic theory*. New York: Holt, Rinehart and Winston.

Grice, H.P. (1975) Logic and conversation. In P. Cole, & J.L. Morgan (Eds.), *Syntax and semantics, Vol. 3: Speech acts*. New York: Academic Press.

Gustafsson, M. (1975) *Some syntactic properties of English law language*, No. 4. Turku, Finland: University of Turku, Department of English.

Harris, R.J. (1975) *The psychology of pragmatic implications*. Unpublished manuscript.

Heath, S.B. (1979) The context of professional languages: An historical overview. In J. Alatis & G.R. Tucker (Eds.), *Language in public life*. Washington, D.C.: Georgetown University Press.

Holland, V.M. (1981) *A comparison of prose and algorithms for understanding complex instructions*. Paper presented at AERA Annual Meeting, Los Angeles, Ca.

Holland, V.M. & Rose, A. (1980) *Understanding instructions with complex conditions: Document Design Project Technical Report No. 5*. Washington, D.C.: American Institutes for Research.

Just, M.A. & Carpenter, P. (1971) Comprehension of negatives with quantification. *Journal of verbal learning and verbal behavior, 10*, 244–253.

Just, M.A. & Clark, H.H. (1973) Drawing inferences from the presuppositions and implications of affirmative and negative sentences. *Journal of verbal learning and verbal behavior, 12*, 21–31.

Kroll, B. (1975) *A linguist goes to court*. Unpublished manuscript.

Labov, W. (1976) Untitled report to the United States District Court in the case of *Rodgers v. U.S. Steel Corp.* Western District of Pennsylvania #71-793.

Loftus, E.F. (1975) Leading questions and the eyewitness report. *Cognitive psychology, 7*, 560–572.

Loftus, E.F. & Palmer, J.C. (1974) Reconstruction of automobile destruction: An example of the interaction between language and memory. *Journal of verbal learning and verbal behavior, 13*, 585–589.

Mellinkoff, D. (1978) *The language of the law* (Third Paperback Edition). Boston: Little, Brown.

Miller, G.A. (1962) Some psychological studies of grammar. *American psychologist, 17,* 748–762.

Newmeyer, F.J. (1980) *Linguistic theory in America: The first quarter-century of transformation-generative grammar.* New York: Academic Press.

O'Barr, W.M. & Conley, J. (1976) When a juror watches a lawyer. *Barrister, 3,* 8–11.

O'Barr, W.M., Walker, L., Conley, J., Erickson, R. & Lind, A. (1975) *Political aspects of speech styles in American trial courtrooms.* Paper presented at the Conference on Culture and Communication, Temple University, Philadelphia, Pa.

Redish, J.C. (1981) *The language of the bureaucracy.* Paper presented at the Conference on Literacy in the 80s, Ann Arbor, Michigan.

Redish, J.C., Felker, D. & Rose, A. Evaluating the effects of document design principles. *Information design journal.* In press.

Rose, A. & Cox, L.A. (1980) *Following instructions: Document design project technical report No. 4.* Washington, D.C.: American Institutes for Research.

Ross, J.R. A fake NP squish. (1973) In C.J.N. Bailey & R. Shuy (Eds.), *New ways of analyzing variation in English.* Washington, D.C.: Georgetown University Press.

Sales, B.D., Elwork, A. & Alfini, J. (1977) Improving comprehension for jury instructions. In B.D. Sales (Ed.), *Perspectives in law and psychology: The criminal justice system.* New York: Plenum.

Shuy, R.W. & Larkin, D.K. (1978) *Linguistic considerations in the simplification/clarification of insurance policy language.* Washington, D.C.: Georgetown University and the Center for Applied Linguistics.

Swarts, H., Flower, L.S. & Hayes, J.R. (1980) *How headings in documents mislead readers. Document Design Project Technical Report No. 9.* Pittsburgh, Pa.: Carnegie-Mellon University.

Wason, P.C. (1962) *Psychological aspects of negation: An experimental enquiry and some practical applications.* London: Communication Research Center, In-house publication, University College.

Williams, G. (1976) *The opacity of real conspiracies.* Paper presented at the Second Annual Meeting of the Berkeley Linguistics Society, Berkeley, Ca.

7 EDNA AMIR COFFIN

Translation: An Exceptional Form of Language Use

The act of translation is a special speech act, with both the process and the product falling within the general domain of exceptional language. Moreover, it is a speech act produced by an exceptional speaker, who is ideally both bilingual and bicultural. In a sense, the translator acts as both the linguist's "hearer" and "speaker." As speaker, however, the translator is not the originator of the propositional content of the message, but rather its interpreter in the role of encoder into a different language code. The triple role of receiver–interpreter–encoder makes the translator an active participant in a multifaceted, exceptionally complex linguistic act, thus affording the translator with the possibility of viewing two language systems in interaction. This experience serves to highlight both the features of sameness and difference in the languages the translator works with.

Adapting a communication in one language to another language system via the mode of translation demands of the translator two different goals which are at times incompatible. On the one hand, the translator has to render the original message, in both content and form, as literally as possible, faithful to the original intent of the writer who generated it, whereas on the other hand, the translator faces the task of transfering that communication in as natural, readable, and comprehensible a manner as possible to the reader in another language system. The translated product has to reflect the uniqueness of the original, and at the same time must be an independent speech act in its own right. It is

EXCEPTIONAL LANGUAGE AND LINGUISTICS

precisely when tensions arise between the two goals that the linguist becomes interested.

When difficulties arise in translation, linguists ask what these difficulties tell us about the structures of the respective languages. Is it, one might ask, simply the case that differences between cultures underlie the difficulties of translation, for example, is it because we do not have enough experience with different types of snow or camels that we cannot translate the subtleties of Eskimo or Arab poetry? I will argue that cultural differences do play a role in translation difficulties, but that these cultural disparities are reflected in the lexicon and the grammar of a language in ways pertinent to the linguist. Is it simply the case, then, that "surface" structures may be hard to translate, while "deep" structures are universal and thus easy to translate? As will become clear in the examples to be cited, no clear dichotomy between "deep" and "surface" structure is demonstrable in translation data. Certainly, the structures involved lie deeper than the surfaces, in so far as they reflect perceptual differences between cultures. Indeed, study of difficulties in translation sheds light on the interaction of language and cognition in ways that permit a new approach to the Whorf–Sapir hypothesis which, in its more reasonable, weak form, posits an interaction between the structure of a language and the cognitive habits of its speakers.

For examples of difficult points in translation I have chosen the field of metaphor. Metaphors themselves comprise a field of exceptional language recognizable as such in literature, but often occurring, unnoticed, in daily life as well. Thus we may consider the continuum of metaphor from the mundane to the literary, and from the novel to the overused: But all tend to be language/cultural specific, and thus to defy literal translation in ways that are worth exploring. We will structure our examples to move from strictly linguistic voids which render lexical items or idioms untranslatable, toward what we term cultural voids which render utterances or even texts difficult to translate.[1]

In the example of the Hebrew metaphorical utterance *hu qeren 'or,* literally 'he is a ray of light', or more idiomatically "he is a ray of sunshine," aside from the substitution of *light* by *sunshine* to create a similar meaning and natural effect in English, the difference between the two statements involves a formal linguistic feature—that of gender of nouns. In Hebrew, all nouns, both animate and inanimate, have gender features (marked as well as unmarked), while in English, gender features are the property of some animate nouns only. Thus the feminine gender

---

[1] For a fuller discussion of metaphors in translation see M.B. Dagut's article (1976) Can "Metaphor" Be Translated? *Babel,* Vol. XXII, 1, 21–32.

of *qeren* ('ray') and the masculine gender of *or* ('light') are not features
which can be translated. In this case the lack of a corresponding feature
of gender in English cannot be said to be situationally relevant in the
sense that its presence or absence affects the gross communicative function of the utterance. Thus, even though the gender feature is not translated by a corresponding feature in English, the act of translation of this
Hebrew metaphorical utterance into English can be considered adequate. However, we cannot be sure to what extent the "hearers" process
noun-gender features subconsciously, and permit this processing to
subtly color their interpretation of a metaphor differently between a
language with obligatory gender features and one without, or between a
language with a specific gender marking for a noun, and another language with a different gender marking for the noun which describes the
same referent (e.g., French *lune* (f.) 'moon', German *mond* (m.) 'moon').[2]

Translation can fail when it is impossible to find a corresponding
formal feature of the source language in the target language where such
a feature is more functionally relevant. Consider the example of the
metaphorical utterance used in certain dialects of adolescent English: *He
is an it,* where the pronoun *it* is used metaphorically to mean a nonhuman (an excellent example for the seemingly anomalous nature of
metaphorical structure which violates conventional selectional restrictions). Since Hebrew, relative to English, has a grammatical and a lexical void in its paradigm of pronouns, as it contains no neuter pronouns,
this metaphorical utterance cannot be translated literally. The translator
who wishes to communicate the essential meaning of this structure
must resort to the act of paraphrasing the original metaphor, and rendering it by a nonmetaphorical or different metaphorical utterance, which
approximates it but does not constitute an equivalent of the original. It
is paraphrasable in English as *He is not human,* or *He is a beast,* and these
paraphrases can be literally translated into Hebrew.

Failure to translate because of a lack of corresponding linguistic features in the target language to those in the source language can also
occur where there is an ambiguity peculiar to the source language text,
which is a functionally relevant feature. One of the sources for such
ambiguity is polysemy of a source-language item with no corresponding polysemy in the target-language. An example taken from a Hebrew
poem which has been translated into English serves to illustrate this
point. The metaphorical structure *məlo' ḥofnayim ruaḥ,* a title of a He-

---

[2] Interesting research results on the effects of gender marking within languages can be
found in the yet unpublished article by Guiora, A.Z. and Herold, A. (1981), Native Language and Cognitive Structures: A Cross-cultural Inquiry. (The article may be obtained
from Dr. Guiora, University Hospital, The University of Michigan, Ann Arbor, Michigan.)

brew poem translated into English as 'Handfuls of Wind' (in Mintz 1968). In the poem this metaphor appears not only in the title of the poem, thus relating to the entire structure, but also in the first stanza, relating it more directly to this shorter context. The following translation of the first stanza is given:

> *All that I have*
> *Handfuls of wind,*
> *A gift for the kingdom of birds.*

The literal translation of *məlo' ḥofnayim ruaḥ* is 'fulness (of) handfuls (of) wind/spirit'. Ruth Finer Mintz, the translator of this poem, faced several problems and had to make choices in translating the metaphor into its English version. The first problem was that of ordering the lexical units which constitute the metaphorical utterance into an acceptable syntactic arrangement in English. Morphological classes also had to be changed, as the /noun–noun–noun/ construction in Hebrew was changed to /noun + preposition + noun/ in English with the first noun *məlo'* being expressed by the suffix '-ful', and the relationship between the nouns had to be expressed in English by the insertion of the preposition *of* between the last two nouns. Aside from changes on both morphological and syntactic levels, lexical choices had to be made as well, and this is where the question of polysemy comes in. In the choice of the lexical item in English which would translate adequately, both distinct meanings of *ruaḥ* which is an important constituent of the metaphorical utterance, the translator had to consider not only the individual item but also the context in which the item appears. In choosing to look at the context, the translator had to choose between the larger context of the entire poem, and the more restricted one of the individual stanza. The choice of the item *wind* rather than *spirit* was out of a preference for considering the more restricted context over the larger one. *Wind* as an equivalent for *ruaḥ* preserves the unity of the field in the stanza, as both *wind* and *the kingdom of birds* belong to the heavenly sphere, paying full attention to both the communicative and esthetic functions in the text. The translation of *ruaḥ* as 'spirit' has relevance for the interpretation of the meaning of the entire poem. In the universe of the poet, what he is willing to give, *all that I have*, is not handfuls of wind, but rather handfuls of spirit or soul. The change is from objective reality to a subjective one, from one that is not within the power of the poet to give, to one which is more readily accessible to him. The Hebrew metaphor works on both levels, because of its polysemic nature, while the English can work on one level alone.

An additional problem of ambiguity that comes up in the translated English text is that of the meaning of the translated metaphor itself. *Handfuls of wind* would most likely be interpreted by an English speaker to mean 'handfuls of nothing' since one cannot capture the wind by the handful. It is not inconceivable that it should mean 'handfuls of something abundant to which there are no limits', which captures the intent of the original speaker. For the Hebrew speaker–listener the second interpretation of *ruaḥ* as spirit reinforces the meaning of *ruaḥ* as wind, as something without limits, something elusive. There is an additional effect present in the Hebrew interpretation which is lacking in English, and that is the contrast created in the poem between body and soul, between *handfuls* which represent the body as a whole, and *ruaḥ* when interpreted as 'spirit'. This particular tension is absent in translation. However, even in the translation one can sense the tension between handfuls of what can be actually held and grasped and handfuls of wind which cannot be captured. The collocation is clearly a very effective one in Hebrew, while it is ambiguous and not as effective in the translation cited. The translation may be judged as partial but adequate in the sense it has given the reader of the target-language text a sense of the original meaning of the metaphor and its relationship to the rest of the stanza, even though it has not given the metaphor a sense in relation to the entire poem. Such examples give us rich insight into languages' differing distribution of connotational meaning into lexeme or idiom "packages." We may turn to cultural "voids" to illustrate how referential meaning may interact with connotational meaning.

Cultural voids reflected in the target-language can be a result of different geographical, ethnic, social, religious, and historical circumstances of the target-language speech community rather than systematic linguistic features of the target-language. These cultural voids can occur in the material as well as nonmaterial aspects of the target language culture.

A case in point is illustrated in an account of the translation of a passage from the King James Version of the New Testament into Dogrib, an Indian language spoken in the Northwestern territories. The original source text from which the passage was translated into Dogrib, is itself a translation which has achieved its own special status as an "original" authorized version of the New Testament. The translators, members of the Evangelical Free Church of America, undertook the task both because of religious convictions and because Dogrib, a largely unrecorded language, is dying out, and this translation may be the only attempt to record the language. The translators were well aware that their mission went beyond literal translation from one language to another. They

acknowledged that "translating the Bible into another tongue is a difficult assignment in itself," and that they "must also translate the Bible
into another culture, one in which, among other things, kings and
ceremonial footwashing and even shepherds are utterly foreign."

In trying to find meaningful equivalents for much of the Biblical text,
the translators ran into many problems. Besides problems of vocabulary
and grammar, the translators had to deal with features of cross-cultural
communication "rife with traps for misunderstandings." A draft translation of the Passion story was received with amusement since it included a word for simply sticking a cross in the sand instead of the one
for formally erecting a cross. Some terms, such as *public baths*, required
lengthy explanatory notes, while others could be more easily adjusted.
As an example, consider the problem of translating *brother* which in
English has an extended sense of 'spiritual brother'. Dogrib has no
general word for *brother;* its kinship terms include only designations for
brothers who are older, younger, or twins, and nobody outside the
family can conceivably be a brother. The translator attempted to over-
come this difficulty by explaining the extended sense in which these
kinship terms were used, as well as by doing considerable research in
Biblical families, for the sake of accuracy in translating terms of older
and younger brothers, features which had no relevance for the extended
meaning of 'spiritual brother'.

A second example which illustrates difficulty in translating metaphorical language for cultural reasons is the attempt of the translators to find
metaphorical language corresponding to utterances which included the
items *shepherd* and *sheep* as used in the figurative sense in a passage
from Mark 6:34:

> *And Jesus, when he came out, saw much people,*
> *and was moved with compassion toward them,*
> *because they were a sheep not having a shepherd;*
> *and he began to teach them many things.*

The following is a literal rendition into English of the translation of the
same passage into Dogrib, reflecting grammar and word order of the
target-language.

> *Jesus came out when people many they were,*
> *there he saw them,*
> *They are pitiful is how he felt toward them,*
> *sheep, one who cares for them, was missing,*

that is how they were since.
That way he felt since things many he taught them. [3]

In the English translation both *shepherd* and *sheep* come from the same semantic field, and also share the same lexical base. Harmony is created both by the complementary roles of sheep and shepherd, as well as by their common etymology. In Dogrib the two lexical items have no equivalents. The word *shepherd* does not exist at all, and therefore its extension to the realm of the metaphoric is not possible. It is impossible in Dogrib to express the notion of tending to the spiritual needs of a community by referring to tending sheep. Further, being nomadic, the Indian speakers of Dogrib have no domesticated animals, and therefore the notion of sheep as an animal to be herded does not exist in the language. The word used by the translators to convey the meaning of *sheep* was the Dogrib lexeme used to denote wild mountain sheep, which would ordinarily be slain by the Indians and eaten rather than tended. Thus, while sharing certain qualities with the sheep of the Biblical text, this creature did not share the essential features of its extended meaning, that of being a tended animal, willing to follow the shepherd.

The task before the translators was to find a realm of social experience from which two such complementary terms could be drawn. Note that these terms need not so much convey the meaning of each distinct individual item as the relationship between the two. These equivalences would have to work in the METAPHORIC as well as in the LITERARY senses to convey the meaningful extension of their sense into the realm of human activities which center around the spiritual needs of the community.

The translators settled on the Dogrib word *gikedi* for *shepherd;* the term means 'one who cares for people,' and is usually used to describe a communal baby sitter. This particular solution raises several questions which are at the heart of cross-cultural transfer problems, notably the problem of conveying both the literal meaning of a term and its relationship to another term. As is always the case in rendering metaphorical language, the possibility of extending the meaning from one area of experience to a new realm of experience is crucial. Instead of finding equivalents which come from the same realm of experience, the translators opted for approximations of the distinct parts of the underlying metaphor, and ended up violating the unity of the original text. Dealing with the whole as the total of two separate parts produced an aberration

---

[3] *New York Times,* February 1, 1981, Section C., p. 10.

in the conceptual framework of Dogrib. *Gikedi* ('one who cares for people') cannot possibly make good sense in relation to wild sheep. If indeed *gikedi* approximated shepherd, especially in its extended sense, it follows that its complement should have been young children rather than wild sheep, especially since the latter translation is objectionable on other grounds. It is also necessary to ask whether the *gikedi* has the same status in the Dogrib speaking community and can be applied to somebody who is a spiritual leader; *gikedi* may be inappropriate in the same way as a term for inserting a cross in the sand cannot be used for formally erecting a cross. This example illustrates the difficulties of translation and the pitfalls in translating metaphors without adequate attention to the entire utterance and its overall metaphoric burden. The force and impact of the basic metaphor is weakened by the violation of the unity of expression, a unity which also enhances its esthetic qualities. Such examples highlight the importance of context in realizing meaning in an utterance. The association network each lexical item brings to a sentence interacts with the association network of other lexical items in ways which remain to be fully detailed.

Whereas the previous example was taken from a literary text, it is important to note that problems arise in translating metaphors of everyday language as well. An example of cultural features which render common metaphors of spoken language untranslatable is brought here in the case of the expression *He is cool,* commonly used in American English and untranslatable into Hebrew, despite the many shared features of the two cultures.[4] We have asked native speakers of American English to paraphrase the meaning of the expression *He is cool,* and to include mention of the intention of the speaker. Responses included such essentially positive paraphrases as *He has a lot of class, He is publicly esteemed, He is good looking, He is calm, relaxed, and unperturbed, He smokes pot and is easy going, He presents a neat appearance,* and *He smokes pot and accepts other people.* All of the respondents agreed on the positive qualities implied by such a metaphoric statement. The same metaphoric statement was translated literally into Hebrew, *hu qarīr* ('He is cool'): although not considered by Israeli native spakers of Hebrew to be semantically or pragmatically deviant, this expression was considered somewhat irregular. The implied meaning of this metaphorical utterance was perceived by the native speakers of Hebrew as being an essentially negative comment on a person. Responses included paraphrases and interpretations such as *He is distant, He is not a warm person,*

[4] Data collected by author from Hebrew and English native speakers at The University of Michigan, March, 1981.

He does not socialize with people, He is inwardly directed, He is withdrawn, He is not pleasant, and *He is not sexy.* The contrast of these sets of paraphrases is easy to interpret in cultural terms. The perception of human relationships in connection with warmth and coldness was judged differently in the two cultures. Whereas a certain distance or control was highly valued by American English speakers, such qualities were viewed as basically negative in Hebrew-speaking culture. An entire cultural attitude is summarized in the contrasting senses of this seemingly simple metaphor. Gradations of temperature are physical phenomena which exist outside of language and are universally recognized in language: when used as metaphors for emotional and social attitudes they are not universally viewed in the same manner. The metaphorical utterance *He is cool* has its origin in American English: Borrowed from the world of music, where it is used metaphorically as well, it was extended to the more general realm of human experience. The same collocation in Hebrew joins the field of related metaphors, all of which belong to gradations of temperature. While *ham* ('hot') in Hebrew connotes intensity of emotion, be it either of affection or anger, *qar* ('cold') connotes a lack of feeling for other human beings, and indifference as well as cruelty. On this scale of human emotions, *qarīr* ('cool') falls near the negative pole and though *qar* ('cold') occupies a more extreme position in the ladder of disengagement, *qarīr* has basically the same attributes. The translation of *cool* from American English into Hebrew in the sense in which it is used as a personal quality is extremely difficult, if not impossible.

Work with translation, we may conclude, highlights the arbitrariness of certain linguistic structures such as gender. It also exposes the effects of polysemy, or how meaning gets differently bundled into the lexical items, idioms, and even syntactic structures of different languages. Further, it provides evidence of the subtle semantic interactions among occurring lexical items, and between lexical items and their (con)text. On a broader scale, study of translation elucidates the interactions between the real world, our perception of it, and our language labelling of that perception.

References

Dagut, M.B. (1976) Can "Metaphor" Be Translated? *Babel,* Vol. XXII, No. 1. 21–32.

Guiora, A. & Herold, A. (1981) Native language and cognitive structures: A cross-cultural inquiry. Unpublished manuscript.

Mintz, R.F. (Ed. & Tr.) (1968) *Modern Hebrew poetry.* Los Angeles, CA: University of California Press. Pp. 344–345.

Part II

8
ARNOLD M. ZWICKY

Classical Malapropisms and the Creation of a Mental Lexicon[1]

Introduction

Popular writing about language often concerns itself with mistakes, sometimes light-heartedly, sometimes in a horror-stricken or sternly corrective vein. Lumped together as "mistakes," however, are phenomena of very different sorts. In *The Joy of Lex* (Brandreth 1980), for instance, the reader is entertained with spelling errors (*The Indians live very froogley*, p. 56), double entendres and other ambiguous sentences (*If the baby does not thrive on raw milk, boil it*, p. 129), spoonerisms (*Is the bean dizzy?*, p. 130), malapropisms (*He had to use biceps to deliver the baby*, p. 131), schoolboy howlers of the malaprop variety (*Pasteur found a cure for rabbis*, p. 215), and mixed metaphors, including some with a malapropistic bent (*The problem started small, but it is baseballing*, p. 227). Here we have errors in writing (the misspellings) and errors in speech (the spoonerisms); errors which were surely inadvertent (the spoonerisms), and others which were almost as surely intended just as said or written (most of the malapropisms); slips in phonology (the spoonerisms), errors in lexical selection (the malapropisms), and inattention to the effect on the hearer or reader (unintended ambiguities and garden-variety mixed metaphors like *The Internal Revenue Service appears to be totally impaled in the quicksands of absolute inertia—*

[1] The material in this chapter owes much to two earlier publications of mine (Zwicky 1979 and 1980). Special thanks to Marlene Deetz Payha, who typed all three manuscripts, developing in the process a (fortunately temporary) inability to write or type coherently; we suffered together, but I brought it on myself, while she was an innocent victim.

Follett 1966, p. 215). Indeed it is common to lump nonstandard dialect forms with errors of the types already illustrated: *A(i)n't . . . as used for isn't is an uneducated blunder and serves no useful purpose* (Fowler 1937, p. 45).

The view of the common person—and I include in this category Bolinger's (1980) "shamans" of language, those professional experts on language, like Fowler and Follett, whose prescriptions are grounded in a scrupulous development of commonsense notions about language—appears to be: "Anything that deviates from what I think I ought to say is a mistake." But this will not do for linguists, who want to understand the system of a language, how it is acquired, how it is produced, how it is understood, and so on. For these purposes, the common person's giant "errors" category has no utility. If, for example, we propose to use errors as evidence bearing on what happens in the production of speech—that is, if we propose to understand the way speech production works by studying the ways in which it is most inclined to fail—then we cannot include as relevant data forms appropriate to particular regional or social dialects, unintendedly ambiguous sentences, or idiosyncratic but intended lexical items. Rather, we need examples that arise from some malfunction in the processes that select lexical items, place them in syntactic structures, and transform them into the neural activity that results in the articulation of speech. This line of inquiry is familiar from the (largely phonological) papers in Fromkin (1973) and the syntactic explorations of Foss & Fay (1975) and Fay (1980). Foss and Fay, for instance, examine errors like *And when they chew coca, which they chew coca all day long, then . . .* and *Why do you be an oaf sometimes?* which they attempt to relate to transformational analyses and to differences between children's utterances and adult models, as well as to processes involved in production.

In the following, I first present a scheme for the classification of linguistic errors, in the course of which I introduce a distinction between **classical malapropisms**—the sorts of errors that made Mrs. Malaprop into a common noun—and a class of production errors studied by Fay and Cutler (1977) under the plain title of **malapropisms.** I then investigate classical malapropisms in some detail, speculating on the ways in which they might arise in the creation of a mental lexicon. A concluding section details a series of problems affecting the analysis and interpretation of error data.

The Classification of Linguistic Errors

Taking "errors" in a broad sense, linguistic errors can be classified according to whether they appear in a **single modality** of linguistic performance or in a **bimodal** performance (where two functions must be coordinated). What I have in mind for the latter category are errors that arise when some type of perception must be coordinated with some type of production: reading and writing, as in copying; reading and speaking, as in reading out loud; listening and speaking, as in shadowing or (at some remove in time) verbatim recall; and listening and writing, as in transcribing.

If we consider only the simpler case of errors in monomodal performance, we see that they may present themselves either in **production** or in **perception,** and that crosscutting these distinctions is one of **medium,** spoken versus written. The result is the familiar four-way division into speaking and writing (both modes of production), listening and reading (both modes of perception). From here on I will be concerned primarily with errors manifested in speaking, though not without attention to their relationship to functioning in modes other than speaking.

Errors can also be classified according to whether some linguistic form or feature is **present** in a context where it would not be expected (the usual situation, illustrated by the examples already given), **absent** in contexts where it would be expected (an error of avoidance or omission), or present in appropriate contexts but **statistically aberrant** (either occurring much more or much less frequently than one would expect). Errors of omission have been observed in the process of first language acquisition (Drachman 1973) and are well known in second language learning (Kleinmann 1978). Gross underuse, short of total absence, as well as gross overuse seem not to have been studied systematically as aspects of individual speech style, though probably everyone has had the experience of feeling overwhelmed by the frequency of particular words, expressions, or syntactic constructions in someone else's speech.

There are at least four further crosscutting distinctions, rather more problematic than those I have already mentioned, but nevertheless very important if we are to understand what happens when people make linguistic mistakes.

The first distinction, common to both production and perception errors, concerns the **linguistic basis** of an error: Does it arise, speaking generally, on the basis of phonological relationships, orthographic relationships, semantic relationships, or something else? And within these broad categories, which specific relationships figure in this error?

Consider, for instance, the production of *easily* instead of *early* (an example from Fay and Cutler 1977, p. 519). Assuming that both are adverbs (*early,* of course, can be used as either an adverb or an adjective), we are dealing with a replacement of a word in one syntactic category by another word in that category. Their morphological structures are different, however; *easily* is bimorphemic, *early* monomorphemic. Phonologically, they share their final syllables, /li/ in both cases, but are otherwise quite different—the two syllables /izɪ/ versus the one syllable /ər/ (though it must be admitted that /r/ and /z/ are not very distant phonologically). Orthographically, they share a final *ly* corresponding to the final shared /li/, **and** an initial *ea* corresponding to nothing the two words share phonologically. The point is that there are several possible linguistic bases for the error: shared syntactic category, shared (or related) phonological segments, or shared spelling. One or more of these linguistic dimensions might have served as the basis for a malfunction in the recall or production of a word. It is customary to classify errors according to their linguistic basis; thus, these distinctions figure prominently in the literature. Fay and Cutler, for instance, distinguish **malapropisms** from **semantic errors.** "In compiling the data used in this study we have relied on our intuitions as to what words were semantically related; where we have considered that a semantic relation existed, the error was eliminated from our list." Their intention was to separate errors with a semantic basis (*fingers* for *toes*) from those with a nonsemantic, presumably phonological, basis, and they appear to have largely achieved their goal. But there is no way to decide clearly in some cases, and many examples could well have more than one basis. The Fay–Cutler errors *summer* for *Sunday*, *got* for *gave*, and *happy* for *healthy* might be semantically as well as phonologically based; *happy* for *healthy* might also be based on associations in the lexicon; *easily* for *early* might be orthographically as well as phonologically based; and so on. Like Fay and Cutler, I am interested in errors that are primarily phonologically based, though I must concede that this is not always easy to determine.

The linguistic basis of an error can be classified in many further and finer ways, of course: by the type of unit involved (phonological feature, single phoneme, syllable nucleus, syllable onset, whole syllable, semantic feature, morpheme, word, phrase, etc.) and by specific relationships or properties within that type (specific phonological feature distinction, specific morpheme class, and so on). My attention here is focused largely on word errors, and the more specific properties of words I will mention include number of syllables, stress pattern, syntactic category, inflectional affixes, and derivational affixes.

The second distinction (not applicable to all error types) concerns the **physical relationship** between the target and the error—between what someone else produced and what was perceived, in the case of a perception error, or between what should have been produced and what actually was produced, in the case of an error manifested in production. The relationship may be **syntagmatic,** having to do with material surrounding the locus of the error, or **paradigmatic,** involving the substitution of one unit for another without influence from surrounding material. Anticipations (*basis on an error* written for *basis of an error*), perseverations (*pale skay* said for *pale sky*), reversals (*the wadar reather watch* said for *the radar weather watch*), and movements (*How much will it cost to buy a dog for a seeing-eye person?* for *How much will it cost to buy a seeing-eye dog for a person?*) are clearly syntagmatic in nature. Omissions and additions are hard to classify. I will group omissions with syntagmatic errors, on the grounds that an omission is a sort of anticipation of material to come. This classification will permit telescopings, like *freech* for *fresh speech*, to be grouped with other omissions, as syntagmatic. Additions, on the other hand, I will classify with paradigmatic errors, on the grounds that they often appear to represent interference from a competing plan of production or strategy of perception, as do paradigmatic errors in general (I shall say more on this in the following). In any event, substitution errors (*Deaf in Venice* misheard for *Death in Venice*) and blends (*They will have to let the reactor to cool down* as a blend of *let the reactor cool down* and *allow the reactor to cool down*) are paradigmatic in nature. My interest here is in paradigmatic errors, in particular, substitution errors.

The classification of particular examples can also be difficult. In particular, it is hard to exclude syntagmatic effects in substitutions—*Deaf* for *Death*, for example, might have been promoted by the later labiodental /v/ in *Venice*—and it is hard to be sure that the special relationships exhibited by paradigmatic errors have no effect on syntagmatic errors— the phonological closeness of /r/ and /w/ might have promoted reversal in *wadar reather*. It is also true that examples classed together as paradigmatic or syntagmatic may arise from quite different mechanisms. MacKay (1980, pp. 323f.) points out that though blends and word substitutions group together by virtue of the fact that semantic similarity plays a systematic role in both cases, still there are important differences (frequent antonym substitutions, as in *open* for *closed*, but no antonym blends at all) suggesting different underlying mechanisms.

The third distinction, specific to errors manifested in production, concerns the **intentions** of the producer: Did the speaker/writer intend to say this thing, or was it inadvertent? (I will assume that errors manifested in perception are inadvertent also.) Inadvertent errors might shed some light on the processes of recall and production, but if the production is as intended, no such inferences can be drawn. The freshman who wrote, "Since this course is required I mine as well take a positive approach to it," and who later read it out loud just as written, and who saw nothing in the least odd about it when questioned, exhibited no failure in recall or production, though certainly the error presented itself in production. This was an **advertent** error, a classical malapropism, in fact, and it is much more likely to show us something about the writer's original hearing and storage of the idiom *might as well* than it is to teach us anything about recall and production. Classical malapropisms contrast with Fay–Cutler malapropisms in this respect, since the former are advertent, the latter inadvertent.

Inadvertent errors include mishearings and misreadings (as when I read the headline *Kin of Slain Nuns Denounce Haig for "Smear Campaign,"* first as *Kin of Slain Nuts . . .*, then as *King of Slain Nuns . . .*), as well as failures to come up with lexical items during speech (the tip-of-the-tongue phenomenon investigated by Brown & McNeill 1966), semantic errors, syntactic blends, reversals, and Fay–Cutler malapropisms.

Advertent errors are quite diverse. First we must separate the special case of **deliberate errors** from other advertent errors: material produced with the understanding that others would find it ungrammatical, unacceptable, or unsuitable in some way—as when someone says *show snoveling* for *snow shoveling* as a joke, or when one person mimics another's dialect or foreign accent, or when a Frenchman insults a friend by addressing him or her as *vous* rather than *tu,* or when a poet requires his or her reader or listener to create coherence out of superficially incoherent discourse—

> *The way I denote him*
> *is by starting fires. I burn the toast*
> *in my oven while daydreaming about a cardinal flying through*
> *a winter tree. My paper towels of yellow or red*
> *catch on fire while I stand blazing*
> *in a yellow kimono*
> *hardly aware of anything but love.*
> [Diane Wakoski, from "Burning My Bridges Behind Me," in
>   *Waiting for the King of Spain*]

or intentionally ungrammatical material—

> *I liked the way he made love then he knew*
> *the way to take a woman when he sent*
> *me the 8 big poppies because mine was*
> *the 8th then I wrote the night he kissed*
> *my heart at Dolphins barn I couldnt*
> *describe it simply it makes you feel like*
> *nothing on earth but he never knew how*
> *to embrace well like Gardner . . .*
> [from page 731 of the 1934 American edition of *Ulysses,* by James
>   Joyce]

Of nondeliberate, but still advertent, errors there are many varieties. What they share is that they are "errors" not from the point of view of the producer, but only from the point of view of an audience. Here fall all the aspects of social and geographical dialects that are subject to negative evaluation by speakers of other dialects. It is scarcely useful to group these sociolinguistic, or **varietal,** differences (which are certainly not mistakes in any psychological sense) together with the many cases of psychological malfunctioning we have mentioned. But there are closely related errors that are of some interest, because they arise in the psychological functioning of an individual; these are **idiosyncratic** advertent errors, including those based on phonological relationships (classical malapropisms) or based on semantic relationships (private meanings). That is, classical malapropisms—*alibi* for *alimony*—are advertent errors parallel to the inadvertent Fay–Cutler malapropisms, and private meanings—*ritzy* meaning 'in poor taste'—are advertent errors parallel to the inadvertent semantic errors. Other sorts of idiosyncratic advertent errors can be catalogued, of course; these include a wide variety of errors in the speech of children acquiring their first language and of adults learning an additional one.

The fourth dimension, almost surely the hardest to determine, concerns the **cause** of the error. Paradigmatic errors, for instance, presumably arise through **competition** between alternative plans (in production) or strategies (in perception), whereas syntagmatic errors presumably arise from **malfunctioning** in the realization of some plan or strategy. As a special case of malfunctioning I will include the complete failure to select a plan or strategy: The listener or reader simply fails to comprehend a stretch, or the speaker or writer is at a loss for (a stretch of) words, as in the tip-of-the-tongue phenomenon.

Competititon and malfunctioning can often be assigned to deeper causes, of course: to physical defects (like missing teeth), or interference (like loud background noise), aphasias, schizophrenias, dyslexias, fatigue, drunkenness, and so on. My interest here is in a more superficial taxonomy of causes, however.

Two classes of phenomena are not in a narrow sense mistakes, and should be separated from other phenomena in this discussion of causes: the deliberate errors already mentioned, and the ordinary dysfluencies of speech (unfilled and filled pauses, restarts, and corrections, for instance). Dysfluencies appear to serve as signals of the speaker's active management of discourse—of turn offering and turn holding, in particular (Rochester 1973; Jefferson 1975). It would be misleading to classify these as errors (though they are so classified by the common person, and even Clark & Clark 1977, p. 273 treat them as a species of extralinguistic performance error).

What are the causes of advertent (but nondeliberate) errors? There is, first, **ignorance,** accompanied by some extension of what is known to the linguistic situation at hand. If you are ignorant of the full set of relevant aspects of the meaning of *apotheosis,* but have discerned its component of positive evaluation and its learned, elegant stylistic character, you might be moved to write something like the following, part of an advertisement for the Côte d'Azur restaurant in Georgetown: *It is here where the apotheosis of gastronomy has reached its apex.* I will assume that this idiosyncratic creation of a sense 'height' (roughly) for *apotheosis* is a typical instance of the development of private meanings. The overregularizations of first- and second-language learners are further examples of advertent errors arising from ignorance (of exceptional formations) combined with knowledge (of the regular formations); Richards (1971) subdivides the "types and causes of intralingual and developmental errors" into four groups—overgeneralizations (*He can sings*), ignorance of rule restrictions (*I made him to do it*), incomplete application of rules (*What you can see?*), and false concepts hypothesized (*One day it was happened* resulting from interpreting *was* as a marker of the past tense). Hypercorrections and spelling pronunciations also fall into the class of ignorance errors. And, in fact, all sorts of imperfect learning can be subsumed under this heading. I will not develop a taxonomy of ignorance errors here; clearly there are many types.

Closely related to ignorance errors are those of **interference,** in which one (perhaps partial) linguistic system in some sense influences productions in another. Interference errors in second-language learning are familiar examples: these involve the carry-over of principles from the first language, which then interact with some (more or less correctly induced) principles of the second. Presumably this is what happens when a speaker of English learning German uses the interrogative *wann* (instead of a subordinating conjunction like *als* or *wenn*) to introduce an adverbial subordinate clause; in English there is a single word *when* with both interrogative and subordinating uses.

Finally, idiosyncratic advertent errors can arise from some **misperception, misanalysis,** or **misproduction.** The classical malapropism *O lever mind* for *O never mind* almost surely originated in a mishearing of this idiomatic expression. The classical malapropism *television scream* for *television screen* probably originated in the listener's analysis of occurrences of [skrī], produced as instances of the word *screen;* [skrī] could realize either /skrim/ or /skrin/, and a listener who does not make the appropriate semantic connections is free to analyze [skrī] as /skrim/. One person's classical malapropisms could also arise in response to another person's production errors. Finally, if a speaker is somewhat unsure

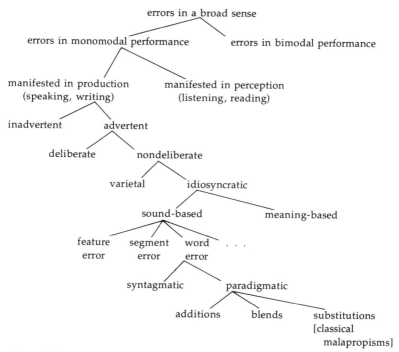

Figure 8.1. Partial classification of errors, focused on the classical malapropism.

about the word he wants, a tip-of-the-tongue approximation could be pressed into service and then provide the model for future productions by that speaker.

So far I have presented a series of classifications of linguistic errors, pausing at each step to fit classical malapropisms into the scheme being developed. The major points in these classifications as they concern classical malapropisms are summarized in Figure 8.1.

The Classical Malapropism Data

I now turn to the analysis of a sample of 158 classical malapropisms, collected from various sources and described in somewhat greater detail in Zwicky (1979). Though I tried to exclude inadvertent errors, private meanings, and varietal differences from the sample, the data are nevertheless very noisy. In the analysis that follows I will refer to a classical malapropism as an **error** and to the word which should have appeared in its place as the **model**.

There is significant agreement between errors and models on at least six linguistic dimensions:

1. *Number of syllables.* The following table shows the difference between the number of syllables in the error and the number in the model.

error minus model:	+2	+1	0	−1	−2
number of examples:	6	23	112	16	1

2. *Stress pattern,* for the 100 errors with more than one syllable that agreed in number of syllables with their models:

stress pattern:	*agrees*	*disagrees*
number of examples:	93	7

3. *Vowel with the primary stress:*

stressed vowel:	*agrees*	*disagrees*
number of examples:	110	48

4. *Word-initial segments.* For the 38 models beginning with vowels, over four-fifths of the errors had matching vowels:

word-initial vowel:	*agrees*	*disagrees*
number of examples:	30	8

   For the 120 beginning with consonants, over three-fourths of the errors had matching consonantal onsets (here I counted initial clusters as matching only if they matched completely)—

consonantal onset:	*agrees*	*disagrees*
#CV	73	22
#CCV	19	6
total	92	28

   (If only the initial consonant is counted the figures are 103 agree, 17 disagree.)

5. *Wordhood.* Eighty-seven percent of the errors are, like the models, existing words of English.

wordhood:	*preserved*	*not preserved*
number of examples:	138	20

6. *Grammatical category.* For the 138 errors that are existing words:

category:	*preserved*	*not preserved*
number of examples:	126	12

(Chi-square tests give results significant at the .001 level or better in all six categories.)

These same dimensions figure in several other types of phenomena: Fay–Cutler malapropisms, tip-of-the-tongue approximations (words offered during a search for the word on the tip of the subject's tongue), and slips of the ear, in particular. Direct comparison to slips of the ear (Garnes & Bond 1980) is impossible, since so many of these slips involve alterations in several words, including word boundary shifts (*herb and spice* heard as *urban spice, descriptive* heard as *the script of*). Still, Garnes and Bond report that only a handful of their 890 slips of the ear do not preserve stress and intonation patterns, and they observe that errors involving the perception of stressed vowels are rare (from their Table 1, pp. 234–235, I would estimate the incidence of these errors to be about 25% of the sample, roughly comparable to the 30% in my classical malapropisms collection). Their data also include 106 slips (12%) classified as syllable deletions and insertions, so that approximately 88% of the slips preserve number of syllables. Almost all of the slips involve words heard as other existing words.

As for the Fay–Cutler malapropisms, they are significantly different from classical malapropisms on almost every linguistic dimension: All 183 of their examples preserved wordhood (significantly more than the 87% in my data); 99% of their examples preserved grammatical category (significantly more than the 91% in my data); 87% of their examples agreed in number of syllables with the target word (significantly more than the 71% agreement in my data); only 54% of the stressed vowels agreed with those in the target words (significantly less than the 71% agreement in my data); and only 50% of the consonantal onsets match completely those in the target words (significantly less than the 77% in my data). Fay–Cutler and classical malapropisms do not differ significantly with respect to agreement in stress pattern (98% and 93%, respectively).

Brown and McNeill's (1966) tip-of-the-tongue results are less easy to compare with the classical malapropism data. Subjects were asked to supply all the words that came to mind while they were in the tip-of-the-tongue state, and responses were divided into "words of similar sound" and "words of similar meaning" categories, only the former being comparable to classical malapropisms. Of these, a fair number seem to be nonexistent words; in this respect, the tip-of-the-tongue and classical malapropism data stand together against the slip-of-the-ear and Fay–Cutler malapropism data. Agreement on grammatical category cannot be judged from Brown and McNeill's article; almost all the target words seem to have been nouns, in any case. The subjects were explicitly asked if they could supply the number of syllables in the target word; 57% of these estimates were correct, and 48% of the similar-sound responses agreed with the targets in number of syllables, both figures significantly lower than the agreements in the three other data sets I have been considering, but comparable to the figures in Browman's (1978) analysis of a corpus of 484 fortuitously collected tip-of-the-tongue approximations (56% agreement in number of syllables). Agreement in stress pattern was calculated for Brown & McNeill's similar-sound responses; the 75.5% figure is substantially lower than the corresponding figures for the other data sets (Browman's figure is 82%). Agreement in stressed vowel was not calculated, but from some examples provided—*Saipan, Siam, Cheyenne, sarong, sanching,* and *sympoon* as stabs at *sampan,* for instance—it is clear that the figure cannot be very high, probably comparable to the 54% for Fay–Cutler malapropisms. Subjects were asked about the beginnings of words, but since they were asked to supply the first LETTER of the target word, the results are hard to compare with those for other data sets; the figures of 57% correct for these explicit guesses and 49% agreement for similar-sound responses are low, in the same range as the Fay–Cutler malapropism data for agreement in consonantal onset. Browman obtained very similar figures—50% agreement on initial phones, 51% for initial letters.

I will now summarize these very rough comparisons by linguistic dimension, letting CM stand for classical malapropisms, SE for slips of the ear, FC for Fay–Cutler malapropisms, and TT for similar-sound tip-of-the-tongue responses.

1. Agreement in number of syllables:

$$\text{TT} < \text{CM} < \left\{ \begin{array}{l} \text{FC} \\ \text{SE} \end{array} \right\}$$

2. Agreement in stress pattern:

$$\text{TT} < \left\{ \begin{array}{l} \text{CM} \\ \text{FC} \\ \text{SE} \end{array} \right\}$$

3. Agreement in stressed vowel:

$$\left\{ \begin{array}{l} \text{TT} \\ \text{FC} \end{array} \right\} < \left\{ \begin{array}{l} \text{CM} \\ \text{SE} \end{array} \right\}$$

4. Agreement in word-initial segments:

$$\left\{ \begin{array}{l} \text{TT} \\ \text{FC} \end{array} \right\} < \text{CM}$$

5. Wordhood:

$$\begin{Bmatrix} TT \\ CM \end{Bmatrix} < \begin{Bmatrix} FC \\ SE \end{Bmatrix}$$

6. Agreement in grammatical category:

CM < FC

There are six two-way comparisons of data sets to be made with respect to these dimensions. In five of the six comparisons, the two data sets are compatible, in the sense that they are either roughly identical or are ordered only one way: TT is always below SE (on four dimensions); TT is below CM on four dimensions, at the same level in two; TT is below FC on three dimensions, at the same level in two; CM is below SE on two dimensions, at the same level in two; and FC is below SE on one dimension, at the same level in three. The one incompatible comparison is between FC and CM: CM is below FC on three dimensions, above it on two, and at the same level in one. This suggests that the mechanisms involved in classical malapropisms and Fay–Cutler malapropisms are quite different. Otherwise, classical malapropisms are most like slips of the ear with respect to phonological properties, but like tip-of-the-tongue approximations with respect to the preservation of wordhood. Although it is hazardous to speculate on the basis of such noisy and only roughly comparable data, my feeling is that these relationships support the suggestion made previously that classical malapropisms have several sources, some in perception (as various types of "frozen" slips of the ear) and some in a recall phase of production (as "frozen" tip-of-the-tongue approximations).

On the Analysis and Interpretation of Classical Malapropisms

It is time to ask the question: What can classical malapropisms tell us about linguistic theory? Since classical malapropisms are performance phenomena, this question naturally breaks down into two questions, one for psycholinguistics, the other for linguistics:

Question P: *What can classical malapropisms tell us about a theory of linguistic functioning (speech perception, speech production, memory for language)?*

Question L: *What can the resultant theory or theories of linguistic functioning tell us about a theory of language structure?*

To begin with Question P: Classical malapropisms, essentially by definition, are not errors in speech production. The involvement of speech perception in classical malapropisms is probably not negligible (as I suggested in the earlier sections of this chapter), and memory for language, in particular, memory for individual words and fixed phrases, clearly plays an important role. Answering Question P then breaks down into three further questions:

Question P1: *What are the relative roles of speech perception and lexical memory in the phenomenon of classical malapropism?*

Question P2: *What can classical malapropisms tell us about a theory of speech perception?*

Question P3: *What can they tell us about a theory of lexical memory?*

Even here at the outset, difficulties and perplexities abound. In particular, there are serious problems, already hinted at, with raw data. The problems begin with the very **definition** of the categories putatively relevant to the collection and analysis of data. I have been assuming without argument that there is some distinguishable class (or classes) of classical malapropisms (that they are, in principle, distinguishable from Fay–Cutler malapropisms, for example) and that they are relevant to perception and memory (whereas the class of errors affecting odd-numbered words in sentences, or the class of errors occurring in warm rooms or in conversational groups of more than three people, while distinguishable from other classes of errors, is presumably not relevant). Next there are problems with the **classification** of particular examples. The assignment of individual errors to the class of classical mala-propisms is often unsure. If the speaker corrects himself or accepts correction from others, it is fair to class the error as a Fay–Cutler malapropism, and if the speaker resolutely maintains that the word uttered was the one intended, it is fair to identify the error as a classical malapropism. If an error is repeated within a discourse, or if a written error survives editing by the original writer, it is usually fair to identify it as a classical malapropism (though, as David Fay has pointed out to me, Fay–Cutler malapropisms sometimes persevere). The ideal form of data collection would accept only errors where the speaker or writer was questioned about what was intended; most of my sample met this requirement, but in order to get reasonable numbers of examples, I found myself obliged to use my judgment about some cases.

There are, in fact, problems in the very **recognition** of examples. To collect my classical malapropisms I had to perceive some disparity between what was said (or in a few cases, written) and what I judged to be appropriate in the context—but this method of collection nets only the most striking instances, and I have no way of knowing the frequency and characteristics of more subtle errors (the same problem exists for the study of private meanings). What is needed is some more controlled form of data collection, as has been explored by Brown & McNeill (1966) for tip-of-the-tongue phenomena, by Baars and his collaborators for spoonerisms (see the summary in Baars 1980), by Kupin (1979) for errors induced by tongue twisters, and by MacKay for a number of error types (surveyed in MacKay 1980, sec. 2). Ideally, one would like a method for exposing the entire mental lexica of individual subjects (or some large and representative samples of these) and comparing one person's linkages of meaning and phonological form with those of the larger speech community. The difficulties in realizing such a project are manifold and obvious, but I see no way of answering questions P1 through P3 without investigations of this sort.

Finally, Question P1 requires an **interpretation** of particular examples as frozen slips of the ear (resulting from original errors in perception) or as frozen tip-of-the-tongue phenomena (resulting from original errors in lexical recall). I know of no principled way to make this distinction in the data.

With these important preliminaries out of the way, our task is to devise theories of speech perception and lexical memory consistent with what is known about classical malapropisms. I assume here that classical malapropisms have nothing much to say in answer to Question P2 that cannot be obtained from more direct studies of slips of the ear, though I should add that such work is still very much in its infancy (both the Garnes–Bond corpus and Browman's data are composed of fortuitously collected examples, and the extensive literature on perceptual confusions deals with the perception of single words or very short phrases in an artificial laboratory setting, rather than with the perception of connected natural speech). That is, I assume that the primary value of classical malapropisms will be in approaching an answer to Question P3.

Question P3 needs some sharpening. Classical malapropisms will tell us no more about lexical **retrieval** than does the production of any other lexical item: speakers producing classical malapropisms are, from their own points of view, simply retrieving and producing ordinary lexical items. The value of these errors lies in what we can learn about the way a mental lexicon is **created** and **maintained** (the maintenance of the lexicon surely in turn involves retrieval, as I have already suggested, so that we might learn something about retrieval indirectly from examining classical malapropisms).

At this point, further difficulties arise. The creation and refinement of lexical entries is a lifelong process, but we do not know whether the mechanisms by which adults acquire new lexical items and alter existing ones are really comparable to the mechanisms guiding the young child. The issue is important, because classical malapropisms could be traceable back to any point in language acquisition, and there is no way to tell from the form of an error when in the course of a life it might have originated. It is sometimes assumed that classical malapropisms are primarily adult creations—as when Evans and Evans (1957) maintain that these errors are "likely to occur in the speech of those who, ambitious to use fine language but not industrious enough to consult a dictionary, soar above their abilities and display, in the malapropism, not only their ignorance but their vanity as well [p. 288]"—but I know of no reason to think this is so. In fact, a substantial portion of my sample involves nontechnical model words (*collier* for *collie, apartment store* for *department store*). I conclude that classical malapropisms can arise from additions to or alterations in the mental lexicon at any age and that consequently they can originate against very different sets of background knowledge and experience and possibly also by means of different acquisitional strategies. My feeling is then that observations about classical malapropisms will become truly useful only when they are much more extensive than at present, particularly when they include substantial longitudinal data (beyond the enormous amount of information we now have about the earliest stages of vocabulary development).

We have many windows on the mental lexicon, including Fay–Cutler malapropisms, semantic errors, the tip-of-the-tongue phenomenon, word associations, and the response time data of semantic memory studies. These appear to look in upon different rooms of the lexical mansion, or upon the same rooms from strikingly different angles: Fay–Cutler malapropisms exhibit phonological relationships, word associations tap semantic relationships (most outstandingly the relationship of opposition), and so on. As essentially everyone who has written on the mental lexicon has admitted, people know an extraordinary number of different things about words—for example, how they are spelled, with what sort of company they are appropriate, whether they are inflectionally regular, in addition to the aspects already mentioned—and people also know a great deal about the things these words refer to, and they remember a good bit about past situations involving those words and those things (see the survey discussion in Miller & Johnson-Laird, 1976, sec. 3.3). Any mental lexicon study must somehow confront this multiplicity of relevant factors; classical malapropism studies must take change and development into account as well. It is apparent that analyzing a set of classical malapropisms (even a much larger or more rigorously collected set than mine was), with data from many subjects lumped together, can provide only limited evidence bearing on an account of how a mental lexicon is created and how it changes over time.

So far I have addressed myself to Question P3, which is psycholinguistic in character. Question L follows upon P: I assume that performance data bear on psycholinguistic theories, and that the choice of a linguistic theory may depend in part on its compatibility with particular psycholinguistic theories (with its "psychological reality" in a weak sense; see Bresnan 1978; p. 2ff.; Cutler 1979; Levelt 1974, p. 69ff.) framed by linguists, but that performance data bear on the choice of a linguistic theory only through the mediation of some psycholinguistic theory, and not directly (I should point out that the choice of a psycholinguistic theory may depend in part on its compatibility with some linguistic theory supported by other, non-psychological, lines of evidence). It follows that classical malapropism data bear only at great remove and in a limited way on issues of linguistic theory. I do not believe the situation is in principle different for classical malapropisms than for any other sort of performance data. The information now available on classical malapropisms, while entertaining, is desperately scanty, but could be improved in a number of ways I have detailed here. When this is done, such data could be used to choose among alternative conceptions of the way in which the mental lexicon is organized and accessed, and by a further step in argumentation, among alternative conceptions of the lexicon in linguistic theory. We have, however, scarcely taken the first step on this path.

References

Baars, B.J. (1980) On eliciting predictable speech errors in the laboratory. In V. Fromkin (Ed.), *Errors in linguistic performance*. New York: Academic Press. Pp. 307–318.

Bolinger, D. (1980) *Language: The loaded weapon*. London and New York: Longman.

Brandreth, G. (1980) *The joy of lex*. New York: William Morrow.

Bresnan, J. (1978) A realistic transformational grammar. In M. Halle, J. Bresnan, and G.A. Miller (Eds.), *Linguistic theory and psychological reality*. Cambridge, Mass.: MIT Press. Pp. 1–59.

Browman, C.P. (1978) Tips of the tongue and slips of the ear: implications for language processing. UCLA *working papers in phonetics and phonology #42*.

Brown, R. & McNeill, D. (1966) The tip of the tongue phenomenon. *Journal of verbal learning and verbal behavior, 5,* 325–337.

Clark, H.H. & Clark, E.V. (1977) *Psychology and language*. New York: Harcourt Brace Jovanovich.

Cutler, A. (1979) The psychological reality of word formation and lexical stress rules. Paper presented at International Congress of Phonetics, Copenhagen.

Drachman, G. (1973) Some strategies in the acquisition of phonology. In M.J. Kenstowicz, & C.W. Kisseberth (Eds.), *Issues in phonological theory: Proceedings of the Urbana conference on phonology.* The Hague: Mouton. Pp. 145–159.

Evans, B. & Evans, C. (1957) *A dictionary of contemporary American usage.* New York: Random House.

Fay, D. (1980) Transformational errors. In V. Fromkin (Ed.), *Errors in linguistic performance.* New York: Academic Press. Pp. 111–122.

Fay, D. & Cutler, A. (1977) Malapropisms and the structure of the mental lexicon. *Linguistic inquiry, 8, No. 3,* 505–520.

Follett, W. (1966) *Modern American usage.* New York: Hill and Wang.

Foss, D.J. & Fay, D. (1975) Linguistic theory and performance models. In D. Cohen, & J.R. Wirth (Eds.), *Testing linguistic hypotheses.* Washington, D.C.: Hemisphere Publishing Co. Pp. 65–91.

Fowler, H.W. (1937) *A dictionary of modern English usage.* London: Oxford University Press.

Fromkin, V.A. (ed.) (1973) *Speech errors as linguistic evidence.* The Hague: Mouton.

Fromkin, V.A. (ed.) (1980) *Errors in linguistic performance.* New York: Academic Press.

Garnes, S. & Bond, Z.S. (1980) A slip of the ear: A snip of the ear? A slip of the year? In V. Fromkin (Ed.), *Errors in linguistic performance.* New York: Academic Press. Pp. 231–239.

Jefferson, G. (1975) Error correction as an interactional resource. *Language in society, 3,* 181–199.

Kleinmann, H.H. (1978) The strategy of avoidance in adult second language acquisition. In W.C. Ritchie (Ed.), *Second language acquisition research: Issues and implications.* New York: Academic Press. Pp. 157–174.

Kupin, J.J. (1979) Tongue twisters as a source of information about speech production. Ph.D. dissertation, University of Connecticut.

Levelt, W.J.M. (1974) *Formal grammar in linguistics and psycholinguistics, Vol. 3: Psycholinguistic applications.* The Hague: Mouton.

MacKay, D.G. (1980) Speech errors: retrospect and prospect. In V. Fromkin (Ed.), *Errors in linguistic performance.* New York: Academic Press. Pp. 319–332.

Miller, G.A. & Johnson-Laird, P.N. (1976) *Language and perception.* Cambridge, Mass.: Harvard University Press.

Richards, J.C. (1971) A noncontrastive approach to error analysis. *English language teaching, 25, No. 3,* 204–19. [Reprinted in J.C. Richards (Ed.). (1974) *Error analysis: Perspectives on second language acquisition.* London: Longman. Pp. 172–188.]

Rochester, S.R. (1973) The significance of pauses in spontaneous speech. *Journal of Psychological Research,* Vol. 2, No. 1, 51–81.

Safire, W. (1980) *On language.* New York: Times Books.

Zwicky, A.M. (1979) Classical malapropisms. *Language sciences,* Vol. 1, No. 2, 339–48.

Zwicky, A.M. (1980) *Mistakes.* Reynoldsburg, Ohio: Advocate Publishing Group.

9
STEFANIE
SHATTUCK-HUFNAGEL

Three Kinds of Speech Error Evidence for the Role of Grammatical Elements in Processing

In the decade since Fromkin (1971) brought speech errors to the attention of modern linguistics and psycholinguistics, there has been a steady growth of interest and work in the application of speech error evidence to the question of how the grammar participates in sentence processing (Baars & Motley 1976; Cutler 1980; Dell & Reich (1981); Ellis 1979; Fromkin 1973; Garrett 1975; 1976; 1980; Goldstein 1977; Shattuck-Hufnagel 1979; Shattuck-Hufnagel & Klatt 1979; Stemberger 1980). Among the reasons for this increasing interest are (a) a gradual recovery from disappointment at the early failure of the direct incorporation model in which the steps in the linguistic derivation of a sentence were hypothesized to correspond closely to the processing steps in the comprehension or production planning of an utterance, (b) a growing data base of speech errors, which now, after 10 years of observation, analysis and experimentation, includes a number of corpora collected by investigators in German, English, Dutch, and Portugese, and (c) the fact that speech error data arise in otherwise normal speaking circumstances, without the unusual influences which might be imposed by laboratory surroundings (e.g., focusing attention on the act of language use.) For these and other reasons, speech error studies have been multiplying, despite the obvious difficulties in dealing with naturalistic data, filtered through the ears and memories of human listeners, which often display tendencies and assymetries rather than absolute constraints. The purpose of this chapter is to illustrate the claim that speech error data can now be used to go beyond the simple demonstration of "psychological

EXCEPTIONAL LANGUAGE AND LINGUISTICS

reality" for various components of the grammar. We are now in a position to specify the contrasting roles that different grammatical components might play in processing. For example, early studies of speech errors cited the distinctive feature, the phonemic segment, and the syllable as "error units," since all three of these elements move and change in spontaneous speech errors. We are now able to see that these three elements may function in very different ways in production planning, by noting that the error evidence which supports them is of three very different kinds.

Error Evidence for a Sublexical Serial Ordering Mechanism

Among the types of errors which occur in spontaneous speech, one of the most surprising involves the misordering of fragments of words and morphemes like the following:

(1)   . . . *ponato* . . .   (tomato)
(2)   . . . *a wed-rine drinker* . . .   (red-wine)
(3)   *I'm a waple-malnut fan.*   (maple walnut)
(4)   *I'm going to keel my parrots.*   (peel my carrots)
(5)   *He met for dinner with Kenry Hissinger.*   (Henry Kissinger)
(6)   *Let me give it a krick skwub.*   (quick scrub)
(7)   . . . *the flouse with the American hag* . . .   (house with the American flag)
(8)   . . . *Glon Jenn Boulevard* . . .   (John Glenn)
(9)   . . . *you mean he's not smowing floothly along?*   (flowing smoothly)
(10)   . . . *an early-moning phorn call* . . .   (early-morning phone call)
(11)   . . . *autism is the most sevore feerm* . . .   (severe form)
(12)   . . . *for pay-chub stecks* . . .   (pay-check stubs)
(13)   *My sole has a hock* . . .   (sock has a hole)
(14)   *You got a piece of papel and a pencer?*   (piece of paper and a pencil)
(15)   *I have to coaten the tight rack.*   (tighten the coat rack)

The reason these exchange errors are unexpected is that information about the order in which the segments of a word or morpheme appear must surely be a part of its lexical representation in order to distinguish e.g. *pat* from 'tap.' Why, then, need the production planning mechanism include a component which reorders the pieces of a lexical item, as these misordering errors seem to suggest? Although we do not have a clear answer to this question, I will argue in this chapter that speech error patterns provide a considerable amount of information about the nature and operation of this **sublexical** serial ordering mechanism. (Sublexical exchange errors are those that involve fragments smaller than a single lexical entry. Since the question of whether lexical entries consist of words or morphemes is still under dispute, we will avoid ambiguity by defining sublexical errors as those which involve fragments smaller than a morpheme: single features, phonemic segments, clusters and longer sequences of segments which do not make up a full morpheme.)

What are the characteristics of sublexical exchange errors that reveal aspects of the serial ordering mechanism? The first thing to notice is that by far the majority of these errors involve single phonemic segments. As is obvious from the previous list of examples, other sublexical error units do arise, but single V and single C errors account for two-thirds of these errors in the MIT corpus of spontaneous speech errors (Shattuck-Hufnagel 1979, 1980). Other units, including distinctive features, consonant clusters, syllables, and other sublexical strings account for only one third of the total, with a small number in each category. Because of the predominance of word onset errors in words that begin with a single consonant, the data are also consistent with the syllable onset, nucleus and coda as processing units, but the syllable (or other unit made up of both C's and V's) appears only rarely in sublexical exchanges.

Further support for the segments or onsets, nuclei and codas as the primary units of serial misordering in speech errors, and thus as the primary unit of serial ordering in normal error-free speech, comes from elicitation experiments. When four-syllable tongue twisters like /pim fan fum pon/ are repeated several times, exchanges of single C or V segments are common but CV-, -VC and CVC exchanges made up only 1% of the total (Shattuck-Hufnagel 1980). Thus, observational and experimental data seem to converge on individual phonemic segments or syllabic subcomponents as the primary units of sublexical misordering errors, and thus as the unit of normal sublexical ordering processes.

A more serious challenge to the phonemic segment as the computational unit for sublexical serial ordering comes from a set of errors in which the single distinctive feature appears to be the unit of exchange. As Fromkin (1971; 1973) has pointed out, errors like *glear plue sky* for 'clear blue sky' are easily accounted for as the exchange of two feature values (in this case, the voicing feature changes places, leaving the remaining feature specifications of the two affected segments intact.) It is more difficult to account for errors like this, and like 'ponato' cited previously, as whole-segment errors. To do so, the two parts of the error would have to be seen as independently occurring substitution errors, /k/ → /g/ and /b/ → /p/. Yet if this were the case, such errors should be part of a larger set of double substitutions that show no such feature symmetry, with the apparent feature exchanges resulting from the coincidental occurrence of two unrelated substitutions. However, no such set of double substitutions occurs in the MIT corpus of errors, and this explanation must be ruled out.

The possibility that the distinctive feature is the element of sublexical serial ordering is kept alive by the observation that many sublexical exchange errors could be described either as segment exchanges or feature exchanges, because the two target segments differ by only one feature value, as in *keel my parrots* for 'peel my carrots'. Taking the unambiguous feature exchanges and the exchanges ambiguous between feature and segment together, why not postulate that the feature is the normal element of sublexical serial ordering?

There are several arguments against making this move. First, a substantial number of exchanged pairs differ by two or more features. More compelling is the argument put forward by Klatt (Shattuck-Hufnagel & Klatt 1979). He showed that among the exchanged pairs in the MIT corpus for which we can be sure whether it was a segment or a feature exchange (like the pair /g/–/n/), the proportion of feature exchanges is very small, only 3 of 70. Most of these errors involve the entire segment instead. This finding suggests that the ambiguous exchanges, which could be analysed either as feature or whole-segment errors, are largely made up of whole-segment errors as well. Finally, in the elicitation experiments previously described, which used four-syllable CVC tongue twisters, no single-feature exchanges were obtained.

Against these arguments for maintaining phonemic segments (or syllabic onset, nucleus and coda) as the units over which sublexical serial order is computed, we have only the existence of a small number of very clear single feature exchanges like *ponato*. Faced with this pattern of observations, we can do one of three things: We can postulate a separate serial ordering mechanism for each observed error unit type, including the feature; we can back off altogether and admit the possibility that any fragment of a morpheme can participate in an exchange error; or we can attempt to account for the small but persistent number of nonsegmental errors in some other way. Since the first alternative involves an unattractive multiplication of processes to account for a relatively small number of errors, we will reject it. The second is not quite accurate, since a number of sublexical fragments (e.g., cv from the context CCV) do not appear as error units at all. Thus, the third alternative appears to be the most reasonable one, and it is not difficult to derive accounts of feature exchanges and other rare error types within the model we have proposed. For example, if the phonemic segments undergoing serial ordering are represented with at least some of their feature values, then occasionally these values could be symmetrically misread. For this to occur, it is not necessary that the feature be the normal element of serial ordering, but only that the feature values be discretely represented, at least some of the time. Alternatively, segments might be read out one feature value at a time, under certain circumstances. In any case, the bulk of the evidence from speech error data supports the existence of a sublexical serial ordering mechanism which operates over units that contain either C's or V's, but not both. What might the details of such a mechanism look like?

Consider what exchange errors like *I never had a pooth tulled* for '. . . tooth pulled' imply about this mechanism. In order for the first part of the exchange to occur, the intruding segment /p/ which appears there must have been available to the planning mechanism while the utterance of "tooth" was being planned. In fact, any error with an anticipatory component implies such a planning span, as Lashley (1951) persuasively pointed out. An exchange, however, gives us even more information about the planning mechanisms involved. Note that the displaced target segment /t/ does not disappear, nor does it appear in some random location in the utterance. Instead, it appears in precisely the location where the intruding segment /p/ SHOULD have appeared, at the beginning of *-ulled*. The fact that a displaced segment always appears in this slot if it appears at all, suggests that the serial ordering mechanism can maintain segments independent of their locations, and locations independent of their target segments. One way of assuring that the ordering mechanism will have this capacity is to allow it to operate over a dual representation of the utterance, with one representation consisting of the candidate segments and the other as an ordered set of slots (Shattuck 1975, Shattuck-Hufnagel 1979). The serial ordering mechanism itself then must consist of an integrator, which scans the available segments and fits them into their appropriate slots. I have argued in earlier papers that such a model can account for all the observed types of sublexical error, as well as for the nonoccurrence of other types, and the similarity constraints governing those that do occur. It is to three of these similarity constraints, and their implications for the role of the segment, the feature and the syllable in production planning, that we now turn.

Three Types of Similarity Constraints on
Interacting Sublexical Elements

In a corpus of sublexical exchange errors, several different kinds of constraints on the relationship between interacting elements can be observed. For example, there is the **Unit Similarity Constraint:** When two elements exchange, they are both single elements at the same level of description. For example, single segments do not exchange with long sequences of C's and V's. Instead, clusters exchange with clusters (*fline swu* for 'swine flue'), longer sequences with other longer sequences (*intax into synsights* for 'insights into syntax'), and, predominantly, single segments with other single segments.[1] This similarity constraint suggests that the integration mechanism which matches elements to slots in the serial ordering process is sensitive to the size of those items.

A second kind of constraint on sublexical exchange errors is the **Intrinsic Similarity Constraint:** When two segments exchange, they tend to share many of their distinctive feature values. This finding has been reported for several speech corpora in English (Goldstein 1977; Shattuck-Hufnagel & Klatt 1975), German (MacKay 1970), Dutch (Nooteboom 1969), and Portugese (Johns 1973). The fact that similarities between interacting segments can be captured by featurelike dimensions is compatible with the hypothesis that the segments are represented along these dimensions at the point in production planning when sublexical exchange errors occur. However, present methods do not allow us to compare the relative efficacy of different dimension systems in accounting for the constraints on interacting target pairs; we can only say whether a given dimension significantly constrains the matrix of interacting pairs (Klatt 1968). Since dimensions like articulatory similarity overlap heavily with distinctive feature similarity, we can expect that both sets of dimensions will significantly constrain the interaction matrix, and we cannot be sure which set is the most appropriate one. At the very least, however, the constraints on which segments can interact in exchange errors is compatible with the hypothesis that the segments are represented in terms of their distinctive feature values.

---

[1] The major exception to this constraint is a set of errors in which the initial consonant of one word exchanges with the initial consonant cluster of another, as in *lightly brit* for 'brightly lit', and *show snovelling* for 'snow shovelling'. These errors suggest the syllable onset rather than the single segment as the appropriate descriptive unit, and the predominance of single consonant onsets among the single segment errors is also compatible with this description. Yet, consonant exchanges also break up onset clusters, as in *peel like flaying* for 'feel like playing'. No single characterization will explain all sublexical exchange units; see Shattuck-Hufnagel (1980) for further discussion.

Finally, there is the **Extrinsic Similarity Constraint:** Two segments which exchange are almost always drawn from similar positions in their respective syllables. While the majority of sublexical exchanges occur in word- and morpheme-initial position (88% in the MIT corpus of complete single-consonant exchanges), there is a small but persistent proportion of exchange errors in noninitial position, such as *stick neff* for 'stiff neck'. In all of these errors, the position constraint could be stated equally easily over the syllable, the morpheme, or the word. In a few errors, however, like *wern-fidal* for 'word-final' or *refeat the peet* for 'repeat the feet', only the syllable constraint appears to hold. Finally, there is a remainder of fewer than five errors in the MIT corpus for which no position constraint seems to hold, as in *I should ashk Slomo* for ' . . . ask Schlomo'. This pattern suggests that the syllable serves to define the ordered-slot representation which guides the serial ordering of sublexical elements.

Further evidence for the syllable as the serial ordering framework comes from error types other than exchanges. These errors seem to require that a framework in terms of canonical syllable shape be available. For example, in shift errors like *using chomatric—chromatic stimuli* and *most claudal side* for '. . . caudal slide', a single segment disappears from its target location and appears instead in a structurally similar nearby slot which was not destined to be filled by any segment in the target string. In other words, the serial ordering mechanism appears to have available slots into which shifted segments may be inserted. A similar argument can be made for addition errors, either with reduplication (*my flace flushed*), or with no apparent source (*to repray the Lapps* for '. . . repay . . .')

Further evidence for the syllable position constraint is provided by the elicitation experiments described previously. In some of the four-syllable stimuli used to elicit exchange errors, a pair of highly confusing target segments appeared in opposite syllable positions, so that one of the pair appeared only in initial slots and the other only in final ones. Even though the segments were highly confusable, no interaction across syllable positions occurred. Thus, all of the available evidence suggests that the syllable is a prime candidate for the unit in terms of which the ordered sequence of slots is represented.

Discussion

We have argued that three different kinds of speech error evidence suggest different roles for the distinctive feature, the phonemic segment (or cluster), and the syllable, in speech production planning. The predominance of single segment units among sublexical errors suggests that syllabic constituents made up of either C's or V's are the normal units of sublexical serial ordering; the feature similarity of interacting segment pairs suggests that the segments are represented at least partially in terms of featurelike dimensions at the point where exchange errors occur, and the syllable-position similarity constraint on interacting segments points to a syllabic framework to guide the serial ordering process. Several other lines of evidence were adduced in support of each of these hypotheses. It is clear, however, that much remains to be discovered about the sublexical serial ordering mechanism. For example, how are the two representations (segments and slots) generated? What does each representation look like in detail? And most importantly, why is the generation of a dual representation and the subsequent reintegration into a single string a necessary part of the normal speech planning process? Discussion of these questions is outside the scope of this chapter; further analysis of existing error corpora and experimentation to test hypotheses in this area are currently under way. It may be worth noting, in the meantime, the general relationship between grammars and processing mechanisms with which this proposed model is compatible.

Garrett (in press) and Garrett and Kean (1980) have suggested a view of the relationship between transformational generative grammar and production processing which draws a distinction between the levels of representation employed in the grammar, and the mechanisms which generate those representations. In their view, we can reasonably expect to find a correspondence between processing representations and the several autonomous LEVELS of description posited by the grammar. However, there is no reason to expect that the MECHANISMS by which the grammar generates its descriptions will correspond to the ones a language user has recourse to in the processing of sentences. Thus,

> We accept the hypothesis that the levels of representation generated by the grammar are the levels of representation in processing.

> There are two distinct issues which are to be considered in the analysis of error data. On the one hand,. . . the objects of the operations of the various components of the processing system. . . . On the other hand, the types of operations which are available to the processor in its component systems. These two types of consideration are, to some extent at least, logically independent [Garrett & Kean 1980, p. 87].

In this view of the role of the grammar in processing, grammatical derivations and psychological mechanisms make contact at critical points during the planning of an utterance, and these points correspond to the levels of description or representation that each would generate. While the generation process in a grammatical derivation might be very different from the corresponding psychological processing for the same utterance, the two kinds of operations make reference to the same kinds of information and generate similar products (the "objects" referred to previously.) Thus, "For each rule system [i.e., in the grammar] there is a corresponding autonomous component of the language processing system whose computational responsibility is to provide a representation equivalent to that of [i.e., provided by] the grammatical rule system" [Garrett, in press].

The sublexical serial-ordering mechanism described in the present paper is not incompatible with such a view of the grammar-processor relationship. While the operations of a sublexical serial ordering mechanism certainly do not correspond to any grammatical rule or derivational process, it is plausible to imagine that the representation operated on by the ordering mechanism closely resembles a level of description posited by the grammar. This claim can be subjected to rigorous testing only to the extent that linguistic formulations of the details of these levels of representation are available. In particular, we need to know more about the internal structure of morphemes, the relationship between syntactic, morphological, and metrical units, and the precise nature of the theoretical entity "level of description." As these issues become clearer, we will be better able to use psychological evidence like that from speech errors to illuminate the relationship between the grammar and the processing mechanism in production planning.

References

Baars, B.J., & Motley, M.T. (1976) Spoonerisms as sequencer conflicts: Evidence from artificially elicited errors. *American journal of psychology, 83,* 467–84.

Cutler, A. (1980) Errors of stress and intonation. In V.A. Fromkin (Ed.), *Errors in linguistic performance*. New York: Academic Press.

Dell, G.S., & Reich, P.A., (1981). Stages in sentence production: An analysis of speech error data. *Journal of verbal learning and verbal behavior, 20,* 611–629.

Ellis, A.W. (1979) Speech production and short-term memory. In J. Morton and J.C. Marshall (Eds.), *Psycholinguistic Series* (Vol. 2): *Structures and Processes*. Cambridge, Mass.: MIT Press.

Fromkin, V.A. (1971) The non-anomalous nature of anomalous utterances, *Language, 47,* 27–52.

Fromkin, V.A. (1973) Introduction. In V.A. Fromkin (Ed.), *Speech errors as linguistic evidence*. The Hague: Mouton.

Garrett, M.F. (1975) The analysis of sentence production. In G. Bower (Ed.), *Psychology of learning and motivation, Vol. 9,* New York: Academic Press.

Garrett, M.F. (1976) Syntactic processes in sentence production. In R. Wales & E. Walker (Eds.), *New approaches to language mechanisms*. Amsterdam: North Holland.

Garrett, M.F. (1980) Levels of processing in sentence production. In B. Butterworth (Ed.), *Language production*, Vol. 1. London: Academic Press.

Garrett, M.F. (in press). Production of speech: Observations from normal and pathological language use. In A.W. Ellis (Ed.), *Normality and pathology in cognitive functions*. London: Academic Press.

Garrett, M.F., & Kean, M.L. (1980) Linguistic representation and the analysis of speech errors. In M. Aronoff & M.L. Kean, (Eds.), *On juncture*. Cambridge, Mass.: MIT Press.

Goldstein, L. (1977) Features, salience and bias. *UCLA working papers in phonetics #39*.

Johns, C.M. (1972) Slips of the tongue in Portugese. M. Litt. thesis, University of Edinburgh.

Klatt, D.H. (1968) The structure of confusions in short-term memory between English consonants. *Journal of the Acoustical Society of America, 44*, 401–407.

Lashley, K.S. (1951) The problem of serial order in behavior. In L.A. Jeffress (Ed.), *Cerebral mechanisms in behavior*. New York: Wiley.

MacKay, D.G. (1970) Spoonerisms: The structure of errors in the serial order of speech. *Neuropsychologia, 8*, 323–350.

Nooteboom, S.G. (1969) The tongue slips into patterns. In A.G. Sciarone, *et al.* (Eds.), *Nomen: Leyden studies in linguistics and phonetics*. The Hague: Mouton.

Shattuck, S.R. (1975) Speech errors and sentence processing. Unpublished Ph.D. thesis, Massachusetts Institute of Technology.

Shattuck-Hufnagel, S. (1979) Speech errors as evidence for a serial-ordering mechanism in sentence production. In W.E. Cooper & E.C.T. Walker (Eds.), *Sentence processing*. Cambridge, Mass.: MIT Press.

Shattuck-Hufnagel, S. (1980) Sublexical structure in speech production planning. Paper presented at the Conference on Speech Production, Austin, Texas, April 1980 [(to appear in P. MacNeilage, (Ed.), *Proceedings of the Conference on Speech Production*.)]

Shattuck-Hufnagel, S. & Klatt, D.H. (1975) An analysis of 1500 phonetic speech errors. *Journal of the Acoustical Society of American, 58*, S(1), 66.

Shattuck-Hufnagel, S. & Klatt, D.H. (1979) The limited use of distinctive features and markedness in speech production: Evidence from speech production, *Journal of verbal learning and verbal behavior, 18*, 41–55.

Stemberger, J.P. (1980) Length as a suprasegmental evidence: from speech errors. Manuscript, University of California at San Diego, La Jolla, California.

10 M. P. O'CONNOR

"Unanswerable the Knack of Tongues": The Linguistic Study of Verse

Thus laudable the trodden bone thus
Unanswerable the knack of tongues.
—GEOFFREY HILL

Literature is a central manifestation of both language and culture, and poetry is the central manifestation of literature. The necessary tie between the study of language and the study of poetry would be apparent in a history of linguistics that acknowledged South Asian roots. The Sanskrit grammarians sought mnemotechnic phonological rules in order to preserve sacred poetic texts. The tie manifested itself often in nineteenth-century linguistics: Sievers and Saussure were assiduous, if eccentric, students of verse. Probably at no time in the history of linguistic thought has the study of poetry been as far from its proper central position as it is today. That it has not failed entirely from that position is due in large part to Roman Jakobson, the scholar who is easily first among "exceptional linguists," the only one who is entirely worthy of Obler and Menn's pun.

In this modest endeavor to frame a case for the usefulness and interest of poetry in language science, I will delineate three areas of comment. First, I will consider the crucial and overriding features of poetry as a linguistic activity. I will ask, to frame the question more formally than I shall try to answer it, "What are the features of poetry that must be accounted for in a theory of language?" Second, I will review some of the types of contributions the study of poetry can make to linguistics and will ask: "What are the varieties of poetic evidence that linguists can draw on?" I will turn in conclusion to some peculiar contemporary interactions of linguistics and literary criticism and inquire into the

143

conflicts among students of verse. I cannot hope to eliminate the attendant acerbity but I do want to cite some causes pertinent to linguists.

I will draw throughout this chapter on the latest full-scale volume from the pen of Roman Jakobson, prepared in collaboration with Linda Waugh, *The Sound Shape of Language* (1979, henceforth SSL), though my plunder of the volume will not exhaust its relevant interest, for I cannot reproduce the ease and urgency with which verse is handled in it. Nor will my exposition exhaust the richness of the range of verse it draws on, from the great Romantics Goethe and Hugo through major Moderns, early and late, Rimbaud and Valéry, and Valéry's younger contemporaries in Russia who were friends of Jakobson's youth. Christian Morgenstern, Gerard Manley Hopkins, Elena Guro, and e.e. cummings are cited alongside children's rhymes and those most rarified of extracts from ancient poetry, Saussure's "anagrams." The latest poet quoted in the book is Jack Spicer (1925–1965), who was trained as a linguist and made youthful contributions to dialectology (e.g., Reed & Spicer 1952) and who later produced a significant body of poetry (Spicer 1975). At the time of his death, his language use was nearly vestigial due to the ravages of Korsakoff's Syndrome. Let Jack Spicer's acceding to the demands of language, an acceding both Romantic and Modern, both enriching and chastening, stand as a sign of the weight of those demands.

The Central Features of Poetry

Literature and a fortiori verse are central manifestations of both language and culture, but in a properly Jakobsonian perspective verse is the central manifestation of language alone. The conceptual framework I shall sketch, of the onomatopoeic and poetic principles and of the notion of a language's resources, can be viewed in the general context of contemporary notions of language. It has its most rigorous formulation, however, in a Jakobsonian setting, one in which the nonarbitrary character of the linguistic sign is acknowledged. The relevant Praguian tradition would recognize Baudouin de Courtenay over Saussure as a crucial predecessor and in American linguistics would look to Sapir and Whorf rather than to Bloomfield.

By way of introduction to the onomatopoeic principle, let me offer a strand of argumentation that proceeds from the core of Praguian phonology through a statement of that principle to one definition of poetic activity. I present the strand in the form it is given by Jakobson and Waugh in order to show the governing necessity of its understanding of language.

> The distinctive features . . . differ from all other constituents of language through the lack of their proper, immediate signification. Their only *signatum* [thing signified] is that of 'mere otherness', or in Sapir's terms, they carry "no singleness of reference." . . . Their inner organization is built on the principle of most effective perception and recollection. And this merely mediate characteristic appears as their only load so long as language is taken in its narrowly rational application.
>
> However, any distinctive feature is built on an opposition which, taken apart from its basic and conventional linguistic usage, carries a latent synesthetic association and thus an immediate, semantic usage. This *immediacy* in signification of the distinctive features acquires an autonomous role in the more or less onomatopoeic strata of ordinary language. The habitual relation of *contiguity* between sound and meaning yields to a bond of *similarity*. . . .
>
> The tension between two structural principles—contiguity and similarity—permeates the whole of language. If, as mediate building blocks of meaningful entities, the distinctive features serve to connect sound and meaning by virtue solely of contiguity, the inner sound symbolism peculiar to these features strives to burst forth and to sustain an immediate similarity relation [SSL, pp. 235–236].

This, then, is the onomatopoeic principle: That alongside the apparently arbitrary functioning of the sound sign, it possesses and seeks continually to manifest a nonarbitrary, synesthetic function. The study of the implications of this function for the shaping of utterances and the structuring of the lexicon is a largely neglected field of linguistics. Only Dwight Bolinger among our older contemporaries has pursued it with rigor. The highest manifestation of the onomatopoeic principle, however, is not in ordinary-language syntax or in the lexicon but in verse.

Before I resume my citation of Jakobson and Waugh, let me offer a summary of the argument so far and anticipate its resolution by citing some lines from Wallace Stevens's major poem, "Notes Toward A Supreme Fiction" (1942/1972, p. 210).

> From this the poem springs: that we live in a place
> That is not our own and, much more, not ourselves
> And hard it is in spite of blazoned days.

Language (I am skewing Stevens's argument) is the place, and it has neither adequate contiguity (it is *not our own*) nor, more crucially, adequate immediacy (it is *not ourselves*). Jakobson and Waugh offer a positive version of Stevens's despair in asserting, "Poetry, as a purposeful, mythopoeic play, is the fullest, universal accomplishment of the synthesis between contiguity and similarity [SSL, p. 236]." The onomatopoeic principle at work throughout language attains a shaping mastery only in verse.

The second principle involved in the most intense of linguistic activities differs from the first in being more strictly limited to poetry. The poetic principle, as it is called, also differs from the first principle in not referring so much to the material of language as to the material's use in the realization of language. Jakobson's central formulation of this principle has achieved some notoriety as an oracular utterance but it is rather a model of conciseness. "The poetic function," he wrote, "projects the principle of equivalence from the axis of selection [a paradigmatic axis] into the axis of combination [a syntagmatic axis]. Equivalence is promoted to the constitutive device of the sequence [Jakobson 1967, p. 303]." Kiparsky usefully paraphrases: "various aspects of poetic form all involve some kind of recurrence of equivalent linguistic elements [1974, p. 235]." Poetic activity isolates those classes from which linguistic tokens are chosen in the building-up of an utterance on all its levels. On the phonological level, syllables, stressed syllables, syllables beginning with a stop, or a particular stop, are examples of classes which are linguistically definable but which are not made the bases of utterances in ordinary language. In syllabic meter, all syllables are chosen as a group to be numerically regulated, "whereas speakers do not measure the number of syllables in their ordinary speech [SSL, p. 216]"; in accentual meter, all stressed syllables form the class to be manipulated in small patterns rather than selected among; in various types of alliterative verse and rarely elsewhere in language use, are words beginning with (say) *t* taken as a class of equivalent members in a way that patterns the surface of an utterance.

Tokens from such linguistically definable classes as these and similar, morphologically or syntactically distinct classes, are combined in accord with underlying patterns of meter and the like. Since patterning is at work on all linguistic levels at once (though never to the same degree), the results are not merely (for example) banal, if charming subsets of the lexicon, but highly charged language. Equivalence in ordinary speech serves to isolate relevant classes and subclasses and subsubclasses as an utterance is shaped. In poetic activity much more is made of that isolation than in ordinary speech: The unity of a given class is validated not merely as useful to the task of organizing speech-in-process but as integral to a form of speech.

These two principles form the ground of a programmatic statement Jakobson and Waugh offer.

The analysis of the two closely interconnected synthetic powers of poetry—that of similarity and contiguity and that of selection and combination—is a burning task faced by our science. Any fear of or reluctance about the analysis of the poetic transformation of language impairs the scientific program of those linguists who pull back from the pivotal problem of this vital transformation; and likewise it curtails the research of those literary scholars who, in treating poetry, pull back from the innermost problems of language [SSL, p. 236].

The theoretical importance of the collocation of these "synthetic powers" or, as I have called them, principles, is plain. Both principles offer a distinctive over-against to the study of ordinary language. Most linguists, for example, would not be inclined to deny the existence in ordinary language of the phenomena explained by the onomatopoeic principle. They would, however, I think tend to regard those phenomena as too eccentric for linguistic investigation. Jakobson's formulation makes that impossible (or should make it impossible), for it claims that there is a sphere of language activity where the onomatopoeic principle in some sense takes over. "In what sense?" linguists and literary scholars have repeatedly asked. Here is the answer Jakobson and Waugh offer when they assert that poetic language is the "one kind of verbal activity which is . . . necessarily characterized by the greater or less self-determination of speech sounds."

> This statement . . . does not mean that the role of poetry is conceived of as reduced to the sound-form or that the meaning loses its import. Rather, the notion of verse implies the indispensable presence of a certain specific, *ad hoc* organization of the verbal sound matter [SSL, p. 215].

This carefully qualified recognition of the onomatopoeic principle makes it compulsory to track that principle as it operates elsewhere in language and to consider how those operations share in the character of verse. If the poetic principle has a less strict demand to make of linguistic theory, that is chiefly because current approaches take account of relevant linguistic phenomena: linguistic levels and their constitutive elements on the one hand, and on the other, similarities of processing operations across all levels.

Implicit in the disjunction of the onomatopoeic and poetic principles is a third focus of interest. The onomatopoeic principle operates throughout language to varying degrees and involves only fundamental units, the sounds, whereas the poetic principle operates in rigorous fashion only in verse and involves all elements of language except the sounds. This exception to the poetic principle follows from the onomatopoeic principle itself: The fullest operation of the onomatopoeic principle blocks, as it were, the workings of the poetic principle. Important features of these workings and of the class of phenomena subject to them have been worked out, notably by two of Jakobson's colleagues, the late John Lotz (1913–1973) and Paul Kiparsky; Kiparsky (1974) and Lotz (1972a) are basic guides. I shall follow them, confining my attention to fine, or low-level poetic structure, i.e., to those problems that involve chiefly the line or a small number of lines (O'Connor 1980 [henceforth HVS], pp. 137–146).

Before we consider the notion of poetic resources, let us note one further feature of the onomatopoeic principle. Just as in connection with poetry, there is a disjunction between the two cardinal principles, so in the operation of the onomatopoeic principle, there is a disjunction between the realms of operation, though it is not a radical disjunction. In poetry, the onomatopoeic principle works across the nexus of other relations that constitute the text; it must perform its operations through them, because after all, even nonsense verse or comparable "prose" usages like rhyming slang are far from being non-sense in any linguistic sense. The opposite case of the onomatopoeic principle is provided by the sound-symbolic use of certain consonant or vowel alternations in Amerindian and African languages (and perhaps also in *emesal*, the drag dialect of Sumerian). These alternations MUST NOT WORK AS part of the ordinary system of the language (as the poetic phenomena must); they must be superadded independent features of the phonology. Jakobson and Waugh, following Sapir's work on this class of phenomena, offer this suggestion. "The presence of a conventional grammatical alternation in a given language seems to preclude the occurrence of an identical sound-symbolic ablaut in the same language and in this way to limit the repertory of such ablauts [SSL, p. 203]." In ordinary language, the onomatopoeic principle in purest form must deal with exactly the subset of relations between pairs of phonological features which ARE NOT relevant grammatically in the language, just as in verse (where the principle is necessarily pure) it must deal with those which ARE grammatically relevant. This description of the onomatopoeic principle, although making allowances for intermediate cases, does require that sound-symbolic alternations which are meaningful elsewhere in the language are largely swamped in the complexities of verse.

Let us return to the poetic principle in the pure form quoted above: "The poetic function projects the principle of equivalence from the axis of selection into the axis of combination." The most arresting feature of this statement is its abstractness: It is designedly powerful in its reticence to specify WHAT is made equivalent, what things are combined that might have been chosen among, and so on, and it predicts that all linguistic levels will be relevant. In fact, the poetic principle, in being powerful enough to account for all the activity in a poetic text, is too powerful by itself to allow us to isolate the working levels of equivalence on which a given poem or body of poems is structured. There is a subset of equivalence relations which is peculiarly functional in any given verse form. In the most common English verse line, these equivalence relations involve the number of syllables in a line—roughly, there must be ten—and the patterning of their stresses—roughly, stresses must alternate with unstressed syllables, and the first syllable in the sequence must be unstressed. Jakobson has protested against strict isolation of the structural level of equivalence relations: "Any attempts to confine such poetic conventions as meter, alliteration, or rhyme to the sound level are speculative reasonings without any empirical justification [1967, p. 312]." However, we cannot deny the usefulness of focusing attention on poetic conventions at the linguistic level where they are most manifest.

What we find when we do restrict our primary attention is the interaction of a class of patterns and a class of linguistic phenomena. One formalism for the class of patterns is familiar from the conventions of rhyme-scheme abbreviation: A quatrain in alternating rhyme is said to have an *abab* scheme. The pattern *abab*, however, can be considered separately from the linguistic phenomena used to fill it out, given the implicit suggestion of Jakobson's formulation that the poetic principle operates irrespective of the linguistic phenomena it operates with. The pattern *abab* can describe not only rhyme across a stanza but also the internal structure of a line of poetry (e.g., the unstress-stress pattern of iambic dimeter) or part of the structure of a line (e.g., in a poetic system where only the end of a line is structurally determined). There need be no variation in the parts of a pattern: *aaaa* is as distinct a pattern as *abab*. There are distinct limits on the number of different tokens which can be used in a pattern, and Kiparsky has suggested that generally no more than three tokens are involved (Kiparsky 1974, p. 236; HVS, pp. 13–20). A pattern may be structurally functional alone in a poetic passage but often there are two or more patterns interacting at the same time. Sometimes patterns of the same order co-occur; often one pattern, a frame (e.g., the English pentameter line), is coextensive with another, active within it, a modulation (e.g., the iambic pattern). (See further HVS, pp. 137–139, 146–150, 156–159.) The character of these patterns, alone and in their various combinations, seems to be among the category of phenomena that should be amenable to psycholinguistic investigation.

The class of linguistic phenomena used in filling out abstract patterns is a diverse one; we have already mentioned rhyme and word-stress, and there are many others. All have in common, however, a distinct relation to the language in which they are used, or, in Kiparsky's statement, "the linguistic sames which are potentially relevant in poetry are

just those which are potentially relevant in grammar [1974, p. 237]." In
fact, the relations between the class of linguistic sames used in poetry
and those used in grammar are diverse. Some facts are obvious and
banal: Word length cannot be a functional aspect of Classical Chinese
poetic patterning since all words are monosyllabic. Others are
obvious—word length in poetic patterns is reckoned in terms of syllables, not in terms of the number of sounds per word—but hardly clear,
given the difficulty of clarifying the concept of the syllable.

In some cases, the poetic sames are binary in character (masculine or
final-stress line endings versus feminine or penultimate stress endings),
while in others, the sames are rather diverse (permissible rhymes in
English). If the pool of tokens in a class of sames is neither binary nor
diverse enough (the vagueness seems necessary for the moment), then
the class must be binarized. This process is complex enough when the
binarization is synchronic, as is the English conversion of four or five
levels of speech stress into two levels of metrical stress, namely, stress/
unstress (Kiparsky 1975). Because of verse's status as a cultural artifact,
potential complexities do not stop here. In Classical Chinese verse, four
classes of speech tone have been binarized into two classes of metrical
tones; however, the classes which underwent the binarization have
since been realigned in the language in such a way that the four tones of
Mandarin cannot be mapped directly onto the metrical tones. The
greater number of tones preserved in most other dialects can be mapped
onto the metrical tones because of transparent sound correspondences,
but note that the language has to be mapped through the medium of
Mandarin in respect to all features but the tonal. This historical/
polydialectal binarization process needs attention in its own right. The
contention that tonal complexity simply "overtook" the verse system in
Mandarin would be based on the dubious assumptions that poetry is a
marginal phenomenon and that monodialectialism is a norm for Chinese
literati. (My informant in Chinese matters is a poet, tridialectal in
Chinese, Li Ch'i; the relevant facts can also be seen in the linguistic
autobiography of the distinguished linguist Chao Yuen Ren [1976, pp.
3–10]; see also Frankel 1972, pp. 22–23.) Thus the operation of the poetic
principle requires either binarity or diversity, but the cutoff point is not
clear; the link between binarization as it operates across time and as it
operates across dialects at single point in time is also obscure.

The byplay, on the level of basic structure, between abstract patterns
and the linguistic entities used to fill them out is repeated on the lower
level of poetic ornamentation. Basic structural features tend to characterize with fairly strict regularity the whole of poetic texts, whereas

ornaments are used over shorter spans of the text to provide additional coherence (HVS, pp. 139–144). Thus alliteration in Modern English texts is never a compulsory structural feature but is often present. The class of structural features can overlap with that of ornaments—internal rhyme is a common ornament in English and differs in instantiation rather than linguistic character from end rhyme—but again the classes of relevant features, though assuredly small, remain to be defined, both descriptively and linguistically.

In discussing the poetic principle, we have introduced two delimitations of the vast range of phenomena it describes, one isolating structural features of a piece of verse or a verse system and the other isolating ornaments. Other equivalences are to be seen in poetic texts, some covering greater portions of the texts than those we have separated and some much smaller portions. The delimited areas have in common their importance in the structure of texts and systems of texts; they enable readers (and hearers) to know a tradition and move through it, and it is thus important to recognize these delimitations both in order to describe how readers read (and hearers hear) and to help them to do so with more perspicuity.

One feature of our exposition so far needs comment as we return again to the poetic principle: "The poetic function projects the principle of equivalence from the axis of selection into the axis of combination." There is not implicit here any restriction of the possible levels of equivalence to the phonological realm, and yet all our examples have been drawn from that realm. In fact, although most poetic systems have a phonological base, all have some syntactic constraints and some are ordered syntactically. The syntactic requirement that the last syllable of a verse line coincide with the end of a word is common in metrical systems, and fairly obvious. More complex examples involve Serbo-Croatian and Homeric Greek epic verse (Halle 1970, pp. 67–68; Nagy 1974, p. 56). The most complex example so far described is the Monosyllable Constraint in English iambic pentameter (Kiparsky 1975; cf. 1977; 1979). Though the study of syntactically-based systems is resistant to the elementary formalisms that so aid the working out of phonological systems, it nonetheless seems clear that "the numerical regulation of certain properties of the linguistic form" to create poetic structure is as possible on the syntactic level as on any other level (Lotz 1972a, p. 2).

It is easiest for a contemporary reader of poetry to recognize the role of syntax in Euroamerican poetry of the last century, as Jakobson and Waugh do.

> Any vers libre in order to be sensed as verse must, despite its relative
> freedom, display certain formal constants, or at least nearly constant ten-
> dencies, especially in the prosodic organization of syntactic groups and
> their intonations. . . . Free verse is an attenuated form of verse, a com-
> promise between poetic and ordinary language, and presupposes the
> copresence of stricter verse forms in any given speech community [SSL,
> p. 216].

The modern case of free verse, of which some examples are treated by
Kiparsky (1974, pp. 237–242), is not so isolated as it may seem. The
simplest type of syntactic system uses as its primary structural feature
the constriction of grammatical material in a line and complements that
restriction with the requirement of rhyme. In many such cases, the
"copresence of stricter verse forms" in the "speech community" is evident: the best known of these verse forms are Chinese *fu* and Arabic *saj*ᶜ,
both terms translated with the unfortunate English 'rhyme(d) prose'.
The presence of rhyme seems to make such systems mixed in character,
but the frequent laxity of the rhyme rules combined with the stringency
and complexity of the syntactic regulations makes it clear that syntax is
the controlling structural force.

Systems with primarily syntactic determinants and without any
phonological structural base may be expected. The verse of the Hebrew
Bible, and of congeneric dialects, displays such a system. In part, the
syntactic usage is responsible for the vast array of regularities gathered
together under the traditional heading of parallelism, though in part,
various of those regularities constitute a system of modulations within
the framework of the syntactic constraints. Recognition of the Hebrew
case has prompted tentative notice of other similar systems (HVS, pp.
146–159).

Given the rigor of the Hebrew verse system, it seems unlikely that the
term "attenuated" is appropriate here. The implicit linguistic question
the term raises is suggestive nonetheless and I want to turn to it in
conclusion. Is there some overall amount of coherence (or perhaps capacity for coherence versus adaptability) to be expected of a verse form or
system? The same question can be raised of a language as a whole, and
the answer is not easy in either case. The notion of examining the whole
of a system is implicit, for example, in much argumentation about language change, where one hears of the simplification of x being a trade-
off for the rising complexity of y, where x and y have some intuitively
satisfying connection. But where does this class of arguments lead in the
end, especially as we know the problems of strictly Meilletian push- and
pull-chain historical phonology? The fact that such a question could
arise of both a language system and a verse system should by now be no

surprise. The homologies that must exist between these types of systems may be the most intractable of the systemic relations of poetic language to language as a whole.

Poetry and the Central Features of Language

Given that poetry is the central manifestation of language, it follows that what happens in poetry will reveal aspects of language behavior. Investigation of these aspects requires sufficient knowledge of poetry to be able to profit from Lotz's warning that "verse is the most idiosyncratic use of language and is subject to extreme individual manipulation [1972b, p. 119]," while persisting in the effort to grasp regularities of the verse system realized in the texts. The locus of greatest regularity in verse is metrical systems, and in modern linguistics, the rise of metrical studies was coordinate in the late nineteenth century with Karl Verner's elucidation, around 1875, of the ties between the Proto–Indo-European and Germanic stop series on the basis of accent. The extreme regularity of many metrical systems puts them in the class of phenomena accessible to linguistic scholars who believed (in Brugmann's formulation of the Neogrammarian postulate) that "every sound change . . . takes place according to laws that admit no exception [Lehmann 1967, p. 204]." Metrics remains an important focus of linguistic investigation. The ways in which information about poetry is incorporated into linguistic theory vary in relation to the kinds of information involved. In some cases, facts about poetry offer a sort of terminus giving shape to a series of other facts about language or languages. In other cases, rigorous argumentation is applied to bring features of poetry to bear on fundamental points of linguistic theory.

Most of the accessible facts about poetry refer to phonological phenomena. Verse as a special form of speech production, for example, often requires the use of extraordinary sounds or even broader alterations of a sound system. The simplest case involves sounds which are used only in poetry and never elsewhere in the language (SSL, pp. 204–208). Linguists might dismiss such phenomena as marginal, but consider the celebrated nasal generalization: All languages of the world make regular use of at least one nasal consonant except for a cluster of Northwest Amerindian languages. In this cluster, at least the Salishan dialects spoken around Puget Sound do use nasal consonants but only in one word of ordinary language, in baby talk, and in songs and related high-style utterances (SSL, p. 132 and refs.; Thompson 1973, p. 1023). Linguists have generally treated the universality of nasal consonants as implicational because of these exceptions (Jakobson 1966a), but the child-language and poetic usage provides an instructive complement to this understanding.

However the Salish nasals are assessed, there are clear cases of what I have called terminal arguments which involve phenomena both proper to and extrinsic to ordinary usage. Kalmyk vowel harmony is of the second type. Systems of vowel (and consonant) harmony are generally limited in operation to the word unit; minor exceptions to this general rule have been noted in various languages but the systemic exception is found in the verse of the Kalmyk, a western Mongol Buddhist community located in the Volga valley northeast of the Caspian (and latterly in Philadelphia and northern New Jersey). "Kalmyk folklore . . . extends the monopoly of grave or acute vowels to a whole verse line. . . . Such extension is telling proof of the actual creative vitality and productivity of vowel harmony and of the distinctive features underlying it [SSL, p. 150]." This extension offers a boundary to vowel harmony: In ordinary language, it is a device to aid word-unit discrimination and thus must be confined largely to words, while in verse, its function can be transcended and it can be used to mark off that polyform entity, the verse line. Before turning to the corresponding French example, we can note here, as with the Salish case, relevant child-language facts. Generalization over an entire short utterance of a feature proper to single units or small groups of them is common in children's speech. Vihman (1982) instances her Estonian-speaking child as adding an r-glide across an utterance in English, the child's second language; nasalization is common in English-language taunting, especially in association with the melodic chain of four ɲǽ, with a medial ɲə̃.

The French glide system includes a tense:lax pair: a lax ∅ sound opposed to a tense sound alternately realized as *h aspiré* and *e muet* (SSL, p. 152). The tense member of the pair can be almost completely lost in fast speech (i.e., realized as its lax partner); correspondingly, the tense glide must almost always be realized in the reading of verse. All other speech styles in standard French fall between these two extremes. The verse usage here provides a terminus which is within the boundaries of common use.

Terminal arguments and citations balance references to core features of language use. Again, an instructive language-particular case is afforded by a situation in which verse speaking makes different demands than ordinary production. There is a distinction between languages with free stress, e.g., Russian, in which "the opposition of stressed and unstressed vowels fulfills both a sense-discriminative and an integrational . . . function," and languages with fixed stress, e.g., Czech, in which "the difference between stressed and unstressed vowels . . . serves only for the demarcation and integration of vowels (SSL, pp. 38–39)." From this second pattern of use it might be argued that in these languages the existence of stress determines word boundaries and thus the reality of word units is a function of the realization of stress. Jakobson and Waugh argue conversely "that grammatical units and their boundaries exist for the speaker and listener even if they are not expressed," drawing crucial evidence from a study of the ways in which the realization of stress is manipulated in Czech verse.

Even broader phenomena can be illuminated on the basis of the diversity of verse systems. In speaking of the universality of distinctive features, Jakobson and Waugh note that the many and diverse systems of vowel harmony resort severally "to one or two (even three) of all the inherent oppositions existing in the vocalic patterns of the world." They parallel this with an argument for the universality of the quite different class of prosodic features, including length, stress, and tone, from the fact that the many systems of verse which discriminate vowel classes use these and only these features to do so (SSL, pp. 50–51). (This class of features contrasts with the subgroup of distinctive features functional only for consonants, the tonal feature of sharpness, and the features of abruptness and stridency.) There are no verse systems which crucially require a sequence of alternating oral and nasal vowels, or of alternating acute and compact vowels, whereas there are systems which alternate unstressed and stressed vowels, short and long vowels, and low-tone and high-tone vowels. (English, Greek, and Yoruba are obvious examples).

Arguments drawn from poetry can deal closely with the understanding of language processing. Predictably these engagements have often involved metrics, both because meter is the best understood of poetic phenomena and because some notion of processing has always (or at least since the medieval Arab grammarians) seemed a necessary part of metrical explanation. Kiparsky has shown that the poetic processing of an utterance as a linguistic operation must take place as part of the phonological processing, that is, that metrical and other rules do not apply to surface structures but to partly-processed underlying forms.

The case of the Finnish folk poetry preserved in the national epic cycle the *Kalevala* and in the form of field transcriptions is clearest (Kiparsky 1970). The metrically relevant forms are not the surface forms: Their structure is "wrong" in that the meter fails to consider the effects of certain phonological rules. Thus it makes sense to think of the metrical judgment of these lines as applying to a form several stages removed from the surface. This approach demonstrates the necessity of viewing poetic processes as a special subclass of language operations. Kiparsky (1972) has suggested that a similar explanation is needed for the case of certain forms of Ṛg-Vedic meter; the objections raised by Hock (1977), far from discomfitting Kiparsky's explanation, reveal again that verse systems, like many other features of language, resist a simple split between synchronic and diachronic inspection. As in the Mandarin tone case, it will not do to assert simply that a Golden Horde of phonological changes swept across the barren fields of poetry and left them bloodily historicized. The complexities of Resistance and Collaboration movements are surely immense, but reckoning with verse as language demands that the reverse accounting take place: language must be studied in the special guise of verse; verse usage cannot be set aside as irrelevantly weird (if indeed any weird language phenomenon is ever irrelevantly—as opposed to intractably—so). Other examples of metrics-and-morphophonemics arguments have been offered, notably by Zeps (1973). Kiparsky (1974, p. 244) has extended the form of argument to account for the unusual rhyme schemes of Stefan George, and S.R. Anderson (1973) has treated the alliteration of late Old Norse poetry. Halle (1972, pp. 150–151) adduces examples from Old English alliteration and from Russian rhymes. These cases show that poetic processing is not only a part of phonological processing, but that it must be in some sense of a piece with it. The class of phenomena regarded by poetic processing, then, is the same as that regarded in phonological processing. This is an independent argument for Kiparsky's contention that the class of phenomena usable in poetry is a grammatically definable one.

Another example of poetic phenomena being judged by canons of linguistic processes is cross-linguistic. Cooper & Ross (1975) show that a simple series of phonological rules serves to describe the ordering of English words used in pairs where semantic factors are not relevant. Such dyads include *kit and caboodle* (short word before long word; this rule is traditionally called Pāṇini's Law); *harum-scarum* (initial cluster internal); *wing-ding* (initial obstruent internal), and so on. This same set of rules serves also to predict the ordering of "parallel pairs" in Hebrew verse, words used in matching (syntactically parallel) slots, in pairs or triplets of lines (HVS, pp. 96–109). The difference here between the languages refers to differences of use for which any explanation must be ad hoc: English happens to use many nonce combinations and Hebrew happens to need pairs of words for verse. Both languages use the same ordering principles to meet these diverse needs.

Another example refers to a more strictly definable area of language behavior. Gapping, the rule which deletes repeated information from syntactically parallel constructions or clauses, is a fairly ordinary phenomenon in the languages of the world (Ross 1970), e.g., the verb gapping in *Rimbaud loved vowels and Mayakovskij, New York*. This rule evidently exists to satisfy a need for economy in language, a rubric under which we gather such diverse rules as the fast-speech elision of final stops in many languages that allow final continuant-stop clusters and Grice's Second Maxim of Quantity ("Do not make your contribution [to a conversation] more informative than is required," Grice 1975, p. 45). Given this range of economical traits, we could claim that gapping exists to satisfy a fairly low-level demand for economy in syntax; the demand can be called low-level because syntax is as rich with redundancy as all other segments of language, and in particular because the situation for gapping exists in all languages but not all languages have gapping. The intermediate situation (intermediate as the Salishan nasal pattern is) manifests itself in Classical Hebrew: gapping never occurs in that language (or in many of its congeners, from Middle Egyptian to Akkadian) except in verse. Thus what may be reckoned a universal syntactic option, exercised freely in many languages, is licensed to only limited, and thus highly marked, use in Hebrew poetry (HVS, pp. 122–129, 401–407).

All of the cases of poetic and ordinary language phenomena cited so far have been susceptible to more or less clear conceptualization, but there is no reason, given the realms of discussion, to look for clarity as a rule. One example of a class of entities crucial to both everyday language and verse is afforded by Harris's "long units," groups of words used regularly in concatenation. In everyday use, formulas are a strategy to permit what Ruth Clark calls "performing without competence," and C.J. Fillmore, Bolinger, and F. Goldman-Eisler have all recently focused on this capacity. L.W. Fillmore, Ann Peters, and Ruth Clark have treated the role of formulas in first- and second-language acquisition by children, and Vihman (1982) reviews and advances their work. There is no reason to separate this "noncreative" use of language from poetic systems of formulas, but examining the usages together will not make the task easier. The pioneer work in the area is Kiparsky's (1976) commentary on formulas in Ingermanland Finnish and Homeric Greek verse, in which he scrutinizes formulas in the context of idiomatic ordinary language usage; other papers in the Stolz and Shannon collection (1976) are instructive. The necessarily complex range of phenomena must be extended to include fully formulaic utterances on the one hand, and on the other, subformulaic systems of usage like the Hebrew "parallel pairs" system previously described.

One caution must balance this vivid imaging of the vistas of information linguists will find on first looking into verse. A system of verse must never be expected to isolate categories relevant to the linguist. The

loud and bold proposal to hear "psychologically real" phonological phenomena in some canons of rhyme falls foul of the fact that rhyming
conventions are far from universal (Lotz 1972a, p. 20; Kiparsky 1974, pp.
241–245; SSL, p. 50). Syllables of the shape . . . VC, for example, can
rhyme if the vowels are (a) identical acoustically, (b) similar acoustically,
or (c) similar in stress, pitch, or tone; or if the consonants are (a), (b), or
(d) similar in place or (e) manner of articulation; or if the vowels and
consonants are both (a) or both (b); and so on. A set of rhyming conventions will be amenable to linguistic explanation but there is little reason to expect it or any other poetic phenomenon to do a linguist's job
of explaining. Jakobson and Waugh misstep along these lines in reprimanding Rimbaud for his sonnet "Voyelles," said to be a "backwards proclamation," "strained and deliberately made à rebours [SSL,
p. 194]." They are correct in reprimanding those who take Rimbaud's
poem as offering a report on audition colorée, but the mistakes of naive
readers are not Rimbaud's. The poet at age seventeen was concerned not
with any merely human faculties of perception but with listening,
through the vowels, to "Silences traversés des Mondes et des Anges [1871/
1957, p. 119]."

The failure to appreciate the potential extent of a poet's grasp of
linguistic reality could lead linguists astray. It is distressing to find
Critchley (1974) asserting that "no one has ever attained a supremacy in
verse or fine writing in more than one linguistic medium." Though the
chances are slight that rigorous evidence for neuropsychology proper
could be derived from bilingual writers, such writers do exist and have
been profitably studied. Albert & Obler (1978, p. 106), in discussing
Critchley's remark, offer as a potential source of counterexamples the
Islamic world, and the medieval Persian-Turkic poet Ali Shir Nava'i has
been studied in the context of bilingualism by Fearey (1977), who can-
nily focuses on aspects of strict metrical forms likely to be beyond conscious control. Major bilingual writers of our own time such as Vladimir
Nabokov and Samuel Beckett have tended to work in prose. Though
both these writers have either prepared or supervised second-language
editions of their works and thus offered the boon of authorized texts in
two languages, notions of transfer and interference are not readily
adaptable as philological or critical tools for the study of their prose.
Similarly, Rainer Maria Rilke's poetry written in French, though part of
his second-language acquisition strategy, would probably resist all
psycholinguists save the few who undertook to master the overbearing
body of his German verse (see Rilke 1902/1969, p. 87).

The range of poetic phenomena examined here is but a small segment
of that found in the recorded verse systems of the world. The service

they have done can be done by all. Poetic phenomena are related to all features of language; we have examined phonological and syntactic features, pragmatic and neurolinguistic data. Poetry may offer the ultimate extension of a language trait or may utilize its exceptional status to stand over against everyday language. Arguments about many features of poetry are of a piece with linguistic arguments, and the constructs of linguists may be verified or discomfitted in considering verse. One language's most ordinary linguistic operation may be in another language a rare and strictly poetic mechanism, but much of the range of phenomena that work in poetry also make everyday speech work, though the phenomena may change their appearance to fit the occasion.

The range of speech forms between poetry and plain speech has been neglected here, save for a few references to child language. The field of child language has profited immensely from the work of Charles Ferguson. Ferguson has paid relevant attention, too, to other special speech forms, such as ritual prayers and other religious forms (1973; 1976a, b) and foreigner talk (1975). Jakobson and Waugh discuss children's word games and rhymes, and glossolalia. The fields of oral and written prose in myths, tales, and legends are also relevant; the work of ethnographers sampled in Bauman & Sherzer (1974) is illuminating. I mention last the form of language I deem closest to verse, naming. Jakobson and Waugh correctly point to "the utterly particular position of names in our vocabulary (SSL, p. 229)." Over the past dozen years, K. O'Nolan and Gregory Nagy have presented some arguments linking naming and Indo-European verse forms; the convergence of my treatment of Semitic names and verse with theirs, though it is a skewed convergence, offers the possibility of both historical and typological connections which will affirm the continued interest of anthropologists in both these areas (O'Nolan 1969; 1978; Nagy 1974; 1979; HVS, pp. 159–163).

Some Difficulties Proper to the Linguistic Study of Poetry

The programmatic statement of Jakobson and Waugh, calling linguists and literary scholars to investigate poetry ever more intensively, was issued into a complex field of work. First I must record that many more linguists than I have been able to take note of have contributed valuable research. I have given some references below; a range of work can be sampled in the anthologies of Chatman & Levin (1967), Freeman (1970), and, most recently, Ching, Haley, & Lunsford (1980).

The Jakobsonian programme has not, however, met with universal approbation; here Jakobson and Waugh move from programme to polemic.

> Poetic language has forcefully entered into the field of linguistic research, and notwithstanding the objections, as multiple as they are vapid, of some literary critics shockingly unfamiliar with the new vistas and even with the primary principles of the science of language, linguists are assessing more and more systematically the manifold and intertwined problems of poetic sound shape and grammar [SSL, pp. 221–222].

This polemic can be put in its context precisely: Jakobson (1980) has written "A Postscript to the Discussion on Grammar of Poetry," addressed to critics who have attacked or dismissed his celebrated reading of "Les Chats" of Charles Baudelaire, prepared with Claude Lévi-Strauss in 1962. It is not to this context that I want to speak, but to the more general situation that finds linguists and literary scholars at a loss with one another's work. Since this situation is far from universal, I will be rehearsing points amply understood by some.

The problems at hand are in part problems created by disciplinary boundaries. In translating a Jakobsonian understanding to the level of "what is to be done?" it may be useful to address those boundaries directly. In so doing, I do not mean to apologize for the stupidity or timidity Jakobson has found in his critics. I offer this treatment in lieu of a proper conclusion because it seems to me neither possible nor desirable to direct linguists' attention to particular phenomena, given the reassessment of theoretical presuppositions currently underway. When the full range of verse in the languages of the world is seriously embraced by language study, linguists will be able to grasp the import of the fact that what happens in language happens more so in literature. An anecdote about C.G. Jung's Zurich practice is suggestive in more than one way. Jung came to know James Joyce's work at the same time he was treating Joyce's schizophrenic daughter, and he said that daughter and father were two swimmers diving to the bottom of a river, the father swimming freely and the daughter bound in shackles and hung with lead weights.

Let us note first of all that Jakobson's writings have been badly read. The remarks of Whitman, made eight years ago on the occasion of the publication of *Selected Writings I* [2] and *II*, are pertinent.

> There has been a tendency among all too many scholars . . . to consider only those parts of his work which bear in some direct fashion on their own special fields. It is some measure of Jakobson's creativity that despite

this he has been able to influence the thinking of researchers in so many diverse fields. But this does not justify the continuation of myopic habits [1973, p. 680].

Not only are these lines pertinent: they are probably truer today than when they were written, precisely because literary scholars have turned to Jakobson ever more intensively in the last decade. Reading Jakobson only on verse, as many of them do, is as unsatisfactory as reading Freud only on daVinci and Moses. There are, I think, no adequate readers of all of Jakobson, but some corrections for myopic habits may be found. Before looking elsewhere, I wish to note one feature of his work which must be attended to if linguistics is to bring its resources to bear on verse. Never has Jakobson failed to see the universality of verse and the necessity which follows from it, the necessity to inspect all variety of verse, not just the written verse of high Euroamerican cultures. The assiduity with which Kiparsky, Halle, and Lotz have followed this Jakobsonian tradition is all too rare a trait.

Let us turn to the language sciences as they are pursued, more or less, here and now. H.A. Gleason has remarked that "one of the failings of recent North American linguistics" has been "its almost total neglect of its market [1980, p. 126]." I offer this jolting allusion to commerce and society as a necessary counterpoint to Jakobsonian vision. Having attended to the Praguian call, the linguist–ephebe is still left with the questions, what shall I study (since one cannot study everything)? and for whom shall I formulate my study, both as I undertake it and as I bring it to term? The ephebe who turns to literature and expects to be listened to by literary scholars will soon find they do not grasp the conceptual formulation the ephebe has presented. It is not so much that they reject the ephebe's labor, but that they do not find it interesting, though they are in part loath and in part unable to say why. It is then up to linguists to try to say WHY, vis-à-vis the state of their discipline. There are three major reasons, each connected to an area of research which has only intermittently been an active focus of linguistic science; this intermittence is comprehensible and in most cases current attention is being directed to those areas.

The first reason is that literary scholars are interested in a nexus of phenomena associated by neurolinguists with nondominant hemisphere activity and modern linguistics has been canonically concerned with dominant hemisphere functions. This nexus includes (a) the perception and production of rhythm, stress, intonation, and speech melody (apparently insofar as they are not sense-distinctive), (b) the manipulation of discourse forms and shapes, notably (c) the distinguishing of literal and non-literal senses of utterances, and (*d*) a host of other discriminations which have largely "affective" roots. Blumstein (1982) reviews this group in a neurolinguistic context. Clearly none of these features of language is foreign to linguistics if it is to be, as it must be, an accounting for all of language. A great many of them, however, are foreign to mainstream modern inquiry. In the early seventies, recall, contrastive stress was disallowed from commentary on utterances claimed to be ambiguous in written form; the removal of what most linguists would now agree was a rather silly restriction led to the acknowledgment of pragmatic considerations. The incorporation into grammar of such considerations and closely related semantic facts is not easy. Sadock has pointed out recently how the role and reference grammar of Foley and Van Valin, by conceiving of syntax in pragmatic and semantic terms, is in imminent danger of losing track of most language-particular grammatical facts (Sadock 1980).

The second of the three reasons involves the lexicon: literary scholars have an interest in words one at a time exceeding that of even a child acquiring a first language or a psychologist testing semantic satiation. Most linguists have not shared this concern; again I quote H.A. Gleason as a senior observer.

> Many . . . linguists . . . have let speculation guide their thinking about the lexicon more than solid empirical research. . . . The issue . . . is not a theoretical issue at all. There is essentially no body of observation and experimentation that would allow it to be framed as a theoretical issue. It is rather a human issue, a matter of professional neglect, of the greater attractiveness of other lines of investigation. Most modern linguists continue the old adage: If it is tractable put it in the grammar, if not assume that it will be taken care of in the dictionary—and keep the dictionary at the bottom of the agenda [1980, pp. 128–129].

The accuracy of Gleason's observation of neglect will be conceded even by those with qualms about his theoretical claim. The lexicon is unlike the set of nondominant hemisphere functions in that linguists have always known it was a problem to be reckoned with, and recent scholars as diverse as Eugene Nida and J.R. Ross have contributed to the reckoning. The deficit remains: We have no globally usable and generally recognized notions of how a speaker of a language structures knowledge of its vocabulary. (See Jakobson 1980, p. 25 further on this point.)

The third reason has to do with linguistics' apparent restriction to what is at hand, where literary scholars attend to what is not at hand, not available. Let me exemplify what I mean by quoting a remark from one of the most perspicuous critics of her generation, Helen Vendler.

If linguists can add to our comprehension of literature, someone trained in linguistics should be able to point out to us, in poems we already know well, significant features we have missed because of our amateurish ignorance of the workings of language. Attempts in this line . . . adopt a complacent tone implying that the authors have come to give a great light to the people who walk in darkness [1966, p. 457].

At the risk of being tedious, let me explicate Vendler's acidic conclusion. She quotes here from Isaiah 9:2, "The people that walked in darkness have seen a great light: they that dwell in the land of the shadow of death, upon them hath the light shined." The words are those of the Authorized Version of the English Bible, but the force of her sarcasm is completely lost if the passage is read as it is in Isaiah, since the birth of a royal heir in Jerusalem some two and a half millennia ago is hardly an interesting occurrence for Vendler's readers, no matter how movingly it is described. The passage has its sense for contemporary readers of English as one of the supposed prophecies of Jesus in the Hebrew Bible, alluded to in the Christian scriptures, cited in the Advent and Christmas liturgies of all high Christian churches, set to music, most memorably by Handel, and so on, and it retains the weight of that sense even if the event proleptically described in the passage is of no direct interest to the reader. All this interpretive context (and all of its self-emptying) is absent from Vendler's remark, but it is all present to a literate reader. Vendler has made an icon of linguistics' greatest deficit in the face of literature, to preface her concession that "linguistics will certainly in the end be of immense use to literary criticism, as all information about language must be [1966, p. 458]."

This deficit is related to a great variety of literary phenomena, and those phenomena are close to the core of literary scholarship's most enduring concerns. From the viewpoint of linguistics, it is all one whether literary scholars allude to the phenomena under the rubrics of literary history or intertextuality, tradition, canon, or quotation. These phenomena, with or without direct verbal base, are central to literary scholars and largely alien to linguists. Consider, for example, this sentence from Zellig Harris's seminal paper on discourse analysis: "The analysis of the occurrence of elements in the text is applied only in respect to that text alone—that is, in respect to the other elements in the same text, and not in respect to anything else in the language (1952, p. 1)." The phenomena are not, to be sure, entirely alien. The connection I made earlier between "long units" in ordinary speech and formulas in poetry involves a subset of relations which must extend to include literary quotation, allusion, and dependency. This task is the most far-

reaching of those I have cited, but it may be the one for which linguists
are best equipped by their tradition of study.

These three deficits linguists must own up to, not only in the marketplace of knowledge, but also, it should be clear, at home. To remedy
these deficits would not require linguists to take up phenomena extrinsic to their proper concerns, but only extrinsic to the bulk of their previous concerns.

Let us consider briefly to whom linguists might talk about literature. I
have used, with wooden inflexibility, the term literary scholars, taking
it from Jakobson and Waugh (who, it is true, borrow it from the population in question) and preserving it for the sake of simplicity. There are,
however, few people who can BEST be called literary scholars; the uses of
reading and listening to verse are so diverse that the linguistic ephebe
had best approach an audience not merely with attention to its degree of
sophistication, but also with an eye to why it takes up works of verbal
art. Philologists, or more simply readers, are engaged with a canon
already defined while critics in the strict sense are devoted to defining a
canon (Steiner 1979). Teachers can use a plurality of procedures that
would be methodologically beyond the grasp of scholars in other circumstances. Students in a "foreign" culture need to know, both
explicitly AND accessibly, things a native would find it otiose to mention; the double demand makes this need different from a linguist's
concern, which is for explicitness regardless of accessibility. (See Chambers 1979 on both these points.) How the linguistic ephebe addresses
these audiences or interlocking sets of them is more than I can say; I can
say that recognition of them would be a useful preliminary.

These notes on disciplinary boundaries aim to make it easier to communicate across and under them. The notion of the marketplace is a
banalizing one, but we have Jakobson's word for it that only poetry
fully affirms "language liberated from all infusion of banality (SSL, p.
231)." Banality then is a concomitant feature of linguistic discourse and
it is useful to temper Jakobson's ambitions to escape it. I conclude by
returning to what I have several times called a Jakobsonian vision, first
to make explicit what careful readers know, that none of the deficits in
linguistic research I have mentioned is the result of any narrowing of
focus encouraged by him, and second, to remark on the form of his
vision, or perhaps better, its source. It is Baudelairean in a sense that
is not evident despite all Jakobson's assiduous study and careful
quotation of Baudelaire. Language is both the garb that covers the spirit
in Poem XXVII of *Les Fleurs du Mal,* and the spirit that reveals itself
beneath the garb.

Avec ses vêtements ondoyants et nacrés,
Meme quand elle marche on dirait qu'elle danse.

(Baudelaire 1857/1954, pp. 103–104; cf. Chambers 1980.) I cannot here explicate the text in relation to Jakobson's labor. Perhaps those opening lines will suffice to isolate the binarity at the center of an understanding of language that has so long and variously instructed us in the relation of verse to its medium.

Postscriptum. Over half of the Autumn 1980 issue of Benjamin Hrushovski's journal *Poetics Today* (2 #1a) is devoted to Roman Jakobson; it includes eight pieces by Jakobson, written alone and in collaboration with G. Lübbe-Grothues, K. Pomorska, S. Rudy, and Ju. Tynjanov, dated between 1928 and the present; many are available in English translation only here. There is also an important paper by L. R. Waugh on "The Poetic Function and the Nature of Language." (The journal is available from Schenkman Publishing, 3 Mount Auburn St., Cambridge, Massachusetts 02138.)

References

In citations of literary texts, the first data indicates the date of composition or publication; the second is the bibliographic reference.

Albert, M.L. & Obler, L.K. (1978) *The bilingual brain: Neuropsychological and neurolinguistic aspects of bilingualism.* New York: Academic Press.
Anderson, S.R. (1973) *u-* Umlaut and Skaldic Verse. In S.R. Anderson & P. Kiparsky, (Eds.) *A Festschrift for Morris Halle.* New York: Holt, Rinehart & Winston. Pp. 3–13.
Baudelaire, C. (1954) *Oeuvres.* Edited by Y.-G. LeDantec. Paris: Gallimard.
Bauman, R. & Sherzer, J. (Eds.) (1974) *Explorations in the ethnography of speaking.* Cambridge: Cambridge University Press.
Blumstein, S.E. (1982) Dissolution of language and aphasia: Evidence for linguistic theory. (In this volume.)
Chambers, R. (1979) *Meaning and meaningfulness: Studies in the analysis and interpretation of texts. French Forum Monographs 15.* Lexington: French Forum.
Chambers, R. (1980) Pour une poetique du vêtement. *Poétiques: Michigan Romance Studies 1,* 18–46.
Chatman, S. & Levin, S.R. (Eds.) (1967) *Essays on the language of literature.* Boston: Houghton Mifflin.
Chao Yuen Ren. (1976) My linguistic autobiography. In his *Aspects of Chinese Sociolinguistics.* Edited by A.S. Dil. Stanford: Stanford University Press. Pp. 1–20.
Chen, M.Y. (1979) Metrical structure: Evidence from Chinese poetry. *Linguistic inquiry, 10,* 371–420.
Ching, M.K.L., Haley, M.C. & Lunsford, R.F. (Eds.) (1980) *Linguistic perspectives on literature.* London: Routledge and Kegan Paul.
Cooper, W.E. & Ross, J.R. (1975) World Order. In R.E. Grossman, L.J. San, & T.J. Vance (Eds.), *Papers from the Eleventh Regional Meeting.* Chicago: Chicago Linguistic Society. Pp. 63–111.
Critchley, M. (1974) Aphasia in polyglots and bilinguals. *Brain and language, 1,* 15–27.

Fearey, M.S. (1977) *Nava'i's Turkic and Persian quatrains: Discourse typology and the bilingual poet*. Doctoral dissertation, University of Michigan.

Ferguson, C. (1973) Some forms of religious discourse. *Internationales Jahrbuch für Religionssoziologie/International yearbook for the sociology of religion, 8*, 224–35.

Ferguson, C. (1975) Toward a characterization of English foreigner talk. *Anthropological linguistics, 17*, 1–14.

Ferguson, C. (1976a) The blessing of the Lord be upon you. In Alphone Juilland *et al.* (Eds.), *Linguistic studies offered to Joseph Greenberg. Studia linguistica et philologica 4*. Saratoga, California: Anma Libri. Vol. 1 pp. 21–26.

Ferguson, C. (1976b) The collect as a form of discourse. In M.A. Jazayery, E.C. Polome, & W. Winter (Eds.), *Linguistic and literary studies in honor of Archibald A. Hill*. Lisse: de Ridder. Pp. 127–137.

Frankel, H.H. (1972) Classical Chinese. In W.K. Wimsatt (Ed.), *Versification: Major language types*. New York: Modern Language Association/New York University Press. Pp. 22–37.

Freeman, D.C. (Ed.) (1970) *Linguistics and literary style*. New York: Holt, Rinehart and Winston.

Gleason, H.A., Jr. (1980) Comments on . . . syntax and linguistic semantics in stratificational theory. In M.Kac (Ed.), *Current syntactic theories: Discussion papers from the 1979 Milwaukee Syntax Conference*. Bloomington: Indiana University Linguistics Club. Pp. 113–133.

Grice, H.P. (1975) Logic and conversation. In P. Cole & J.L. Morgan (Eds.), *Syntax and semantics 3: Speech acts*. New York: Academic Press. Pp. 41–58.

Halle, M. (1970) On meter and prosody. In M. Bierwisch & K.S. Heidolph (Eds.), (1980) *Progress in linguistics*. The Hague: Mouton. Pp. 64–80.

Halle, M. (1972) On a parallel between conventions of versification and orthography; and on literary among the Cherokee. In J.F. Kavanaugh & I.G. Mattingly (Eds.), *Language by ear and by eye: The relationships between speech and reading*. Cambridge: MIT Press. Pp. 149–154.

Halle, M. & Keyser, S.J. (1971) *English stress: Its form, its growth and its role in verse*. New York: Harper and Row.

Halle, M. & Keyser, S.J. (1972) English III. The iambic pentameter. In W.K. Wimsatt (Ed.), (1972) *Versification: Major language types*. New York: Modern Languages Association/ New York University Press. Pp. 217–237.

Harris, Z.S. (1952) Discourse analysis. *Language, 28*, 1–30. Reprinted in Z.S. Harris. (1970) *Papers in structural and transformational linguistics. Formal Linguistics Series 1*. Dordrecht: Reidel. Pp. 313–348.

Hill, G. (1975) *Somewhere is such a kingdom*. Boston: Houghton Mifflin.

Hock, H.H. (1977) Archaisms, morphophonemic metrics, or variable rules in the Rig-Veda? Paper read at Spring 1977 American Oriental Society Meeting, Ithaca.

HVS *see* O'Connor 1980

Jakobson, R. (1966a) Implications of language universals for linguistics. In J. Greenberg (Ed.), *Universals of language*[2]. Cambridge: MIT Press. Pp. 263–278.

Jakobson, R. (1966b) Grammatical parallelism and its Russian facet. *Language, 42*, 399–429.

Jakobson, R. (1967) Linguistics and poetry. In S. Chatman & S.R. Levin (Eds.), *Essays on the language of literature*. Boston: Houghton Mifflin. Pp. 296–322.

Jakobson, R. (1968) Poetry of grammar and grammar of poetry. *Lingua, 21*, 597–609.

Jakobson, R. (1980) A postscript to the discussion on grammar of poetry. *Diacritics, 10*, #1, 22–35.

Jakobson, R. & Waugh, L. (1979) *The sound shape of language*. Bloomington: Indiana University Press.

Kiparsky, P. (1970) Metrics and morphophonemics in the Kalevala. In D.C. Freeman (Ed.), (1970) *Linguistics and literary style*. New York: Holt Rinehart & Winston.

Kiparsky, P. (1972) Metrics and morphophonemics in the Rigveda. In M.K. Brame (Ed.), *Contributions to Generative Phonology*. Austin: University of Texas Press. Pp. 171–200.

Kiparsky, P. (1973–1974) Commentary. *New literary history, 5*, 177–85.

Kiparsky, P. (1974) The role of linguistics in a theory of poetry. In E. Haugen & M. Bloomfield (Eds.), *Language as a human problem*. New York: Norton. Pp. 233–246.

Kiparsky, P. (1975) Stress, syntax and meter. *Language, 51*, 576–616.

Kiparsky, P. (1976) Oral poetry: Some linguistic and typological considerations. In B.A. Stolz & R.S. Shannon (Eds.), *Oral literature and the formula*. Ann Arbor: Center for the Coordination of Ancient and Modern Studies of the University of Michigan. Pp. 73–106.

Kiparsky, P. (1977) The rhythmic structure of English verse. *Linguistic inquiry, 8*, 189–247.

Kiparsky, P. (1979) Metrical structure assignment is cyclic. *Linguistic inquiry, 10*, 421–41.

Lehmann, W.P. (1967) *A reader in nineteenth-century historical Indo-European linguistics*. Bloomington: Indiana University Press.

Liberman, M. & Prince, A. (1977) On stress and linguistic rhythm. *Linguistic inquiry, 8*, 249–336.

Lotz, J. (1960) Metric typology. In T.A. Sebeok (Ed.), *Style in language*. Cambridge: MIT Press. Pp. 135–148.

Lotz, J. (1972a) Elements of versification. In W.K. Wimsatt (Ed.), *Versification: Major language types*. New York: Modern Language Association/New York University Press. Pp. 1–21.

Lotz, J. (1972b) Uralic. In W.K. Wimsatt (Ed.), *Versification: Major language types*. New York: Modern Language Association/New York University Press. Pp. 100–121.

McCarthy, J.J. (1979) On stress and syllabification. *Linguistic inquiry, 10*, 443–65.

Maling, J.M. (1973) *The theory of classical Arabic metrics*. Doctoral dissertation, MIT, Cambridge, MA.

Nagy, G. (1974) *Comparative studies in Greek and Indic meter. Harvard Studies in Comparative Literature 33*. Cambridge: Harvard University Press.

Nagy, G. (1976) Formula and meter. In B.A. Stolz & R.S. Shannon (Eds.), *Oral literature and the formula*. Ann Arbor: Center for the Coordination of Ancient and Modern Studies of the University of Michigan. Pp. 239–260.

Nagy, G. (1979) *The best of the Achaeans: Concepts of the hero in archaic Greek poetry*. Baltimore: Johns Hopkins University Press.

O'Connor, M. (1980) *Hebrew verse structure*. Winona Lake, Indiana: Eisenbrauns.

O'Nolan, K. (1969) Homer and Irish heroic narrative. *Classical quarterly, 19*, 1–19.

O'Nolan, K. (1978) Doublets in the *Odyssey*. *Classical quarterly 28*, 23–27.

Reed, D.W. & Spicer, J.L. (1952) Correlation methods of comparing idiolects in a transition area. *Language, 28*, 348–59.

Rilke, R.M. (1969) *Letters . . . 1892–1910*. Translated by J.B. Greene & M.D. Herder Norton. New York: W.W. Norton.

Rimbaud, A. (1957) *Oeuvres*. Edited by M. Raymond. Lausanne: La Guilde du Livre.

Ross, J.R. (1970) Gapping and the order of constituents. In M. Bierwisch & K.S. Heidolph (Eds.), *Progress in linguistics*. The Hague: Mouton. Pp. 249–259.

Sadock, J.M. (1980) Discussion of 'role and reference grammar'. . . . In M. Kac (Ed.), *Current syntactic theories: Discussion papers from the 1979 Milwaukee Syntax Conference*. Bloomington: Indiana University Linguistics Club. Pp. 1–6.

Sapir, E. (1949) *Selected Writings.* Edited by D. Mandelbaum. Berkeley: University of California Press.

SSL *see* Jakobson & Waugh (1979).

Spicer, J. (1975) *The collected books.* Edited with a memoir by R. Blaser. Los Angeles: Black Sparrow.

Steiner, G. (1979) "Critic"/"Reader." *New literary history, 10,* 423–452. Reprinted in *PNReview, 17,* (1980), 39–50.

Stevens, W. (1972) *The palm at the end of the mind.* Edited by Holly Stevens. New York: Random House/Vintage.

Stolz, B.A. & Shannon, R.S. (Eds.) (1976) *Oral literature and the formula.* Ann Arbor: Center for the Coordination of Ancient and Modern Studies of The University of Michigan.

Thompson, L.C. (1973) The northwest. In T.A. Sebeok *et al.* (Eds.), *Current Trends in Linguistics. 10. Linguistics in North America.* The Hague: Mouton. Pp. 979–1045.

Van Valin, R.D. Reply to Sadock (1980). In M. Kac (Ed.), *Current syntactic theories: Discussion papers from the 1979 Milwaukee Syntax Conference.* Bloomington: Indiana University Linguistics Club. Pp. 7–13.

Vendler, H.H. (1966) Review of R. Fowler (Ed.), *Essays on style and language.* In *Essays in criticism, 16,* 457–463.

Vihman, M.M. (1982) Formulas in first and second language acquisition. (In this volume).

Whitman, R.H. (1973) Review of R. Jakobson's *Selected writings* I², II. In *Language, 49,* 679–682.

Zeps, V.J. (1973) Latvian folk meters and style. In S.R. Anderson & P. Kiparsky (Eds.), *A Festschrift for Morris Halle.* New York: Holt, Rinehart & Winston. Pp. 207–211.

11 GALIT HASAN-ROKEM

The Pragmatics of Proverbs: How the Proverb Gets Its Meaning

A common genre of folk literature is the proverb, a multivalent poetical summary of a community's collective experience. It is precisely the multivalence of the proverb which determines the potency of its meaning; proverbs combine poetic structure with frozen meaning in ways that render their usage linguistically exceptional.

Proverbs may either be used alone, as an utterance in an appropriate situational context, or they may be used at a structural juncture in a folktale. The specific application of a proverb is a collocation of an element already existing in the folk literary tradition, namely, the proverb, and of a conceptual structure by which the situation is experienced. That application imbues the unique situation with cultural meaning by linking it to a chain of situations all of which may be interpreted by the same proverb. This is the paradigmatic aspect of proverb usage. The specific meaning of a proverb, which itself is a poetic wording for a conceptual structure, is thus dependent on the context in which it is used. The use of a proverb within a folk narrative stresses the paradigmatic, cultural aspect of the proverb. The proverb within the narrative creates an effect of intertextuality—a relationship among several texts (Morawski 1970; Abrahams & Babcock 1977; Hasan-Rokem 1981).

The syntagmatic aspect of the proverb is revealed in the capacity of an individual acquainted with the paradigmatic range of the proverb to use it in acceptable contexts. This ability could be termed the individual's proverb competence, and it naturally varies with the tale-teller's memory, knowledge, and creativity.

169

We may consider how both the paradigmatic and syntagmatic aspects of a proverb's use contribute to its meaning. Two methods of approach will prove fruitful. In the first we will consider the individual proverb in the light of its appropriate range of usages. In the second we will consider a cluster of proverbs which share a core semantic meaning, and will see how they may be differentiated from each other. The first approach, we should note, is analogous to considering the meaning of a lexical item in the light of the range of contexts in which it is used (Krikmann 1974; Szemérkenyi & Voigt 1972); the second approach treats meaning in terms of the psychologists' "association networks," as with lexical items distinguishable from each other by few semantic features.

That we may appropriately analogize from the lexical item to the proverb is clear in that the proverb bears many markers of a tight linguistic entity. Even more than the idiom, the proverb has a fixed word order which is not subject to inflectional changes according to linguistic context. Indeed, the proverb is generally marked as such by one of a set of fixed formulas to introduce it: *Like they say . . . My mother (father, grandmother, etc.) used to say . . .* , or in Hebrew: *Our sages said . . ., It is said . . . .* Not only are the lexical items and their syntax fixed, intonation also marks a setting apart of the proverb-sentence as something impersonal, stemming from an authority. But the meaning of the proverb derives only minimally from the sum of its parts. The main features by which the proverb is distinguished as such by the audience, are its poetic nature (including semantic and syntactic markers; Silvermann-Weinreich 1971) and the fact that it is recognized as being recurrently used in that specific ethnic group.

Consider how the frozen syntax of the proverb may be superceded by discourse necessities: Basically, proverbs are affirmatives even when formulated as a question, an order, a request, etc. The affirmative nature of the proverb derives from the fact that it is based on and summarizes a collective experience. The sentence *Is Saul also among the prophets* (I Sam. 10:11–12) when used as a proverb does not pose a question but states affirmatively: *Not every X is among the prophets*. The proverb: *Look not at the flask but at what is therein* (Mishna, Avot, Ch. 4) is not an imperative although syntactically it is a conjoining of negative and positive imperatives. Rather, it says look not at the flask, it pays to look at what is in it. The motivation for what is said does not, as in an imperative, stem from the will of the speaker, but rather it refers to a reality in which the affirmative has been demonstrated.

Thus, syntactic analysis of the proverb, alone, is relatively unhelpful in discerning its meaning. Rather, I will argue, the syntax of the proverb AS A UNIT within a discourse bears the greater semantic weight. Indeed it is not the proverb which is generated by the user, but rather the fact of inserting it in a particular behavioral or tale-performance context.

Not only is syntactic analysis of the proverb per se unfruitful; but simple lexical analysis is also. Semantic analysis of the lexical items within the proverb is unfruitful unless the items are considered in the light of other lexical items both within and outside the proverb, precisely because the proverb is a poetic utterance which often exploits metaphor, another instance of exceptional language use. The discrepancy between the metaphoric and the literal interpretations of proverbs is vividly demonstrated in Breughel's painting "The Dutch Proverbs." Consider literal interpretations of: *Opportunity knocks but once, A penny saved is a penny earned, A bird in the hand is worth two in the bush.* Even if we were to treat the "internal metaphors" of the proverb (Silvermann-Weinreich 1971), we would still need to treat the interplay of literal and metaphoric elements in the proverb's usage, as in the following tale of a man who dug a pit and fell into it. As lexical and syntactic analysis will not suffice to catch/interpret the meaning of the proverb, let us turn to analysis of the range of usage. In the course of our data collection in Israel (Hasan-Rokem 1978) we have come across numerous instances of proverbs derived from Ecclesiastes 10:8 *He who diggeth a pit shall fall himself therein.* As reported by one informant, this proverb is used in a situation "when somebody tries to harm somebody else and he himself is harmed." In one specific instance an informant reported that somebody had tried to give the impression that she, the informant, then a school girl, had stolen money from the class, but later it was revealed that the slanderer herself had taken the money and was then punished.

The proverb also appears in an Iraqi–Jewish tale in which the father of the bride is not happy with his new son-in-law and he prepares an actual pit behind the synagogue for him. But the digger forgets all about it and when he is suddenly called out by somebody, he himself falls into the well-hidden pit. It is characteristic that for this proverb, the behavioral–situational use is more abstract that the folktale use. That is, the folktale concretizes the metaphor. We have observed (Hasan-Rokem 1982) that proverbs in folktales are more likely to become exemplified both negatively and positively, while proverbs in behavioral contexts are generally limited to comments on negative functions.

Let us turn then to analysis of a cluster of proverbs on fate, as they may be used to demonstrate how semantic interpretation of proverbs must take into account cultural traditions and the norms of specific ethnic groups. The fate-proverbs I have collected in Israel come primarily from informants from Islamic countries, in keeping with the folk beliefs of Islamic Culture. (*Encyclopedia of Religion and Ethics,* "Fate,

Islam"; *Encyclopedia of Islam,* "Kadar"; G. Basile *The Pentamerone,* tr. B. Croce, ed. N.M. Penzer, London 1932, III, 3, Penzer's note). For example from Morocco: *Fate cannot be avoided;* [1] from Iraq: *Fate is inscribed on the day of birth and cannot be erased.* [2] In these proverbs fate is anonymous and is conceived of as an independent power.

An analysis of the set of proverbs which express the general function "Everything depends on fate" reveals the belief of the users of the proverbs that fate reigns over three main domains of human life: marriage, death, and economy. The different uses, narrative and behavioral, of the same proverb, *Fate is inscribed on the day of birth and cannot be erased* (or: *Fate is written on the brow; it cannot be erased*) may be used in tales with regard to death, marriage, wealth, and poverty. However, in the behavioral contexts recorded in our field work, only negative possibilities were concretized, namely, those regarding death or poverty. That is, the proverb *Fate is inscribed . . .* is applied on the occasion of somebody's (often untimely) death, or when somebody loses property. This confirms our earlier point about the broader range of proverb meaning in tales as compared to behavioral contexts.

What controls fate changes from one tale to another. Thus, in a tale told by an Iraqi informant about King Solomon's daughter[3], the closing statement is: *He could not fight fate, God is the one who gives it.* By subjecting fate to God's will and by denying its autonomous power, humans are able to influence fate, by means of the normative religion with its clearcut system of reward and punishment. People can alter fate by moral actions or by observing religious precepts. However the act which alters fate may also be morally neutral, as in the proverb from Central Asia: *Change of locality changes luck.* [4] The view that fate is determined by God is expressed again in the following proverb from Egypt: *God impoverishes and enriches.* [5]

The view that man's actions change his fate (for the better) is seen in the proverb reported from Egypt, Palestine, and Morocco: *Charity saves from death.* [6] This possibility of avoiding fate's total control by means of moral and religious values leads toward another outlook on this theme: *Man is rewarded according to his deeds.* Thus we reach dialectically the

---

[1] Israeli Folklore Archives = IFA, text nr. 6732.

[2] IFA 338, Iraq.

[3] A version of the international folktale type nr. 930, according to the Aarne and Thompson (1973) index of folktale types.

[4] 1FA 7254, Bukhara.

[5] 1FA 1224, Egypt; Samuel I, 2:7.

[6] 1FA 1226, Egypt: 1FA 6596, Palestinian Sephardic; 1FA 7388, Morocco; Proverbs 6:2; Proverbs 11:4.

semantic opposite of the function with which we started, *Fate controls everything* (*Everything depends on fate.*). As with lexical items, then, the individual proverb may be closely related to its semantic opposite.

The utterance of proverbs, we conclude, is folk discourse in miniature. While analysis of lexical and syntactic meaning within the proverb may be of interest, and is certainly necessary for a thorough understanding of the proverb's multi-level meaning, it is the discourse and pragmatic aspects of proverb use which bring heavy accretions to meaning in any given usage instance. Thus by studying the way meaning inheres in the proverb, we are opening the way for incorporation of discourse and broader pragmatic principles into linguistic theory.

References

Aarne, A., & Thompson, S. (1973) The types of the folk-tale. *Folklore Fellows Communications* nr. 184, Helsinki: Academia Scientiarum Fennica.

Abrahams, R.D., & Babcock, B.A. (1977) The literary use of proverbs. *Journal of American folklore, 90,* 414–429.

Hasan-Rokem, G. (1981) The Biblical verse—proverb and quotation. In *Jerusalem studies in Hebrew literature* 1. Jerusalem: The Magnes Press. Pp. 155–166.

Hasan-Rokem, G. (1982) Proverbs in Israeli folktales: A Structural model for folklore. *Folklore Fellows Communications* nr. 232, Helsinki: Academia Scientiarum Fennica.

Krikmann, A. (1974) On denotative indefiniteness of proverbs. *Proverbium, 23,* 865–879.

Morawski, S. (1970) The basic functions of quotation. In A. Greimas *et al.* (Eds.), *Sign, language, culture.* Janua linguarum series maior 1. The Hague: Mouton. Pp. 690–705.

Silvermann-Weinreich, B. (1971) Formal problems in the study of the Jewish proverb. *Hasifrut, 3,* 85–92. Translated and elaborated version of the Yiddish article printed in *For Max Weinreich.* (1964) The Hague: Mouton. Pp. 383–392.

Szemérkenyi, A. & Voigt, V. (1972) The connections of theme and language in proverb transformations. *Acta ethnographica academiae scientiarum Hungaricae.* 21, 95–108.

12 JOEL SHERZER

Play Languages: With a Note on Ritual Languages[1]

SPEECH PLAY defines a broad area of language usage in which linguistic forms at any level are purposely manipulated. Speech play thus defined can be understood in terms of what Jakobson (1960) calls the poetic function of language. For Jakobson, this poetic function, which occurs in many verbal genres in addition to poetry, involves the projection of paradigmatic linguistic axes onto syntagmatic axes, resulting in a focus, foregrounding, and/or manipulation of any aspect of language (phonetics, lexicon, syntax, etc.) for its own sake. In speech play, the poetic function of language becomes so predominant that one might say it is on display. There is an interesting relationship between speech play and verbal art. Verbal art often, but not always, involves speech play. On the other hand, speech play also occurs in speech usages which particular societies may not consider to be verbal art, for example play languages. (For further discussion of speech play and its relationship to verbal art, see Kirshenblatt-Gimblett 1976). Furthermore, the play involved need not necessarily be humorous; for example, serious messages are communicated in the play languages described in this paper.

Play languages are a form of speech play in which a new linguistic code is created by derivation from a real language by means of definable

[1] An earlier version of this chapter (without the note on ritual languages) appears as "Play languages: Implications for (socio) linguistics." In Barbara Kirshenblatt-Gimblett (Ed.) (1976) *Speech Play*. Phila.: University of Pennsylvania Press. Those segments of that paper duplicated here are published with the permission of the publisher.

EXCEPTIONAL LANGUAGE AND LINGUISTICS

rules. (For an exception, see Price & Price 1976 who describe how new linguistic material is created for the express purpose of deriving a play language from it.) Native speakers of play languages can often articulate the language's rules, as they have to, for example, in teaching the language to others. The native version of the rules is usually simpler than that which a linguist would construct. The native version enumerates the major linguistic transformations or derivations involved in the play language, while the linguist's version, in addition to these, enumerates minor morphophonemic adjustment rules. In the scholarship, PLAY LANGUAGES are also called "disguised speech" (Haas 1967; 1969); "linguistic games" (Burling 1970; Sherzer *et al.* 1971); "ludling" (Laycock 1965; Laycock, Lloyd, & Staalsen 1969); "pig latins," "secret codes," "secret languages" (Opie & Opie 1959; Berkovits 1970); "speech disguise" (Conklin 1956); and other names. I prefer the term PLAY LANGUAGE (which I borrow from Price & Price 1976) as a general term because, first, play languages are not games strictly speaking. They do not necessarily involve competition, two or more sides, and criteria for determining the winner (see Roberts, Arth, & Bush 1959, p. 597). Second, play languages are not necessarily or exclusively used for purposes of secrecy. They may be widely understood and used primarily for fun. Third, not all methods of disguising speech need produce play languages.

Although play languages have attracted the attention of folklorists, they have not been a central concern of linguists. Halle (1962) uses PIG LATIN to argue for the necessity of ordered rules in phonological descriptions. Burling (1970), Chao (1931, 1968), Conklin (1956; 1959), Coupez (1981) Hale (1971), Haas (1967; 1969), Hombert (1973), and Laycock (1965) describe play languages in nonwestern societies and Campbell (1974) describes an American Indian play language. Haas (1967) suggests a typology of play languages (see also Laycock 1972). Burling (1970) argues that investigation of play languages would provide data for the analysis of the linguistic structures on which they are based and Coupez (1981) and Hombert (1973) discuss the implications of play languages for the analysis of particular natural languages.

In this chapter, I will discuss play languages from three points of view: First, their inherent properties, that is, the kinds of linguistic rules that are involved in the generation of play languages; second, the relevance of play languages to theoretical linguistic concerns, both within particular languages and concerning language in general; third, the place of play languages in the overall speech patterns of a community.

Since a play language is a coded version of a particular variety of a language, the rules for each play language are derivations from that variety to the play language forms. In contrast with some other types of speech play, for example, counting out rhymes, play languages are used by speakers to transfer novel messages to one another. Examples of play languages from Kuna, French, Javanese, English, Spanish, and Portuguese will illustrate the types of phenomena involved.

Five Kuna Play Languages[2]

The first play language is called *sorsik summakke* or *arepecunmakke*, 'talking backwards'. *Arepecunmakke* is derived from Spanish *al revés* ('backwards') plus Kuna *sunmakke* ('to speak'). This play language and especially its implications for sociolinguistic theory is investigated in greater detail in Sherzer (1970). It consists of taking the first syllable of a word and placing it at the end of the word. The following rule generates the forms used:

$$\#S1 \quad S2 \quad S3 \ldots Sn \rightarrow S2 \quad S3 \ldots Sn \quad S1\#$$

where S signifies syllable and # signifies word boundary. Some examples are:

> *osi* ('pineapple') → *sio*
> *ope* ('to bathe') → *peo*
> *takke* ('to see') → *ketak*
> *take* ('to come') → *keta*
> *ipya* ('eye') → *yaip*
> *uwaya* ('ear') → *wayau*

(The examples represent but one way of forming words in this play language—see Sherzer 1970. They are represented in a more phonological than phonetic form. Kuna phonemes are p, t, k, k^w, s, m, n, w, y, r, l, a, e, i, o, u. The phoneme c results from a cluster of s plus s. Stress usually falls on the penultimate syllable of the word.)

The rule for this first play language is written above in terms of syllables and the language is indeed based on the syllable. Let us consider describing it another way. Kuna words have the following properties with regard to permitted consonant clusters. No more than one consonant can begin or end a word. Words may have, internally, that is, intervocalically, clusters of two consonants, but not more than

[2] Kuna is an American Indian language spoken in Colombia and Panama. The Kuna data for this chapter were gathered on the islands of Sasartii-Malatuppu and Niatuppu in San Blas, Panama. The research was supported by NSF Grant GU-1598 to the University of Texas.

two. Canonic shapes for Kuna words include, for example:

VC:	*an*	('I, my')
CVC:	*nek*	('house')
VV:	*ia*	('older brother')
CVV:	*poe*	('to cry')
CVCV:	*kape*	('to sleep')
CVCCV:	*warpo*	('two pole-like objects')
CVCCVC:	*sorsik*	('backward')

The maximal canonic shape with regard to consonant clusters is:

$$\#C1 \ V \ C2 \ C3 \ V \ C4 \cdots VCn\#$$

It is possible to represent every Kuna word with this maximal phono-logical structure if those places where consonants can potentially occur but happen not to are filled in with zeros: $\emptyset$. This would not entail a boundless or unstructured use of $\emptyset$ but rather a logical one based on the canonic shape of Kuna words. (I suggest then "another use of nothing," following Hoenigswald 1959.) In the following examples the $\emptyset$ will be placed IN FRONT OF single, intervocalic consonants. This will enable the proper generation of play language forms in the rules to be stated below. The placing of the $\emptyset$ is of course directly related to the fact that single, intervocalic consonants serve as the first consonant of the fol-lowing syllable and not the final consonant of the preceding syllable. Examples are:

ia	('older brother')	$(\emptyset i\emptyset\emptyset a\emptyset)$
ope	('to bathe')	$(\emptyset o\emptyset pe\emptyset)$
kape	('to sleep')	$(ka\emptyset pe\emptyset)$
uwaya	('ear')	$(\emptyset u\emptyset wa\emptyset ya\emptyset)$

The rule for this play language can now be rewritten in terms of the canonic shape of the Kuna word; namely, in terms of a shifting of consonants and vowels and without reference to syllables.

$$\#C1VC2C3VC4 \cdots VCn\# \rightarrow \#C3VC4 \cdots VCn C1VC2\#$$

Repeating the previous examples of the play language with inserted zeros:

osi	('pineapple')	$(\emptyset o\emptyset si\emptyset)$	$\rightarrow sio$
ope	('to bathe')	$(\emptyset o\emptyset pe\emptyset)$	$\rightarrow peo$
takke	('to see')	$(takke\emptyset)$	$\rightarrow ketak$
take	('to come')	$(ta\emptyset ke\emptyset)$	$\rightarrow keta$
ipya	('eye')	$(\emptyset ipya\emptyset)$	$\rightarrow yaip$
uwaya	('ear')	$(\emptyset u\emptyset wa\emptyset ya\emptyset)$	$\rightarrow wayau$

The resulting "backwards" words for the most part fit the phonological canons of ordinary Kuna speech. They could be and at times actually are perfectly good words in Kuna. This gives the hearer of the play language the superficial impression that the player is speaking normal Kuna.

The second Kuna play language is called *ottukkuar sunmakke*, ('concealed talking') and consists of inserting a sound sequence after the initial consonant-vowel sequence of each syllable. The inserted sequence consists of *pp* plus the vowel of the preceding syllable. In terms of the canonic shape of Kuna words, the rule for play language 2 is:

$$\#C1V1C2C3V2C4 \cdots Cn\# \rightarrow \#C1V1pp\,V1C2C3V2pp\,V2C4 \cdots Cn\#$$

Some examples are:

merki	('North American')	(*merki*∅)	→ *mepperkippi*
pia	('where')	(*pi*∅∅*a*∅)	→ *pippiappa*
ua	('fish')	(∅*u*∅∅*a*∅)	→ *uppuappa*
perkʷaple	('all')	(*perkʷaple*∅)	→ *pepperkʷappapleppe*

Although the forms used in this play language theoretically fit Kuna phonological canons, they are marked by alliteration and rhyme because of the constant repetition of *pp* V.

The third Kuna play language has no name; it is the same as the second except that the inserted sound sequence is *r* plus the vowel of the previous syllable. The rule is thus:

$$\#C1V1C2C3V2C4 \cdots Cn\# \rightarrow \#C1V1r\,V1C2C3V2r\,V2C4 \cdots Cn\#$$

Examples are:

merki	('North American')	(*merki*∅)	→ *mererkiri*
pe	('you')	(*pe*∅)	→ *pere*
pia	('where')	(*pi*∅∅*a*∅)	→ *piriara*
tanikki	('he's coming')	(*ta*∅*nikki*∅)	→ *taranirikkiri*

Like those of play language 2, the forms of play language 3 fit Kuna phonological canons but exhibit marked alliteration and rhyme.

The fourth Kuna play language has no name and involves the prefixation of *ci*- before every syllable. Furthermore, each syllable in the source or original Kuna word receives primary stress in the play language form. The rule for this play language, stated in terms of syllables, is:

$$\#S1 \quad S2 \quad S3 \cdots Sn\# \rightarrow \#ci\acute{S}1 \quad ci\acute{S}2 \quad ci\acute{S}3 \cdots ci\acute{S}n\#$$

or stated in terms of the canonic shape of Kuna words:

$$\#C1VC2C3VC4 \cdots VCn\# \rightarrow \#ci\,C1\acute{V}C2ci\,C3\acute{V}C4 \cdots Cn\#$$

Examples are:

ina	('medicine')	(ⱷiⱷnaⱷ)	→ cííchiná
ai	('friend')	(ⱷaⱷⱷiⱷ)	→ ciáchií
naipe	('snake')	(naⱷⱷiⱷpeⱷ)	→ cináchiíchipé
maceret	('man')	(maceⱷret)	→ cimácicécirét

The forms of this play language ring quite differently from ordinary, spoken Kuna, because of both the repeated *ci* and the positioning of the stressed syllables.

The fifth Kuna play language, like the first, is called *sorsik sunmakke*, although it is actually quite different from the first. It is the only one of the five Kuna play languages which is not based on the syllable. Rather it is based on the vowel. It is important to note, however, the following relationship between Kuna vowels and syllables. Each short vowel forms the nucleus of a single syllable. Long vowels are phonologically two vowels and are two syllables in length. There is variation within the Kuna speech community, though, in the treatment of long vowels. For a discussion of this variation see Sherzer (1970, pp. 346–347).

In this instance, every vowel becomes *i*. Stated in terms of the canonic shape of Kuna words, the rule is:

$$\#C1V1C2C3V2C4 \cdots Cn\# \rightarrow \#C1i\,C2C3i\,C4 \cdots Cn\#$$

or, more simply, without reference to context:

$$V \rightarrow i$$

Examples are:

pia	('where')	→ pii
pe	('you')	→ pi
tanikki	('he's coming')	→ tinikki
iki	('how')	→ iki
nuka	('name')	→ niki

The forms used in this play language have a strange ring to them due to the fact that *i* is the only vowel used.

Two Variants of a Complicated French Play Language

French backwards talk is called *langage à l'envers* ('backwards language'), *parler à l'envers* ('speak backwards'), or, in the code itself, *verlen* or *larper*. There are variants of this play language, one of which involves a switching of syllables. Dubois *et al.* (1970, p. 65) describe this version. (See also Guiraud 1973.) In it:

l'envers	('backwards')	→ *verlen*
pedes	('pederast')	→ *dépés*
mari	('husband')	→ *rima*
copains	('friends')	→ *painsco*
cul	('ass')	→ *luc*

(All French play language forms are written here in normal French orthography and the ordinary orthographic to pronunciation canons can be followed in reading them.) Notice that French orthography plays a role in this play language. The *s* of *copains*, for example, is not pronounced in ordinary French but it is pronounced in the backwards *painsco*. Similarly with regard to the *l* of *cul*. Some function words, such as prepositions, are not affected and are deleted in the play language outputs. Thus, *peau de balle* ('nothing') becomes *balpeau*. This variant of the play language has three rules, which operate in the following order:

1. Delete those words not to be affected.

   By this rule, *peau de balle* → *peau balle*

2. Number the pairs of syllables which are to be switched.

   By this rule, *peau balle* → *peau balle* (with 1 over *peau*, 2 over *balle*)

3. Switch each syllable numbered 1 with the following syllable numbered 2.

   By this rule, *peau balle* (with 1 over *peau*, 2 over *balle*) → *balpeau*, which is the desired play language output.

Another version of this play language is even more complicated. Basically, it consists of switching the initial consonants or consonant clusters of two consecutive syllables.[3] *Parler,* ('to speak') for example, becomes *larper*. In words of a single syllable, it is the initial and final consonants or consonant clusters of this syllable which are switched. Thus: *boire* ('drink') → *roib* and *mec* ('guy') → *quem*. As in the version previously described, certain classes of words are not affected; in this version, however, they still appear in the play language outputs. Thus *je bouffe pas* ('I'm not eating') → *je foub pas,* only the verb being

---

[3] The examples which appear here were collected by the author in August, 1970.

affected. Pronouns and definite articles are generally not affected, except when they are phonetically linked with the next form by vowel elision (*j'* and *l'*):

le mec	('the guy')	→ *le quem*
but *l'école*	('the school')	→ *qu'élole*
je bouffe pas	('I'm not eating')	→ *je foub pas*
but *j'entends*	('I hear')	→ *t'enjends*

Note that this play language is derived from an extremely colloquial variety of French. (See following discussion.) Thus the rather formal negative *ne* is not involved. This variant of talking backward requires the following ordered rules:

1. Mark all words as to whether or not they are to be affected. By this rule (using parentheses to mark unaffected words), examples are:

je vois   ('I see')   → *(je) vois*
je parle   ('I speak')   → *(je) parle*
le mec   ('the guy')   → *(le) mec*
je te pissais à la raie   ('I pissed in your face')
              → *(je) (te) pissais (à) (la) raie*
passe moi la bouteille   ('pass me the bottle')
              → *passe (moi) (la) bouteille*
je te crache à la gueule   ('I spit in your face')
              → *(je) (te) crache (à) (la) gueule*

2. Assign the number 1 to the initial consonant or consonant cluster of each affected word and the number 2 to the initial consonant or consonant cluster of the second syllable of each affected word. If the affected word has only one syllable, assign the number 2 to the terminal consonant or consonant cluster of this syllable.
By this rule,

(je) vois	→ $(je)\ \overset{1}{v}ois$
(je) parle	→ $(je)\ \overset{1\ \ 2}{parle}$
(le) mec	→ $(le)\ \overset{1\ \ 2}{mec}$
(je) (te) pissais (à) (la) raie	→ $(je)\ (te)\ \overset{1\ 2}{pissais}\ (à)\ (la)\ \overset{1}{raie}$
passe (moi) (la) bouteille	→ $\overset{1\ \ 2}{passe}\ (moi)\ (la)\ \overset{1\ \ 2}{bouteille}$
(je) (te) crache (à) (la) gueule	→ $(je)\ (te)\ \overset{1\ \ 2}{crache}\ (à)\ (la)\ \overset{1\ \ 2}{gueule}$

3. If any affected word has only one number, erase the first set of parentheses to its left and renumber, beginning with the newly affected word.[4]

By this rule,

$(je) \overset{1}{v}ois$ $\quad\quad\quad\quad\quad\quad \rightarrow je \overset{1}{v}\overset{2}{o}is$

$(je)\,(te)\overset{1}{p}\overset{2}{i}ssais\,(\acute{a})\,(la)\overset{1}{r}aie \rightarrow (je)\,(te)\overset{1}{p}\overset{2}{i}ssais\,(\grave{a})\,la\,\overset{1}{r}\overset{2}{a}ie$

4. Switch each consonant or consonant cluster numbered 1 with the next consonant or consonant cluster numbered 2.

By this rule,

$\overset{1}{j}e\,\overset{2}{v}ois$ $\quad\quad\quad\quad\quad \rightarrow ve\,jois$

$(je)\,\overset{1}{p}ar\overset{2}{l}e$ $\quad\quad\quad\quad \rightarrow je\,larpe$

$(le)\,\overset{1}{m}e\overset{2}{c}$ $\quad\quad\quad\quad \rightarrow le\,quem$

$(je)\,(te)\overset{1}{p}\overset{2}{i}ssais\,(\grave{a})\,\overset{1}{l}a\,\overset{2}{r}aie \rightarrow je\,te\,sipais\,\grave{a}\,ra\,laie$

$\overset{1}{p}\overset{2}{a}sse\,(moi)\,(la)\overset{1}{b}ou\overset{2}{t}eille \rightarrow sap\,moi\,la\,toubeille$

$(je)\,(te)\overset{1}{c}ra\overset{2}{ch}e\,(\grave{a})\,(la)\overset{1}{g}ueu\overset{2}{l}e \rightarrow je\,te\,chacre\,\grave{a}\,la\,lueugue$

Seven Javanese Play Languages of Increasing Complexity

The following Javanese play languages are described by Sadtono (1971). In the first Javanese play language, every vowel of the source word is followed by a syllable which consists of *f* plus a repetition of the vowel. The rule for this play language is as follows:

$$V \rightarrow VfV$$

An example is:

aku arep tuku klambi ('I want to buy a dress')
$\rightarrow$ *afakufu afarefep tufukufu klafambifi*

Like many play languages, this one is based on the syllable. Here, every open syllable is followed by *f* plus the vowel which is the nucleus of the syllable. Every closed syllable inserts such a new syllable (e.g., *fV*) before its final consonant.

---

[4] Notice that the rules for this play language are then cyclic in the sense that this notion is used in generative-transformational grammar. I am grateful to Lawrence Foley for calling this fact to my attention.

The second Javanese play language is identical to the first, except that the inserted syllable begins with p.
The rule is thus:

$$V \rightarrow VpV$$

Example:

kikik anak nakal   ('Kikik is a naughty boy')
→ *kipikipik apanapak napakapal*

The third Javanese play language is similar to the first two although it is somewhat more complicated. Analogous to the first two, every noninitial syllable of each word adds *s* plus a repetition of the vowel which is the nucleus of the syllable. The first syllable of the word is treated as follows. If the syllable is open, it is closed with *s*. If the syllable is closed, the closing consonant is replaced by *s*, the replaced consonant in turn becoming the initial consonant of the following syllable, sometimes preceding the original initial consonant of this syllable, sometimes replacing it. This play language may be described in terms of the following two rules:

1. #CV − CVC · · · # → #CVs − CVsVC · · · #

where − signifies syllable boundary and # signifies word boundary.

2. #CVC^a − C^{b}VC · · · # → #CVs − C^a(C^b)VsVC · · · #

where parentheses signify that C^b is sometimes deleted.
Example:

aku arep tuku klambi karo sepatu kembaran karo bocah akeh ('I want to buy a dress and a pair of shoes that are identical with those of my friends')

→

askusu asresep tuskusu klasmbisi kasroso sespasatusu kesmbasarasan kasroso boscasah askeseh

The two rules are not ordered with respect to one another but rather deal with two different possibilities. The first accounts for initial syllables which are open. The second accounts for initial syllables which are closed. The two rules could of course be conflated into a single one. Regardless, this play language involves more complicated operations than the first two Javanese ones described.

In the fourth Javanese play language, every syllable of every word except the initial one is deleted. Furthermore, every syllable in the play language output must be closed; this is done by retaining the initial consonant of the second syllable of the source word, if needed. The two rules for this play language are:

1. $\#C1V1 - C2V2C3 \cdots \# \rightarrow \#C1V1C2 \cdots \#$
2. $\#C1V1C2 - C3V2C4 \cdots \# \rightarrow \#C1V1C2 \cdots \#$

Example:

> *aku arep luŋo* ('I am going to go') → *ak ar luŋ*

The fifth Javanese play language involves a switching of the kind already encountered in one version of French backwards talk. The consonant or consonant cluster (or Ø) which begins each word is switched with the consonant or consonant cluster which begins the second syllable of the same word.

The rule for this play language is:

$$\#C1VCC2V \cdots \# \rightarrow \#C2VCC1V \cdots \#$$

where C signifies consonant or consonant cluster.
Examples are:

> *nduwe* ('have') → *wunde*
> *rupiah* ('rupees') → *puriah*

The sixth Javanese play language is based on the word; in it every word is pronounced completely backwards. The rule is:

$$\#C1V1C2C3V2C4 \cdot \cdot \cdot Cn\# \rightarrow \#Cn \cdot \cdot \cdot C4V2C3C2V1C1\#$$

Example:

> *bocah iku dolanan asu*   ('the boy is playing with a dog')
> → *hacob uki nanalod usa*

The seventh Javanese play language is based on the order of the Javanese consonant alphabet. This alphabet is as follows:

> 1.*h* 2.*d* 3.*p* 4.*m* 5.*n* 6.*t* 7.*d* 8.*g* 9.*c* 10.*s* 11.*j*
> 12.*b* 13.*r* 14.*w* 15.*y* 16.*ṭ* 17.*k* 18.*l* 19.*ñ* 20.*ŋ*

The play language associates with every consonant an equivalent derived by superimposing the alphabet in reverse order onto the normal order. Play language equivalent consonants are thus

> *h:* *ŋ* *d:ñ* *p:l* *m:k* *n:ṭ* *t:y* *ḍ:w* *g:r* *c:b* *s:j*

In the play language, vowels are unaltered and all non-word final consonants are replaced by their alphabetically derived equivalents.

Example:

aku gawe layaŋ ('I'm writing a letter') → *ŋamu raḍe pataŋ*

(In Javanese orthography, *aku* ('I') is written *haku*. Therefore in this play language *aku* → *ŋamu*.)

At first glance, this play language seems so complicated that it is hard to believe that individuals actually speak it rapidly. However, there are several facilitating factors. First, the alphabet contains twenty letters; therefore only ten interchanges must be learned. The second ten are merely the reverse of the first ten. Second, if all twenty sounds are grouped into two classes,

1. all nonnasal stops
2. all other sounds: nasal stops, semivowels, affricates, fricatives, and *r* sound.

then eight of the ten interchanges involve exchange from class 1 to class 2 or vice versa. The exception are *s:j* and *h:* , both within class 2. These involve, however, shifts from fricative to homorganic voiced affricate and from fricative to almost homorganic nasal stop. The remaining eight interchanges involve some homorganic or almost homorganic shifts and some not at all homorganic shifts. Finally, all but three interchanges (*d:ñ ḍ:w g:r*) involve shifts in voicing. Thus, although this is undoubtedly an intriguingly complicated play language, there are, nonetheless, some regular patterns which facilitate its learning.

Some English Play Languages

The most commonly known English play language is probably PIG LATIN in which the first consonant or consonant cluster of a word is shifted to the end of the word and *-ey* is added to it. The following example is written in English orthography:

The man is home → *ethey anmey isey omehey.*

In England, BACK SLANG is a term used to label several play languages. Opie and Opie (1959, p. 320) report that BACK SLANG proper is "employed by barrow-boys and hawkers" and is "indigenous to certain trades such as the greengrocers and the butchers, where it is spoken to ensure that the customer shall not understand what is being said." The rule for this form of BACK SLANG is identical to that used in the sixth Javanese play language described above, namely each word is said entirely backwards. Opie and Opie provide the following example:

Give her some old scrag end → evig reh emos delo garcs dene.

Notice that in unpronounceable (according to English canons of pronunciation) consonant clusters such as *dl* and *dn*, the orthographic letter is pronounced, thus providing an epenthetic vowel.

BACK SLANG is also used in England to refer to play languages which insert sound sequences into words. A common variant involves the insertion of stressed ág before every vowel. Thus:

thank you very much → thágank yágou vágerágy máguch.

Sound sequences inserted before vowels often provide the principle underlying the derivation of American English play languages. ABI DABI, known by many American children, inserts *ab* before every vowel. One version stresses the inserted syllable:

street → strábeet   language → lábanguábage

Another version stresses each syllable of the original word in English:

street → strabeét   language → labánguabáge

It is interesting that the two versions of ADI DABI sound quite different and are not always mutually intelligible, even though the only difference between them is stress placement.

Play Languages in Spanish and Portuguese

A very common Spanish play language, spoken in Latin America, is the F LANGUAGE. In this play language, *f* plus the vowel of the source syllable is inserted after the initial consonant-vowel sequence of each syllable. (Compare with the second and third Kuna play languages.) Thus:

la casa grande → lafa cafasafa grafandefe.

A quite similar P LANGUAGE is spoken in Brazil, derived from Portuguese. Thus:

menina → mepenipinapa

Another variant of this play language, without the vowel echoing, inserts *pe* before each vowel. Thus:

menina → pemepenipena

Returning to Latin American Spanish, the following play languages are reported to be spoken among Mexican Americans in Texas.[5] KUTI inserts the nonsense word *kuti* before each syllable. Thus:

rosa → *kutirokutisa*

MARACAIBO is different from any of the play languages I have described so far. In it each vowel in the source word is replaced by a nonsense word. The replacements are:

> *a: agwara*
> *e: emuger*
> *i: isimil*
> *o: ofo*
> *u: ugacher*

Thus:

rosa → *rofosagwara*   *dalia* → *dagwaralisimilagwara*

Significance and Implications

All of the play languages described here are rule-governed in the precise sense that this notion is currently used in generative phonology. The rules operate on a particular phonological or phonetic input, changing the order or sequencing of sounds and/or their nature (constituent features), thereby producing new outputs. Furthermore, the order in which the rules apply may be crucial. (For a discussion of generative phonological rules and their occurrence in play languages, see Haas 1969; and Halle 1962.)

Haas (1967) provides a taxonomy of the mechanisms or rules generally involved in play languages. These are addition, subtraction, reversal, and substitution. Most of the play languages I describe here can be accounted for in terms of these mechanisms. But other phenomena are also involved in these play languages. In French backwards talk, for example, there is first a rule which marks which categories of words are to be affected by the later reversal rule and which are not. It is interesting that this rule must operate after the ordinary French rules of elision. The seventh Javanese play language depends on knowledge of the Javanese alphabet and an ability to associate with each consonant in this alphabet another consonant, derived by superimpos-

[5] I am indebted to Margaret Medrano for these examples.

ing a backward order of the alphabet onto the normal order. The substitution rule applies after the alphabetic operation. That the ortho-graphic representation of a word (rather than its pronunciation) some-times plays a role in play languages is demonstrated by the first version of French backward talk described above. (See also Foley 1971; N. Johnson 1971; and C. Johnson 1971.)

Although the forms that the rules for play languages take are very much like those written by generative phonologists in their descriptions of language (whether synchronic or diachronic), the actual substance or details of the rules are unlike those typically found in ordinary language (again, viewed from either a synchronic or a diachronic perspective). That is, there are no documented cases of ordinary linguistic processes in which the syllables of all or most words are reversed or the same sound sequence is prefixed to all or most syllables of words. The explanation for this difference between ordinary linguistic processes and those that occur in play languages cannot be given in purely linguistic terms. Rather it has to do with one of the common social functions of play languages: concealment. Most ordinary phonological rules (e.g., the voicing of intervocalic consonants or the merger of two similar vowels) do not result in a new language so different from the original as to be difficult for native speakers to understand. On the other hand, most play languages are unintelligible to persons who do not know them (even if they are native speakers of the source language). Thus one major linguistic task of a play language is to produce distinct and hard-to-recognize forms by means of one or two relatively simple rules.[6] This is done most efficiently by making use of the rule structure or rule format of ordinary language but at the same time filling in this structure or format with possibilities not exploited in ordinary language. This is a particularly striking case of creativity in language use, especially when one considers that the play languages in question are usually played by relatively young children. It is also interesting that although the play languages typically involve only one, two, or three rules, these rules can be somewhat complex, as is illustrated above in the French and Javanese examples.

The play languages described here (and most of those discussed in the literature) involve relatively superficial and essentially phonological aspects of language. On the other hand, Hale (1971) and Joly (1981) describe play languages which operate at the level of underlying semantic contrasts, one among the central Australian Walbiri, the other

---

[6] This point is missed by Halle (1962) who labels PIG LATIN a "special dialect," but does not note the special nature of the rule which generates it and makes it incomprehensible to noninitiates.

among Blacks of the Atlantic coast of Panama. The play language of the ritual Congo drama described by Joly also utilizes considerable phonetic and phonological modification.

Play languages are relevant to the theoretical concerns of linguists for a number of reasons. First, they are a valuable source of data crucial to the solution of such basic problems as the definition and structure of syllables and words, the abstract representation of sounds, the grouping of morphemes and words into classes, and the semantic analysis of the lexicon. Many play languages are based on the syllable. The permutation of syllables or the insertion of a sound sequence at the boundaries of syllables aids the analyst of a particular language to arrive at a definition of this basic phonological unit. For example, the Kuna play languages discussed previously demonstrate that the Kuna syllable has a basic CVC structure; and that words of the shape CVCCVC are always syllabically CVC#-#CVC; and words of the shape CVCVC, CV#-#CVC. Thus in Kuna talking backwards, which moves the first syllable of every word to the end of the word, *ipya* ('eye') becomes *yaip* and *ome* ('woman') becomes *meo*.

By throwing sounds into new environments, in which they usually undergo the ordinary morphophonemic rules of the particular language, (cf. Haas 1969, for an exception to this) the play languages provide rich evidence of the kinds of patterned phonetic alternation used by linguists to posit abstract phonemes or morphophonemes. The Kuna word *in·a* ('chicha') when pronounced backwards, becomes *nain*. We have here evidence for the argument that a lengthened *n* at the surface phonetic level is represented by two short *n: nn,* at a more abstract phonological level. At this abstract level *in·a* is represented *inna*.

Play languages, such as French backwards talk, which affect certain words in sentences and not others, effectively group all words into two classes. It is interesting that in the French play language the affected words are MAJOR or CONTENT words (nouns, adjectives, verbs, and adverbs) while the unaffected words are relatively MINOR or FUNCTION words (articles and prepositions) but also pronouns, which straddle the content–function boundary. The distinction between major and minor classes of words is of course one that has been made by many theoretical linguists. (See, for example, Weinreich 1966, p. 432. Lyons 1968, pp. 435–442 discusses the related question of grammatical versus lexical meaning.)

Play languages also provide insights concerning the psychological reality of linguistic descriptions. Much of the discussion of this issue has tended toward a circular trap. The most popular view is probably that the best or in some sense the most economical linguistic description

MUST be the one employed by native speakers. (See, for example, Chomsky 1964; 1965; See Linell 1979 for another view.) This argument must be accepted or rejected on faith. Play languages, on the other hand, in which native speakers manipulate such linguistic units as syllables and abstract phonemes, offer direct evidence of how the speakers themselves actually represent these units. Coupez (1981) uses Sanga play languages to argue for the psychological reality of his analysis of Sanga syllable boundaries, the phonological status of tone, and the definition of words. (See also Campbell 1974, pp. 276–277 and Chao 1968, p. 21.)

It is rather interesting then that careful investigation of variation in the speaking of play languages strongly suggests the possibility that there is a corresponding variation in native speaker linguistic models, from the perspective of both the individual speaker and the speech community at large. Thus, for example, there is in Kuna a surface distinction between voiceless and voiced stops intervocalically: *dage* ('to come'); *dake* ('to see'). In 'talking backwards' (Kuna play language 1), all speakers say *geda* for *dage*; but for *dake* some speakers say *gedag* and others *geda* or *keda*. It is as if some speakers represent voiceless stops as underlying or abstract sequences of two identical voiced stops, while others do not. The first model is probably a more efficient and economical one from the point of view of Kuna grammar as a whole; both models, however, are descriptively adequate.

A particularly interesting example of the existence of variation in underlying models of linguistic structure is the following, revealed by an investigation of two Kuna play languages. The Kuna word for 'mangrove' is *aili*. It does not alternate with any other form. There are three possible underlying phonological representations (written here with dashes to indicate syllable boundaries):

(1)   *ak-li* (since *k* becomes *i* before any consonant other than *k*),
(2)   *ai-li*,
(3)   *a-i-li*.

In *sorsik sunmakke* (Kuna play language 1) there are two ways of saying *aili*: *liak*, which supports solution (1) above, and *liai*, which supports solution (2). In Kuna play language 4 there are also two ways of saying *aili*: *ciaicíli*, which supports solutions (1) or (2), and *ciácíicíli*, which supports solution (3).[7]

[7] See Sherzer (1970) for additional examples of variation in the speaking of this play language, and Sherzer (1975) for another sociolinguistic and ethnographic perspective on Kuna phonology.

In French 'backwards' talk, there is variation with regard to which words are affected and which are not. For all speakers, nouns, verbs, adjectives, and adverbs are always affected; articles, prepositions, object pronouns, emphatic pronouns, and the negative particle *pas* are typically not affected. An interesting category of words in this play language includes subject pronouns, possessive pronouns, and demonstrative adjectives. For some speakers these are affected; for others, they are not. Furthermore, the same speaker will sometimes treat them as affected, sometimes as not. Thus, *ce conard* ('that idiot') becomes either *ce nocard* or *que sonard*. *Mon pinard* ('my booze') becomes either *pon minard* or *mon nipard*. Thus, at least as far as this play language is concerned, subject pronouns, possessive pronouns, and demonstrative adjectives straddle the boundary between the major and the minor word classes. Linguists have alternated between treating these morphemes as prefixes (thus more grammatical, functional, or minor) and as separate, independent words (thus more content or major); it is not surprising that the same variation exists in the minds of native speakers.

The data from play languages thus enable us to reformulate the problem of psychological reality in a way that is socially more sensible. The sociolinguistic reformulation asks, for a particular speech community: What are the areas and aspects of linguistic structure for which there is variation in native speaker models? One suspects that such variation occurs in aspects of rather superficial linguistic structure (such as those typically made use of in play languages) and not in aspects of deeper structure.

Any investigation of play languages must pay attention to the social and cultural contexts and functions of their use. The play languages discussed here are derived from colloquial varieties within the repertoire of linguistic varieties in use in the speech community. Thus no Kuna play language forms are derived from words used in the formal historical–political–religious or magical–curing varieties. The Javanese play languages are played at the *ngoko* level, the lowest level of Javanese varieties on the scale of formality. French talking 'backwards' is based on the extremely colloquial slang of French adolescents. When used by French gangs, many of the source words are in an argot limited to the particular gang. Thus a double code is involved: In order to decipher what is said in the play language, one must first move back up the play language derivation rules to the source word and then translate the source word from the special gang argot into standard French.

A common function of play languages is concealment and a corresponding delineation of social groups and subgroups. That is, a major and public means of demonstrating that one is a member of a particular group is the fluent use of its play language. Children often use such play languages to keep secrets from other children and at times from their parents. Play languages may also play a role in language learning. Some Thai play languages are used by Thai children to help them learn new words and generally improve their competence in speaking. (See Haas 1957; Palakornkul 1971.) Another possible social function is pure fun. For the Kuna, the primary purpose of the play languages described above is not concealment. They are not used by certain groups of children to keep secrets from others. Rather, the play languages seem to be a form of linguistic play for play's sake.

Related to the use of play languages to delineate social groups is their use in ritual. Although most play languages that have been reported in the literature are used in nonritual contexts, two interesting cases of ritual use have been reported. The play language described by Hale (1971) is a significant aspect of male initiation rituals among the Walbiri of central Australia. These Walbiri initiation rituals involve a great deal of secrecy and the play language used in these rituals is an important aspect of this secrecy. Joly (1981) describes a play language, used by adults, as well as children, in the ritual drama of the Congos, acted out by Blacks who inhabit the Atlantic coast of Panama. It is perhaps interesting to note that in both these examples of play languages used in ritual, the play language is based on relatively deep underlying lexical–semantic contrasts.

Finally, play languages provide insights into general patterns and themes of language use and into the role of speaking in the community. For example, the 'backwards' language of the Panamanian Congo is one of the major communicative manifestations (along with clothing and gestures) of this carnival time ritual of reversal. As a second example, Parisian youth gangs are extremely concerned with publicly marking their distinctness as a group. (See Monod 1968.) A major way of doing this is through language, by means of both a special and elaborate argot and the frequent use of the complicated talking 'backwards' play languages, often based on the argot. For the Kuna, play and creativity with language are highly valued. With regard to adults, this play and creativity include expressively altering Kuna sounds, introducing nonKuna sounds, making use of foreign words, altering the names of people and things, developing metaphors, and inserting relevant jokes and anecdotes. Indeed, one way to classify Kuna genres of speaking is according to the types and degrees of linguistic creativity and play (both serious and humorous) involved in them. Although adults do not use the play languages and usually claim not to understand them, they generally consider them acceptable behavior for children and seem amused when they are used. It is as if they recognized them to be a children's variety of Kuna linguistic play. Some traditional leaders are against the use of such play languages, however, especially if they think that obscene words are being concealed in them.[8]

Play languages, then, interesting in and of themselves, also have relevance for various issues that students of language confront today—the nature of linguistic rules, the psychological and sociological reality of linguistic descriptions, and the ethnographic patterns involved in the practice of speaking.[9]

A Note on Ritual Languages

Although I have discussed the social functions and contexts of play languages in this paper, my definition of play languages was essentially a linguistic one. That is, I have defined a play language as a whole new language which is derived from a nonplay (real) language by means of a small, finite set of rules. The play language is an anamorphosis of the language it is derived from, and word-for-word translation from one language to the other is possible by means of application of the rules in either direction. The most commonly reported sociocultural functions of play languages are concealment, marking of group membership, and play and amusement for their own sake. At the same time, since one of the reported functions of play languages is as a ritual language (Hale 1971; Joly 1981), it is interesting to examine the nature of ritual languages as a postscript-note to this paper on play languages.

As distinct from the definition and characterization of play languages I provide here, ritual languages have traditionally been defined

---

[8] At the 'traditional congress' held in Mulatuppu-Sasartii in June, 1970, a visiting official from an extremely traditional village complained publicly about one of the play languages and claimed that it was obscene. Since then I have at times heard Malatuppu parents stopping their children from using the play languages, reminding them that village officials had declared them obscene. The traditional leaders might have been struck by a similarity between play languages and Kuna *sekrettos*. *Sekrettos* are short, charm-like utterances which are used to control objects in nature, animals, and human beings. They are considered both powerful and dangerous. Their effectiveness resides in language, by means of which the origin of the object or individual to be controlled is revealed. The language of each *sekretto* (considered obscene because it deals with sexual origins) is not comprehensible to anyone who has not learned it because it is a secret code—usually containing nonsense syllables or words from languages other than Kuna.

[9] The examples cited in this chapter by no means exhaust the existing cases of play languages. It has been my pleasure, since I began researching this topic several years ago, to continue discovering fascinating examples, in both published literature and personal contacts.

functionally and contextually; that is ritual language (really, the language of ritual) is that language which is used in situations and contexts which members of a society (and the anthropologists who study them) consider to be ritual. This definition enables us to recognize a great variety of types of ritual language, thus contrasting with the much more narrow and limited range of types of play language. The unifying principle of ritual language is probably best conceived in terms akin but not identical to what Malinowski (1935), in his theory of magical language, called the "coefficient of weirdness." In ritual language, we typically encounter what might be called a "coefficient of difference." That is, the language of ritual is usually (always?) different in some way from the ordinary language or languages of everyday communication of a particular community. I offer here a typological overview, illustrating the dimensions required for a cross-cultural perspective.

1. The ritual language(s) is genetically unrelated to the language(s) of ordinary communication in the community.

Example a: The use of Arabic in religious contexts in such nonArabic speaking communities as the Wolof of Senegal.

Example b: In the Xingu area of central Brazil, various indigenous groups use as one of their ritual languages a language no longer spoken which is intelligible to no one, including ritual specialists. (Anthony Seeger and Eduardo Viveiros de Castro, personal communication.)

2. The ritual language(s) is genetically related to the language(s) of ordinary communication in the community, often an archaic version or earlier stage of one of the languages.

Example: The use of Latin in religious contexts in countries where Romance languages are spoken (France, Italy, etc.)

3. The ritual language is a dialect (perhaps mutually intelligible), often including archaisms, of one of the languages of ordinary communication in the community.

Example: The ritual dialect-language of the Yanomami Indians of Brazil and Venezuela. (Ernesto Migliazza, personal communication.)

4. As distinct from types 1, 2, and 3, the ritual language does not have a historical provenance independent of its use in ritual, but rather is found only in ritual. It is distinguished from the language(s) of ordinary communication in the community along one or more linguistic dimensions—phonetic-phonological, morphological, syntactic, semantic, lexical. It is analyzable and translatable. It may or may not be intelligible to noninitiates of the ritual.

Example a: The ritual vocabularies of the Indian communities of the

American Southwest. (See Newman 1955; Opler & Hoijer 1940; White 1944.)

Example b: The three ritual languages (political–historical–religious, magical–curing, puberty rites) of the Kuna Indians of Panama, each of which is characterized by a unique set of phonological, morphological, syntactic, semantic, and lexical features. (See Sherzer 1983.)

5. The ritual language is unintelligible and unanalyzable. The native view might include the possibility of translation.

Example: The glossolalia or "speaking in tongues" of certain North American Protestant religious sects.

6. The ritual language is a play language derived from one of the languages of ordinary communication in the community.

Example a: The Walbiri (central Australian) male initiation language. (See Hale 1971.)

Example b: The ritual language used in the performance of the "Congo" drama and associated activities by Black communities of the Atlantic coast of Panama. (See Joly 1981.)

7. The ritual language is one of the languages of ordinary communication in the community, but involves certain poetic and/or rhetorical features and processes, such as parallelism or metaphor, which are particular to or characteristic of ritual discourse and contexts.

Example a: The metaphors of Ilongot magical discourse. (See Rosaldo 1975.)

Example b: The parallelistic couplets of Mayan ritual speech. (See Bricker 1974; Gossen 1974.)

8. The ritual language is characterized by certain verbal genres and/or forms of verbal interaction.

Example a: The *kabary* (ceremonial speech situation) of the Vakinankaratra area of Madagascar. (See Keenan 1974.)

Example b: The ritual dialogue found in many indigenous societies of Tropical Forest South America. (See Sherzer 1983.)

9. The ritual language is characterized by particular modalities, such as chanting, shouting, whispering, or weeping, or by particular accompaniment, such as musical instruments or gestures.

Example a: The ritual language of Kuna historical and religious discourse is 'chanted,' while the ritual language of Kuna puberty rites is 'shouted' (See Sherzer 1974.)

Example b: Jewish davening (a form of praying) which is characterized by a murmured chanting and a back and forth rocking movement of the body.

This typology is presented in the form of discrete types. In actuality, ritual communication typically involves various combinations of these types, indeed it is characterized by special, often unique constellations of verbal and nonverbal expressive forms, physical and temporal settings, and social and cultural rules for interaction. (Notice that the Kuna appear twice in the typology; Kuna examples can be provided for some of the other categories in the typology as well.) An interesting example is the Rotinese *bini*, a verbal genre characterized by parallel verse based on dyadic lexical sets created out of dialect differences on the island of Roti. (See Fox 1974.) Finally, it is important to recognize that the relationship between ordinary and ritual speech and between the various types of formal and ritual speech use in a society often involves continua and overlaps of various kinds.[10]

In conclusion, this very brief exploration of the language of ritual reveals a broad variety of possibilities involving various uses of the heterogeneous sociolinguistic resources provided by speech communities.

References

Berkovits, R. (1970) Secret languages of school children. *New York folklore quarterly, 26,* 127–152.

Bricker, V.R. (1974) The ethnographic context of some traditional Mayan speech genres. In R. Bauman and J. Sherzer (Eds.) (1974) *Explorations in the ethnography of speaking.* London and New York: Cambridge University Press. Pp. 368–388.

Burling, R. (1970) *Man's many voices.* New York: Holt, Rinehart, and Winston.

Campbell, L. (1974) Theoretical implications of Kekchi phonology. *International Journal of American Linguistics, 40,* 269–278.

Chao, Y.R. (1931) Eight varieties of secret language. (Text in Chinese.) *Academica Sinica, Bulletin of the National Research Institute of History and Philology, 2,* 312–354.

Chao, Y.R. (1968) *A Grammar of spoken chinese.* Berkeley and Los Angeles: University of California Press.

Chomsky, N. (1964) Current issues in linguistic theory. In J.A. Fodor & J.J. Katz (Eds.), *The structure of language: Readings in the philosophy of language.* Englewood Cliffs: Prentice-Hall. Pp 50–118.

Chomsky, N. (1965) *Aspects of the theory of syntax.* Cambridge, Mass.: M.I.T. Press.

Conklin, H.C. (1956) Tagalog Speech Disguise. *Language, 32,* 136–139.

Conklin, H.C. (1959) Linguistic play in its cultural context. *Language, 35,* 631–36. Reprinted in D. Hymes (Ed.) (1964) *Language in culture and society: A reader in linguistics and anthropology.* New York: Harper and Row. Pp. 295–300.

Coupez, A. (1981) A linguistic lesson. In J.P. Angenot, G. Istre, J.J. Spa, & P. Vandresen (Eds.) (1981) *Studies in pure natural phonology and related topics.* (UFSC Working Papers in Linguistics). Florianópolis (Brazil): Núcleo de Estudos Linguísticos.

[10] See Irvine (1979) for a useful discussion.

Dubois, J., Edelin, F., Klinkenberg, J.M., Minguet, P., Pire, F., & Trinon, H. (1970) *Rhétorique générale*. Paris: Larousse.

Foley, L. (1971) Green talk: A sociological and linguistic analysis. In Sherzer *et al.* (1971) *A collection of linguistic games. Penn-Texas working papers in sociolinguistics*, No. 2. Austin, Texas: University of Texas. Pp. 14–23.

Fox, J.J. (1974) "Our ancestors spoke in pairs": Rotinese views of language, dialect, and code. In R. Bauman & J. Sherzer (Eds.) (1974) *Explorations in the ethnography of speaking*. London and New York: Cambridge University Press. Pp. 65–85.

Gossen, G.H. (1974) *Chamulas in the world of the sun: Time and space in a Maya oral tradition*. Cambridge, Mass.: Harvard University Press.

Guiraud, P. (1973) *L'Argot*. Paris: Presses Universitaires de France.

Haas, M.R. (1957) Thai Word Games. *Journal of American folklore, 70*, 173–175. (Reprinted in D. Hymes (Ed.) (1964) *Language in culture and society: A reader in linguistics and anthropology*. New York: Harper and Row. Pp. 301–304.)

Haas, M.R. (1967) A taxonomy of disguised speech. Paper presented to the Linguistic Society of America.

Haas, M.R. (1969) Burmese disguised speech. *Bulletin of the Institue of History and Philology (Academic Sinica 39*, Part 2): 277–285.

Hale, K. (1971) A note on a Walbiri tradition of antonymy. In D.D. Steinberg & L.A. Jakobovits (Eds.), *Semantics: An interdisciplinary reader*. London and New York: Cambridge University Press. Pp. 472–482.

Halle, M. (1962) Phonology in generative grammar. *Word, 18*, 54–72. (Reprinted in J.A. Fodor & J.J. Katz (Eds.) (1964) *The structure of language: readings in the philosophy of language*. Englewood Cliffs: Prentice-Hall, Pp. 334–352.

Hoenigswald, H. (1959) Some Uses of Nothing. *Language, 35*, 409–421.

Hombert, J.M. (1973) Speaking backwards in Bakwiri. *Studies in African Linguistics, 4*, (3) 227–236.

Irvine, J.T. (1979) Formality and informality in communicative events. *American Anthropologist, 81*, 773–790.

Jakobson, R. (1960) Closing statement: Linguistics and poetics. In T.A. Sebcok (Ed.), *Style in language*. Cambridge, Mass.: M.I.T. Press. Pp. 350–377.

Johnson, N. (1971) You can say S F D in Corsicana, Texas. In Sherzer *et al.* (1971) *A collection of linguistic games. Penn-Texas working papers in sociolinguistics*, No. 2 Austin, Texas: University of Texas. Pp. 8–13.

Johnson, Sister C. (1971) Doggie Language. In Sherzer *et al.* (1971) *A collection of linguistic games. Penn-Texas working papers in sociolinguistics*, No. 2 Austin, Texas: University of Texas. Pp. 4–7.

Joly, L.G. (1983) The ritual "Play of the Congos" of North Central Panama: Its sociolinguistic implications. *Working papers in sociolinguistics*, No. 85. Austin, Texas.

Keenan, E. (1974) Norm-Makers, norm-Breakers: Uses of speech by men and women in a Malagasy community. In R. Bauman & J. Sherzer (Eds.) (1974) *Explorations in the ethnography of speaking*. London and New York: Cambridge University Press. Pp. 125–143.

Kirshenblatt-Gimblett, B. (1976) *Speech play: Research and resources for studying linguistic creativity*. Philadelphia: University of Pennsylvania Press.

Laycock, D. (1965) Back and fill: A cross-linguistic look at ludlings. Paper delivered to the Australian and New Zealand Association for the Advancement of Science, Hobart.

Laycock, D. (1972) Toward a typology of ludlings, or play-languages. *Linguistic communications, working papers of the Linguistic Society of Australia 6*, 61–113. Clayton, Victoria: Monash University.

Laycock, D., Lloyd, R.G., & Staalsen, P. (1969) Sub-languages in Buin: Play, poetry and preservation. *Papers in New Guinea Linguistics* 10 (Series A: Occasional Papers 22), 1–23.

Linell, P. (1979) *Psychological reality in phonology*. Cambridge: Cambridge University Press.

Lyons, J. (1968) *Introduction to theoretical linguistics*. Cambridge: Cambridge University Press.

Malinowski, B. (1935) *Coral Gardens and their magic*, Vol. II: *The language of magic and gardening*. London: Allen and Unwin.

Monod, J. (1968) *Les Barjots*. Paris: Julliard.

Newman, S. (1955) Vocabulary levels: Zuni sacred and slang usage. *Southwestern journal of anthropology 11*, 345–354. (Reprinted in D. Hymes (Ed.) (1964) *Language in culture and society: A reader in linguistics and anthropology*. New York: Harper and Row. Pp. 397–403.)

Opie, I. & Opie, P. (1959) *The lore and language of schoolchildren*. Oxford: Clarendon Press.

Opler, M.E. & Hoijer, H. (1940) The raid and war-path language of the Chiricahua Apache. *American anthropologist 42*, 617–634.

Palakornkul, A. (1971) Some linguistic games in Thai. In Sherzer et al. (1971) *A collection of linguistic games. Penn-Texas working papers in sociolinguistics*, No. 2. Austin, Texas: University of Texas. Pp. 25–31.

Price, R. & Price, S. (1976) Secret play languages in Saramaka: Linguistic disguise in a Caribbean creole. In B. Kirshenblatt-Gimblett (1976) *Speech play: Research and resources for studying linguistic creativity*. Philadelphia: University of Pennsylvania Press. Pp. 37–50.

Roberts, J.M., Arth, M.J., & Bush, R.R. (1959) Games in culture. *American anthropologist 61*, 597–605.

Rosaldo, M. (1975) It's all uphill: The creative metaphors of Ilongot magical spells. In M. Sanches & B.G. Blount (Eds.), *Sociocultural dimensions of language use*. New York: Academic Press. Pp. 177–203.

Sadtono, E. (1971) Language games in Javanese. In Sherzer et al. (1971) *A collection of linguistic games. Penn-Texas working papers in sociolinguistics*, No. 2. Austin, Texas: University of Texas. Pp. 32–38.

Sherzer, J. (1970) Talking backward in Cuna: The sociological reality of phonological descriptions. *Southwestern journal of anthropology 26*, 343–353.

Sherzer, J. (1974) *Namakke, Sunmakke, Kormakke: Three types of Cuna speech event*. In R. Bauman & J. Sherzer (Eds.) (1974) *Explorations in the ethnography of speaking*. London and New York: Cambridge University Press. Pp. 263–282.

Sherzer, J. (1975) A problem in Cuna phonology. *Journal of the linguistic association of the southwest 1* (2), 45–53.

Sherzer, J. (1983) *Kuna ways of speaking: an ethnographic perspective*. Austin, Texas: University of Texas Press.

Weinreich, U. (1966) Explorations in semantic theory. In T.A. Sebeok (Ed.) *Theoretical foundations. Current trends in linguistics*, Vol. 4. The Hague: Mouton. Pp. 395–477.

White, L.A. (1944) A ceremonial vocabulary among the Pueblos. *International journal of American linguistics 10*, 161–167.

Part III

13 SHEILA E. BLUMSTEIN

Language Dissolution in Aphasia: Evidence for Linguistic Theory

Language presents itself in the healthy adult as an indissoluble whole. Only in the context of speech errors or in the psycholinguistics laboratory do we see the fractionalization of the system and begin to gain some insight into the organization of the language processing mechanism. In contrast, in the study of aphasia we see the dissolution of the language system as the direct consequence of localized brain pathology. Aphasia then affords, as it were, an "experiment in nature" in which it is possible to explore directly the effects of brain damage on the adult linguistic grammar. Such study can provide important insights into the nature of the linguistic system and the structure and organization of its linguistic primitives. Further, it provides important evidence reflecting how the linguistic system interfaces with the cognitive system, on the one hand, and with speech physiology and acoustics, on the other. In this chapter, I will attempt to address several issues which bear directly on linguistic theory. The first issue concerns the semiautonomy of linguistic levels. The second issue focuses on the nature of the primitives representing these linguistic levels. And the third issue concerns the dissociation of the components of the grammar found in the aphasias but not necessarily compartmentalized in the same way by current linguistic theory.

Traditionally, the linguistic grammar is divided into various levels of analysis including phonology, morphology, syntax, and semantics. Following Chomsky's (1965) model, these levels of analysis are

203

incorporated into components of the grammar including syntax with a level of representation in the phrase structure rules and transformations, phonology as an interpretive component of the surface structure, and semantics as an interpretive component of the deep structure. While morphology does not constitute a separate level of representation, morphological processes are reflected in word formation rules in the lexicon, and in agreement and inflectional rules in the transformation component. Structural approaches to language have maintained a strict dissociation of levels of grammar (Joos 1963). However, current generative approaches indicate that from both a theoretical and methodological point of view these levels are not completely dissociable. Thus, although the levels of grammar are at some level independent, it is clear in the elaboration of the grammar that they are in reality only semiautonomous. For example, stress assignment rules in the phonological component require labelled brackets indicating constituent structure in order to produce the correct output (Chomsky & Halle 1968). Similarly, selectional restriction rules are determined largely by semantic constraints or real-world facts rather than by syntactic rules of the grammar (Chomsky 1965).

In accord with this notion, evidence from aphasia suggests that although linguistic levels or components of the grammar are separable components, they are not, as it were, of a piece, but rather are indeed semiautonomous. The separability of linguistic levels is seen most notably in the dissociation of syntactic and semantic components as evidenced by two distinct clinical types of aphasia—Broca's aphasia and Wernicke's aphasia. Clinically, Broca's aphasia can be characterized by the following set of characteristics: Patients show an expressive disorder which is described as agrammatic, primarily because grammatical markers such as grammatical morphemes and small lexical items functioning as grammatical markers are lost. Speech output is also often slow, labored, and dysarthric, showing a distinct phonetic disorder in addition to a syntactic disorder (Goodglass 1976; Blumstein 1981). In contrast to the poor speech output, language comprehension is relatively spared (although, see discussion of this later in the chapter, Goodglass & Kaplan 1972 example). An example of a typical speech output of a patient with Broca's aphasia is presented here; the patient was asked to describe a picture showing a little boy standing on a stool that is tipping over while he was stealing cookies from a cookie jar. To his left is a little girl aiding him and to his right is a woman washing the dishes with water overflowing in the sink. She is unaware of the children's activities as well as the water overflowing.

*Cookie jar . . . fall over . . . chair . . . water . . . empty . . . ov
. . . ov . . . ?* [Examiner: "overflow?"] *Yeah*
[Goodglass & Kaplan 1972, p. 56].

Wernicke's aphasia, in contrast, is characterized by fluently articulated but paraphasic speech. Speech output, although grammatically correct, is often described as circumlocutory and empty of semantic content. Language comprehension, however, is severely impaired. The following is an example of a Wernicke's aphasic's description of the cookie theft picture.

Well, this is . . . mother is away here working out o'here to get her better, but when she's working, the two boys looking in the other part. One their small tile into her time here. She's working another time because she's getting, too [Goodglass and Kaplan 1972, p. 61].

Several experiments have shown that not only the speech output but also the comprehension of Broca's aphasics may be subserved by a deficit in syntax and morphology. As indicated by the example, these patients are agrammatic in their speech output (Goodglass 1968; 1976). However, it has only recently been noted that these patients may have a morphological–syntactic deficit at the input level as well. Perhaps the first study to address this issue directly was conducted by Zurif, Caramazza, & Myerson (1972). They used a hierarchical clustering methodology to assess the linguistic intuitions of aphasic patients. Basically, if a subject is given a simple sentence as *The dog chases a cat*, as shown in Figure 13.1, and is asked to cluster the two words of an array of three taken from a sentence written in front of them, the patient normally clusters the words in terms of their implicit hierarchical organization, i.e., similar to a phrase structure tree. Given the same task, Broca's do not know what do to with the "small" words. As Figure 13.1 shows, they randomly assign the articles *the* and *a* with other words in the sentence. Thus, Broca's aphasics are as agrammatic in their intuitions about grammar, as they are in their speech output.

In contrast, Wernicke's aphasics seem to have basically a semantic disorder. With regard to speech production, their expressive speech suggests an impairment in the integration of the semantic properties of words within a particular grammatical framework. Thus, sentences may show an intact syntactic structure; however, they may be empty of semantic content, for example *he hit me in the thing*, or even semantically

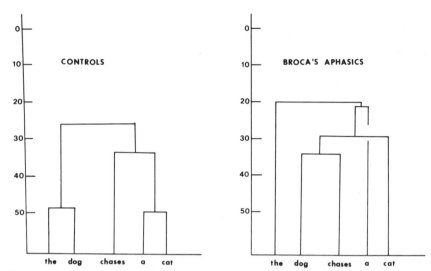

Figure 13.1. Hierarchical clustering schema for normal controls and Broca's aphasics for the sentence *the dog chases a cat.* Reprinted with permission from Neurolinguistic Disorders: Language Brain Relationships, in *Handbook of Clinical Neuropsychology,* ed. S.B. Filskov and T.J. Boll, Wiley and Sons, 1981, p. 245.

anomalous, for example *I surprise no new glamour.* At the input level, it has also been shown that Wernicke's patients have a deficit in semantic processing (cf. Goodglass & Baker 1976; Whitehouse, Caramazza, & Zurif 1978; Zurif & Caramazza 1976). One study used the hierarchical clustering methodology described previously to assess how aphasics structured lexical items sharing various semantic dimensions (Zurif, Caramazza, Myerson, & Galvin 1974). The words used (*mother, wife, cook, partner, knight, husband, shark, trout, dog, tiger, turtle, crocodile*) varied along the semantic dimensions human–nonhuman, gender, mammal–nonmammal. Nonaphasic adults group these words along the human–nonhuman dimension, and within the animal class according to species membership. When this task was given to Broca's and Wernicke's aphasics, two distinct patterns of clustering emerged. Broca's aphasics cluster the words as do normals along the human–nonhuman dimension (save for the word *dog*). The animal terms were grouped along the emotive or functional feature "ferocity" rather than species membership, i.e., mammal–nonmammal. In contrast, the Wernicke's performance was random—they were as likely to cluster *husband* with *trout* as with *wife.*

There have been a number of studies which support the idea that Wernicke's aphasics have a deficit in metalinguistic tasks requiring semantic judgments of words. These patients have shown impaired performance in tasks requiring them to categorize objects varying in perceptual and functional attributes (Whitehouse *et al.* 1978), or to judge whether a particular word was related to another word varying by associative types (Goodglass & Baker 1976). The results of these studies have shown that these patients demonstrate a restricted access to the underlying semantic relations of words in the lexicon (Milberg & Blumstein 1981).

Comparing the two components of the grammar—syntax and semantics—it seems that the language deficit of aphasic patients reflects a double dissociation. Broca's show a relatively preserved semantic component in the face of a severely impaired syntactic component. In contrast, Wernicke's show a relatively spared syntactic component with an impaired semantic component.

Nevertheless, although one can find a fairly selective deficit in components of the grammar, evidence from aphasia does not support the view that the linguistic levels are completely autonomous, nor that deficits occur in only one component of the grammar, while the remainder of the linguistic system remains intact. With regard to the semiautonomy of levels, it has been shown that the syntactic deficits found in Broca's aphasics turn crucially on the semantic reversibility of the sentence. That is, Broca's aphasics show significant deficits when the test sentences are semantically reversible, or when they have to rely on syntactic information, for example, *the boy was hit by the girl* compared to when they are semantically nonreversible, *the dog was hit by the girl* (Zurif & Caramazza, 1976). Similarly, Wernicke's aphasics do not show normal syntactic organization when given the syntactic clustering task previously discussed (Kurowski 1981). In particular, some Wernicke's patients cluster as agrammatically as do Broca's. Further, most of them have difficulty apprehending the constituency of the VP, and are as likely to cluster the verb with the subject NP as with the object NP.

These sets of results for both Broca's and Wernicke's aphasics are not all that surprising. After all, when the lexical items are susceptible to only one plausible semantic interpretation, a complete syntactic analysis can be by-passed in on-line processing. Similarly, a deficit in accessing the semantic representation of a word would likely have repercussions on correct assignment of its constituent structure. Because language is a structured system, a deficit in one component will have its effects on another. In this sense, the levels can never be completely autonomous.

However, in addition to the interaction of linguistic levels, it is never the case that aphasic patients show a deficit in one level or component of the grammar and normal processing at the other levels. That is, aphasics may show deficits of varying degrees at all levels of the linguistic grammar, and these deficits may not be attributable to the interaction of levels we have discussed. For example, in addition to a morphosyntactic deficit, Broca's aphasics show moderate to severe phonetic (Blumstein, Cooper, Goodglass, Statlender, & Gottlieb 1980) and phonological deficits (Blumstein 1973), as well as some impairments in making judgments on the semantic relatedness of words (Zurif et al. 1974). Similarly, Wernicke's aphasics show not only deficits in accessing semantic information (Milberg & Blumstein 1981), but also a limitation in the syntactic routines they have available in speech production (Gleason, Goodglass, Obler, Green, Hyde & Weintraub 1980) and a phonological deficit in speech production (Blumstein 1973). Further, it has been shown that the patterns of linguistic behavior may be remarkably similar across the different clinical groups. For example, studies on the comprehension and production of morphological endings in English have shown similar patterns of performance among aphasic patients with different syndromes (Goodglass 1968). In particular, given the third singular of the verb, and the possessive and plural of nouns, all of which follow the same morphophonemic rules, Broca's aphasics show a hierarchy of deficit in which the plural is the most preserved form, then the third singular, and last, the possessive. Such a hierarchy is not at all surprising and can be explained in terms of either morphological complexity or a theory of grammatical markedness. However, it has been shown that Wernicke's aphasics, given similar tests of production and comprehension, show an error distribution similar to that of Broca's aphasics. That is, they also find the third singular easiest, and the possessive the most difficult. Thus, their performance is hierarchically organized as well, and the nature of this hierarchical dissolution cannot discriminate across types of aphasia.

Given that the facts of aphasia support the view that the components of the grammar have relatively separate levels of representation, it is useful to consider whether the primitives operating within each component are also reflected in the aphasic's language. Linguistic primitives are part of the universal properties of grammar and have been motivated primarily by theoretical considerations internal to linguistics proper, i.e., in relation to the processes and patterns found in natural language. Each linguistic component has its set of primitives. For example, in the phonological component, the distinctive features are primitives, whereas in the syntactic component, syntactic constituents are primitives.

Performance of aphasic patients clearly shows that most of the linguistic primitives elaborated in current theories of grammar are instantiated in the grammar of aphasics. Perhaps the clearest example can be found concerning the distinctive features of the phonological component. From the time of the Prague school, linguists have suggested that the minimum phonological unit is not the segment or phoneme (Vachek 1966; Jakobson 1968). Rather, phonemes are further divisible into a finite set of acoustic–articulatory distinctive features. Studies of both the production and perception of speech in aphasia support the view that the distinctive feature is a basic processing unit. In particular, errors of speech production and speech perception may be defined by the phonological relations between the target or test stimulus and the patient's response. These errors can be characterized in terms of a distance metric based on distinctive feature relations, that is, errors are more likely to occur between segments related by one distinctive feature than by more than one distinctive feature, and also in terms of a hierarchy of feature contrasts, for example, particular types of feature contrasts, such as place of articulation, seem to be more vulnerable than other feature contrasts, such as manner of articulation. In speech production, all aphasics, regardless of clinical type, are more likely to produce errors of phoneme substitution that are one distinctive feature apart from the target than they are to produce substitutions that are more than one distinctive feature apart, e.g., *peel* → /bil/, distinguished by one feature (voice) versus *peel* → /dil/ distinguished by two features, voice and place (Blumstein 1973). Furthermore, all patients make more place than manner errors, and voicing and nasal errors occur less frequently than either place or fricative/stop manner errors. Similar patterns emerge in perception. Again, an aphasic patient is more likely to show discrimination deficits for single feature contrasts compared to feature contrasts of more than one distinctive feature (Blumstein, Baker, & Goodglass 1977). Similarly, place contrasts are much harder to perceive or discriminate than are voice contrasts.

Grammatical and lexical formatives that characterize morphological processes in language also seem to function as linguistic processing units. Traditionally, the distinction between lexical and grammatical morphemes has been used to elucidate various types of grammatical distinctions (Lyons 1971). What is of interest is that the dichotomy between these two primitives seems to be psychologically real and to function importantly in the processing of linguistic grammar. Basically, the distinction between grammatical and lexical morphemes turns on the contrast between open and closed class word items. Grammatical words or morphemes such as the copula, articles, and prepositions, contrast with lexical morphemes involving major class categories such as nouns and verbs. With a lexical decision task in which subjects are required to determine if a four or five letter string is a real word or not, normals show a different pattern of response to lexical and grammatical morphemes (Bradley & Garrett 1980). In particular, reaction time to lexical morphemes is dictated by frequency effects whereas reaction time to grammatical morphemes is not. These results were interpreted in terms of the differential role of these primitives. In this view, lexical morphemes are processed in terms of their underlying semantic representation, whereas grammatical morphemes are processed as input to a syntactic parser. This latter function critically contributes to syntactic processing of sentences.

When Broca's aphasics are tested on the same task, they do NOT show the distinction between lexical and grammatical morphemes (Bradley, Garrett, & Zurif 1980). Instead, for them, both types of words show frequency effects. Thus, these words function as part of the lexicon for the Broca's aphasics, but for these patients the function of grammatical morphemes as input to a parser seems to be selectively impaired. Such an impairment is consistent with the agrammatic performance of these patients described earlier, and suggests that it may provide the basis for the syntactic deficits they display.

The results I have treated thus far suggest that the components of the grammar and linguistic primitives elaborated by linguistic theory seem to be uniquely organized and directly reflected in the language processing mechanism. Nevertheless, it is not always the case that language behavior in aphasia may simply reflect the theoretical constructs and theoretical organization of the grammar postulated by linguistic theory. This is where aphasia may contribute importantly to the development of a theory of language processing.

There are two specific examples that can be explored, each emphasizing a different type of disparity between the theory of grammar and language breakdown in aphasia. The first concerns a language impairment in aphasia which does not have a comparable level of representation in the theory of grammar, and the second concerns a dissociation of impairments in aphasia which are not separable in the linguistic grammar.

With regard to the first, it has generally been hypothesized that the facts of aphasia would mirror the organizational principles of the linguistic grammar. Generally speaking, as elucidated previously, this seems to be the case. However, the agrammatism of Broca's aphasics does not reflect a deficit at a particular level of representation. As discussed by Kean (1980), the distinction between the major lexical categories such as N or V and the grammatical words such as Det, Prep is not a syntactic primitive. That is, there is no formal distinction in the current linguistic grammar between these two types of word classes. As a result, the deficit of these patients cannot be formally defined in terms of these theories. Furthermore, morphological processes, as such, do not have a systematic level of representation in the grammar. That is, inflectional affixes are assigned as features to constituents on the basis of syntactic structure, whereas grammatical formatives such as Det are generated in the base as feature complexes. The characteristic features of agrammatism include omission of both certain bound morphemes, e.g. *he goes* → *he go*, and of function or grammatical words, *the book is on the table* → *book on table*, as well as the replacement of morphologically marked forms with unmarked forms, e.g. replacing a verb inflected for tense with the infinitive. Thus, it is impossible to describe the agrammatism of Broca's aphasia in terms of a single level of representation. Kean (1980) discusses this issue and suggests that agrammatism can be characterized at a single level of representation in the phonological component of the grammar. In particular, in this component there is a formal distinction between phonological words and nonphonological words. She suggests that it is the phonological words which are retained in aphasia and the nonphonological words which are dropped (Kean 1979; 1980). While such an analysis may account for a number of the characteristics of agrammatism, it cannot capture the full range of deficits occurring in this syndrome. Namely, agrammatic patients have deficits in both the production and comprehension of syntactically complex sentences as well as a morphological impairment. Although one could maintain that the morphological impairment reflects a deficit in the phonological component and the syntactic deficit an impairment in the syntactic component, doing so implies that the two characteristics of agrammatism are in some sense separable and unrelated. Yet, intuitively, both the morphological and syntactic deficits seem to reflect a single impairment, namely, an inability to handle grammatical relations. The fact that the linguistic grammar cannot represent this phenomenon in a simple way could be used as evidence that the linguistic grammar is not currently appropriately elaborated, and that the formal properties of both morphological and syntactic processes must be elucidated in one component of the grammar. Such a view is consistent with more traditional descriptions of language organization (Jakobson 1964; Bloomfield 1933).

The second example showing a disparity between the organization of current theories of grammar and language breakdown in aphasia concerns the relation between speech production and perception. These theories of grammar generally assume that both speech production and perception are subserved by the same underlying mechanisms or at least share a common final pathway where the organization and processing occurs in terms of the same underlying primitives and rules. In effect, the breakdown of phonological relations characterized in terms of distinctive features and a hierarchy of features in both speech production and perception would support this notion. However, clear dissociations between speech production and speech perception abilities can be shown in aphasic patients. For example, comparison of the perception and production of voice-onset time, an important cue subserving the voiced–voiceless distinction, has shown that Broca's aphasics generally perceive the category of voice-onset time normally, but show a deficit in voice-onset time production (Blumstein, Cooper, Zurif, & Caramazza 1977). Their production deficit seems to occur both at the level of articulatory implementation and phonological planning. Wernicke's patients, on the other hand, show a relatively spared ability to discriminate the phonological contrast of voiced–voiceless, but an inability to use these contrasts in speech perception to label the contrast, namely, to indicate whether a particular acoustic signal is [d] or [t]. These same patients show nearly normal production of voice-onset time with only a few errors in phonological planning. Thus, at the level of speech processing, one can see a double dissociation between the ability to perceive and produce the sounds of speech with Broca's aphasics showing a production deficit in the face of relatively spared perception, and Wernicke's showing a perception deficit with relatively spared production.

These findings suggest that at some stage of processing there are separate grammars for perception and for production, and despite the fact that the production and perception grammars seem to be operating under similar organizational principles, they are not necessarily subserved by the same mechanism. To be sure, it can be argued that the distinction between grammars of perception and production reflects a fact about linguistic performance and not linguistic competence. Competence in this view is modality-free and only reflects the knowledge speaker–hearers have of their grammar, not how they use it or how it is instantiated in language processing. Although a distinction between linguistic competence and performance may be useful for elaborating a theory of grammar, it is less clear that it is a useful or valid construct with regard to language processing. The problem lies with the fact that in current theories of grammar, one can ignore language processing and just study language knowledge. However, with linguistic performance, it is impossible to titrate out performance from competence. Is an aphasic's deficit a competence or performance deficit? If language deficits in aphasia were due solely to a performance deficit, then linguistic competence would have to either be located in areas of the brain other than the so-called language areas, or not be located in the brain at all. The latter possibility is ludicrous. That the former possibility is not the case can be shown by evidence that damage to these "nonlanguage" areas produces minimal, if any, language deficits and further, such deficits are transient in nature (Luria 1970). Thus, one must consider that aphasics can have a partially impaired competence. But how is this formally distinguished from impaired performance? In short, we are claiming that the failure to distinguish competence and performance in aphasia does not reflect a methodological limitation, but rather reflects the fact that in language processing, there is no clear-cut distinction between competence and performance. Rather, language competence is instantiated in language performance, and the knowledge a speaker–hearer has is derived from his language processing system.

An example may help clarify this point. Recursion has been built into a competence grammar to capture the observation that sentence length theoretically has no upper bound or limit, that is, a sentence can potentially be infinite in length. The obvious fact that a speaker–hearer can neither understand nor produce an infinitely long sentence (or even one with 6 embeddings) is interpreted as a performance variable. But how can this view be incorporated into a theory of language processing? It is counterintuitive to assume that there is a limitless language mechanism which is in some way connected to a memory component that constrains the length of language input or output. Sentences are in fact finite in length and the linguistic processing mechanism is a limited-capacity system. As a result, a basic property of the linguistic grammar should be that it is syntactically finite. Recursion, then, is not a fundamental property, but a derived notion, derived presumably from the "logical" application of rules of embedding. In short, our argument is that a theory of grammar should not be more powerful than the actual instantiation of that grammar in language processing.

Returning to our original point, given that linguistic competence and performance are not dissociable constructs in a theory of language processing, then the facts of aphasia suggest that the speech production and speech perception systems do not share the same grammar. Rather they seem to be two separate components. The fact that they may share certain fundamental properties or characteristics does not mean that they perforce are part of a single mechanism. A theory of grammar must be able to characterize in an explicit way the types of dissociations which can and do occur in language processing. In this sense, aphasia provides a testing ground for both the formal properties and organizational principles that comprise a theory of grammar.

Acknowledgments

This work was supported in part by Grant NS07615 to Clark University and NS06209 to the Boston University School of Medicine. Many thanks to Philip Lieberman, Jack Ryalls, and Aditi Lahiri for their comments on an earlier draft of this chapter.

References

Bloomfield, L. (1933) *Language*. New York: Holt, Rinehart, and Winston.

Blumstein, S.E. (1973) *A phonological investigation of aphasic speech*. The Hague: Mouton.

Blumstein, S.E. (1981) Phonological aspects of aphasia. In M.T. Sarno (Ed.), *Acquired aphasia*. New York: Academic Press.

Blumstein, S.E., Baker, E. & Goodglass, H. (1977) Phonological factors in auditory comprehension in aphasia. *Neuropsychologia, 15*, 19–30.

Blumstein, S.E., Cooper, W.E., Goodglass, H., Statlender, S. & Gottlieb, J. (1980) Production deficits in aphasia: A voice-onset time analysis. *Brain and language, 9*, 153–170.

Blumstein, S.E., Cooper, W.E., Zurif, E.B. and Caramazza, A. (1977) The perception and production of voice-onset time in aphasia. *Neuropsychologia, 15*, 371–383.

Bradley, D.C. & Garrett, M. (1980) Lexical recognition for open and closed class vocabularies. In preparation.

Bradley, D.C., Garrett, M. & Zurif, E.B. (1980) Syntactic deficits in Broca's aphasia. In D. Caplan (Ed.), *Biological Studies of Mental Processes*. Cambridge: MIT Press.

Chomsky, N. (1965) *Aspects of the theory of syntax*. Cambridge: MIT Press.

Chomsky, N. & Halle, M. (1968) *The sound pattern of English*. New York: Harper and Row.

Gleason, J.B., Goodglass, H., Obler, L., Green, E., Hyde, M.R. & Weintraub, S. (1980) Narrative strategies of aphasic and normal-speaking subjects. *Journal of speech and hearing research, 23*, 370–382.

Goodglass, H. (1968) Studies in the grammar of aphasics. In S. Rosenberg & J. Koplin (Eds.), *Developments in applied psycholinguistics*. New York: MacMillan.

Goodglass, H. (1976) Agrammatism. In H. Whitaker & H.A. Whitaker (Eds.), *Studies in neurolinguistics, Vol. I*. New York: Academic Press.

Goodglass, H. & Baker, E. (1976) Semantic field, naming, and auditory comprehension in aphasia. *Brain and language, 3*, 359–374.

Goodglass, H. and Kaplan, E. (1972) *The Assessment of Aphasia and Related Disorders*. Philadelphia: Lea and Febiger.

Jakobson, R. (1964) Toward a linguistic typology of aphasic impairments. In A.V.S. de-Reuck & M. O'Connor (Eds.), *Disorders of language*. Boston: Little, Brown.

Jakobson, R. (1968) *Child language, aphasia, and phonological universals*. Translated by A.R. Keiler. The Hague: Mouton.

Joos, M. (1963) *Readings in linguistics, I*. New York: American Council of Learned Societies.

Kean, M.L. (1979) Agrammatism: A phonological deficit? *Cognition, 7*, 69–83.

Kean, M.L. (1980) Grammatical representations and the description of language processing. In D. Caplan (Ed.), *Biological studies of mental processes*. Cambridge: MIT Press.

Kurowski, K. (1981) *A contrastive analysis of the comprehension deficit in posterior and anterior aphasia.* Unpublished Master's thesis. Brown University, Providence, R.I.

Luria, A.R. (1970) *Traumatic aphasia.* The Hague: Mouton.

Lyons, J. (1971) *Introduction to theoretical linguistics.* Cambridge: Cambridge University Press.

Milberg, W. & Blumstein, S.E. (1981) Lexical decision and aphasia: Evidence for semantic processing. *Brain and language, 14,* 371–385.

Vachek, J. (1966) *The linguistic school of Prague.* Bloomington: Indiana University Press.

Whitehouse, P., Caramazza, A. & Zurif, E.B. (1978) Naming in aphasia: Interacting effects of form and function. *Brain and language, 6,* 63–74.

Zurif, E.B. & Caramazza, A. (1976) Psycholinguistic structures in aphasia. In H. Whitaker & H.A. Whitaker (Eds.), *Studies in syntax and semantics.* Vol. I. New York: Academic Press.

Zurif, E.B., Caramazza, A. & Myerson, R. (1972) Grammatical judgements of agrammatic aphasics. *Neuropsychologia, 10,* 405–418.

Zurif, E.B., Caramazza, A., Myerson, R. & Galvin, Jr. (1974) Semantic feature representation for normal and aphasic language. *Brain and language, 1,* 167–187.

14

ROBERT K. HERBERT

KAREN Z. WALTENSPERGER

Linguistics, Psychiatry, and Psychopathology: The Case of Schizophrenic Language

Introduction

The history of interest in schizophrenic-like behavioral disturbances can be read as the history of psychiatry as a field of inquiry and practice in the same way that the history of aphasiology can be read as the history of neuropsychology. Although the writings of Hippocrates (ca. 460–377 B.C.) distinguish between a select number of psychotic conditions (and there are much earlier observations in Indian and Chinese documents), it was not until the first century A.D. physician Aretaeus of Cappadocia that the essential clinical difference was articulated between patients suffering from mania and those described as *stupid, absent, and musing*—which Lehmann (1980) suggests might translate as 'stuporous, preoccupied, and in poor contact with reality.'

Most modern clinical investigators in the Western medical tradition agree that one of the clinical symptoms of schizophrenia is observed in the language and language behavior of schizophrenics. Unfortunately, the boundary between a language disturbance per se and a thought disorder expressed in language is not always clearly marked in patients' behavior or in the clinical literature. This demarcation is least clear in the semantic realm since it is here, for example, in word associations, that thought processes interface most directly with the linguistic system. Many researchers have named both syntactic and semantic disorders as characteristic of schizophrenia (e.g., Bleuler 1950), and Critchley (1964) states that aberrations of thought or personality are mirrored in all levels

217

of language—phonetic, phonemic, semantic, syntactic, and pragmantic. To be sure, Kraepelin (1917) lists phenomena of pitch, rate, rhythm, loudness, and timbre of spoken language in his concept of DERAILMENT. Clinicians frequently describe an individual as "sounding schizophrenic," but no one has successfully defined the objective components of that "sound." Vetter (1970) points to increased sophistication in techniques of acoustic analysis as potentially contributing to the description and therefore diagnostic value of this symptom, and a number of researchers are turning their attention to this problem (e.g., Clemmer 1980).

In this chapter, after a brief treatment of some of the definitional problems inherent in the diagnostic category of SCHIZOPHRENIA and in the symptom manifest SCHIZOPHRENIC LANGUAGE, we will provide a review of illustrative case studies and theoretical formulations of schizophrenic language, attempting to evaluate their practical applications for linguistic theory and clinical practice. Additionally, comparisons will be drawn between language disturbances in schizophrenia and those observed in aphasia and other organically based syndromes, for example, dementia, retardation, autism, etc. The interest in such comparisons, seem from the vantage point of neurolinguistics and neuropsychology, is in what the language behavior of schizophrenics can tell researchers about schizophrenia as an organic disease. Although the distinction between functional and organic disorders has traditionally been drawn with schizophrenia falling into the category "functional disorder," it is clear that every abnormal emotional state is produced by one or more neurological syndromes, i.e., behavioral syndromes, regardless of etiology, are mediated by the central nervous system (Pincus & Tucker 1978).

History and Definition

Many of the symptoms that characterize schizophrenia have been described since antiquity, but there is by no means agreement as to what the precise clinical definition of the term SCHIZOPHRENIA should be. Kraepelin (1917) was the first to integrate the various behavioral symptoms, unifying all primary and secondary dementias into one disease process, DEMENTIA PRAECOX, or premature mental deterioration. Kraepelin's definition includes observed clinical phenomena such as hallucinations, delusions, stereotypies, disordered affect, and negativism, as well as a prognostic factor of final deterioration. Focusing on the progressive deterioration and predominance of the disease amongst the young, Kraepelin succeeded in recognizing that a number of clinical syndromes could be viewed as forms of one disease, and in differentiating this entity from other psychoses.

In contrast to this model, Bleuler (1950/1911) provided three major modifications of Kraepelin's conceptualization. First, he noted that the disease is not confined to the young, and he substituted the term *schizophrenia* (<Greek *schizein*, 'to divide', and *phren*, 'mind'), believing that the fundamental defect is a splitting of the functions of personality. Second, he deemphasized the progressive deteriorating aspects of the disease. Bleuler regarded any individual presenting the major symptoms as suffering from the disease, regardless of the prognosis for recovery; Kraepelin, on the other hand, thought that a clinician might have to wait for several years to observe the outcome of dementia and confirm the diagnosis of dementia praecox (Lehmann 1980). According to this latter view, schizophrenics who exhibit recovery have been misdiagnosed. Bleuler's final contribution was to view schizophrenia as a group of related disorders in place of Kraepelin's single disease concept. The common features in all the schizophrenias include disturbances of affect, association, and volition; Bleuler considered the clinical picture described by Kraepelin, which included hallucinations, negativism, delusions, stupor, etc., as constituting secondary symptoms.

Further contributions to the diagnosis and treatment of schizophrenia were made by Freud, by Bleuler's student Jung, and by the American Adolph Meyer, the father of the psychobiological school of psychiatry. In large part, however, all modern approaches to the study of schizophrenia derive, directly or indirectly, from the work of Kraepelin and Bleuler, with differences in diagnostic symptoms reflecting differences in conceptualization of the disease schema. The most restricted diagnostic systems for schizophrenia emphasize thought disorders exclusively (e.g., Schneider 1959). More flexible systems recognize a broader symptomological base. For example, the World Health Organization's *International Classification of Diseases* (ICD-9) lists ten subdivisions under the general heading of schizophrenic disorders, e.g., disorganized type, catatonic type, paranoid type, etc., and the *Diagnostic and Statistical Manual of Mental Disorders* (DSM-III) (1980) mentions a wide range of characteristic symptoms involving multiple psychological processes, including: content and form of thought, perception, affect, sense of self, volition, relationship to the external world, and psychomotor behavior. The diagnosis of a particular subtype is based on the predominate clinical picture although the classificatory type 295.9x (Undifferentiated type) is designed for those patients judged to be schizophrenic, but who do not fit into one of the more narrowly defined groups. Due to such imprecise categorization and basic definitional problems, some researchers have suggested that the label SCHIZOPHRENIA be dropped entirely (Szasz 1961). However, there is now convincing evidence that schizophrenics can be reliably diagnosed by clinicians with common training, even in diverse national and cultural settings (WHO 1973). For purposes of the present chapter, we may define schizophrenia as a disease "characterized by a special type of alienation of thinking, feeling and relation to the external world which appears nowhere else in this particular fashion [Bleuler 1950]" affecting approximately 1% of the world's population.

It is interesting to note that clinical practicioners agree that the linguistic systems of schizophrenics are in some ways aberrant, but language disturbances do not function significantly within the lists of behavioral symptoms (Bernheim & Lewine 1979; Chapman & Chapman 1973; Salzinger 1973) or among the diagnostic symptoms listed in the DSM-III, the diagnostic manual most commonly used in psychiatric facilities and mental health centers in the U.S., or in the ICD-9. According to Pincus & Tucker (1978), schizophrenia continues to be considered a "functional" (i.e., psychogenic) disorder, "the product of environmental stress," rather than a neurological dysfunction, largely because the means of establishing the diagnosis have been limited exclusively to history and observation, age of onset, clinical course, family history, phenomenology of symptoms, and response to treatment. They argue, however, that schizophrenia must be considered a dysfunction of the brain which is easier to diagnose than to define. The consistency in constellation of symptoms, only slight cross-cultural variation, and only small changes in the clinical picture over time support the disease concept of schizophrenia.

Research interest in schizophrenia has frequently focused on the aberrant communications that schizophrenics sometimes produce (Chaika 1974, 1977; Kasanin 1944; Maher 1973; Pavy 1968; Schwartz 1978; Vetter 1968, 1970, etc.). Part of the difficulty in providing a synthesis of the various reports derives from differences in definition, as well as imprecise reports of symptomotology and the data on which conclusions are based. Further, there is a frequent confusion in the literature between the terms LANGUAGE, a symbolic communication system characterizable by general rules, and THOUGHT, that which is made public by language (cf. Brown 1973); many studies which purport to deal with the language aspects of schizophrenia actually focus on word associations, memory structure, encoding processes, and so on, or deal with discourse aspects of schizophrenic language, such as flight of ideas and circumstantiality, thus investigating the links between linguistic and cognitive functions (e.g., Rochester & Martin 1979). This terminological confusion is sometimes resolved by a distinction between *schizophrenic language* and *schizophrenic speech, schizophrasia, schizophasia, "schizophrenese"*, and so on. However, individual authors may or may not use the latter terms interchangeably, a situation which only confounds the basic definitional quagmire. For the sake of convenience, the present authors use the term *schizophrasia* interchangeably with *schizophrenic language,* and reserve *schizophrenic speech* to refer to the vocal aspects of the communications of schizophrenic individuals.

Linguistic Features of Schizophrasia

The following sections will present illustrative examples from the clinical and experimental literature which seek to describe and delimit the range of aberration observed in the language behavior of schizophrenics. Before proceeding to such description, it is appropriate to address a few words to the various sources of data in the relevant literature. One of the outstanding features of schizophrenic language research by linguists and nonlinguists alike is the heavy, though not exclusive, reliance on written texts. There are presumably a number of factors which explain this situation: First, a nonlinguist may not be sensitive to observed differences in spoken and written media and may assume identity between the two; second, researchers may choose to work with a written corpus because of its greater reliability, the transcription of oral data being complicated by the use of neologisms and the general problems in transcribing suprasegmental features essential to schizophrenic speech; third, the visuo-graphic character of texts authored by schizophrenics is interesting and often enlightening, frequently testifying to the schizophrenic's distorted sense of conventional organization and world view. This factor was first noted by Bleuler (1950). Examples of typical bizarre use of space and graphic characters are found in Figures 14.1 and 14.2. An additional explanation for the heavy reliance on written texts is an apparent assumption that, in principle, written data provide more direct access to schizophrenics' linguistic "competence" as opposed to the initial performance character of much schizophrenic speech.

Three further facts require mention at this time. First, most of the major studies of schizophrasia have been conducted with speakers of Indo-European languages, especially German, French, and English. Second, much of the data available in English, particularly from the earlier works, have been translated from other languages. Third, there is

Figure 14.1. Illustrative example of one schizophrenic subject's written composition and use of space.

a noticeable difference in the types of linguistic observations cited in the various reporting formats: detailed case studies of a single individual, generalizations based on the behavior of large, heterogeneous, usually institutionalized, psychotic populations, experimental manipulations of linguistic perception and production, as well as the expected difference

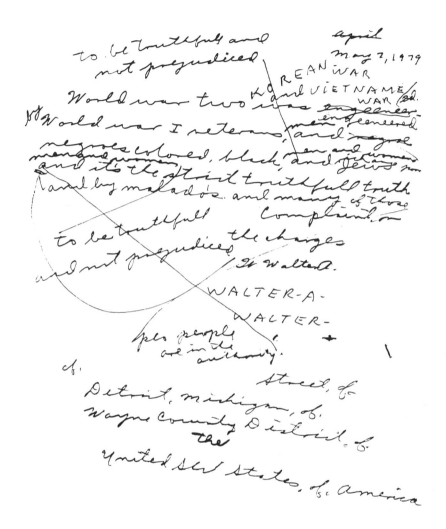

Figure 14.2. Second example of the writing of a schizophrenic subject.

in detail and type of data cited by linguists and clinical investigators or practitioners. All of these factors, as well as the previously described definitional issues, contribute to the initial impression of confusion that follows from a reading of the literature on schizophrenic language.

For the sake of expository clarity, we have attempted to classify the relevant studies into categories corresponding to conventional levels of linguistic description; however, it will be clear that there is some overlap in classification. For example, the phenomenon of LOOSENING OF ASSOCIATION has been described at the lexical, semantic, syntactic, and morphological levels. Moreover, it must be stressed that the following is by no means a comprehensive review or synthesis of the literature; constraints of space, coupled with the conceptual complications described earlier, preclude such a treatment at this time.

Semantic Aspects of Schizophrasia

The preponderance of work on schizophrenic thought and language disturbances focuses on semantic aspects of linguistic behavior, particularly in relation to loosening of associations. The classic psychiatric diagnostic technique of word association has been extensively employed in research with schizophrenic subjects, attempting to demonstrate that schizophrenics give fewer common word association responses than nonschizophrenics. However, the bulk of studies in this tradition seem to indicate that the associational mediations of schizophrenics do not differ significantly from normal subjects. Indeed, as Schwartz (1978) points out, schizophrenics' associations may be more common than those of some college students.

This finding is seemingly in conflict with the numerous reports in the clinical literature of irrelevant associations frequently produced by schizophrenic patients. For example, one of Bleuler's patients, when asked with whom she had been walking the previous day, referred to members of her family, listing "father, son", and then adding, "and the Holy Ghost." Similarly, Maher (1973), citing an earlier study, reported that one of his patients wrote: "I like coffee, cream, cows, Elizabeth Taylor." Maher suggested that what is bizarre about such associations is not the associations themselves, but rather the fact that they intrude into schizophrenics' utterances. Several theories have been developed to explain such intrusion, e.g., Salzinger et al., (1970) presented the immediacy hypothesis, which contends that schizophrenic behavior is controlled by stimuli in the immediate environment. In the case of schizophrasia, this means that any individual word may be a response to some immediately preceding word rather than to the semantic intention of the utterance as a whole. This may relate to the observed frequency of puns in schizophenic utterances, for example, "Canada look for peace and piece of ass," produced by one of the present authors' subjects. However, Chapman & Chapman (1973) hypothesized that schizophrenics' associations are explained instead by an inability to inhibit the dominant meaning of a multiple-meaning word; they suggest that intrusion of association with a dominant meaning is most common when a word is used with one of its less common meanings, e.g., the word *date* used in its gastronomic sense may elicit an association with another meaning (either calendar or social).

Another proposed explanation for this phenomenon is based on a distinction between literal and figurative meanings; however, there is little evidence to support this interpretation at present. Other investigators have attempted to view schizophrenics' associations as a shift to more concrete and less abstract modes of thought. While it appears that schizophrenic thought tends to be "concrete," there are no empirical studies that satisfactorily extend this concept to an explanation of word associations. A strict word association model would seem, in fact, to have little to contribute to a comprehensive theory of language in psychopathology.

Closely related to "word associations" are two other phenomena observed in some patients. The first has been termed a "klang association" of a word to the initial syllable of a previous word, for example, *subterfuge—substitution, contention—contradiction*. Second, there is the well-known tendency of many schizophrenics to perseverate, which might also be considered as a type of association, especially since schizophrenics, in experimental settings, are often observed to respond to a stimulus with a repetition of the stimulus, i.e., the first word that comes to mind is the word itself. This phenomenon will be treated in greater detail on page 237.

Many investigations have been conducted on the relative lack of redundancy in schizophrenic language; these studies are based on the observed tendency of schizophrenic patients to be disorganized and hence less redundant when communicating about ambiguous or complex events. One of the more common measurements of redundancy in language is achieved through the use of cloze analysis. In this technique, a transcript of the text to be measured is presented with every nth (usually fifth) word omitted; normal readers are then given the text and asked to judge what the missing words might be. Salzinger, Portnoy, & Feldman (1964) reported that the speech of schizophrenics is less redundant (i.e. harder to predict) than the speech of normals. Other studies have attempted to demonstrate that schizophrenic patients also benefit less from redundancy in language than do normal individuals; cf. page 229.

Also within the semantic field of behavior, many investigators have noted a common difficulty of schizophrenics in interpreting or explaining proverbs. For example, Forrest, Hay, & Kushner (1971) asked one subject to explain the meaning of "a rolling stone gathers no moss," and the patient responded *a rolling stone is a new moon—which is other side, and blue on the far side, where are the Russians.* This observed difficulty has frequently been related to the figurative–literal or concrete–abstract continua discussed previously: one subject explained *people in glass houses shouldn't throw stones* by saying *because people would see me in my house and throw stones at me* (Pincus & Tucker 1978). This proposed explanation, referring to concrete–abstract difficulties, is not easy to accept when one considers that schizophrenics often respond in a bizarre fashion when asked for the definition of a single common noun. For example,

Q: *What is a shop?*
A: (Pause) *Well, I suppose a shop was where somebody who couldn't get past the bank examiners who had to come down through the banks and shown a shop at some borderline examination shopping bar. However, somebody had broken down the manifold and overclaimed in somebody's life and had got in a muddle and we think scouts should be called in to organize their sorts of imposition bar migraines as in connection with the shops.* [Forrest, Hay, & Kushner 1971].

Such utterances, coupled with the bizarre associations and low redundancy found in much schizophrasia, along with the tendency to perseverate, contribute to the general clinical symptoms which has been described as "incoherence" (Lehmann 1980). This supports the conclusion drawn by Salzinger *et al.* (1964) who found that schizophrenics' "ability to communicate" is lower than that of normal persons.

The semantic properties previously listed all interface with the thought process and are less than purely linguistic in nature. Among the true linguistic features considered to have diagnostic value is the phenomenon of NEOLOGISM, that is, the coinage of new words or the use of accepted words in a bizarre and unusual manner. Herbert & Waltensperger (1980a) reported the following neologisms in one of their subjects:

*I'm don't like the way I'm **pupped** today.*

*. . . with syndicates organized and **subsicates** in the way that look for a civil war.*

*. . . **wared** me.* ('made war on me')

It is noteworthy that when speech and language are mentioned as diagnostically critical, it is generally an impairment at the semantic level of analysis that receives attention. So, for example, a primary diagnostic criterion for schizophrenia in the DSM-III (1980) reads: "incoherence, marked loosening of associations, marked illogical thinking, or marked poverty of content of speech . . ." Similarly, Lehmann (1980), under the heading "Disorders of Verbal Behavior," lists the following clinical features: excessive concreteness and symbolism, incoherence, neologisms, mutism, echolalia, verbigeration, and stilted language. This list is typical of that found in the psychiatric literature, which tends to view the bizarre language of schizophrenics as resulting from the interaction of various factors on cognitive processes. This is certainly in keeping with Bleuler's view that one of the primary features of schizophrenia is a disorder of thinking. Although theoretical linguists might question the accuracy and value of categorizing several of the above phenomena as semantic in nature, this disagreement points to the fact that it is not always possible to separate linguistic and nonlinguistic aspects of cognitive impairment. In part, this is due simply to the fact that cognitive impairment is most frequently manifested in the vehicle of language, but some of the blame must be attributed to linguists, who have not precisely defined the boundaries of semantics, which, in fact, change from one theoretical model to the next. The phenomena classed as semantic impairment in schizophrasia point to the need for linguists to address this question more seriously; the imprecision generated by a lack of coherent definition contributes to the more basic definitional problems associated with the terms SCHIZOPHRASIA and SCHIZOPHRENIC LANGUAGE previously discussed. Ultimately, it may not be possible to completely separate that which is linguistic from that which is thought-symbolic, but this is certainly a topic which deserves more serious attention from linguists than it has received in recent models, especially since this is one of the most vexing issues in clinical linguistics. Although they are not frequently mentioned in the diagnostic literature, it is certainly true that grammatical disturbances appear in the language of schizophrenics, and these will be discussed on page 229.

Discourse and Pragmatic Features of Schizophrasia

No review of language in schizophrenia would be complete without some mention of the pragmatic and discourse features of communication. The complexity of this topic, as well as constraints of space, preclude a comprehensive overview. Therefore, the following discussion will be restricted to a few representative concerns.

There is no doubt that the thought disorder typical of schizophrenia compromises an individual's communicative competence. Such symptomatic features as thought blocking, flight of ideas, loosening of associations, and poverty of content of speech have major implications for conversational behavior. In addition, the schizophrenic individual's common autistic tendencies, disturbances of affect, delusions, hallucinations, and impaired sense of self (loss of ego boundaries) make relating to others fundamentally problematic. Bizarre language features such as echolalia, perseverating, and "klanging" further contribute to a schizophrenic's overwhelming difficulty in maintaining contact and rapport with the surrounding world.

Chaika (1974) discusses the seeming breakdown in hierarchical linguistic rules in schizophrenic syntax and discourse; she notes that the schizophrenic appears unable to control or suppress focusing on inappropriate semantic features and phonological features (e.g. punning, alliteration, rhyming) and allows these disruptive trends to govern his discourse. Some clinical investigators, emphasizing the autistic tendencies of schizophrenics, have suggested that bizarre use of language functions as a defense mechanism to insulate them from others and the outside world. Sullivan (1944), for example, noted that the schizophrenic, as a result of experiences and emotional disorder, is convinced that it is impossible to gain satisfaction from interactions with other people; consequently, he ceases to use language to communicate and he increasingly uses language for the purpose of obtaining security by manipulating it for magical operations. This is similar to Cameron's (1944) view that, in schizophrenic disorganization, "social communication is gradually crowded out by fantasy" and that the schizophrenic, in the course of progressive isolation, comes to speak an "asocial dialect full of idioms that have value only for himself." This strategy is very well illustrated by the case of M.M., one of the patients described by Herbert & Waltensperger (1980b). M.M is a 29-year old black male, who lives in an abandoned car in a vacant lot adjacent to a community mental health center. The patient reports hearing voices in a secret language which only he understands. M.M is quite willing to demonstrate this language upon request, and the authors have elicited long lists of lexical items but little narrative text, so that the structure of this "language" remains M.M.'s secret. When questioned about the language's origins, Mr. M.M. volunteered that it was a mixture of "Hebrew and the Swiss" and was spoken only by himself and the invisible people who live in his hair or on various other parts of his body. M.M. characterizes the voices as friendly and supportive in nature and generally takes a protective attitude toward the welfare of the invisible speakers. For example, on one occasion, while being fingerprinted, M.M. became distraught and accused a police officer of having "killed three little people on the end of my finger." Mr. M.M. is severely alienated from society, and he therefore finds solace, friendship, and support, in the idioglossic voices of his hallucinations.

Although there is general agreement that schizophrenics have difficulty in forming and maintaining human relationships, not all clinical investigators support the notion that schizophrenics desire a communicative distance from the world at large. For example, Lehmann (1980) interprets "schizophrenic echolalia" (cf. the following) as well as "stilted use of language", e.g.

a real magnanamous good morning to you on this first Wednesday of our glorious New Year

I have not yet heard . . . from any one of my own colleagues when I am leaving this noble institution of the healing arts

as extraordinary efforts to maintain social relations.

For a detailed review and analysis of schizophrenic discourse, cast in a particular theoretical framework, see Rochester & Martin (1979).

Syntactic Aspects of Schizophrasia

An early psycholinguistic study by Gerver (1967) tested recall in schizophrenics, nonschizophrenic psychiatric patients, and normals under different noise conditions for three sentence types: (1) grammatical and meaningful, (2) grammatical and meaningless, (3) ungrammatical and meaningless. The three subject groups present similar profiles, scoring highest for recall on Type 1, and lowest for Type 3 sentences. Schizophrenics showed very poor performance for Type 3 sentences, perhaps due to associational mediations not found in the other two subject groups. However, it is certainly worth noting here that schizophrenics have significantly more misperceptions of stimulus words than normals with whom they are matched for auditory acuity; the misperceptions are presumably due to difficulties in recognition (Maher 1973). Attempting to demonstrate that schizophrenics benefit less from redundancy in language than normal individuals, Truscott (1970) employed four classes of material: (*a*) normal sentences, (*b*) anomalous sentences, (*c*) anomalous but semantically related word strings, (*d*) random word strings, e.g.,

(*a*)   *Snug rings bind chubby fingers.*
(*b*)   *Snug olives spread splintered splintered subdivisions.*

(c)   *Rings snug fingers chubby bind.*
(d)   *Olives snug subdivisions splintered spread.*

Schizophrenic patients were inferior to normals in recall for all of the four types, with the greatest difference being found for Type (*a*), where normal subjects showed markedly increased performance, but the schizophrenics performed only slightly better than in Types (*c*) and (*d*).

Many investigators have noted the ungrammatical character of many schizophrenic utterances (e.g., Bleuler 1950; Chaika 1974; Critchley 1964; Lehmann 1980), but relatively little data are available from which to draw conclusions regarding the degree and type of syntactic impairment in linguistic production. Fromkin (1975), Maher (1973), Rochester & Martin (1979), and Shapiro (1979), claim that there is very little in syntactic organization that can be described in psychotic language. In fact, Shapiro maintains that grammar, once learned, is a remarkably stable feature of the human mind. Disorders of anaphora and ellipsis are generally treated within the semantic, rather than syntactic, framework in schizophrenic language research.

A recent report of a longitudinal case study of a single paranoid schizophrenic individual (DSM-III: 295.3x) by Herbert & Waltensperger (1980) listed numerous examples of morphological and syntactic aberrations. For example, verbs often appear in their uninflected form:

> *I'm write letters in self defense and have been write for 25 years already*
> *Russia and Israel is try to drive me to approve of war against Canada*
> *I'm not interested in become a socialist*

Other errors in tense and aspect marking are also apparent in the subject's language:

> [She] *has been blackmail me . . .*
> [They] *are got FBI credentials on my name*
> *I'm was railroad*
> *. . . the letter I'm wrote*

The contracted form *I'm* seems to be reanalyzed and functions as the first person singular pronominal subject marker, e.g.:

> *I'm could*
> *I'm was die*
> *I'm was a Catholic Church annulment*
> *the money I'm inherited from my pa*
> *my ma . . . used rat poison to get the _____ family and I'm the last man*
> *   of it and I'm don't feel so good*

As Critchley (1964) noted, there is a grossly heightened incidence of the first person singular in schizophrasia that is not found in other organic disorders. However, it should be noted that the above reanalysis also occurs with less frequent non–first person singular items, e.g.:

> They're threatened me with the mad war weapon
> They're use me as an excuse

This phenomenon of reanalysis is commonly observed in children's early language, where it is explained as a segmentation error, e.g., It's has wheels.

Herbert and Waltensperger noted that the individual in question introduces relative clauses by the marker that or by no marker at all:

> Bishop W _____ that play dead . . .
> It's my brother, etc., Father Emil-Joe _____, plan to kill me because I'm god by heritage and yet by ancestry

The most striking feature of this subject's grammar, however, is his readily apparent difficulties in word class organization and production. For example, the predominant construction for adverbial formation is an idiosyncratic derivational element -way:

> fun way
> sexual way
> medical way
> open way
> Polak national socialist secret way

The more common -ly formation occurs with very few adjectives, e.g., remote and complete. Further, it is interesting to note that adverbial modifiers are commonly misplaced within an utterance:

> Hawaiians are very sick mental way people
> Dominion of Canada gives me a cholera headache m.d.'s way and must be without a reason of a doubt mad completely incurable

There are other problems besides those with adverbs in derivational morphology, e.g., in nominalizations:

> This country is supposed to be based on the give of death to war mongers and not war
> I'm going to stop the letter write since Canada made a sucker out of me with electrical shock treatment shock
> I'm was a Catholic Church annulment without the go to Italy
> . . . and succeed in the pull of a perfect crime

> *I'm had a sexual intercourse with her and was framed the next day by*
> *artificial inseminate*

Syntactic problems are also evident in the subject's bizarre use of prepositions:

> *Some doctor is mad completely for the fix of me m.d.'s way to have an*
> *urge to try have another dose of drug I'm got after prescribed on me*
> *especially if I'm got brainwashed m.d.'s way and wasn't sure if I'm took*
> *a dose of as prescribed.*
> *I'm disqualify into to go of Washington, D.C., one nation indivisible*
> *because of the war letters in self-defense against foreign I'm wrote*
> *. . . atomic plant at Oak Ridge, Tennessee, in Tennessee, went bad with*
> *the experiment of neutralize my health and put on me in severe strain.*

These examples illustrate another organizational problem in the placement of constituents in the subject's discourse, as do the following:

> *A subsidiary of General Electric tried to make me die of despair*
> *in _____ State Mental Hospital . . . over the scrap I took when I'm*
> *worked there for souvenir reasons.*
> *Doctor _____ turned in I'm understand the truth is the books to you.*

On the surface, many of this subject's utterances would be considered "word salad" by practitioners uninterested in identifying underlying structures, but closer examination reveals the frequently disguised semantic intent of such agrammatic strings. The interesting question raised by this phenomenon is whether such anomalous strings of words can be accounted for by an impaired system of linguistic rules or by some other cognitive–organizational deficit. Certainly, the integrity of most major constituent groups and remarks such as Shapiro's on the "indissolubility" of syntax would likely favor aberrant rule explanation. The question then becomes how such aberrations might develop neurologically and neurolinguistically. Further, the fact that the majority of syntactic rule types remain intact whereas others, such as those involving movement, are subject to impairment, suggests a possible hierarchy. Of course, the constraints on movement which produce such normally ungrammatical sentences such as those just cited require further investigation before such an issue can be addressed. In the long run, it will be profitable in discussions of linguistic impairment to separate TYPES of syntactic impairment, e.g., in the transformational component, various types of agrammatism. The question which then arises is whether these types are themselves hierarchically ordered and what the underlying basis of such a hierarchy might be. In order to test the validity of such possibilities, it is necessary to examine similar phenomena in other language disorders, and this task presupposes a greater consensus among linguists as to the precise boundaries of syntax, morphology, semantics, and pragmatics. Such consensus seems remote, but it is certainly a priority in the clinical applications of linguistic models.

It needs to be emphasized that although the extreme syntactic and morphological disorder in the language of the subject previously described is uncommon among schizophrenics, the subject's history and course of treatment over 35 years has been completely consistent with the schizophrenic diagnosis, e.g., the administration of pheno-thiazines, and it seems safe to assume that the label chronic schizo-phrenic, paranoid type (295.3x) is accurate, with the prominent per-secutory delusions and hallucinations expected in this type, as well as the magical thinking more generally characteristic of the schizophrenias as the following selection demonstrates:

> *BENSON-FORD and CLAY-FORD fixed me up so I can't pray and when I'm pray I'm talk prayer words specific as I'm could and they become miracle words and the three sets of miracles clears up the weather when all the clouds run away from above me and in half hour or more the weather gets very clear in the sky and I'm don't drink drinks I'm dies twenty-seven times in hospital and they brought me to life every time and it's the strict truthful truth.*

Phonetic and Phonological Aspects of Schizophrasia

Chaika (1974; 1977) lists two characteristics which relate to the phonological level in schizophrenic language: (*a*) the inappropriate noting of phonological features of words in discourse, and (*b*) the production of sentences according to phonological and semantic features of previously uttered words rather than according to a topic. This latter characteristic relates most directly to the schizophrenic associations discussed previously; at the phonological level of as-sociation, the KLANGING ASSOCIATIONS described by Maher (1973) are relevant examples. Similar phonological focusing is also exhibited in a schizophrenic's tendency to engage in rhyming behavior, mentioned by Forrest (1968) and others, as well as the senseless phonological evolution of Kraepelin's patient, who in response to the German word *Bett* said:

> *Bett, Bett, Bett, dett, dett, dett, ditt, dutt, dutt, daut, daut, daut, dint, dint, dint, dutt, dett, datt. Wenn ich angefangen habe, fahre ich fort bis zu Ende.*

This response is perhaps related to phonological perseveration, common in both the language of schizophrenics and of some aphasic and brain-damaged populations. Perseveration at all levels of linguistic organization is discussed in the following section. Another example of inappropriate noting of phonological features, leading to bizarre associations is seen in the patient whose language was described on page 233.

Dr. _____ that for peace and piece of ass by hand and excuse the vulgar language instead peace in mind.

The exact relationship between phonetic and semantic realms in these examples, where phonological mediation seems to generate word associations, requires further investigation. In addition to the language behavior of other language-impaired populations, a potentially fruitful avenue of investigation would include an examination of environmental factors in this interface. It has frequently been observed that there is great individual variation in linguistic competence in areas such as rhyming behavior and also in other types of linguistic manipulation such as riddling, punning, etc. Longitudinal studies of children's language development demonstrate that such behavior involves both sociolinguistic and linguistic maturation. An interesting question that arises is whether the same underlying mechanisms responsible for the observed maturation are also implicated in the language behavior of schizophrenics.

Phonemic transformations and paraphasias seem to be no more or less common in the speech of schizophrenic subjects than in the speech of normal subjects (Critchley 1964; Fromkin 1975; Lecours & Vanier-Clement 1976). However, as was mentioned in the introduction, this is not to imply that schizophrenics sound "normal" on the phonological level. On the contrary, there is a recognizable deviance to schizophrenic speech, which seems more properly confined to the paraphonological level.

In an informal unpublished study by Waltensperger (1980), 50% of professional and paraprofessional employees of a community mental health center claimed to be able to identify a schizophrenic on the basis of an initial telephone interview. In addition to affective qualities of language, those individuals interviewed cited such features as "flatness of speech," lack of intonation, monotony, and choppy sentences, as diagnostic aids. Rochester et al. (1977) studied pausal durations and frequencies in schizophrenics, and they found that thought-disordered schizophrenics had hesitation patterns different from those of normal speakers. However, as Clemmer (1980) points out, there are certain methodological problems marring their conclusions. In a study of text retelling by schizophrenic and normal subjects, Clemmer found that schizophrenic speech was characterized by a considerably greater number of spoken hesitation syllables per 100 syllables than normal speech. Attributing this difficulty to disruptions in "train of thought" or "sequencing of ideas," Clemmer concludes, somewhat hastily, that it is clear that schizophrenic dysfunction is cognitive rather than linguistic. Certainly, further research in the area of paralinguistic phenomena in schizophrenic speech are in order, particularly in the temporal and rhythmic aspects of speech. The fact that it is the suprasegmental aspects of speech which are frequently implicated in schizophrasia again brings to mind relevant developmental factors. Specifically, since paralinguistic and suprasegmental features are observed earlier than segmental development, it is interesting that these features are commonly first involved in deviant speech. This points once again to the basic untenability of a strict regression hypothesis approach to language dissolution, as one would expect those features first acquired to be the most stable within the linguistic system (Caramazza & Zurif 1978). Along with many other facets of schizophrenic language discussed in this paper, this fact calls into question the hierarchical nature of linguistic phenomena. In terms of a typology of language disturbances, one would want to know, for example, whether certain points within any proposed hierarchy are more liable to disturbance than others, and what the relationships among individual pathologies, their linguistic manifestations, and hierarchical ordering would be. Although strict regressionism cannot be maintained, the inclusion of developmental data would seem to preclude specific proposals at this point. However, it is certainly an area to which linguists must again turn their attention in the future.

Perseverations in Schizophrasia

One of the most outstanding clinical features in the schizophrenic's use of language lies in the tendency to perseverate at all levels of linguistic organization. It is important to note that perseveration is not unique to schizophrasia, but is found widely among brain damaged and organically-impaired populations, e.g., aphasics, autistics, retardates, and so on. Perseveration is particularly common at the clause level, for example, Critchley (1964) reports the following passage:

> *Soon get me home by Easter I hope. Soon may I come home to you at Easter by my birthday I hope to be home. I hope to be home. I hope to be home soon, very soon. I like chocolate eclairs. I fancy chocolate eclairs. Chocolate eclairs. Donuts. I want donuts . . .*

This example clearly demonstrates this particular patient's tendency to lock into a particular idea which then continues to express itself in successive utterances. The more typical perseveration at a phrase level is also apparent in schizophrenic utterances as the following example from Maher (1973) demonstrates:

> *Kindly sent it to me at the hospital. Send it to me, Joseph Nemo, in care of Joseph Nemo and me who answers to the name of Joseph Nemo will care for it myself. Thanks everlasting and Merry New Year to Metholatum Company for my nose, for my nose, for my nose, for my nose, for my nose, for my nose.*

This example involves several types of perseveration: (*a*) the ideational, (*b*) one with slight changes in meaning of a word (*care*), and (*c*) simple phrasal repetition (*for my nose*). Some investigators have suggested a link between these types of perseveration and the associational mediations discussed previously. That is, the perseverated item (sound, syllable, word, phrase, clause, or thought) elicits an associational intrusion, which is a copy or near-copy of itself.

Another common pattern in perseveration is observed in the patient whose language was described by Herbert & Waltensperger (1980a), where the perseveration occurs at the level of fixed, formulaic phrases. Specifically, the patient controls a small repertoire of discourse formulae, which he employs with notable frequency and repetition. This repertoire includes:

> *I'm hope and I'm also pray*
> *and it's the strict truthful truth*
> *to be truthful and not prejudiced*
> *and I'm stay non-partisim* [sic]
> *because there's laws of this land*
> *ever and ever, God forever and ever*
> *complaint on the charges*

The first four examples occur freely anywhere within the discourse, whereas the latter examples tend to function as discourse closers. It should also be mentioned that these fixed phrases may occur perseverated or in combination with one another. The example *ever and ever, God forever and ever* is often elicited when the adverb *ever* occurs within the text. This is similar to the example reported by Bleuler where his patient's description of her family members included *father, son . . . and the Holy Ghost*. Here, too, the associational mediations seem to be present to the extent that the patient is unable to control noncompletion of the formula even though some other meaning is intended.

Perseveration is also noted at the level of single word:

I was under under under as ob observation at [town]
State Hospital, [town], Michigan, Michigan, Michigan
Before the go go go of me to ———— aftercare center
Dominion of Canada government went bad too, too, too
strict truthful truth
electrical shock treatment shock

A general appreciation of the extent to which perseveration may be apparent in schizophrasia is obtained from a consideration of the following letter in the authors' possession:

April 8, 1977

All those that mixed races to become socialists to be truthfull [sic] and not prejudiced are out to doaway [sic] with me the m.d.'s way and tried to kill me already for 22 years already m.d.'s way with the mad war weapon and it's the strict truthfull [sic] truth and segregation is mental health and it's the strict truthful truth, among whites to be specific, and not among Jews a creed to be truthfull [sic] and not prejudiced and colored negro or black to be truthful and not prejudiced and it's the strict truthful truth, especially if with the mix of races causes epilepsy and it's the strict truthful truth. I'm white to be specific and it's the strict truthful truth.

[signed]

In the discussion of associational testing, it was mentioned that certain schizophrenics respond by repeating the stimulus word itself. It has been suggested that this can be explained by the immediacy hypothesis, where the first word to come to the patient's mind is the word which he has just heard. It should be pointed out, however, that such responses might be related to the phenomenon of echolalia sometimes attributed to schizophrenic patients. Certain investigators, e.g. Lehmann (1980), use the term ECHOLALIA to describe the situation in which a patient will respond to an interviewer's questions using many of the same words that the questioner has employed, e.g.

Examiner: *How did you sleep last night?*
Patient: *I slept well last night.*
Examiner: *Can you tell me the name of your head nurse?*
Patient: *The name of my head nurse? The name of my head nurse is Miss Brown.*

Lehmann suggests that the patient, aware of his ideational shortcomings, uses this strategy as a compensatory mechanism in order to maintain a rapport with the interviewer. However, Lehmann's and others' neologistic use of the term ECHOLALIA to describe this phenomenon is certainly at variance with its more common definition as employed in neurolinguistics and aphasia research.

True echolalia is occasionally found in schizophrenics, as is verbigeration, a senseless repetition of the same word or phrase which may go on for days at a time. This latter symptom is rare and generally found only in patients in long-term institutional settings. An equally rare sympton, elective mutism (in noncatatonics), is also observed occasionally in patients in long-term psychiatric inpatient facilities. Many of the more unusual linguistic and behavioral symptoms reported in the early literature on schizophrasia are seen less frequently since the advent of the phenothiazines in the 1950s, which has allowed the wide-scale deinstitutionalization and chemotherapeutic maintenance of large clinical populations in the community. Implications of this important shift in the clinical picture as expressed in treatment modality and functional level will be discussed in the next section. Finally, it will have been noted that many of the previously mentioned phenomena, both as individual symptoms and as constellations of symptoms, also appear in other organically impaired populations. Similarities and differences will be discussed.

Neurolinguistic Aspects of Schizophrasia

It has been well established for almost a century and a half that speech and language functions are lateralized in the left cerebral hemisphere of the human brain. In addition to the necroscopic evidence presented by Dax, Broca, Wernicke, and others, there is now convincing experimental and clinical support for this finding from dichotic listening, tachistoscopic visual hemifield presentations, electroencephalography, hemidecortication, commisurotomy studies, neuropharmacological manipulations, studies of regional cerebral blood flow, and electrical stimulation of the cerebral cortex.

Aphasic disturbances have occupied central positions in the development of the disciplines of neuropsychology and neurolinguistics. Initial interest on the part of linguists in the area of aphasia and other language disturbances seems to focus on theoretical issues in an attempt to find empirical evidence supporting or refuting particular formulations of linguistic models. However, there has been a very noticeable shift in orientation, and linguists now participate in interdisciplinary research teams and make clinical and experimental contributions to the field. By contrast, there has been no such apparent interest in psychotic language, due perhaps to the alleged "functional" (rather than "organic") basis of schizophrenia and related disorders, and also to the very wide variation in the linguistic performances of individual schizophrenics, rendering generalization across types difficult, if not impossible.

There are several tantalizing suggestions in the literature on schizophrenia hinting at similarities between schizophrasia and aphasia: Chaika (1974), Critchley (1964), Forrest, Hay, & Kushner (1971), Herbert and Waltensperger (1980a), Maher (1973), Strub & Black (1977), Pincus & Tucker (1978). However, there exist no comprehensive treatments of this question. Again, due to the extreme difficulty in making valid generalizations about the linguistic behavior of ALL schizophrenics, one is seemingly reduced to comparisons of the language of a single schizophrenic with language performance in the organically based disorders (aphasia, dementia, and so on). Such comparisons would seem to have little clinical or diagnostic value; however, it may be that more sophisticated and precise classification of schizophrenic subtypes will allow for broader-based comparisons.

Meanwhile, we shall restrict ourselves to select comparisons of discrete linguistic features, remaining cognizant of the fact that none of the features described in this paper are observable in the language of schizophrenics of all diagnostic types or in all individuals within a single type. It is hoped that, in the long run, more detailed and controlled descriptions of the language disturbances observed in the range of schizophrenias will have clinical and diagnostic contributions to make.

Improvements in techniques of psychiatric management of acute psychotic episodes and in long-term maintenance and rehabilitation of chronic sufferers reduces the potential variation in the available institutional population and makes the longitudinal study of subjects in acute, fully exacerbated, floridly psychotic states next to impossible to conduct. A further implication of the advances in psychiatric treatment is that subject populations studied by clinical investigators today differ diagnostically, therapeutically, prognostically, and in degree of severity from those classic populations studies by Kraepelin, Bleuler, Freud, Jung, Meyer, and others. The question of populations becomes significant, for example, in the study of differences during stage and course of illness.

For example, Shimkunas (1978) proposes a tentative nomological mapping of the structure of thought disorder in schizophrenia, which he views as an asymmetrical dysfunction in cortico-hemispheric integration. According to this model, overexcitation of the left hemisphere, during acute stages, disrupts the verbal–conceptual reasoning and focal–attentional–informational processing, leading to a breakdown of verbal–temporal information processing strategies and causing the patient to seek compensation in right hemisphere perceptual–emotional mediation. During chronic states, conversely, right hemisphere overexcitation intensifies perceptual–emotional mediation, "potentiating narrowed attention to subcortically stimulated imagery in the context of behavior withdrawal." Such a model has obvious parallels with Chaika's (1974; 1977) largely unsupported view of schizophrasia as an intermittent aphasic disturbance. In Shimkunas' conceptualization, the discontinuity between thought and affect observed in schizophrenia results from a malfunction in inter-hemispheric nerve fibers; this malfunction serves to disconnect con-ceptual from perceptual and emotional mediation. There is some support in the clinical literature for schizophrenia being mediated by abnormal interhemispheric connections, e.g., Rosenthal & Bigelow (1972).

Several investigators have also proposed models of left hemisphere dysfunction for schizophrenia. For example, Gur (1978) found that schizophrenics exhibit left visual field advantage in both syllable recognition and dot localization tasks whereas normal subjects tend to exhibit right visual field advantage for the former, i.e., the schizophrenics tested showed right hemisphere superiority for both linguistic and spatial stimuli. Schweitzer et al. (1978) claimed to have found behavioral evidence for left hemisphere overactivity in schizophrenic patients, and Gur (1977) reported that there is an increased tendency for sinistrality in schizophrenics, which may also point to left hemisphere dysfunction. In a series of studies involving schizophrenics, manic-depressive patients, and normals, Flor-Henry (1976) found predominant left temporal EEG abnormalities in the schizophrenics and right temporal abnormalities in the manic-depressive group. Also of considerable interest in this regard is the study by Bear & Fedio (1977), identifying self-reported and observed psychological features which distinguish epileptic patients with right and left temporal foci. The authors point out there is no reason to believe that schizophrenia and other observationally-based diagnostic categories should mirror the behavioral consequences of neurological processes at specific loci. Still, it is intriguing that right temporal epileptics report more elation whereas left temporal epileptics describe more anger, paranoia, and dependence; the left temporal group was identified with a sense of personal destiny and a concern for meaning and significance behind events. Such patterns are generally consistent with prior studies of emotional differences between patients with right and left hemisphere lesions, although the underlying basis for such differential behavior is unclear. The various experimental methods and measures employed by different researchers makes integration of the experimental literature difficult; Wexler (1980) provides an excellent review of the literature dealing with cerebral laterality and psychiatric disorders.

The view of schizophrenia as a left hemisphere dysfunction, and recent interest in the essential organic, rather than functional (i.e., psychogenic), nature of the disorder, leads directly to a comparison of language behavior in schizophrenia and the aphasias. Critchley (1964) attributes to Rümke and Nijam an early suggestion that the "secret of schizophrenia" might lie in a high level aphasic disturbance. However, as Critchley points out, unlike the situation in aphasia and dementia, there appears to be no true inaccessibility of vocabulary or grammar in schizophrenia; the schizophrenic fails in his communicative intent by virtue of his disordered thinking processes and not linguistic impairment per se. Both schizophrenics and some aphasics engage in neologistic behavior, although schizophrenic neologisms are typically more consistent and recurring (Lecours & Vanier-Clement 1976; Strub & Black 1977) whereas aphasic neologisms tend to be random and nonsymbolic. Chaika (1977) disputes this dichotomy on the basis of her single subject X; the present authors' subjects certainly do exhibit consistent reemployment of neologisms.

Another pathological linguistic feature common to both schizophrasia and some aphasias is perseveration at all levels of linguistic organization (cf. Buckingham, Whitaker, & Whitaker 1979). The seeming behavioral identity in this phenomenon may perhaps be distinguished in aphasia and schizophrasia by underlying psychological and neurological mechanisms of associational mediation in schizophrenia, which is presumably not the case in aphasia perseverations.

Echolalia is also observed in both schizophrenic and aphasic populations. It is difficult to give an adequate appraisal of its dimensions in schizophrenia as it occurs rarely and in only the most severe cases, which again raises the point that psychiatric advancements in symptomatic management compromise accessibility to an adequate subject pool.

At the level of comprehension, testing reveals that some aphasics (e.g., Wernicke's aphasics, jargonaphasics) exhibit gross deficits, whereas the same receptive impairment is not usually observed in schizophrenic populations, though lack of cooperation on the part of subjects makes comprehension frequently difficult to evaluate. Similarly, repetition may be impaired in certain aphasias, but only rarely in the schizophrenias. In naming tasks, aphasics may exhibit difficulties, due either to lexical retrieval deficits, or may produce phonemic paraphasias. Only the former, that is, retrieval difficulties, are observed in dementia, and neither in schizophrenia. Schizophrenics are likely to produce the correct name, although they will frequently embed it in strings of irrelevant or marginally relevant associations:

Q. *And what is this thing?*
A. *That's a cigarette.*
Q. *What are cigarettes used for?*
A. *They are usually used, you can use them for trade with natives, so I believe, or, um, in this country you can use them for smoking.* [Forrest *et al.* 1971]

On the basis of a small survey, Critchley (1964) found no difference in the type/token ratio or verb-adjective ratio in aphasics and schizophrenics.

A striking behavioral difference between aphasics and schizophrenics is that aphasics seem reluctant to express themselves in writing, whereas the opposite is true of schizophrenics, who often produce voluminous written texts. Further, the schizophrenic will frequently embellish penmanship, write in all directions across the page, insert extensions, and so on, suggesting that the written page is barely large enough to contain his or her expression; see Figures 14.1 and 14.2. These peculiarities are typically not observed in aphasic writing (Critchley 1964).

Demented patients frequently exhibit difficulties in praxis and drawing. Whereas the schizophrenic patient may distort graphics, he or she can usually make recognizable copies of designs and figures. Ideational apraxia may be observed in aphasics and demeted patients, but not in schizophrenics (Strub & Black 1977).

The grammatical differences described for schizophrenics are typical, in many instances, of some agrammatic errors reported for Wernicke's aphasics: confusion of verb tense, errors in pronoun, case and gender, and incorrect choice of prepositions. The schizophrasic described on page 230 also produces long syntactic strings replete with lexical substitutions, semantic non-sequiturs, neologisms, conflusion of inflexional morphemes, perseverations, and stereotypic phrases. However, he does not exhibit any of the receptive impairment characteristic of Wernicke's asphasia, and his linguistic symptomatology does not fit well with any other common category of aphasia.

In order to complete the neurological comparison between schizophrenics and other organics, it is necessary to give at least passing mention to other neurological impairments frequently observed in schizophrenia. Pincus & Tucker (1978) report on a series of studies in which neurological "soft signs" were found in 65–75% of the schizophrenics examined. These minor neurological signs included: stereognosis, difficulty in coordination, balance, and gait, tremor, graphasthesia, bilateral marked hyperreflexia, cortical-senroy abnormalities, cranial nerve abnormalities, defective auditory-visual integration, and so on. Pincus and Tucker suggest that these neurological "soft signs" are minor only in their motor and sensory manifestations, but reflect a widespread dysfunction throughout the nervous system which gives rise to serious behavioral and intellectual abnormalities. This view is in keeping with the general belief that behavioral manifestation of symptomatology in the schizophrenias and the dementias does not reflect underlying focal lesions but rather diffuse degeneration or impairment, which in schizophrenia may be mediated by any number of possible factors (e.g., biochemical, metabolic, toxic, genetic, and so on) not yet identified.

Chaika (1974; 1977) suggests that language disorders in schizophrenia should be viewed as "intermittent aphasias" due to the effect of focal "disturbance in those areas of the brain concerned with linguistic production." The view of schizophrasia as an intermittent aphasia is explicitly rejected by Lecours & Vanier-Clement (1976) and by the analysis above, which is not to suggest that language deviance in schizophrenia may not be episodic. Moreover, it should be noted that it remains an empirical question whether the overlap in schizophrasia and aphasia are motivated by the same neurological and neuropsychological mechanisms, or whether the overlap perhaps reflects a simple "common end path" (Forrest et al. 1971), that is, whether there is biological as well as behavioral identity in the symptoms.

Conclusion

In this brief chapter, we have attempted to provide a sketch of the history and clinical and diagnostic significance of the disorder known as schizophrenia. The most salient characteristics of language disturbances observed in schizophrenics were selectively reviewed with particular attention made to structural deficits in schizophrasia. At several points during the course of the discussion, we have stressed that the entire complement of symptoms will not be present in the language of EVERY or, in fact, ANY single schizophrenic patient. Thus, the "checklist" approach to schizophrasia (e.g., Chaika 1974) is inherently unsatisfying.

Comparison of the features of schizophrenic language with language disturbances present in other organic disorders was sketched. Although the view of schizophrasia as an intermittent aphasia is rejected since there is no evidence for focal disturbances in schizophrenia, its biological basis remains to be determined. In addition to the inherent interest in comparisons of aphasia and psychotic language disturbances, this type of research may eventually help to elucidate the underlying neurological and neuropsychological organization of language and speech in normal individuals. That is, as several other chapters in this volume suggest, the study of exceptional language advances our understanding of the nature of "normal language." A unified field approach to the study of language in psychoses, in aphasia, and other pathological organic conditions, as well as in neurologically unimpaired speakers and hearers is a prerequisite to an understanding of linguistic performance and competence in these various individual states as well as to a fuller appreciation of the complex relationship that exists between the symbolic communication system known as LANGUAGE and the biological organ known as the BRAIN.

References

Bear, D.M. & Fedio, P. (1977) Quantitative analysis of interictal behavior in temporal lobe epilepsy. *Archives of neurology, 34,* 454–467.

Bernheim, K. & Lewine, R. (1979) *Schizophrenia: Symptoms, causes, treatment.* New York: W.W. Norton.

Bleuler, E. (1950) [1911]. *Dementia-praecox and the group of schizophrenias.* New York: International Universities Press.

Brown, R. (1973) Schizophrenia, language and reality. *American psychologist, 29,* 395–403.

Brown, J. (1977) *Mind, brain and consciousness: Neuropsychology of consciousness.* New York: Academic Press.

Buckingham, H., Whitaker, H., & Whitaker, H. (1979) On linguistic perseveration. In H. Whitaker & H. Whitaker (Eds.), *Studies in neurolinguistics,* Vol. 4. New York: Academic Press.

Cameron, N. (1944) Experimental analysis of schizophrenic thinking. In J. Kasainin (Ed.), *Language and thought in schizophrenia.* New York: W.W. Norton. Pp. 50–64.

Chaika, E. (1974) A linguist looks at "schizophrenic" language. *Brain and language, 1,* 113–118.

Chaika, E. (1977) Schizophrenic speech, slips of the tongue, and jargonaphasia: A reply to Fromkin and to Lecours & Vanier-Clement. *Brain and language, 4,* 464–475.

Chapman, L. & Chapman, J. (1973) *Disordered thought in schizophrenia.* Englewood Cliffs: Prentice-Hall.

Caramazza, A. & Zurif, E. (Eds.) (1978) *Language acquisition and language breakdown: Parallels and divergencies.* Baltimore: Johns Hopkins University Press.

Clemmer, E. (1980) Psycholinguistic aspects of pauses and temporal patterns in schizophrenic speech. *Journal of psycholinguistic research, 9,* 161–185.

Critchley, M. (1964) The neurology of psychotic language. *British journal of psychiatry, 110,* 353–634.

DSM-III. (1980) *Diagnostic and statistical manual of mental disroders (3rd ed).* Washington, D.C.: American Psychiatric Association.

Flor-Henry, P. (1976) Lateralized temporal-limbic dysfunction and psychopathology. *Annals of the New York Academy of Sciences, 280,* 777–795.

Forrest, D. (1968) Poesis and the language of schizophrenia. In H. Vetter (Ed.), *Language behavior in schizophrenia.* Springfield: Charles C. Thomas. Pp. 153–181.

Forrest, A., Hay, A., & Kushner, A. (1971) Studies in speech disorder in schizophrenia. In R. Cancro (Ed.), *The schizophrenic syndrome: An annual review 1,* 636–651. New York: Brunner/Mazer.

Fromkin, V. (1975) A linguist looks at "A linguist looks at 'schizophrenic' language." *Brain and language, 2,* 495–500.

Gerver, D. (1967) Linguistic rules and the perception and recall of speech by schizophrenic patients. *British journal of social and clinical psychology, 6,* 204–211.

Gur, R. (1977) Motoric laterality imbalance in schizophrenia. *Archives of general psychiatry, 34,* 33–37.

Gur, R. (1978) Left hemisphere dysfunction and left hemisphere overactivation in schizophrenia. *Journal of abnormal psychology, 87,* 226–238.

Herbert, R. & Waltensperger, K. (1980a) Schizophrasia: Case study of a paranoid schizophrenic's language. *Applied psycholinguistics, 1,* 81–93.

Herbert, R. & Waltensperger, K. (1980b) Language in psychopathology: Bilingual auditory hallucinations. Paper presented at American Anthropological Association, Washington, D.C., December 3–7, 1980.

ICD-9. (1979) *International classification of diseases, (9th revision)* Geneva: World Health Organization.

Kasanin, J. (Ed.) (1944) *Language and thought in schizophrenia.* Berkeley: University of California Press.

Kraepelin, E. (1917) *Lectures in clinical psychiatry.* New York: Wood.

Lecours, A. & Vanier-Clement, M. (1976) Schizophasia and jargonaphasia. *Brain and language, 3,* 516–565.

Lehmann, H. (1980) Schizophrenia. In H. Kaplan, A. Freedman, & B. Saddock (Eds.) *Comprehensive textbook of psychiatry/III.* Baltimore: Williams & Williams. Pp. 1104–1113, 1153–1192.

Maher, B. (1973) The language of schizophrenia: A review and interpretation. In R. Cancro (Ed.), *Annual review of the schizophrenic syndrome, 3.* New York: Brunner/Mazel. Pp. 91–114.

Pavy, D. (1968) Verbal behavior in schizophrenia: A review of recent studies. *Psychological bulletin, 70,* 164–178.

Pincus, J. & Tucker, G. (1978) *Behavioral neurology.* New York: Oxford University Press.

Rochester, S. & Martin, J. (1979) *Crazy talk: A study of the discourse of schizophrenic speakers.* New York: Plenum.

Rochester, S., Martin, J., & Thurston, S. (1977) Thought-process disorder in schizophrenia: The listener's task. *Brain and language, 4,* 95–1114.

Rosenthal, R. & Bigelow, L. (1972) Quantitative brain measurements in chronic schizophrenia. *British journal of psychiatry, 121,* 259–264.

Salzinger, K. (1973) *Schizophrenia: Behavioral aspects.* New York: John Wiley.

Salzinger, K., Portnoy, S., & Feldman, R. (1964) Verbal behavior in schizophrenics and some comments toward a theory of schizophrenia. In P. Hoch & J. Zubin (Eds.), *Psychopathology of schizophrenia.* New York: Grune & Stratton. Pp. 92–128.

Salzinger, K., Portnoy, S., Pisoni, D., & Feldman, R. (1970) The immediacy hypothesis and response-produced stimuli in schizophrenic speech. *Journal of abnormal psychology, 76,* 258–264.

Schneider, K. (1959) *Clinical psychopathology.* New York: Grune & Stratton.

Schwartz, S. (1978) Language and cognition in schizophrenia: A review and synthesis. In S. Schwartz (Ed.), *Language and cognition in schizophrenia.* Hillsdale: Lawrence Erlbaum. Pp. 237–276.

Schweitzer, L., Becker, E. & Welsh, H. (1978) Abnormalities of cerebral lateralization in schizophrenia patients. *Archives of general psychiatry, 35,* 982–985.

Shapiro, T. (1979) *Clinical psycholinguistics.* New York: Plenum.

Shimkunas, A. (1978) Hemispheric asymmetry and schizophrenic thought disorder. In S. Schwartz (Ed.), *Language and cognition in schizophrenia.* Hillsdale: Lawrence Erlbaum. Pp. 193–235.

Strub, R. & Black, F.W. (1977) *The mental status examination in neurology.* Philadelphia: F.A. Davis.

Sullivan, H. (1944) The language of schizophrenia. In J. Kasanin (Ed.), *Language and thought in schizophrenia.* New York: W.W. Norton. Pp. 4–16.

Szasz, R. (1961) *The myth of mental illness.* New York: Dell.

Truscott, I. (1970) Contextual constraint and schizophrenic language. *Journal of consulting and clinical psychology, 35,* 189–194.

Vetter, H. (Ed.) (1968) *Language behavior in schizophrenia.* Springfield: Charles C. Thomas.

Vetter, H. (1970) *Language behavior in psychopathology.* Chicago: Rand McNally.

Waltensperger, K. (1980) Language attitudes in the community mental health center. Unpublished manuscript.

Wexler, B. (1980) Cerebral laterality and psychiatry: A review of the literature. *American journal of psychiatry, 137,* 279–291.

WHO. (1973) *Report of the international pilot study of schizophrenia.* Geneva: World Health Organization.

15 LISE MENN

Child Language as a Source of Constraints for Linguistic Theory

Introduction

Unlike many of the areas of exceptional language discussed in this volume, child language has some history of being acknowledged as a potential source of constraint on the construction of linguistic theory. It is invoked with varying degrees of seriousness in a fair number of recent papers in phonology, usually in support of some proposed general constraint on rules. This chapter is concerned with the quality of acquisition-based arguments in current phonological theory: Some invalid arguments will be discussed, and some which I believe to be valid will be presented as examples of the potential usefulness of acquisition considerations. (For semantic and syntactic discussions germane to this topic, see Slobin 1977, 1979; Traugott 1977).

Three tacit assumptions seem to underlie most careless argumentation from child phonology:

1. The properties of child phonology can be derived deductively, by simply "working backwards" from a theory of adult phonology (see Menn 1980).

2. The ways in which child phonology corresponds to adult phonology are obvious.

3. Child phonology is simpler than adult phonology.

The first two of these are false; the third is a slippery half-truth which we will consider further in the concluding section of this paper.

EXCEPTIONAL LANGUAGE AND LINGUISTICS

The basic problem in arguing from acquisition is that we cannot derive "learning principles" and "operating principles" deductively. The human mind, although usefully regarded as an information processing device, was not designed by an artificial intelligence laboratory. Instead, it evolved in response to unfathomed internal and external environmental pressures. Arguments such as Jakobson's in favor of binary phonological features (that 2 is the optimal number for coding decisions) MAY be relevant to the actual working of language users, but such relevance must be supported by argument and evidence in each individual case.

Theory construction in developmental psycholinguistics cannot proceed a priori; instead, the theoretician must operate by observing what children do and then asking "What sort of a creature would be benefitted by following such strategies? If this is the behavior of the device, what kind of device might it be?" In other words, the child must be treated with the respect due any other unknown system.

Current Approaches to Phonological Theory

There are two familiar theoretical approaches to constraining the power of generative phonology. Some phonologists—say Bruce Derwing or Joan Bybee (Hooper)—can be seen as attempting to minimize the distance between underlying and surface representation (Derwing 1973; Hooper 1979). Others—for example Sanders, Dinnsen, Donegan & Stampe (all in Dinnsen 1979)—constrain the steps within a derivation, requiring them to bear certain relations to one another, to be of a certain type, or to be small in some sense. For each approach, developmental psycholinguistic rationales are customarily offered, and up to a point, there are merits to be found in those rationales. No one can deny that children must start figuring out how the phonology of their language works by starting from the presented surface, or the generalizations which are true on the surface should, other things being equal, be easier to acquire than generalizations made opaque by surface exceptions. One must grant a first round to those who want their phonology and morphology concrete. And when we consider the shallower parts of phonology, dealing with co-articulation and other phenomena of phonetic realization, natural rules may reasonably be supposed to be preferred by the learner as far as the pronunciation side of "acquiring a rule" is concerned. The cognitive allomorph-connecting aspect of rule acquisition, however, seems to be governed by other principles—see Slobin (1973), MacWhinney (1978), Kiparsky & Menn (1977).

And here we come to the point: Acquisition, although it surely affects the eventual shape of language, is such a rich process of analysis and reanalysis that we cannot go beyond the most elementary level of armchair consideration without intensive fieldwork and laboratory work. Furthermore, there is absolutely no justification in what is presently known about the acquisition of phonology for the strict formal constraints on rules that some theorists urge.

The Acquisition of Morphophonemic Rules

A good start on a data-based model for the acquisition of morphophonology has been made by Brian MacWhinney in his 1978 monograph of that name. He worked with extensive diary and experimental materials from Hungarian, German, and other languages with a richer morphophonology than English. On the basis of these data he suggests, I think correctly, that the acquisition of even the simplest productive patterns of morphological marking require several passes or "cycles" through the same material. Each live rule, then, will pass through two or more cycles (whether they do so one at a time or whether similar ones "go through" in groups remains to be studied).

Cycle 1: The child learns some inflected or derived forms by rote as wholes. This notion, although it seems radical to most generativists, is supported by all observation and experimentation (e.g., Berko 1958; Cazden 1968). MacWhinney's terms for these items is "amalgams"; one might also paraphrase Moskowitz (1970) and call them "morphological idioms." At this stage with respect to pluralization, for example, a child might use *apple* versus *apples* correctly, having learned that *apple* is for one apple and *apples* is for referring to two or more of them. But she would omit the plural marker on some regular-plural words; crucially, there would be no overgeneralizations or generalizations to new words.

Such a rudimentary level of knowledge is sometimes spoken of as being "contextually determined"—but that must be understood as referring to semantic context (presence of one versus several apples) as well as syntagmatic context (selection of the word "apple"). Again, this level is one in which both the inflected word and the marked meaning are still unanalyzed gestalts; the marked forms are presumably associated with the unmarked forms, but they are not derived from them yet. A comparably primitive state of knowledge for some adult English speakers might exist, say, with respect to the *-ceive, -cept* allomorphy: an association exists between the morphs and there is a contextual "feeling" for when each is to be used, but there is no apparent ability to generalize that knowledge.

Cycle 2: (For each rule), the child begins to analyze words morphemically. In doing so, she will also run across some instances of allomorphy if there are any, but she will not at this level have discovered which allomorph to use in which context. Overgeneralization of one allomorph to inappropriate contexts now occurs; for the child learning the English plural, for example, we now get both generalization of *s/z* to new words and overgeneralization of it to words with irregular plurals.

Cycle 3: Rules governing allomorphy (if any) appear in place of gross overgeneralizations. It is important to note that MacWhinney has a good many claims (which I will not enumerate here) about which hypotheses a child will make first: other things being equal, the earlier ones will be those applying most generally (in several senses of the word). There is NO blanket statement that one or another type of rule has absolute priority in the child's discovery procedure.

Cycle 4: Case by case, the child finds out whether the allomorphy rules that she formulated on Cycle 3 still lead to error. Phonological conditions on rules are refined, and lexical exceptions are noted; irregular forms are produced correctly.

Cycle 5: Lexical exceptions to a rule are collected into lexical classes (declension classes, gender classes, lexical strata) if phonological rules cannot predict the allomorphies (and if there are enough lexical exceptions to warrant the formation of lexical classes).

Argumentation about Constraints on Rule-ordering

Now: Extrinsic rule ordering, as the reader knows, arises when we attempt to capture patterns existing among exceptions to a rule. MacWhinney's third, fourth, and fifth cycles all involve the discovery of such patterns. For example, cycle 3 overgeneralization of the vowel change in *sing, sang, sung; ring, rang, rung;* to *bring, brang, brung* shows that English learners are sensitive to this irregular tense marker as a pattern. Translation of this fact about English speakers into standard generative formalism is done by ordering the vowel-change tense-marking rule before the regular suffixation tense-marking rule.

This simple demonstration shows that rule-ordering in morphology (and I think in general) CAN be learned. The question is, in each specific instance, HAS it been learned? That is, has the connection among various exceptions to a rule been apprehended by a given speaker or not? And at what level has it been apprehended—as a list or as a generalizable pattern? These are psycholinguistic questions, not meta-theoretical ones.

In connection with rule-ordering, we should consider a good example of flawed argumentation from child phonology. Bruce Derwing caught me in an incorrect argument for the learnability of rule-ordering, and the mistake I made is worth examining since it is one of a prevalent and tempting type.

It is well known that very young children coping with the problems of pronouncing their language often develop fairly elaborate procedures for "transducing" the words that they hear into something that they can pronounce. In most cases we can capture these procedures in the all-powerful notation of generative phonology. Frequently, there are patterned sets of exceptions to these transduction procedures, and as we have just noted, rule-ordering is the way to capture those patterns without generative formalism. The "psychological reality" of the exception patterns cannot be denied, since the child herself has created them.

The above sequence of true propositions about child phonology was offered, unfortunately, as an argument for the admissibility of ordered rules in adult generative theory. And Derwing was quite right to complain at that point: One cannot correctly argue from these cases of rule INVENTION to the case in which children must APPREHEND rule ordering in the language "out there" around them. The two cases have only a formal resemblance; the "reality" of rule-ordering in each must be argued on its own merits.

Abstractness

Let us now return to the problem of abstractness in phonology, raised previously as the problem of trying to decide when to ascribe knowledge of a rule to a speaker—that is, the problem of psychological reality. Here I have a new proposal for some acquisition-based research.

There was a superb set of position statements on "psychological reality" in phonology which can be found in Volume II of the *Proceedings of the Ninth International Congress of Phonetic Sciences*. Yet in spite of all the well-made points in that psychological reality symposium, something was missing which an acquisition perspective could have supplied: a confrontation with the complexity of the notion "knowledge of a rule." (See, however, Cutler 1979.)

Ronnie Wilbur and I suggested in a pair of papers some years ago (Wilbur & Menn 1974; 1975) that linguists are not merely faced with the problem of deciding whether or not to take "psychological reality" tests into account in our formulation of underlying forms and rules; we must also deal with the fact that speakers know some rules sketchily and others thoroughly. That is the nature of human knowledge; we can hum along with more tunes than we can sing solo, we can understand more words than we can use properly, and Dorian (this volume) has now shown that some people fully understand a second language that they can barely speak. Similarly, Wilbur and I demonstrated experimentally that speakers have a passive knowledge of some of the submerged morphemic relationships that they do not command actively. We had nonlinguists pick out one of three meanings for some made-up words (for example, they were given the form *retent* and asked to guess whether the best meaning for it was (*a*) that which is *spent*, (*b*) that which is *kept*, (*c*) that which is *spoken of*.) In all eleven made-up words, the etymologically optimal choice was made significantly more often than the others, and on some items it was chosen about 90% of the time. Yet informal discussion with some of the subjects showed that they were unable to explain on what basis they had made their choices. Their analogies or analyses were not made at a conscious level—they just had a "feeling" about what the forms ought to mean.

Myerson (1975) used another technique to study partial knowledge of nonproductive patterns. She taught subjects pairs of words with made-up meanings; some were taught, for example, a "verb" *inclort* and a related "noun" /inklɔršʌn/, while others were taught the pair as inclort, /inklɔrtiʌn/. She then tested recall of the word pairs over several weeks, and found that her fourteen-year-old subject group recalled the noun as /inklɔršʌn/ regardless of whether they had been taught the /_šʌn/ form or the /_tiʌn/ form; her oldest subjects, seventeen-year-olds, recalled whichever one they had been taught, but those who had been given the /tiʌn/ form commented that it was peculiar and that it seemed as though it should have been /šʌn/.

Work of increasing psychological and linguistic sophistication, such as Jaeger's (1980) dissertation, will undoubtedly continue to be produced, but the point at issue is already clear: Knowledge of morphophonemic patterns is not an all-or-nothing matter. There can be partial or partially accessible knowledge of some of them. And for this reason, we cannot simply say that we will represent the speaker's knowledge in grammar.[1] Unless we go to the Lightnerian extreme of representing every pattern that the best historical linguist can detect, we must face the problem of deciding how much knowledge is enough. In fact, there are two axes of variation: Within the individual, we must deal with the fact that one person knows some rules better than others, and across individuals we must deal with the fact that some speakers know more rules and/or know some rules better than other speakers.

It will be necessary to decide whether differing degrees of knowledge along either axis of variation should be represented by differing formal devices in our grammars. Furthermore, we cannot begin to cope with this new indeterminacy until the following question is settled: Can the different degrees of knowledge tapped by different experimental tasks really be linearly ordered?

After all, consider: The meaning-guessing task in Wilbur and Menn, the word-memory task in Myerson, and the concept-formation task used by Moskowitz (1973) as well as by Jaeger do not give any hint in themselves as to which requires the greater degree of partial knowledge. We would need to rank them in order of difficulty in order to have a single parameter of "degree of knowledge." At present, we cannot do this, and we also must entertain the disconcerting possibility that it cannot be done—that perhaps there are several dimensions to the individual's (or the group's) knowledge continuum.

I propose a hypothesis which, IF true, would help to solve this problem of deciding whether one performance represents a greater degree of partial knowledge than another.

Hypothesis (a): If one follows the course of development of knowledge of morphophonemic rules that do clearly become productive by adulthood in some individuals, that knowledge will go through a definable succession of stages over time.

Hypothesis (b): Rules which do not become productive will be describable as having been "arrested" at one of the earlier stages of development.

Neither part of this hypothesis need be true. But suppose they both are. Then we could study behavior on various psycholinguistic probes for a rule as it approaches and reaches productivity; the probes could be "calibrated," as it were. In fact, Myerson has already studied how children from 8 to 17 years of age change in their ability to handle her task, and other probes for partial knowledge could be calibrated with stages of acquisition in the same way.

Abstractness/psychological reality, then, is one persistent issue of phonological theory which can be approached through analysis of an experimentation with language acquisition.

254   Lise Menn

Output Constraints

Another classical issue in phonology which can be clarified by acquisition considerations is one most notably raised by Kisseberth (1970): the relationship of phonotactic constraints (constraints on possible sequences of segments) to generative phonological rules. (Here I apologize for having to use CONSTRAINT as a construct within phonological theory when in the title and up until now I have used it in a metatheoretical sense. *Caveat lector.*) The argument I am about to present is made at greater length in Menn (1979); it is summarized and offered here as a constructive proof that valid arguments from child phonology to general phonology are possible.

In discussing rule ordering and abstractness previously, we were concerned with the child's acquisition of knowledge about the relations between morphs as she hears them in the speech of others.[1] Now we are considering "learning to pronounce"; that is, the control of the output phonetics of one's own speech. A phonotactic constraint or phonological output constraint is a statement describing some of the logically possible configurations of segments and boundaries that do not and apparently cannot appear on the surface of the language under consideration. They can be quite particular—for example the inadmissibility of initial /ŋ/ in English—or very general—e.g., the fact that consonant clusters are "forbidden" in many languages of the world.

To convey this sort of information formally, one uses either "the string XY is not permitted" or "if property A holds of a string, then property B holds also" (these being mutually translatable types of expressions).

Output constraints, though studied intensely as descriptions of words and syllables (Kahn 1976; Bell 1971; etc.) have no formal position in standard generative phonology, for they cannot generally in themselves be part of an ordered-rule derivation. A derivation must be determinate; but an output constraint by itself does not determine what rule a language will use to deal with underlying forms or borrowed forms which violate that constraint. The only way an output constraint can be part of a top-down derivation is as a filter to throw away ill-formed strings; but when ill-formed strings are modified rather than discarded, the output constraint cannot be part of the derivation.

Nevertheless, Kisseberth (and others since) have argued convincingly that formal output constraints should be incorporated into linguistic

---

[1] (Or perhaps as she apprehends them through reading? Linguistics has not come to terms with the enriched knowledge of one's language provided by diglossia, and literacy can well be thought of as a form of diglossia.)

theory, because without them, important generalizations are missed in the frequent case where a number of rules in a language "conspire" to "correct" potential violations of some single phonotactic generalization.

It is usually said that output constraints "motivate" derivational rules. But this figure of speech may lure us into committing a category error. Speakers and linguists may be motivated, but rules? How are rules motivated?

Finding the answer to this question requires both synchronic and diachronic considerations, and a distinctly psycholinguistic approach to both. Consider the beginning speaker, first. Evidence summarized in Menn (1979) indicates that children in the first few months of speaking have a very small repretory of output forms, which Ingram (1974) calls "canonical forms." These are likely to include CV, CVCV, (perhaps with a consonant harmony restriction); possibly CVC with harmony restriction or a proviso that only certain segments such as /s/, /n/, or /?/ can occupy the second C position; and VC with the same sort of restrictions as CVC. More intricate restrictions for particular children have been documented by Macken (1979), Vihman (1976), and Fey & Gandour (1979).

The repertory of canonical forms is enlarged steadily—in other words, the variety of segment sequences which the child can produce is increased steadily—so that the phonotactic capacity of the child who has been speaking for nine months or a year will differ from the adult English-speaker's phonotactic capacity primarily in having fewer consonant clusters (for example, absence of consonant clusters is the only salient phonotactic constraint in N.V. Smith's (1973) study, which begins when his child had been speaking for about 9 months).

The child's phonotactic restrictions do not in any way determine the rules that she will use to render adult speech. Confronted with an adult form that does not match any of her canonical forms, a child may avoid saving it or invent a variety of rules such as deletion, harmony, epenthesis, and even metathesis to adapt it. These adaption or transduction rules, once invented, have considerable "life" of their own—that is, they may continue in effect and even generalize long after the phonotactic restriction which "motivated" them has been relaxed. (There are certainly also rules which do not have any phonotactic motivation; some of these are apparently contrast-preserving devices, and others are presently not understood at all.)

Recall that rules such as these are not analogous to most of the rules of adult phonology. These are rules to render surface forms that the child hears but cannot say "properly"; their closest analogues in adult language are rules for adapting words in a foreign language or certain

"difficult" learned words (*auxiliary* /ɔksiləˈrerij/, *nuclear* /ˈnukjʌlər/).
These all, I suggest, belong to a class of "pronunciation rules" which
interrelate surface forms, and which also include "fast speech" rules,
hypercorrection rules, and dialect-correspondence rules. They contrast
with rules which relate abstract underlying forms to pronounced forms,
that is, with derivational rules; derivational rules are concerned with
capturing allomorphy (conditioned variation), but pronunciation rules
are concerned with what used to be called "free variation" until
sociolinguistics suggested that there was no such thing. Pronunciation
rules are invented by the individual attempting to realize a certain
phonetic surface (perhaps succeeding, perhaps not); derivational rules
and the underlying form that they "operate" on are derived by the
unconscious equivalent of historical internal reconstruction.[2]

Given that derivational rules and pronunciation rules are such
conceptually distinct entities, one should expect that the output
constraints invoked by conspiracy theory would bear only a formal
resemblance to the output constraints of child phonology. That being
the case, our discussion of the way in which output constraints motivate
child-phonology rules would not be of much help in dealing with the
problem we set out to solve: How do output constraints "motivate"
derivational rules?

However, further diachronic consideration allows us to find an
essential connection between these two notions after all. First, let us
pursue the course of the acquisition of the ability to pronounce one's
native language. If a child becomes a normal adult speaker of her
language, whatever it is, she must develop the articulatory agility to
produce all the native phonotactic patterns without effort. However, she
need never acquire the ability to perform articulatory gymnastics that
are not required by her language; she may remain quite innocent of the
fact that there are consonant clusters or voiced final consonants in the
world. If, as an adult, the speaker is confronted with a new sequence of
segments that goes beyond the production ability that she has
acquired—in other words, a sequence that violates the phonotactic
constraints of the language, she is again confronted with the same
situation as a child: She must either master this new sequence or adapt
it to her existing phonotactics; if she adapts it, she has a choice of rules,
but the need to use some rule or other can properly be said to have been
motivated by the output constraint violation.

Now let us recall where derivational rules come from historically

---

[2] (Refinement of this idea is needed. There are accidental phonotactic gaps and there
are essential ones; English speakers can produce /#pw/ but not /#tl/.)

rather than ontogenetically; they are, of course, the fossils of changes in pronunciation that took place in the past; somewhat degraded and restructured, to be sure, but quite recognizable. They were once rules relating surface variants, or else rules created to deal with potential violations of phonotactic constraints which had just arisen. (They might eliminate the violation entirely or the speakers might learn to produce some novel configurations and invent rules to reduce the difficulty of others.) In short, at the historical point of origin, the rules that we think of as derivational were subject to the same forces of naturalness as any other pronunciation rules, and were motivated in the same way. In their acquisition by a speaker of later generations, the fact that a certain set of derivational rules was once motivated by some output constraint is (probably) irrelevant; they are acquired by "working backward" from the surface, and the surface is in compliance with that constraint already. Once a rule has been established, its relation to an output constraint is redundant, and of course the rule may persist when the constraint is lost.

Conclusion

Child language, and considerations of learning in general, have a role to play in helping to explore and explain the phenomena of language; we have seen that the nature of rule ordering and of output constraints can both be understood better with the help of an acquisition perspective, and we have suggested that an experimental acquisition study could also contribute to the resolution of the abstractness/psychological reality question.

In the course of discussing these points, we have demonstrated the untenability of the "tacit assumptions" that were criticized in the introduction. First, we have seen that such a basic property of child phonology as the presence of massive output constraints cannot be derived from anything in adult phonology. Second, in contrasting the roles played by rules in child phonology and adult phonology, and in citing an erroneous argument from one to the other we have demonstrated that the ways that child phonology corresponds to adult phonology are not obvious. And finally, in tracing the broad outlines of the acquisition of morphophonology and phonotactics we have seen that the "simplicity" of child phonology is not sufficient to make it possible to discover its nature without intensive fieldwork and analysis. In particular, we have seen that the acquisition process is very rich, and that children in fact learn rather complicated things in cycles of successive refinements of rule-knowledge. Children certainly find some kinds of rules easier to learn than others, but nothing in our research to date hints at whether there is a limit to the complexity of what they can learn given enough time and relevant input. Putting constraints on one or another type of phonological rules on the a priori grounds that children cannot learn them is completely unjustified given our present knowledge and ignorance. I would argue instead in favor of John Goldsmith's "current approach" (1979); describe what's out there in all its richness, create the most perspicuous possible notation to represent it, and don't look yet to formal constraints from any source as the way to truth about language. The only source of constraints that will eventually serve us will be psycholinguistic studies of children and adults, and given the continuum nature of knowledge discussed earlier, designing and interpreting such studies will not be easy.

References

Bell, A. (1971) Some patterns of occurrence and formation of syllable structures. In *Working Papers on Linguistic Universals, 6*. Linguistics Department, Stanford University. Pp. 23–137.

Berko, J. (1958) The child's learning of English morphology. *Word, 14*, 150–157. Reprinted in A. Bar-Adon & W. Leopold (Eds.) (1971) *Child language: A book of readings.* Pp. 153–167.

Cazden, C. B. (1968) The acquisition of noun and verb inflections. *Child development, 39*, 433–438.

Cutler, A. (1979) The psychological reality of word formation and lexical stress. In E. Fischer-Jorgensen et al. (Eds.), *Proceedings of the Ninth International Congress of Phonetic Sciences.* Copenhagen.

Derwing, B.L. (1973) *Transformational grammar as a theory of language acquisition.* Cambridge: Cambridge University Press.

Dinnsen, D.A. (Ed.) (1979) *Current approaches to phonological theory.* Bloomington: Indiana University Press.

Dinnsen, D.A. (1979) Atomic phonology. In D.A. Dinnsen (Ed.) (1979) *Current approaches to phonological theory.* Bloomington: Indiana University Press.

Donegen, P. & Stampe, D. The study of natural phonology. In D.A. Dinnsen (Ed.) (1979) *Current approaches to phonological theory.* Bloomington: Indiana University Press.

Fey, M. E. & Gandour, J. (1982) Rule discovery in phonological acquisition. *Journal of Child Language 9*, 71–82.

Goldsmith, J. The aims of autosegmental phonology. In D.A. Dinnsen (Ed.) (1979) *Current approaches to phonological theory.* Bloomington: Indiana University Press.

Hooper, J.B. Substantive principals in natural generative phonology. In D.A. Dinnsen (Ed.) (1979) *Current approaches to phonological theory.* Bloomington: Indiana University Press.

Ingram, D. (1974) Phonological rules in young children. *Journal of child language, 1*, 49–64.

Jaeger, J.J. (1980) Categorization in phonology: An experimental approach. Doctoral dissertation. University of California/Berkeley.

Kahn, D. (1976) Syllable-based generalizations in English phonology. MIT doctoral dissertation, circulated in mimeo by Indiana University Linguistics Club, Bloomington.

Kiparsky, P. & Menn, L. (1977) On the acquisition of phonology. In J. Macnamara (Ed.), *Language learning and thought.* New York: Academic Press.

Kisseberth, C.W. (1970) On the functional unity of phonological rules. *Linguistic inquiry, 1,* 291–306.

Linell, P. (1979) Panel discussion, Symposium No. 2, *Proceedings of the ninth international congress of phonetic sciences,* Vol. III. Copenhagen: University of Copenhagen Institute of Phonetics. P. 209.

Macken, M. (1979) Permitted complexity in phonological development: One child's acquisition of Spanish consonants. *Lingua, 49,* 11–19.

MacWhinney, B. (1978) The acquisition of morphophonology. *Monographs of the Society for Research in Child Development, 43,* 1–2.

Menn, L. (1979) Toward a psychology of phonology: Child phonology as a first step. In R. Herbert (Ed.), *Applications of linguistic theory in the human sciences.* Linguistics Department, Michigan State University.

Menn, L. (1980) Child phonology and phonological theory. In G. Yeni-Komshian, J. Kavanagh, & C.A. Ferguson (Eds.), *Child phonology: Perception and production.* New York: Academic Press.

Moskowitz, A. (1970) The acquisition of phonology. *Working paper #34.* Language-behavior Research Laboratory, University of California at Berkeley.

Moskowitz, B.A. (1973) On the status of vowel shift in English. In T.E. Moore (Ed.), *Cognitive development and the acquisition of language.* New York: Academic Press.

Myerson, R. (1975) A developmental study of children's knowledge of complex derived words of English. Doctoral dissertation, Harvard Graduate School of Education.

Sanders, G.A. (1979) Equational rules and rule functions in phonology. In D.A. Dinnsen (Ed.) Current approaches to phonological theory. Bloomington: Indiana University Press.

Slobin, D.I. (1971) Cognitive prerequisites for the development of grammar. In W.O. Dingwall (Ed.), *Survey of linguistic science.* University of Maryland. Also in C.A. Ferguson & D.I. Slobin (Eds.) (1973) *Studies of child language development.* New York: Holt, Rinehart, and Winston.

Slobin, D.I. (1977) Language change in childhood and in history. In J. Macnamara (Ed.), *Language learning and thought.* New York: Academic Press.

Slobin, D.I. The role of language in language acquisition. Invited address to the Eastern Psychological Association, 50th Annual Meeting, April 1979.

Smith, N.V. (1973) *The acquisition of phonology: A case study.* Cambridge: Cambridge University Press.

Vihman, M.M. (1976) From prespeech to speech: On early phonology. Stanford Papers and Reports on Child Language Development 12, 230–243.

Wilbur, R.B., & Menn, L. (1974) The roles of rules in generative phonology. Paper read at the 1974 summer meeting of the Linguistic Society of America.

Wilbur, R.B., & Menn, L. (1975) Psychological reality, linguistic theory, and the internal structure of the lexicon. *San Jose State University occasional papers in linguistics.*

16   MARILYN MAY VIHMAN

Formulas in First and Second Language Acquisition[1]

In the past few years a number of writers have pointed out that not all of language is generated afresh each time we speak, starting with a unique combination of meanings and working through from a deep to a surface structure. Instead, it has been suggested that a great deal of ordinary language consists of well-worn cliches and idioms, quotations, allusions, and other routines. In Charles Fillmore's words, "an enormously large amount of natural language is formulaic, automatic, and rehearsed, rather than propositional, creative, or freely generated [1976, p. 9]."[2] As examples of formulaic language we might cite such old American rejoinders as *You're telling me?*, *No kidding!*, or *Nothing doing!* (though none of these is as popular now as fifty years ago; the last expression has been eclipsed by the ubiquitous *No way!*), as well as such more current expressions as *what's it TO you?* or *I could care less* (which has been tolerated in that anomalous form for over two decades now); formulas may also range from such deliberately vivid phrases as *He cried all the way to the bank* or *Butter wouldn't melt in her mouth* (which, for most American speakers, at least, seems to imply a calculated appearance of sweetness and innocence: the route from literal to

---

[1] This chapter was presented at the Symposium on Exceptional Language and Linguistic Theory, LSA Annual Meeting, Los Angeles, Calif., Dec. 27, 1979. It has benefitted considerably from the critical comments of Dwight Bolinger, Marvin J. Homzie, and Loraine K. Obler on earlier drafts.

[2] Cf. also Bolinger 1976 and 1977; Coulmas 1979; Ferguson 1976; Fillmore 1979a and b; Olson 1973; and Ruhl 1977.

idiomatic meaning is fairly distant in this case), to the dull but time-honored *Hot enough for you?*

Dwight Bolinger is another major proponent of the view that the role of such prepackaged strings is far more pervasive in language than has been acknowledged by linguists. Applying Ladefoged's remark that "The central nervous system is like a special kind of computer which has rapid access to items in a very large memory, but comparatively little ability to process these items . . ."—which originally related to the issue of distinctive features as opposed to segments—to the area of morphology and syntax, Bolinger insists that "speakers do at least as much remembering as they do putting together [1976, p. 2]." He suggests further that "learning goes on constantly—but especially with young children—in segments of collocation size as much as it does in segments of word size, and . . . much if not most of our later manipulative grasp of words is by way of analysis of collocations [1976, p. 8]."

Bolinger offers little in the way of child language data to support his point, and in fact such data are difficult to obtain from studies of first-language acquisition since, as is well known, most children begin with just "one word at a time [Bloom 1973]."[3] Yet incontrovertible evidence for the prefabricated or memorized nature of much of the material incorporated into the flow of normal adult speech is even more difficult to obtain, since the joints are rarely detectable, except by introspection. In children's speech, however, the small quantity and simple structure of the language produced can sometimes allow an analyst valuable insights into the psychological processes underlying fully competent adult language use. Following up on Bolinger's hint, then, in the present chapter I will begin by reviewing what data can be found regarding the learning of larger-than-word-size chunks in first language acquisition, and I will then go on to focus on the child second-language learner, whose reliance on memorized strings in the early stages is quite indisputable.

Brown (1973) describes in fairly exhaustive detail the morphological and syntactic/semantic properties of the language of three children he and his colleagues at Harvard followed for several years. In *A First*

---

[3] Hence the near-universal dependence on mean length of utterance (MLU), measured in morphemes, as a standard against which to judge the comparability of children in different studies, learning the same or different languages. Though this standard is admittedly flawed (cf. Crystal 1974), it has been repeatedly shown to be far superior to chronological age as an index of the child's relative language development. The absence of any comparable measure is painfully felt in second-language acquisition studies (cf. Larsen-Freeman 1978).

Language he considers only data from the early stages, when the children ranged in age from 20 to 34 months and used an average of up to 2.5 morphemes per utterance. He mentions in passing the use of such "inflexible" forms as *what's that? where* (noun) *go?* at stage I (mean length of utterance =1.75), well before the "flowering of wh- questions" that takes place in Stage III. Brown comments that "the precursors that appear in Stage I must be generated by some simpler mechanism, either as fixed routines or as simple frames in which a set of words could rotate [1973, p. 181. Cf. also Brown 1968; Brown and Hanlon 1970]."

In Stage II, Brown found that one of the children learned *it's* and *that a* as units, and also tended to use several obligatory transitive verbs in combination with the article *a: get-a, got-a, put-a, want-a.* Finally, "There is some evidence from one or more of the children of such other amalgams as *want-to, have-to, going-to, another-one, what-that,* and *let-me*" [1973, p. 305]. Brown points out that all of these amalgams are based on pairs of words that occur AS PAIRS with unusually high frequency in parental speech, so that we have here one exceptional case where frequency of presentation has a direct effect on the child's production. Brown mentions no other instances of rote memorization of multi-morphemic sequences by the children; it seems safe to assume the phenomenon occurred rarely in Brown's data.

In a study of lexical and semantic development, Nelson (1973) drew on data from 18 children producing their first fifty words, and thus was able to hazard some conclusions regarding individual differences. She found a dichotomy between what she termed **referential** and **expressive children,** the distinction being based primarily on the number of common nouns among the first 50 words the child learned (more or less than 50%, respectively). A second characteristic difference dividing the two groups was "the early learning of speech units of two words or more . . . The number of phrases produced by the R[eferential] group during this period ranged from 0 to 5 (mean 2.4), while those of the E[xpressive] group ranged from 6 to 18 (12.6)." Nelson goes on to say that these phrases—many of which she classifies as "personal–social" language, including "expressions useful for dealing with people" (*go away, stop it, don't do it,* as well as *thank you, do it, I want it*)—"may be considered as preformed or stereotyped units . . . which can be combined into larger units but are not themselves analyzable. Thus, they are equivalent to words in their linguistic function [1973, p. 25]."

The children these data come from are younger than Brown's (they ranged from 14 to 24 months at the point where their vocabulary count was 50 words, the words in unit-phrases being counted separately) but, presumably because the sample is larger, we find several children who learned whole phrases at the outset of language acquisition (cf. also the discussion of "rote productions" in Dore *et al.* 1976).

A third observer, Ann Peters, followed just one child, but that child proved to have two strategies in early language learning which corresponded roughly to the two strategies identified by Nelson.

> The first kind . . . was the nice, neat one-word utterance which began occurring . . . when he was about 14 months old . . . I will call this kind of speech ANALYTIC . . . The second type of speech was beginning to appear even earlier . . . In this type, each target phrase has a very characteristic intonation contour . . . Minh . . . apparently attempted to extend this strategy of extracting the melody, at the expense of the individual segments, to those cases where the target sentence was NOT so reliably characterized by its intonation contour, and hence was not recognizable except in very context-bound situations. The result was utterances in which, though the segmental fidelity was not very great, the combination of number of syllables, stress, intonation and such segments as could be distinguished combined to give a very good impression of sentencehood. I will call this the GESTALT type of speech since . . . it seems to aim at whole phrases or sentences rather than single words. [Peters 1977, p. 563f.]

Some of Minh's phrases are clearly formulas like those Nelson's expressive children used—*look at that!, what's that?, silly, isn't it?*—though others, more specific in reference, seem less likely candidates for unit-learning or rote memorization—e.g., *open the door!*

Cazden (1968) has commented, in an analysis of the development of inflection in the children of the Harvard study, that "The pattern of no use, followed by infrequent but invariably correct use, followed only later by evidence of productivity, characterizes the development of many features of the children's speech." She goes on to remark that one might infer from these data "that the child begins to operate with stored fragments of speech he has heard . . . which are somehow tagged liberally for semantic information on the verbal and nonverbal context and only later are gradually subjected to analysis for the acquisition of productive rules [Cazden 1968, p. 437]." Similarly, Olson (1973), citing an atypically complex negative from Bloom's (1970) data, ə *don't want baby*, supposes that such unanalyzed units "may be precursors of the preprogrammed routines" which he believes adults use to achieve "encoding economies"; they would provide "an example of how the child can produce longer or more complicated utterances by, in a sense, avoiding the computation of all the internal structure of the string [Olson 1973, p. 156]."

Cazden's sketch of the learning process as involving, first, memory (coding of unanalyzed units) and then analysis (productive use, marked by overgeneralization) can be seen to apply to phonology and semantics as well as to inflectional morphology. Thus, Ferguson and Macken (1982) describe early phonological acquisition in these terms:

> We begin with the observation that the data from a very young child—one just learning to talk—are piecemeal and apparently unintegrated. It seems that the child initially analyzes word shapes on an individual basis . . . At some point, the child begins to recognize similarities between classes of sounds and sounds-in-combination, and to construct rules for relating similar sounds and word shapes . . .

Similarly, Carey (1978) has offered a theory of semantic acquisition that involves "missing features and haphazard examples": "On this view, the child learns, object by object and particular part by particular part, what spatial adjective applies to what kinds of variation . . . [1978, p. 286]." This information is at first encoded "in an unanalyzed format," just as the early use of causative verbs may involve "notions of causation, but only as part of unanalyzed conceptual packages [p. 289]." Carey outlines three stages in the acquisition of causation by Bowerman's daughter Christy: "The representation of causative verbs as unanalyzed cognitive units, the abstraction of the lexical feature [cause], and finally the long-drawn-out process of working out the details of the semantics of causatives [p. 291]" (or the idiosyncracies of their morpho-lexical mapping in English).

Drawing on Karmiloff-Smith and Inhelder's studies of cognitive abilities outside the realm of language (specifically, the development of understanding of properties of weight and balance), Ferguson and Macken outline a seven-step acquisition process, beginning with "(a) single item match, (b) gradual recognition of a pattern, (c) period of exploration, (d) construction of a theory, followed by generalization . . . and loss of ability . . .". If we view the rote-learning of irregular verbs, whole sound-shapes, "haphazard examples," and routine syntactic units as instances of the first step, we can readily grant that memory seems to pave the entry-way to system-building or productive grammar. Yet, as Krashen and Scarcella (1978) have forcefully argued, the process of analysis need not BEGIN with units already available for productive use. Rather, in phonology we see the child SELECTING words to attempt partly on the basis of the sounds he can handle—showing some awareness of the sound system prior to the development of a productive repertoire (cf. Celce-Murcia 1978; Drachman 1973; Ferguson & Farwell 1975; Macken 1976; Menn 1976; Vihman 1976). Similarly, "Bowerman argues that Christy's mastery of the syntax of coordinated [causative] structures was a prerequisite to . . . her abstraction of [cause] as a lexical organizer [Carey 1978, p. 290]." Thus, we can agree with Krashen and Scarcella that "prefabricated routines may evolve into patterns, but at the same time, independently, the creative construction process develops [1978, p. 284]." Rote-learning of shorter and longer, simpler and more complex units, at the various levels of sound and meaning, syntax and lexicon, must go on simultaneously with analysis, the latter based at first on the words, sounds, meanings, and constructions in the perception- or comprehension-based store that antedates the first productive uses of language (Huttenlocher 1974; Nelson *et al.* 1978).

To turn to one last example from the first-language acquisition literature, Ruth Clark (1974) found that her son Adam, at age 2;9 to 3;0, often incorporated into his utterances whole strings from a preceding adult utterance, e.g.:

> Mother (attempting to take the coat her son has laid on the floor, preparatory to putting it on): *That's upside down.*
> Child: *No, I want to upside down.*

In addition, Adam used utterances such as *Sit my knee* to mean 'I want to sit on your knee'. Such utterances "were quite clearly copied as incompletely analysed units, and given only a global interpretation with reference to the situation . . . The fact that copied utterances were retained intact for several weeks without other lexical items being substituted suggests that such utterances . . . function as units with limited internal structure [Clark 1974, p. 4]." Writing as if in direct illustration of Bolinger's point, Clark comments:

> In Adam's speech at this time a number of routine unproductive sequences seemed to coexist with a few simple productive rules. Many, though not necessarily all, the productive rules originated as invariable routines, which were in use for some time with the original lexical items before new lexical items were inserted [p. 4]

Adam's strategy is clearly a form of imitation, though much of his "copying" is delayed imitation. Nelson (1973, pp. 49ff.) found that imitation correlated significantly with vocabulary level and, to a much smaller extent, also with child's age. The children who were more advanced in terms of vocabulary were more likely to imitate, and were also most likely to imitate familiar words. This would suggest that children are most likely to learn whole strings or collocations once they are launched on language acquisition—after Stage II, say, in Brown's terms—and would tend to explain why one finds a one-word and a two-word stage but not such clear-cut three- or four-word stages: At that point the child is likely to be making use of "unopened packages," as Clark calls them, which can be combined to produce long, superficially complex utterances such as *I don't know where's Emma gone* or *That a bunny taking a book home* (Clark 1974, pp. 5ff; cf. also Clark 1977). Because such utterances are often apparently well-formed, they are difficult to detect. A good deal of what Clark calls "performing without competence" must pass unnoticed.

It is unclear why multimorphemic lexical units or formulas should be fairly seldom used at the outset in first language acquisition, or to put it differently, why children do tend to begin with one word at a time. Memory span has most often been implicated (cf. especially Brown & Fraser 1963), but this position has recently been challenged (Olson 1973; Braine 1974). Olson points out that studies of memory which use nonverbal stimuli show relatively little development from three-year-olds to seven-year-olds and even to adults. (Cf. also Flavell & Wellman 1977.) He suggests that "the performance deficits that we find in younger children's remembering are due to their failure to organize, plan, monitor, and integrate their information processing and remembering as effectively as older children and adults [Olson 1973, p. 151]" (but, as he also notes, the evidence for that point is largely drawn from experiments with children aged 3½ or 4 at the youngest). Furthermore, there is evidence that even very young children can sometimes remember impressively long strings: See, for example, "Eric's ability to 'recite' accurately from memory long passages of text in his favorite story books, turning the pages at the appropriate juncture, when he was two and one-half years old. But he was unable to answer specific questions about the text, and certain phrase structures he recited—sentence adverbials for example—did not appear in his spontaneous utterances (Bloom 1970, pp. 168ff.)." Ann Peters suggests that formulas may not in fact be uncommon in early child language; it may be that they are rarely reported simply because linguists have been biased to expect single words or morphemes and are inclined to view other kinds of data as "noise" or a residue of "unintelligible utterance" (Peters, 1980). As Peters notes, the difficulty a child typically experiences with phonological control in the early stages adds to the linguist's difficulty in "recogniz[ing] the multimorphemic nature of the target [1980, p. 10]."

In any case, there is one kind of language learning that appears to begin, most typically, with the use of memorized strings: This is naturalistic second-language acquisition by children.[4] The first study to remark on this was no doubt the Kenyeres' (1938) diary account of their six-year-old Hungarian-speaking daughter's acquisition of French. In the first month in Geneva, Eva asked her parents the meaning of *tout le monde à sa place* ('everyone to his own seat'), *qui c'est qui joue à l'école?* ('who plays at school?'), and *feuille d'où viens-tu?* ('leaf, where do you come from?', the title of a song). In the next month she attempted to make up with her mother after a quarrel, using strikingly formulaic French: *Maman, s'il vous plait, qu'est-ce que c'est, voulez-vous?* ('Mother, please, what is it, would you like?') In another early attempt at constructing a sentence she modified one element in a memorized string, asking *Où sont les mamans?* ('where are the mothers' instead of 'where is mother'), based on a sentence learned at school, *où sont les ciseaux?* ('where are the scissors?').

In a 1970 UCLA masters thesis, Huang found that his five-year-old Chinese subject "was capable of imitating amazingly complex sentences almost from the start and to attach a global meaning to them [Huang & Hatch 1978, p. 131]." In the first month of exposure to English, Huang's subject used the following imitated strings ("rule-formed utterances" began to occur only in the sixth week): *Get out of here!*, *It's time to eat and drink.*, *Let's go!*, *Don't do that!*, *Don't touch!* Kenji Hakuta (1974) has also presented data to demonstrate the use of "pre-fabricated patterns" by a five-year-old Japanese girl learning English. Hakuta analyzes three such patterns, those using the copula, the string *do you* in questions, and the string *how to* in embedded how-questions, showing that, though well-formed on the surface, each of these was in fact memorized without internal analysis, so that *do you*, for example, functioned as a question marker, turning up as an error only in the few cases where the child attempted a question with a third person subject, such as *What do you do it, this, froggie?*, *What do you doing, this boy?*

Lily Wong Fillmore's (1976) Stanford thesis provides the most extensive documentation of the use of formulas by children learning a

---

[4] Observational data on naturalistic second language acquisition by adults are practically nonexistent, though one study of a 19-year-old Arabic speaker learning English does report heavy dependence on formulaic speech at the outset (Hanania & Gradman 1977). Scarcella (1979) used some simple drawings to test 60 adult learners of English on their knowledge of such formulas as *Watch out!*, *Fill 'er up*, *Keep the change*, *I'm sorry I'm late*. She found that her subjects made full, accurate use of the formulas only about 34% of the time. For the remainder, the adults avoided the expected routine by resorting to paraphrase (44% of the errors), or aimed at but just missed the expected wording of the formula (25%), or used the wrong formula (10%), or translated word-for-word from a corresponding formula in their first language (9%). Scarcella concludes that "many adult second language acquirers have difficulty acquiring very common routines [p. 84]."

second language. Presenting data from five Mexican children, each recorded while interacting with the observer and an English-speaking friend, Fillmore emphasizes the vital function formulas serve in opening communication channels with speakers of the second language, and thus in securing access to second language input.[5] Like Bolinger and Clark, she sees formulas as an entry to grammar, a data-bank to be used for later analysis and reorganization. As an example of the uninhibited use of a formulaic frame with minimal knowledge of English structure we can cite her subject Alej: *Is a coffee me?* (holding out a cup, pretending to ask for coffee) and *Is a playground me.* (speaking to Fillmore on return from a playground melee). Fillmore comments, regarding the most effective language learner, Nora, who had the greatest number of formulas:

> It seems that having a few formulaic expressions which could be used facilitated the acquisition of a variety of similar forms. The evidence of this can be seen in a rather consistent pattern [in which Nora would] acquire and overuse a few formulaic expressions of a new structural type during one period, and amass a variety of similar forms during the next. Perhaps having a few formulaic expressions of a particular type permitted her to notice, interpret, and pick up like expressions [Fillmore 1976, p. 508].

Fillmore maintains that "the strategy of acquiring formulaic speech is central to the learning of language . . . it is this step that puts the learner in a position to perform the analysis which is prerequisite to acquisition [p. 640]." She indicates that in the first two of the eight months of observation the children's utterances ranged (across the children) from 53% to 100% formulaic; in the last two months the range was from 37% to 81%.

In Hatch's recent anthology of second-language acquisition studies we find the use of formulas further documented for several children, including two Japanese boys learning English, one a 3½-year-old, the other 2½ (cf. Yoshida 1978; and Itoh & Hatch 1978). The study of the latter is grouped by Hatch under instances of "simultaneous acquisition of two languages," presumably in accordance with the principle of drawing an arbitrary line at age three for sequential acquisition of a

[5] A French engineer visiting Stanford for a year with his family reports that his son, aged 5;9, learned as his first English expression, upon starting first grade about two months after arrival in the United States, *What's your name?*, which the father heard him make use of as he wrestled another child to the ground. The younger son, aged 3, attended a day care center, where he became convinced that *It's clean-up time!* was an English expression signalling the advent of lunch.

second language (cf. McLaughlin 1978). Yet that two-year-old subject made ample use of formulaic patterns, like other second language learners, whereas the accounts of children exposed to two languages from the start—that is, children acquiring "bilingualism as a first language," to use Swain's (1972) expression—have not generally noted any extensive use of unit-phrases. (Cf. Celce-Murcia 1978, Imedadze 1967, Leopold 1939–49, Murrell 1966, Padilla & Liebman 1975, Pavlovitch 1920, Ronjat 1913, Swain 1972, Tabouret-Keller 1963, Volterra & Taeschner 1978.) Burling (1959) constitutes an exception of sorts: With regards to Garo, his son's dominant language during the period in question, Burling comments that the child, between age 1;11 and 2;3 "apparently always used the [syntactic] construction first in certain specific examples which he learned as a whole and by rote. After using several of these for a while, he would learn to generalize on the construction, and to substitute different morphemes or words in the same construction [Burling 1959, p. 67.]." At the same time, he made productive use of only one English construction (*more* + N): "The few other English phrases which he used, including even such complex ones as *What are you doing,* had been memorized as units and the parts were not separable [1959, p. 67]." In other words, Burling's son is following the route Cazden outlines for the acquisition of English inflectional morphology in his acquisition of Garo morphology and syntax, while in his weaker language, English, he behaves much like other children learning a second language, who seem universally to make use of a formula strategy for a while. Thus, to add to the cases already cited, we can mention Oksaar's son, who first learned to speak Estonian and Swedish at the same time and who then was exposed to his third language, German, at 3:11: "The first striking difference [between his simultaneous acquisition of the first two languages and his subsequent acquisition of German] is that instead of single items blocks of utterances were produced after just two or three weeks in Hamburg. Only 30% were two-word sequences of the type *grosse Treppe; nicht treten; guck mal;* 70% were three-word sequences of the type: *was ist das?; ich komm runter* [Oksaar 1977, p. 301]."

The study of a child learning a second language before age 2 would be of particular interest in view of the memory span issue: Such a child must be still well within the period of intensive first language acquisition, if indeed he has already acquired a sizeable first-language lexicon and has begun combining words into sentences. In fact, as we shall see, at least one such child did use acquisition strategies with regard to the second language which resemble those of older children more than they do her own first language strategies.

The child in question is my daughter Virve, who, at 21 months, had a recorded vocabulary of about 260 words in her first language, Estonian, and a mean length of utterance of 2.05 when she began spending four hours daily at a day care center where only English was spoken. V. had learned about 17 English words by the time she entered the center, but she made regular use of only four or five—*no, hi, bye, mine, come*—and her comprehension of English was minimal.[6]

In the first month V. made use of 7 new English lexical units, every one of them morphologically complex words or even multi-word strings, though they seemed clearly to be single, unanalyzed units for V.: *happy birthday to you, Jingle Bells, pattycake, thank you, what's that, six-nine* (referring to numbers on a calculator), *Mickey Mouse*. In the second month the "lexical opacity index," as we might call it, was lower: Of 15 new items, 8 were actually phrases, namely, *come on, stop it, that's mine, jump down, Happy New Year, my goodness, apple juice, lunch time*. The fact that the first influx of new vocabulary consisted exclusively of complex words or phrases is suggestive: We might suppose that the lack of analysis was related to V's lack of significant previous exposure to English, as compared with the first language learner, who generally has a several month lead in comprehension by the time he begins to produce adult-based words in quantity. The drop in number of morphemes per unit could indicate a growing ability to separate out the parts of lexical items of interest—although the fact that all but two of the items used in

[6] Virve's acquisition of English is described in greater detail in Vihman (in preparation), where the circumstances of data collection are set forth as follows:

The methodology of this study was dictated by the circumstances. First, since my husband and I had established a policy of speaking only Estonian with V. from the time of her birth, unless monolingual English-speakers were present, I was loath to "elicit" any English from her myself. Second, because V. was so shy of strangers, it was unlikely an unknown English-speaking adult would have much luck eliciting speech, unless that person were to do so regularly over an extended period—and then the elicitation sessions would likely take on the nature of language lessons But I was interested in following V.'s progress in English in a completely natural setting, motivated by V.'s communicative needs rather than by my own need for quantifiable data. As a result, the information I have is fragmentary . . . Nevertheless, because V. felt quite unconstrained about practicing her English at home (where she received no encouragement to do so; quite the reverse), and because she proved an adept learner with a high degree of interest in language, the data are plentiful, though not, on the whole, quantifiable [p. 3].

In addition to recording whatever English V. used at home, in the car, or on visits, whether she was speaking to her parents, to herself, or to others, I worked at V.'s cooperative daycare center for a few hours each week and had no difficulty noting down the little English she used in that context.

the first month were proper names or routine formulas in the adult language rather weakens this argument in the present instance.

In any case we can note that V. made no use of phrases in her early first-language lexicon, though her choice of words qualified her as "expressive," like those of Nelson's children who did use phrases.[7] How, then, shall we explain this shift in strategy over the mere seven or eight months that separate the initial stages of first and second language acquisition in V.'s case? The structure of English as opposed to Estonian may be relevant: MacWhinney (1978) has claimed that "if a language uses relatively unambiguous intonational cues to mark words as basic units, the intonational units acquired by children will be words [p. 10]." Estonian would be such a language, since its core vocabulary is characterized by strong demarcative (first syllable) stress on content words. Of three Estonian-speaking children I have observed (see Vihman 1971; 1976; 1981), none appeared to learn whole unit-phrases at the start. In fact, at least one, Linda V., was misled by the absence of stress on the negative particle: for *ei taha* ('[I] don't want'), lit. ('no want'), she produced *taha,* with strong stress and an emphatic shaking of the head to make the negative meaning clear. My own second child, Raivo, who was exposed to at least four hours of English a day from the age of six months on, through baby-sitters and other children, and who had an average of 24% English words in his lexicon over the first 10 months of language use (with 26% active English words at 2;0, out of a recorded vocabulary of 489 words), used only one unit-phrase in his first fifty words: *what's this?* By 2;0 he has used 24 such expressions, all English, the longest being *Billy goat, Nanny goat,* from a nursery school chant of his older sister's. There were virtually no prefabricated phrases apparent in his Estonian lexicon. Similarly, in the published vocabulary of a two-year-old Romanian- and English-speaking child (Vogel 1975) we find just two multi-word units cited for Romanian (out of 85 words), though there are multimorphemic units, such as noun + article suffix; out of the 70 English words listed, nine are clearly multiword units (*bad*

---

[7] V. proved far more clearly "expressive" in her second-language lexical choices, inasmuch as only 28% of the first 50 English words she produced after 1;9 were general nominals, while 36% fell in the personal–social category (the figures for the first fifty words she produced when she began speaking—including five English words—are 48% general nominal and 22% personal–social). Contrast Yoshida (1978), whose 3½-year-old male subject had 60% general nominals in his second language (English), and was thus clearly "referential." The number of personal–social expressions, which is not reported, was presumably insignificant; we have no information on the make-up of his first language lexicon. But this Japanese-speaker, like V., exhibited the learning of unit phrases, which appears to be highly characteristic of second-language learners regardless of differences in cognitive and linguistic style or strategies.

boy, I got it, I had it, look at, right here, sit down, up here, and *yes-or-no*),
and an additional three verbs optionally include the pronoun *I.*
Disregarding the latter, the English vocabulary consists of 13%
unit-phrases. Finally, in the small English vocabulary V. acquired
before entering day-care at 1;9 she had four unit-phrases—*peek-a-boo,
all done, more juice,* and *all fall down;* this amounts to 24% of her English
lexicon.

These figures do seem to implicate the structure of English as a factor
in V.'s use of formulas in her second-language acquisition, but the fact
that the same strategy is reported for the acquisition of French
(Ervin-Tripp 1974, Valette 1964), German (Oksaar 1977), and Hebrew
(Berman 1979), seems to tip the balance in favor of a universal strategy
for successive acquisition of a second language by children. Certainly a
broader sampling of children learning languages of various structural
types will be needed to fairly evaluate this factor.

A simple increase in articulatory control could also be involved here,
enabling V. to "get her mouth around" longer strings, so to speak. But
clarity of enunciation was an outstanding property of V.'s earliest
speech; I encountered nothing remotely resembling the "mush-mouth"
problems Peter faced with Minh.

It could be argued that input was the significant variable: L. Fillmore,
for example, maintains that the formulaic speech of child second
language learners derives from the more complex language addressed to
them, as compared with that directed at a one-year-old acquiring his
first language (personal communication). Yet in V.'s case, again, the
time interval between first and second language acquisition was only a
few months. Is it likely that a 21-month-old who understands very little
English would be addressed, by adult caretakers, very differently from
any other infant just learning his first language? On the other hand, the
amount of one-to-one adult-to-child speech at a day care center is
significantly lower than the amount an only child receives from a
parent–caretaker at home, and in fact many of V.'s unit-phrases clearly
derive from the speech of the other children (e. g., *that's mine, stop it*) as
well as from routines addressed to the group of 9-month to 3-year-olds
indiscriminately, such as *lunch time!*

Could it be that sheer short-term memory span had increased? Or is it
more likely that V.'s experience in combining words in her first
language led her to look for longer chunks with which to express herself
in English? This latter explanation seems closest to Olson's (1973)
hypothesis that "limits on information processing are ontogenetically
invariant, . . . nominal quantitative changes in the amount of
externally defined information that can be handled have to do with the

nature of the child's internal representations [p. 150]." That is, rather than credit simple memory for digits, as in Brown's work cited earlier (cf. also Hakuta's reference to "a developed processing span [which] enables memorization of longer speech segments. . . . Segments . . . like *this is* would be not too different from individual lexical items [1975, p. 22]," it may be that we should look specifically to an expanded memory-for-language, based on experience with form-meaning (or form-situation) pairings in the first language. Generally speaking, for children learning a second language we can appreciate the increased ease experienced in pairing a situation-based meaning with the several-syllables-long string which expresses it as compared with the first language learner, for whom linguistic difficulties are initially present at both the phonetic and the semantic levels (assuming, with Bates 1976; Bruner 1975; Snow 1977; and many others, that certain basic pragmatic aspects of language—such as the nature of communication, the structuring of dialogue or conversation, etc.—are the earliest aspects of language to be understood by the child, somewhat before the onset of productive speech-with-adult-models). In this framework V. clearly is more like the older second-language learner: Despite her age, she could produce strings of up to five or six morphemes in her first language, and thus had to have a fairly well-developed capacity for internally representing (her first) language by the time she began seriously grappling with her second language.

In contrast, Fantini (1974) reports on the progress of his son Mario, who learned Spanish (as well as a little Italian) at home and English in the community. Though, like V., he had contact with English-speaking relatives and other visitors from the start, Mario, also like V., began to make regular use of English only when he entered nursery school, at 2;6. Unlike V., however, he was still at an early stage of first language acquisition at that point. Fantini does not directly report on the size of the child's lexical store or his mean length of utterance at 2;6, but he notes a total of about 50 recorded words (including five unit-phrases, one the English *don't touch*) as of 2;3; and he comments that "by 2;7 four-word utterances were common, marking the upper limits of sentences produced during his first three years [pp. 190ff.]." Fantini remarks on the early unit-phrases, or "imitative expressions, requiring no knowledge of underlying syntactic rules [p. 89]," in Spanish, but reports no such strategy in Mario's acquisition of English from 2;6 on. These data, alongside my own observations of V.'s second-language learning, seem to suggest that chronological age is less important than stage of linguistic development in determining whether or not a child will use a formula strategy in acquiring productive use of a second language.

Though V.'s second-language learning seems in some ways in the nature of a test case of Olson's position, the "natural experiment" is, as usual, too ill-defined, too compounded with external factors (such as the phonological and morphological make-up of the two languages in question and the relative complexity of the input she received) to afford a satisfyingly clear or conclusive answer to the question of growth in memory capacity in the one-to-two-year old.

In the third month, V. began to construct simple English sentences: On hearing *everybody out* (of the car), she said, *Linda out* (V.'s age was 2;0.4 at this point); in response to another child who said *That's not my lunch*, V. said, *no, mine lunch* (2:0;6); and initiating with her mother the naming game her English-speaking relatives often played with her, *what's that—shirt?* (lifting the hem of her shirt: 2:0;27). The following month her constructed sentences had already become more complex as well as more numerous: Raising a warning finger to her cousin Jeff, *Jeff, no nose* ('don't touch my nose') (2;1.0); *Anjalee, it's yours baby* (returning a doll to a friend: 2;1.3); *no hold Virve* (wrestling with her father: 2;1.5); *book fell down* (2;1.8); *no, no, mama, no, you throw no* (as her mother throws her a ball: 2;1.15). At the same time V. in this month used 63 new items, which consisted of 111 words, or 1.76 words per utterance. There was no indication that any of these complex units were fully constructed, and clear evidence that some were memorized, such as *roll it, roll it, and mark it V* (from Patty-cake: 2;1.1), or partly memorized, partly constructed: Stepping on her mother's foot, V. said, *put-your* [pučʌ] *Virve's foot* (from the song Hokey-Pokey: ('Put your right foot in . . .'):2;1.19. More conversational formulas V. used at this point included *I'll get it*, used several times appropriately but formally invariant; *I will be back; what happened (there)?; what are doing?* which also took the form *what doing?* and *what you doing?*, suggesting some on-going effort at analysis; and *what's the matter?* In two cases V. glossed her phrases in Estonian: *I like it* she rendered as 'Virve wants' (2;1.2),[8] *run away* as 'go away' (2.2,10). Thus V. seems here to be following, at 25 months, a strategy which is typical of second language learners, including the storage and use of unanalyzed complex strings, and the assignment of roughly appropriate global or situational meanings to these strings.

In addition to making fairly rapid lexical and syntactic progress in the fourth month, V. also began to produce strings of distinctively English-sounding jargon; these seemed to arise out of a kind of obsession with the new language, which intruded more and more

---

[8] Note that at this stage, V. had not yet begun to make regular use of personal pronouns in her first language which was largely adult-derived (V. being a first child), whereas in English, a largely peer-derived language for her, the pronouns *I* and *you* appeared among her earliest utterances.

frequently at this time into the otherwise monolingual Estonian home environment.[9] The earliest instance occurred at 2;1.2: With a devilish air, early one morning, she reached for a journal on her mother's bed, saying [a: gadit hɔ̃n pë:k] ('I've got it (one?) book'.) Repeating this two or three times, she proceeded to turn pages and "read" aloud in English-sounding gibberish, making heavy use of the sequence [hɔ̃n]. One could sometimes detect, embedded in such jargon sequences, recognizable strings of English, quite out of context. For example, at dinner at 2;1.7 she played with her fork and spoon, chattering and seeming to say at one point, *do it again, Jennifer.* At lunch at home three days later she said distinctly, *Let's go, lunch time, yes,* quite obviously rehearsing phrases often used at school. At 2;1.22 she spoke some garbled-sounding English to her father, ending with *my house.* To his question as to what this meant, V. replied in Estonian, *You mustn't come into my house take away. The one that's in my room.* At lunch the same day she uttered some strings of jargon, ending with *I want to get down, please* [ayɹwanʌ gEɹdawn, piys], with spread of a gratuitous r-glide across the string. A month later V. was no longer producing jargon, though she still used longer strings in talking aloud while playing alone than when actually communicating with English-speakers, who were necessarily outside her immediate family. For example, playing outdoors while her parents were present but otherwise occupied, V. said *I'm [g]onna come back to see you* ([àymn̩ʌkʌmbǽktʌsíyyuw]) as she went down some steps to get on her tricycle. She then added, *I'm [g]onna bike* ([àymn̩ʌbáyk]) (2;2.3). The first string seems likely to have been fully drawn from memory, the second a two-part construction, *I'm gonna + bike.*[10]

Two qualities differentiate the jargon strings from the English sentences V. built from scratch: Not only were they longer (as compared to her two or three word constructed utterances), but they seemed not to

---

[9] Compare Kenyeres, who writes, "*De ce chaos surgissent . . . les éléments entendus le plus souvent. Ceux-ci se fixent quelquefois dans sa mémoire avant qu'elle en comprenne le sens. Ils résonnent plus tard à ses oreilles. Quelquefois ce sont des phrases entières . . . C'est un grouillement dans son cerveau* [1938, p. 328].''

[10] Berman (1979) also reports the use of jargon by her daughter, Shelli, who reacquired Hebrew after a year of speaking only English. Unlike V., Shelli had made extensive use of jargon earlier, throughout her first year of language use; on return to Israel, at 4;6, Shelli would sing in a kind of gibberish in which were interspersed several words and formulas from Hebrew, seemingly at random; and she would indulge in this kind of chanting-talk when "reading" a book, "talking" on the telephone, or watching a Hebrew show on television. Just as in her original jargon, these vocalizations, too, contained many Hebrew-like sounds such as a low /a/ and velar /x/, and they became increasingly interspersed with Hebrew words . . . By her second month back in Israel, Shelli no longer jargonized. [p. 164].

be filtered through her first language phonology. They quite succesfully rendered the superficial acoustic impression of English, even if individual segments might be misplaced or mispronounced. These strings can be fairly characterized as simple mimicry, or parroting, though they were not prompted by a direct model but were recalled from memory after a delay of unknown length. They differ from the unanalyzed phrases or formulas in that no situational meaning appeared to be attached to them. Since V.'s growing repertoire of individual lexical items were pronounced like Estonian words at first, with gradual substitution of English segments as V. mastered the new phonology, the simultaneous occurrence of these phonetically accurate strings suggests the existence of multiple lexical stores, each with its associated phonetic or phonological processors, much as Moskowitz (1977) has postulated for child language. In adult language, dysfluencies in "propositional" speech as opposed to the fluent production of formulaic or "automatic" speech may point to a similar dichotomy (Goldman-Eisler 1968; Van Lancker 1975; cf. also L. Fillmore 1976, pp. 427ff.)

To consider briefly the operation of a formula strategy, on the one hand, and the co-existence of competing phonological processors, on the other, we can review the development of a particularly high-frequency construction type, that of *I want* + noun and verb complements, over an eight-month period.[11] Within the fourth month two distinct forms of the verb *want* were used: *I wannu*, used at school in response to the question, *Do you want to look at the hamster?*, and *I want more* [ay vant mɔɹ], said to her mother at dinner. For two months thereafter V. used the form *wanna* (or *wannu*) exclusively, whether it was followed by an adverb, a verb, or a noun.

2:1;28 *I wanna down.*
2:2;2   *I wanna here.*
2:2;22 *I wanna home.*
2:2;3   *I wanna go back.*
2:2;14 *I wanna eat-it yoghurt.*
2:2;22 *You wanna see three-jump?* (Posing a toy bear on the edge of a couch)
2:4;16 *I wanna this do.* (This word order, which persisted throughout the period covered here, reflects a common Estonian syntactic choice.)

[11] These were the most common verb constructions for Itoh's subject as well; his use of *I wanna* as a formulaic sentence-opener is very similar to V.'s (see Itoh & Hatch 1978, p. 86).

2;2.4   *I wanna elutoas book.* (*elutoas* 'in the living room')
2;2.14 *I wanna sandals on.*
2;2.14 *I wanna clothes on.* (on hearing *Virve will have to put her clothes on*)
2;2.22 *I don't wannu potty.*
2;4.6   *I wanna my lap, mama.* (asking for a picnic lunch, to eat on her lap)
2;4.6   *I wanna candy.*
2;4.16 *You wanna your lunch?*
2;4.16 *I wanna crayon.*

She then again began to use *want*, now pronounced [uant], but correctly followed by a noun or pronoun complement.

2;4.18 *You want your mama?*
2;2.20 *You want another puzzle?*
2;4.20 *This puzzle you want?*
2;4.25 *I don't want it.*

The following month she overgeneralized her new construction: *You want come my house?* (2;5.0) The remaining recorded instances show *wanna* followed by a verb, with one exception: As her teacher traced the outlines of another child's foot, V. said *I wanna my foot too* (2;7.24), apparently regressing in the face of a more complex construction than she had attempted before, where the subject of the second clause differs from that of the first. Compare the remaining instances:

2;7.11 *I wanna do puzzle.*
2;7.11 *I wanna go.*
2;7.11 *I wanna read a book.*
2;7.13 *I wanna come inside.* (responding to *No one can come inside.*)
2;7.20 *I wanna go back.*
2;7.29 *I wanna play with Linda.*
2;8.15 *I wanna play my room.*
2;8.22 *I wanna this do, you, Jeff.* ('I want to do this with you, Jeff')

What these data suggest is a dynamic interplay between grammar and lexicon, in which the child alternates between the choice of a ready-made formula, *I wanna*, delivered with a fluent approximation to English fast-speech style, and the competing lexical item, *want*, filtered through her existing Estonian-based phonological system (which lacks /w/, but includes both /v/ and /ua/ sequences). Both forms are subject to V.'s emergent syntactic rules or overgeneralizations, with a gradual reorganization in the direction of conventional English grammar. Such an interplay between formulaic or automatic phrasal units and strings constructed out of single lexical items has been detected in adult language as well:

> In the flow of normal speech voluntary and automatic activities are closely interlaced, symbolic behavior alternates with habitual verbalization, the construction of propositions with emotional expression and with the use of ready-made phrases, choice in fitting words to meaning takes turns with submission to the routine course and to the constraints of learned sequences . . . Normal spontaneous speech might be viewed as a highly integrated blend of processes at both levels where results of practice alternate with spontaneous creation [Goldman-Eisler 1968, pp. 9ff; cf. also Bateson 1975, p. 61].[12]

Though idioms, or bound expressions, received some attention within the transformational framework as potential obstructions to the smooth working of a set of generative rules (cf. Fraser 1970; Katz & Postal 1964; Weinreich 1969), it is only in the last decade that simple collocations, including situational or routine formulas, have been cited as a kind of counter-evidence to the creativity and productivity generally claimed for language. For example, Becker (1975), in *The Phrasal Lexicon*, sees the use of language as "based at least as much on memorization as on any impromptu problem-solving [p. 27]"; in his view, "productive processes [or generative rules] have the secondary role of adapting the old phrases [or formulas] to the new situation [p. 1]." (See Nunberg, Sag, & Wasow 1981.) Bolinger's suggestion, quoted earlier, that "learning goes on constantly . . . in segments of collocation size" which yield only gradually to analysis, closely resembles Ferguson's (1977) position regarding phonology: "At the basis of an individual adult's phonology is really something like the phonologically unanalyzed phonetic shapes of whole words, no matter how much phonological order the individual may put into it. All of us make some use of phonetic shapes of whole words unphonologized [p. 287; cf. also Ferguson & Farwell 1975]."

Explaining the results of some psycholinguistic tests on the productivity of English derivational morphophonemics, John Ohala

[12] Wagner-Gough (1975) presents data from a Persian- and Assyrian-speaking child, Homer, who began to learn English at 5:11. Wagner-Gough shows that Homer, who tended to make heavy use of imitation, often incorporated portions of the previous speaker's utterance into his own speech (like Adam Clark, quoted earlier). She further demonstrates the evolution of *wh*-question formation rules in Homer's speech, based on the incorporated patterns. Though Wagner-Gough contrasts her analysis with that of Klima & Bellugi (1966), who derive children's *wh*-questions via transformations from a deep-structure string, it is likely that both juxtaposition of unanalyzed units and creative construction play a role in sentence formation at all ages.

(1974) suggested that there must in some cases be alternate phonological representations of a single word for a single speaker. He represented in flow-chart form a "hypothetical algorithm for analogical derivation," in which the speaker has the option of avoiding the complex analogical (phonological rule) route in favor of a simple addition of affix to stem with no phonetic (or morphophonemic) change [p. 373]. If Goldman-Eisler and the other writers I have cited are right in suggesting that normal spontaneous adult speech typically alternates between creative construction and the use of ready-made formulas, then a model much like that underlying Ohala's flow-chart representation may be needed to express the relation between multiple lexical possibilities, some consisting of collocations and other phrase-length units, and the workings of grammar or syntax.

In short, the use of formulas by children learning a second language is not so remote from ordinary adult language use. A great deal of further work, and some rather clever methodology, will be needed to ascertain the relationship between memory and analysis; the assembling of "formulas, cliches, idioms, allusions, slogans, and so forth [Becker 1975, p. 1] which goes into producing the novel but often familiar-sounding utterances of the practiced speaker is not easily detected, since the process has become deceptively fluent or automatic. Whereas in early first-language learning, memory strategies are inadequate, on the whole, to the task of storing large chunks of unanalyzed material, the child second-language learner comes already prepared with a language-wise memory, a developing need for social intercourse, and an enviable willingness to venture into unexplored territory. These seem to be the right ingredients to afford us a window on the dynamics of memory and generative rules as they interact to create an air of competent performance.

References

Bates, E. (1976) Language and context: The acquisition of pragmatics. New York: Academic Press.

Bateson, M.C. (1975) Linguistic models in the study of joint performances. In M.D. Kinkade, K. L. Hale, & O. Werner (Eds.), Linguistics and anthropology: In Honor of C.F. Voegelin. Lisse: Peter de Ridder Press.

Becker, J. (1975) The phrasal lexicon. Artificial intelligence report no. 28. Bolt Beranek & Newman Inc. Report No. 3081.

Berman, E. (1979) The (re)emergence of a bilingual: A case study of a Hebrew–English speaking child. Working papers in bilingualism, 19, 157–180.

Bloom, L. (1970) Language development: Form and function in emerging grammars. Cambridge, Mass.: MIT Press.

Bloom, L. (1973) *One word at a time*. The Hague: Mouton.

Bolinger, D. (1976) Meaning and memory. *Forum Linguisticum, 1*, 1–14.

Bolinger, D. (1977) Idioms have relations. *Forum Linguisticum, 2*, 157–169.

Braine, M.D.S. (1974) Length constraints, reduction rules, and holophrastic processes in children's word combinations. *Journal of verbal learning and verbal behavior, 13*, 448–456.

Brown, R. (1968) The development of wh-questions in child speech. *Journal of verbal learning and verbal behavior, 7*, 279–290.

Brown, R., & Fraser, C. (1963) The acquisition of syntax. In C.N. Cofer & B. Musgrave (Eds.), *Verbal behavior and learning: Problems and processes*. New York: McGraw-Hill.

Brown, R. & Hanlon, C. (1970) Derivational complexity and order of acquisition in child speech. In J.R. Hayes (Ed.) *Cognition and the development of language*. New York: John Wiley & Sons.

Bruner, J.S. (1975) The ontogenesis of speech acts. *Journal of child language, 2*, 1–19.

Burling, R. (1959) Language development of a Garo and English-speaking child. *Word, 15*, 45–68. Reprinted in E. Hatch (Ed.) (1978) *Second language acquisition: A book of readings*. Rowley, Mass. Newbury House.

Carey, S. (1978) The child as word learner. In M. Halle, J. Bresnan, & G.A. Miller (Eds.), *Linguistic theory and psychological reality*. Cambridge, Mass.: MIT Press.

Cazden, C.B. (1968) The acquisition of noun and verb inflections. *Child development, 39*, 435–448.

Celce-Murcia, M. (1978) The simultaneous acquisition of English and French in a two-year old child. In E. Hatch (Ed.) (1978) *Second language acquisition: A book of readings*. Rowley, Mass.: Newbury House.

Clark, R. (1974) Performing without competence. *Journal of child language, 1*, 1–10.

Clark, R. (1977) What's the use of imitation? *Journal of child language, 4*, 341–358.

Coulmas, F. (1979) On the sociolinguistic relevance of routine formulae. *Journal of pragmatics, 3*, 239–266.

Crystal, D. (1974) Review of Roger Brown, *A First Language*. *Journal of child language, 1*, 289–306.

Dore, J., Franklin, M.B., Miller, R.T., & Ramer, A.L.H. (1976) Transitional phenomena in early language acquisition. *Journal of child language, 3*, 13–28.

Drachman, G. (1973) Some strategies in the acquisition of phonology. In M.J. Kenstowicz & C.W. Kisseberth (Eds.), *Issues in phonological theory*. The Hague: Mouton.

Ervin-Tripp, S. (1974) Is second language learning like the first? *TESOL quarterly, 8*, 111–127. Reprinted in E. Hatch (Ed.) (1978) *Second language acquisition: A book of readings*. Rowley, Mass.: Newbury House.

Fantini, A.E. (1974) *Language acquisition of a bilingual child: A sociolinguistic perspective (to age five)*. Brattleboro, Vt.: The Experiment Press.

Ferguson, C.A. (1976) The structure and use of politeness formulas. *Language in society, 5*, 137–151.

Ferguson, C.A. (1977) New directions in phonological theory: Language acquisition and universals research. In R.W. Cole (Ed.), *Current issues in linguistic theory*. Bloomington: Indiana University Press.

Ferguson, C. A., & C. B. Farwell (1975) Words and sounds in early language acquisition. *Language, 51*, 419–439.

Ferguson, C. A., & Macken, M.A. (1982) Phonological development in children. in K.E. Nelson (Ed.), *Language development, 4*. New York: Garner Press.

Fillmore, C.J. (1976) The need for a frame semantics in linguistics. *Statistical methods in linguistics*. Stockholm: Skriptor.

Fillmore, C.J. (1979a) Innocence: A second idealization for linguistics. *Proceedings of the Fifth Annual Berkeley Linguistic Society*, Feb., 17–19.

Fillmore, C.J. (1979b) On fluency. In C.J. Fillmore, D. Kempler, & W.S.-Y. Wang (Eds.), *Individual differences in language ability and language behavior*. New York: Academic Press.

Fillmore, L.W. (1976) The second time around: Cognitive and social strategies in second language acquisition. Unpublished dissertation, Stanford University.

Flavell, J.H. & Wellman, H.M. (1977) Metamemory. In R.V. Kail, Jr. & J.W. Hagen (Eds.), *Perspectives on the development of memory and cognition*. Hillsdale, New Jersey: Lawrence Erlbaum Associates.

Fraser, B. (1970) Idioms within a transformational grammar. *Foundations of language, 6*, 22–42.

Goldman-Eisler, F. (1968) *Psycholinguistics: Experiments in spontaneous speech*. London: Academic Press.

Hakuta, K. (1974) Prefabricated patterns and the emergence of structure in second language acquisition. *Language learning, 24*, 287–297.

Hakuta, K. (1975) Becoming bilingual at age five: The story of Uguisu. Unpublished Harvard Honors Thesis.

Hanania, E. & Gradman, H. (1977) Acquisition of English structures: A case study of an adult native speaker in an English-speaking environment. *Language learning, 27*, 75–92.

Huang, J. & Hatch, E.M. (1978) A Chinese child's acquisition of English. In E. Hatch (Ed.) (1978) *Second language acquisition: A book of readings*. Rowley, Mass.: Newbury House.

Huttenlocher, J. (1974) The origins of language comprehension. In R.L. Solso (Ed.), *Theories in cognitive psychology*. Hillsdale, New Jersey: Lawrence Erlbaum Associates.

Imedadze, N. (1967) On the psychological nature of child speech formation under condition of exposure to two languages. *International journal of psychology, 2*, 129–132. Reprinted in E. Hatch (Ed.) (1978) *Second language acquisition: A book of readings*. Rowley, Mass.: Newbury House.

Itoh, H. & Hatch, E.M. (1978) Second language acquisition: A case study. In E. Hatch (Ed.) (1978) *Second language acquisition: A book of readings*. Rowley, Mass.: Newbury House.

Katz, J.J. & Postal, P.M. (1964) *An integrated theory of linguistic descriptions*. Cambridge, Mass.: MIT Press.

Kenyeres, A. & Kenyeres, E. (1938) Comment une petite hongroise de sept ans apprend le français. *Archives de psychologie, 26*, 321–366.

Klima, E.S. & Bellugi, U. (1966) Syntactic regularities in the speech of children. In J. Lyons & R.J. Wales (Eds.) *Psycholinguistic papers*. Edinburgh: University Press.

Krashen, S. & Scarcella, R. (1978) On routines and patterns in language acquisition and performance. *Language learning, 28:2*, 283–300.

Larsen-Freeman, D.E. (1978) Evidence of the need for a second language acquisition index of development. In W.C. Ritchie (Ed.), *Second language acquisition research*. New York: Academic Press.

Leopold, W.F. (1939–1949) *Speech development of a bilingual child, Vols. I–IV*. Evanston, Ill.: Northwestern University Press.

McLaughlin, B. (1978) *Second language acquisition in childhood*. Hillsdale, New Jersey: Lawrence Erlbaum Associates.

MacWhinney, B. (1978) *The acquisition of morphology: Monographs of the Society for Research in Child Development, 43*, 1–2.

Macken, M. (1976) Permitted complexity in phonological development: One child's acquisition of Spanish consonants. *Lingua, 44*, 219–253.

Menn, L. (1976) Evidence for an interactionist-discovery theory of child phonology. *Papers and reports on child language development 12*, 169–177.

Moskowitz, B.A. (1977) Idioms in phonology acquisition and phonological change. Unpublished paper, UCLA.

Murrell, M. (1966) Language acquisition in a trilingual environment: Notes from a case study. *Studia linguistica, 20*, 9–34.

Nelson, K. (1973) Structure and strategy in learning to talk. *Monographs of the Society for Research in Child Development, 38.*

Nelson, K., L. Rescorla, J. Gruendiel, & H. Benedict. (1978) Early lexicons: What do they mean? *Child development 48*, 960–968.

Ohala, J. (1974) Explaining historical phonology. In J.M. Anderson & C. Jones (Eds.), *Historical linguistics II: Theory and description in phonology.* (Proceedings of the First International Conference on Historical Linguistics. Edinburgh. 2–7 September 1973.) Amsterdam: North Holland Publishing Co.

Oksaar, E. (1977) On becoming trilingual: A case study. In C. Molony, H. Zobl, & W. Stölting (Eds.), *German in contact with other languages.* Kronberg: Skriptor.

Olson, G.M. (1973) Developmental changes in memory and the acquisition of language. In T.E. Moore (Ed.), *Cognitive development and the acquisition of language.* New York: Academic Press.

Padilla, A.M. & Liebman, E. (1975) Language acquisition and the bilingual child. *Bilingual review*, 34–55.

Pavlovitch, M. (1920) *Le langage enfantin: Acquisition du serbe et du français par un enfant serbe.* Paris: Champion.

Peters. A. (1977) Language learning strategies. *Language, 53*, 560–573.

Peters, A. (1980) Units of acquisition. *Working Papers in Linguistics, 12*, 1–72. University of Hawaii.

Ruhl, C. (1977) Two forms of reductionism. In M. Paradis (Ed.) *The Fourth LACUS Forum.* Columbia, S.C.: Hornbeam Press. Pp. 370–383.

Scarcella, R.C. (1979) "Watch up!": a study of verbal routines in adult second language performance. *Working papers in bilingualism, 19*, 79–88.

Snow, C.E. (1977) The development of conversation between mothers and babies. *Journal of child language, 4*, 1–22.

Swain, M.K. (1972) Bilingualism as a first language. Unpublished dissertation, University of California at Irvine.

Tabouret-Keller, A. (1963) L'acquisition du langage parlé chez un petit enfant en milieu bilingue. In J. de Ajuriaguerra, F. Bresson, P. Fraisse, B. Inhelder, P. Oleron, & J. Piaget (Eds.), *Problèmes de psycho-linguistique: Symposium de l'association de psychologie scientifique de langue française.* Paris: Presses universitaires de France.

Ronjat, J. (1913) *Le développement du langage observé chez un enfant bilingue.* Paris: Champion.

Valette, R.M. (1964) Some reflections on second-language learning in young children. *Language learning, 14*, 91–98.

Van Lancker, D. (1975) Heterogeneity in language and speech: Neurolinguistic studies. *Working papers in phonetics, 29.* University of California at Los Angeles.

Vihman, M.M. (1971) On the acquisition of Estonian. *Papers and reports on child language development, 3*, 51–94. Stanford University.

Vihman, M.M. (1976) From pre-speech to speech: On early phonology. *Papers and reports on child language development 12*, 230–243. Stanford University.

Vihman, M.M. (1981) Phonology and the development of the lexicon: Evidence from children's errors. *Journal of child language 8*, 239–264.

Vihman, M.M. (In preparation) Learning a second language at age two: A diary study.

Vogel, I. (1975) One system or two: An analysis of a two-year old Romanian-English bilingual's phonology. *Papers and reports on child language development, 9,* 43–62. Stanford University.

Volterra, V. & Taeschner, T. (1978) The acquisition and development of language by bilingual children. *Journal of child language, 5,* 33–326.

Wagner-Gough, J. (1975) Comparative studies in second language learning. *CAL–ERIC/CLL Series on Language and Linguistics, 26.* Reprinted in part in E. Hatch (Ed.) (1978) *Second language acquisition: A book of readings.* Rowley, Mass.: Newbury House.

Weinreich, U. (1969) Problems in the analysis of idioms. In J. Puhvel (Ed.) *Substance and structure of language.* Los Angeles: University of California Press.

Yoshida, M. (1978) The acquisition of English vocabulary by a Japanese-speaking child. In E. Hatch (Ed.) (1978) *Second language acquisition: A book of readings.* Rowley, Mass.: Newbury House.

17 SUSAN CURTISS

Developmental Dissociations of Language and Cognition

There are a few questions in linguistic theory which are of particular interest to me and which are, in my opinion, of central importance. Two of these questions are (a) is the human mind innately endowed with knowledge about language, and if so, what is the character of that knowledge, and (b) are there language-specific learning mechanisms? The innateness question and the language-specificity question are closely bound together, for it is difficult to imagine what language-specific learning mechanisms would be or how they would operate without innate knowledge about the possible form of human language or innate predispositions to process linguistic input in highly specific ways. However, it is possible that there is innate knowledge that is implicated in the learning of language that is nonetheless NOT specific to the learning of language. Thus the two questions are separate issues, and attempts can be made to answer each question separately, keeping in mind that the answer to one will probably have direct bearing on the answer to the other.

In this chapter I will address the second of these two questions: Are there language-specific learning mechanisms? This question can be broken down into at least three component questions:

1. Is language acquisition simply one instance of the general cognitive development of the child?

2. Does language acquisition co-occur in development with certain nonlinguistic cognitive attainments (or, are they correlated) because they are based on the same cognitive principles?

EXCEPTIONAL LANGUAGE AND LINGUISTICS

3. If there is such a thing as general intelligence, can the multipurpose learning mechanisms which account for its ontogenesis learn language?

The data I will present come from cases of abnormal language acquisition, cases which manifest a noteworthy dissociation of language from nonlanguage function. Although these cases represent striking divergencies from normal development, such cases of language–nonlanguage dissociations can help to clarify the connections and interdependencies between language and other aspects of mental development in the normal child. They can aid in teasing out those relationships which are necessary from those which may look so, but may instead be artifacts of general maturation. I discuss only three cases here because of space limitations, but we have other, comparable data and are in the process of collecting still more (Curtiss, Yamada, & Fromkin 1979; Curtiss, Kempler, & Yamada 1981).

Genie

The first case is that of Genie, a case of first language acquisition in adolescence. Much has been written about this case and I will not rehash what can easily be found elsewhere (Curtiss 1977; Curtiss, Fromkin, Krashen, Rigler, & Rigler 1974; Fromkin, Krashen, Curtiss, Rigler, & Rigler 1974). For those who are unfamiliar with the case, Genie underwent extreme isolation and deprivation until she was 13½ years of age. Never having had sufficient exposure to language to learn language as a child, she faced the task of first language acquisition as a teenager. Despite her severely limited life experience, however, she had not been asleep during her years of confinement; and in some areas Genie had apparently developed beyond the level of a child beginning to learn language. There are, as a result, aspects of this case which are particularly relevant to the questions at hand.

Genie's language development has been notably abnormal. For one thing, the majority of her utterances are noun phrases, a reflection of her fixation on static visual images, past and present, and possibly the result of her restricted sensorimotor experience. For another, she is very limited in using language as a communicative device. For example, she produces no vocatives or grammatically marked questions and has no topicalization or focusing devices save repetition (c.f. Curtiss 1977; Bennett 1978). This is in striking contrast to her effectiveness, indeed power, as a nonlinguistic communicator. She has, for example, well-developed use of gesture, facial expression, eye gaze, attention-getting devices, and turn-taking knowledge. The most important aspect of her language development for the issues of concern here, however, is the disparity between her lexical semantic, and thematic or relational semantic knowledge on the one hand, and her syntactic abilities, including her ability to map thematic relations onto syntactic structures and to subcategorize lexical items, on the other. This disparity between the aspects of language Genie has readily acquired and those she still has not mastered can perhaps best be generalized as one between conceptual content and grammatical form, a disparity which has been present from the onset of Genie's speech.

The area of language best mastered by Genie, it would appear, is lexical semantics. Genie's early vocabulary acquisition revealed a cognitive sophistication not found in the early vocabularies of children during first language acquisition. For example, children's early vocabulary appears to function both in comprehension and production as narrowly specified subportions of the equivalent adult terms (Clark 1977; Reich 1976; Saltz, Dixon, Klein, & Becker 1977). Naming errors tend to be overdiscrimination errors, although overgeneralizations in word use are frequently reported. Such overgeneralizations, however, probably result mainly from a child's overextending his or her vocabulary to communicate about topics that would otherwise be beyond what his or her small vocabulary would allow (Saltz, Soller, & Siegel 1972; Clark 1975). Genie, however, did not appear to underspecify or overspecify the semantic domain of words in the ways seen with normal children. For example, although she spoke in one-word utterances for several months, at no time did she appear to overextend semantic reference. In contrast, she appeared to seek out vocabulary to differentiate between similar objects which she knew to be different along some parameter—visual, functional, or otherwise, even if it interrupted a communicative interchange. Second, vocabulary in the early stages of language acquisition normally consists of lexical items for general, basic classes (e.g., chair), not superordinate or subordinate terms (e.g., furniture, or rocking chair) (Rosch, Mervis, Gray, Johnson, & Boyes-Braem 1976). Even at the single-word stage, however, Genie learned and appropriately used superordinate, subordinate, and general class terms (e.g., *lion, tiger, cat, dog*, etc. and *animal; coat, jacket, blouse, sweater*, etc. and *clothes*). Fourth, normal children first talk only about the here-and-now (Brown 1973; Gesell 1940; Greenfield & Smith 1976; Weisenburger 1976). But even during Genie's one-word period she often spoke of nonpresent people or objects. Thus in her earliest use of words, Genie displayed elaborate,

TABLE 17.1
Examples of Thematic Relations in Genie's Speech

Utterance	Date	Relations expressed
Spot chew glove.	12/71	Agent–action–object
Miss F. have blue car.	12/72	Possessor–state–object
Play gym.	1/72	Action–Location
Genie bad cold live father house.	10/73	Experiencer–state–time
Mama people not hit big wood.	5/74	Agent–agent–negation–action–instrument
Father hit Genie big stick.	8/74	Agent–action–patient–instrument
Go doctor house tomorrow.	9/77	Action–location–time

adult-like classificatory schemes and the ability to represent the nonpresent in thought and language. From that early point on, Genie has readily acquired new vocabulary, following the path familiar to all of us of continually learning new words that correspond to and represent new nonlinguistic mental knowledge and ever-finer semantic differentiations.

From the range of Genie's vocabulary, her use of vocabulary, and her continuing acquisition of vocabulary, one can conclude that Genie is not impaired in the acquisition of lexical semantics, and that her lexical entries contain adult-like semantic feature specification.

There is one other aspect of language that Genie performs quite well—the expression of combinations of basic semantic (thematic) relations. Examples are presented in Table 17.1.

Genie expresses a substantial range of thematic relations and in some instances has also learned grammatical devices to mark certain relations overtly; namely, adverbials and locative and directional prepositions as seen in Table 17.2.

TABLE 17.2
Examples of Overtly Marked Semantic Relations

Utterance	Date	Relations expressed
See Mama Friday.	9/72	State–patient–time
Mama wash hair in sink.	1/73	Agent–action–object–location
Get out baby buggy.	3/73	Action–direction–location
After dinner use mixmaster.	1/74	Time–action–object
You draw standing Mama on stair.	9/77	Agent–action–action–agent–location
Think about D. swim in ocean.	11/74	State–agent–action–location
At Woolworth big huge truck.	10/73	Location–object

TABLE 17.3

Utterance	Date	Approximate gloss
Applesauce buy store.	4/72	('I want you to buy applesauce at the store'.)
Father house live father Genie bad cold.	10/73	('When I lived at father's house, I had a bad cold'.)
Spool wind thread.	12/76	('One winds thread around a spool'.)
Water think swim think swim.	8/77	('I'm thinking about swimming in the water'.)
Tummy water drink.	8/77	('My tummy drank the (swimming) water'.)
Sick people lady driving ambulance.	9/77	('A lady is driving sick people in the ambulance'.)
Hot dog eat, eat the hot dog, eat hot dog.	11/77	('I ate the hot dog'.)
I want I want big Mama toy.	10/77	('I want a big toy from Mama'.)

Thus we can see that Genie's grammar must contain not only the sense or meaning definitions of words, but also a list of at least potential arguments for verbs and a specification of the semantic relations between arguments. Occurrence restrictions of elements such as articles and progressive marker /-ing/ in Genie's speech indicate that the syntactic category of a word is also included in its stored representation, although /-ing/ is not used consistently or unambiguously to mark progressive aspect.

Note, however, the sentences in Table 17.3. Utterances such as these suggest the absence of subcategorization information and the absence of consistent rules for mapping thematic relations onto subcategorization features or grammatical relations. The "sentences" in Table 17.4 (as well as Table 17.3) indicate the additional absence of other gram-

TABLE 17.4

Utterance	Date	Approximate gloss
Angry burn stove.	1/72	('Grandma was angry at me and said I'd get burned if I stayed by the stove'.)
I supermarket surprise Roy.	4/74	('I was surprised to see Roy at the supermarket'.)
Live father house smell washcloth.	10/73	('When I lived in my father's house I used to smell the washcloth he used'.)
Father house live father Genie bad cold.		('When I lived at my father's house, I had a bad cold'.)
Genie cry ride.	10/77	('I cried when I was on the ride'.)

matical devices or operations for signalling syntactic relations or other than thematic semantic structure (e.g., subordinating conjunctions, tense markers, complementizers). It is worth noting that despite the ill-formed character of many of Genie's utterances, their semantic intent and content is remarkably clear, especially in context. The gap, then, between conceptual/semantic content and grammatical form in Genie's utterances is quite striking. One is led to try and account for such a selective difference between the aspects of language Genie has acquired and those she apparently has not been able to master.

Perhaps Genie's markedly uneven profile is reflective of either a general intellectual deficit or of specific cognitive impairments, i.e., perhaps a nonlinguistic cognitive impairment has prevented her from developing beyond this point linguistically. It is hard to imagine how a general intellectual deficit could account for such a selective linguistic deficit. One should imagine, for example, that the one area of language which might be most affected by or tied to intellectual level would be vocabulary, but that is the area of language most developed in this case. Nonetheless, to address the hypothesis that language development can be accounted for (i.e., learned) by the same mechanisms that account for the development of general intelligence, it is important to determine whether or not Genie might be limited from learning language by her general intellectual level.

Table 17.5 presents Genie's performance on standardized intelligence tests from the time she was first found until the time she was last tested. There are two major points to be made regarding these data. (Genie's performance on these tests is considered in greater detail elsewhere. See Curtiss 1979). First, both her verbal and nonverbal intelligence have developed "normally" in the sense that for every year of chronological age increase since her discovery, there has been a concommitant mental age increase. The difference between the two areas appears to lie primarily in the degree of knowledge or development Genie began with when she emerged into our world. After seven years of "human" social experience, starting with essentially no linguistic knowledge or experience, Genie achieved a mental age of approximately 6 years; and after seven years of new life experience starting with, perhaps, a 4 or 5-year-old level of nonlinguistic ability, Genie attained a mental age of approximately 12 years. Secondly, in both areas she has surely demonstrated sufficient intellectual ability to support a full linguistic system. That is, children with a comparable mental age have language. It appears, then, that Genie's selective linguistic deficits cannot be attributed to lack of sufficient intelligence, and more importantly for the

TABLE 17.5
Intelligence Tests Administered to Genie

Test	Date	M.A.	I.Q.	Score	Other quantification of performance
Preschool Attainment Record (PAR)	11/70	(0–2)			Mean for 13 months; range from 0–24 months
Vineland	11/70	1.05			
Leiter	1/71	(5.2)	38		Mean for 4.9; range 3 yrs. to 5.9 yrs.
PAR	7/71	4.5			
Vineland	7/71	5.2			
French Pictorial Test of Intell.	10/71	(4–9)			Picture Vocab. 4.6; Info and Comp. 5.0; Size + Number 4.6 (short form); Form Discrim. 7.0; Similarities 4.6 (short form, Immed. Recall 9.0
Vineland	1/72	5.6			
Leiter	4/72	(7.5)	53		
WISC	6/72	(6–9)			Picture Arrangement 6.2; Block Design 9.6–9.10; Object Assembly 8.6–8.10
Columbia Mental Maturity Scale (CMMS)	9/72	5.11	38	55	
Vineland	10/72	5.7			
Leiter	5/73	8.3	53		
Bender-Gestalt	5/73	5.6			
WISC	5/73				Below norms verbal; Performance IQ 50; Full scale below norms
CMMS	5/73	6.1		57	
Stanford-Binet	5/73	5.8	38		
PAR	6/73	5.8			
Leiter	2/74	9.7	65		
Raven Coloured Progressive Matrices	1/75			29	25% of 10-yr-olds attain a score of 29 or more
Raven (RCPM)	3/77	(10–11)		32	95th percentile for 10-yr-olds; 75th–90th percentile for 11-yr-olds
Leiter	10/77	12.6	74		

questions at hand, that the mechanisms by which Genie's general intelligence developed were not able to mediate the learning of certain aspects of language.

Perhaps, even though Genie's linguistic profile cannot be accounted for by a general intellectual deficit, it can be tied to her failure to develop certain specific cognitive abilities. According to classical Piagetian theory, language emerges from and is rooted in general sensorimotor intelligence and is only one instance of the semiotic function, which is attained at the end of the sensorimotor period (Inhelder, Lezine, Sinclair & Stamback 1972; Piaget 1980; Sinclair 1975). More recent developmental psycholinguistic work, however, has proposed that the ties between language and nonlanguage cognition are more specific, that particular abilities are prerequisites to language, or share a common cognitive basis with language; e.g. means–ends knowledge (Bates, Benigni, Bretherton, Camaioni, & Volterra 1977; Snyder 1978), drawing (Goodenough 1926; Harris 1963), symbolic play (Hulme & Lunzer 1966; Lovell, Hoyle, & Sidall 1968; Nicolich 1977), knowledge that other people can serve as agents (Bates, Benigni, Bretherton, Camaioni, & Volterra 1979), the attainment of object permanence (Bloom 1973; Corrigan 1978 but cf. Corrigan 1979), classificatory skills (Sinclair 1970), and nesting ability and hierarchical construction ability (Greenfield 1976; 1978; Greenfield & Schneider 1977). Since the bulk of the grammar is normally acquired during the preoperational years, we might also consider a general demonstration of preoperational intelligence as a necessary concommitant to grammar acquisition.

Genie's performance on a variety of relevant tasks is presented in Table 17.6. (See Curtiss 1979 for a more complete description of the material covered in Table 17.6.)

As Table 17.6 indicates, Genie's performance on relevant tasks places her within the stage of concrete operations (i.e. beyond preoperational intelligence). It further indicates a dissociation between some of the very abilities hypothesized to be linked to language and her linguistic disabilities. The small range of semantic abilities Genie demonstrates may be tied to general conceptual level and/or to specific cognitive attainments, but the aspects of language Genie lacks do not evidence this tie. This case, then, supports the hypothesis that there are language-specific learning mechanisms and suggests that these mechanisms may be responsible for the learning of syntax in particular.

If there are language-specific learning mechanisms for the acquisition of certain aspects of language and these same aspects of language are not tied to nonlinguistic cognitive development, it should in principle be possible to find children who show an opposite profile to Genie's—i.e.,

TABLE 17.6

Test/task	Genie's performance level
Drawing (spontaneous)[a]	approximate 6–7-year-old level
Logical sequencing (Curtiss & Yamada, unpublished)	8½–9-year-old level; at ceiling of test presented
Conservation[b]	6–7-year-old level (conserves area and length; number questionable)
Classification (Curtiss, unpublished)	8-year-old level; at ceiling
Spatial operations (Laurendeau & Pinard 1970)	12-year level; appears to have all concrete operational spatial operations.
Nesting (Greenfield, Nelson, & Saltzman 1972)	at ceiling
Hierarchical construction (Greenfield 1976; 1978; Greenfield & Schneider 1977)	able to copy all models, regardless of internal complexity; at least 11–12-year level performance.
Auditory Short Term Memory (I.T.P.A. Kirk, McCarthy, & Kirk 1968)	3.0 year level

[a] Drawing assessed by criteria per Goodenough (1926); Kellogg (1969); Goodnow (1977).

[b] Conservation assessed by a series of tasks modelled after Beard (1963); Goldschmid & Bentler (1968); Elkind (1961); Elkind (1966); Lovell, Healey, & Rowland (1962); Wallach, Wall, & Anderson (1967); Wohlwill & Lowe (1962).

one of mastery of the linguistic system (at least those aspects Genie lacks) despite cognitive deficits even in those areas hypothesized to be linked to language. Such children would in a sense have selectively "intact" linguistic function.

We have been studying several children who appear to fit this description and I will discuss two of them in the following paragraphs. Before doing so, two caveats must be mentioned.

Such cases have been difficult to locate. There are, it seems to me, at least two reasons why this has been so. First, children who "speak well" (fluently, in sentences, but not necessarily communicatively or meaningfully) but who are mentally deficient are an enigma to many professionals. It is assumed by many educators and psychologists that children who "speak well" cannot truly be mentally retarded and so are not labelled as such. The consistent deficient performance of such children on I.Q. tests and in classrooms is attributed to underlying emotional disorders, behavioral disorders, or both. Often these children are placed in special classes or schools with the continual expectation that they will snap out of their social/emotional disorder and their academic performance will improve remarkably, finally matching their linguistic performance. What often results is terrible frustration shared by all concerned, and very few children are considered to fit our description, especially since such children usually develop strategies to compensate for their deficits, strategies based on linguistic and social cunning. Consequently, few children who fit this profile are referred to us.

Second, such children are difficult to locate because they are probably rare. A first step toward extracting meaning from speech input, and a prerequisite, one would think, to seeking and finding structural regularities in this input, would be the acquisition of words, one of the abilities apparently tied strongly to nonlinguistic conceptual development. If a child is mentally retarded, word acquisition will be retarded; and we expect the rest of language acquisition to follow in kind, since without an interpretation of the content words in a sentence, no hypotheses regarding their organization or constraints on their organization could be tested. It is no surprise, therefore, that severely retarded individuals generally develop little language, regardless of whether or not there may be language-specific learning mechanisms, or whether these mechanisms might even be intact.

We have nonetheless found children who are retarded (I.Q.'s from 30–60) whose knowledge of linguistic structure appears to far outstrip almost every other mental ability, in some cases including some of those semantic abilities preserved in Genie.

Antony

The first such child to be discussed is Antony.[1] (See Curtiss and Yamada 1981 for a more detailed description of this case.) Antony was a child of 6–7 years of age when we studied him. Antony's I.Q. estimates range from 50–56 and mental age less than one year prior to our study was 2.9. Surprisingly, parental report of speech onset is one year, with "full sentences" reported at three years.

Antony's language was quite complex in terms of morphological and syntactic structure, although Antony made errors not untypical for his age, suggesting that he was still mastering some grammatical rules, providing evidence also that his language was productive and creative and not simply formulaic echoing. See, for example, the sentences in Table 17.7. His speech includes Wh-pronouns, demonstratives, third person pronouns, anaphoric pronouns, complex complementation,

---

[1] These data were collected in collaboration with J. Yamada, University of California at Los Angeles.

TABLE 17.7
Some Examples of Antony's Speech

I told somebody be quiet.
I would not have an ice cream.
Whyn't you make her hair like that?
Because I want to hate her.
I say you wash your face like that.
I don't got friends, I got my brother named David.
That clock says it's time to get some prizes.
Jeni would you help me draw pictures of Susie?
Didn't ate this one.
I doed this already.

---

relativization, and close to the full range of auxiliary elaboration—all features absent from Genie's speech.

Despite the degree of morphological elaboration and structural complexity, however, in context, Antony's language is often confusing. First of all Antony's lexical choice is frequently inappropriate or incorrect as illustrated in Table 17.8. It is not only the sense definitions of lexical items in Antony's speech that cause confusion, however. In part, communication with Antony is difficult because despite his fluent productive language, he has substantial comprehension problems with individual words as well as larger structures, e.g.,

(1)   A: *We sew this.* (referring to a spool)
        J: *You sew with that, right.*
        A: *No, I don't sew with that.*
        J: *Other people do.*
        A: *No, my Mom do.*

TABLE 17.8
Some Examples of Lexical Errors in Antony's Speech

---

*We saw them on the **birthday**.* (for 'cake')
*He has a **batman**.* (for He has a 'basket')
*He's **cutting** the mail.* (for he's putting a stamp on the letter)
***Watering** it.* (for 'washing it')
Drum (for 'horn')
*A **pie**.* (for 'pear')
***That's** tying his shoe.* (for 'He's' tying)
*Goes **to** the fish.* (for 'with' the fish)
*Goes **in** the broom.* (for 'with' the broom)
*A **grass**, that we drink with it.* (for 'glass')

---

(2)   J: *Draw a picture of Vivian.*
        A: *No. It's not Vivian's, it's mine.*
        S: *Draw a picture of Mrs. W.*
        A: *No. It's not Mrs. W's.*
        S: *Draw a picture of Antony.*
        A: *That's not me.* **This** *is me* (pointing to himself).

(3)   J: *Does your Daddy stay home all day and cook?*
        A: *Nope. He was not comin home.*

and he does not control or grasp presupposition or implicature in his
own speech, e.g.,

(4)   A: *Do you got a brother?*
        J: *Uh huh, I have two brothers.*
        A: *What's his names?*
        J: *My brothers' names are Stephen and Douglas, Steve and Doug.*
        A: *What's your sister's name?* (assuming J. has a sister without
           knowing)
        J: *My sister's name is Hedi.*
        A: *What's your other sister's name?*
        J: *I only have one sister. I have two brothers and one sister. How 'bout
           you?*
        A: *I got two sisters. I got David and Vicky and Ann Margaret.*

In addition, his use of deixis i.e., articles, tense, pronouns, demonstratives, and Wh-words, is often inconsistent and ill-formed, as
illustrated in (5)–(9).

(5)   A: *He's taking a boy. He's taking the boy.*

(6)   A: *He shot him. He shoot him. The police shoot Lucan.*

(7)   M: *That's who?*
        A: *Our father.* (meaning 'his' (Lucan's) father).

(8)   Miss C. enters Antony's class and stands within full view of
        Antony.
        A: *You guys, lookit who's in our class. I want to see who's in that class.*
        S: *Who's in what class?*
        A: *No, in ours.*
        S: *Everybody's here!*
        A: *Not Miss C.*

(9)   A: *Where I took?* (for 'What'd I take?')

It appears that Antony has learned grammatical devices and operations separate from the semantic complexities mapped onto sentences by these very devices. What has resulted is a system in which substantives are usually combined in a structurally well-formed manner, but well-formed often only when abstracted away from context. Thus, although basic sentential and semantic relations appear to be systematically expressed through SVO word order, one is tempted to call Antony's full-blown set of devices at least a partially autonomous syntax.

A look at Antony's nonlanguage functioning illustrates once again a dissociation of grammatical ability from general intelligence and from specific cognitive abilities hypothesized to be linked to language.

Antony's general intelligence is difficult to measure. He has a markedly short attention span and was extremely difficult to test. Many tasks successfully administered to two-year-old children by the same experimenters were found to be too difficult for Antony to grasp. One's impression of Antony's general intelligence is that he is substantially mentally deficient, and that his real intelligence belies his scorable I.Q. This is in marked contrast to one's impression of Genie which is that she is considerably more intelligent than most tests and her scorable I.Q. reflect.

An examination of Antony's specific abilities is consistent with the impression that he is a very low-functioning child, and points again to a separability between language development and development of at least some of the specific cognitive abilities hypothesized to be linked to language development. See Table 17.9.

Antony is severely delayed in every area except language and auditory short term memory. His play, drawing, copying, and general problem-solving behavior place him approximately in sensorimotor

TABLE 17.9
Antony's Nonlanguage Profile

Ability	Antony's performance
Auditory short term memory	7-year level
Drawing and copying	prerepresentational
Nesting	28–32 months
Hierarchical Construction	less than a 2-year level
Conservation	couldn't administer, even à la Gelman
Logical sequencing	2-year level
Classification	unable to perform at all; below 2 years
Play	1–2 year level

stage VI (20–24 months), possibly just beyond. It is important to note that Antony was functioning at this low level during the period of our case study, when he was already 6½–7 years of age, and when he had already attained considerable linguistic mastery. How much had Antony developed beyond the cognitive level of his early years when he reportedly was learning language? And because his vocabulary seemed quite limited in comparison to the structural richness of his speech, one must ask with what even more limited vocabulary was he able to abstract the linguistic regularities and principles of English grammar?

These are questions we do not have answers to. But Antony's case nevertheless bears suggestively on the question of language-specific mechanisms. Like Genie's case, Antony's profile indicates clearly that the acquisition of grammar is not simply one instance of general cognitive development. Like Genie's case, Antony's profile suggests that certain linguistic abilities (i.e., syntax) are unrelated to many of the specific cognitive abilities which have been hypothesized to be based on shared cognitive principles. And like Genie's case, Antony's profile demonstrates that the mechanisms by which syntax is acquired are not general purpose learning mechanisms underlying the development of a general intelligence.

Marta

The second case of "selectively intact" linguistic ability is that of Marta. Marta is the subject of a dissertation in progress (Yamada, forthcoming. See also Yamada 1981 for a more detailed description and analysis of the linguistic and nonlinguistic data on this case.) Only a portion of the data I will discuss was collected jointly, and I am grateful to J. Yamada for allowing me to include some of her data here.

Marta ia a mentally retarded adolescent (I.Q. 44) who has been studied since October, 1979. She is in a sense "hyperverbal," and because she is apparently no longer acquiring language, she offers a rare opportunity to study the nature of and extent to which language can be acquired in the face of severe cognitive deficits.

Marta's lexical abilities appear moderately well-developed, although recent vocabulary assessment (Peabody Picture Vocabulary Test) places her vocabulary at only a 3.11 year level. She occasionally demonstrates word-finding difficulties as illustrated in (10) below, although her word-finding difficulties are most often manifested in attempts to use proper names.

(10)   Marta is being asked to name pictures. She is shown a picture of
        a bed and asked to identify it.
        M: _____ (no response)
        S: *Go to* _____. *It's time to go to . . .*
        M: (Gestures sleeping.)
        S: *That's right. But what's another word?*
        M: *Zonk out.*
        S: *Right.*
        M: *Or sack out.*
        S: *But what's this called? What do you get on?*
        J: *Does anybody ever say, Don't jump on the* _____? *What is*
           this?
        M: _____

Marta's syntactic and morphological abilities are richly developed as
illustrated in Table 17.10. She produces sentences involving full noun
phrase and verb phrase morphological elaboration, and an adult range
of syntactic operations (e.g., subject-auxiliary inversion, relativization,
pronominalization, complementation, passivization, and extrapo-
sition). Marta also uses an abundance of sentence adverbials and semantically rich and sophisticated lexemes, but these are often used inappropriately as are tense markers and pronouns, as illustrated in Table 17.11.

The syntactic devices and operations in Marta's sentences appear not
to be tied to the semantic structures normally being mapped onto them,
suggesting, as with Antony, what might be considered a partially
independent or autonomous syntax, reminiscent of cases of mixed
transcortical aphasia and senile dementia whose performances have
been interpreted as evidence for an autonomous syntactic filter (Davis,
Soldi, Gardner & Zuriff 1978; Whitaker 1976).

TABLE 17.10
Examples of Marta's Utterances

The police pulled my Mother an' so I said he would never remember them as long as we live!
And another home, with the, our second home, now this my (in) fact third home I've ever have
*   lived in.*
I was like 15 or 19 when I started moving out o'home.
Well, we were taking a walk, my Mom, and there was this giant, like my Mother threw a stick.
I haven't shown you my garage yet, but Dad would be really hard.
We should go out an, um go out, and do other things.
Maybe I could play with a friend!
I have like second friends, . . .
. . . Somebody had his bangs trimmed in Iceland.

TABLE 17.11
Examples of Inappropriately Used Adverbs, Tense and Aspects Markers, and Pronouns.

And that's my regular friend, who normally will live by us, I think.
And she asked me out about a month.
And what hot air is rosen it, the air, she rise;
And air, air if you're really are innocent air, . . .
A third year I've ever been a student I've gotten, well, a ticket.
One's got married a week.
And I've/I'm nevers!
After awhile I gotten tried of it.
I like livin' away from home an' met friends.
I have like second friends an' now when I'm 18 or 19 I start moving out of, I think I wasn't, . . .

Marta's general intelligence and nonlinguistic cognitive performance stand in marked contrast to the level of her linguistic knowledge. Like Antony, Marta's general intelligence is difficult to assess, partly because of Marta's limited attention span and frequent failure to grasp the requirements of a task. Like Antony, Marta sometimes fails to understand or perform tasks readily and successfully performed by two-year-olds; like Antony, Marta's overall level of capacity appears to be close to, perhaps just beyond sensorimotor Stage VI; like Antony, Marta's scorable I.Q. belies her observed level of capacity.

Table 17.12 presents a profile of Marta's functioning in more specific cognitive areas. Marta cannot copy anything more complex than a simple bridge structure, draws at a preschool level, cannot count to 5, does not know her own age, cannot successfully attend to tasks involving three or more different items in an array. Once again we find a dramatic and striking contrast between performance on a range of

TABLE 17.12
Marta's Nonlanguage Profile

Ability	Marta's performance
Auditory short term memory	3-year level
Drawing	preschool level
Copying	preschool level
Classification	18-month level
Nesting	28-month level
Hierarchical construction	2-year level
Counting	cannot count to five; does not have one–one principal

cognitive tasks and linguistic performance, a contrast reflective of a dissociation between these areas.

Marta's case perhaps even more than Antony's illustrates the separability of those mechanisms responsible for the learning of syntax from those underlying the development of general intelligence and specific nonlinguistic functions. Like Genie and Antony, Marta's case suggests the existence of learning mechanisms specific to the learning of syntax.

Discussion

Obviously, in normal development, language unfolds in the context of social–communicative development and conceptual–cognitive development. This obvious phenomenological link between linguistic, social, and cognitive development has provided the impetus for the theoretical positions on language development prevalent today—the social/interaction model (Ervin-Tripp & Mitchell-Kernan 1977; Nelson 1977; Newson 1978; Snow 1972; 1977; Snow & Ferguson 1977; Trevarthan & Hubley 1978; Zukow, Reilly & Greenfield in press) and cognitive models (Bates *et al.* 1977; 1979; Corrigan 1978; Cromer 1976; Ingram 1978; Schlesinger 1974). How do data such as those just described bear on these models of language acquisition?

In the interaction model, there have been two major tenets. First, primary linguistic input to children learning language has a number of special properties. It is a greatly reduced, simplified, and repetitive version of the adult system; it is modified to correspond to (or be slightly in advance of) the linguistic level of the language-learner; it serves as an ideal model for presenting the structural regularities of the system to the child; it focuses particular attention on linguistic distinctions which may be difficult to discriminate. Second, the use of the simplified code in the context of familiar and frequently repeated social interactions and routines serves to focus attention on the communicative underpinnings of the code, provides abundant opportunities for imitation and rehearsal, and ties the use of the linguistic code to conversational settings from which to learn the basic principles of speech acts.

This model has typically placed the burden of acquisition on the environment, on factors external to the child which might facilitate the acquisition process for the child. As Bates, Bretherton, Beeghly-Smith, & McNew (in press) point out, however, "the identification of 'social' with 'external' is not logically necessary [p. 21]." The specialized language-learning environment may indeed provide an ideal model for language acquisition, which is nevertheless a child-driven rather than an environmentally-driven process. Since the mechanisms by which the child makes use of this specialized input have not been made explicit in this line of research to date, however, the question of whether there might be language-specific mechanisms at play is left unaddressed.

Cognitive models, in contrast, do address the question of language-specific learning mechanisms. The strongest position holds that there are no language-specific learning mechanisms, that language being simply one instance of the semiotic function is a direct outgrowth of sensorimotor intelligence and is explainable on that basis (e.g., Piaget 1980; Sinclair 1975). All three of our cases, as well as considerable other data, such as data from language impaired children and childhood hemidecorticates demonstrate the untenability of this position.

In a somewhat different cognitive model of language-learning, language is seen as formally parallel and therefore analogous to a number of other cognitive areas, for example, action and interaction schemes (Bruner 1975; 1977; Greenfield 1976; 1978). Here, too, the mechanisms by which the child learns grammar are never made explicit, but the implication is that he or she does so by analogy. Analogy-making, however, involves first recognizing that two systems are similar and then either constructing analogous schemes to represent these systems or mapping one set of schemes onto a formally parallel set of schemes. But to imply that language can be learned by a general learning mechanism of analogy without characterizing or specifying how a child constructs analogies between systems whose similarities are hardly direct or transparent merely begs the question of language-specific mechanisms.[2] Furthermore, our three cases and others like them suggest an underlying independence of action and communicative interaction abilities from the acquisition of syntax, suggesting that the cognitive principles subserving these domains are distinct from one another and require separate mechanisms to account for their development. Thus the "formal parallels" position neither explains nor is supported by our data.

A third differently formulated cognitive model of language acquisition holds that specific cognitive abilities are related to specific linguistic developments not by analogy, but by homology, i.e., an underlying source common to them both (Bates *et al.* 1979; Edwards 1973; Ingram 1978). To some extent, specific proposals made by

---

[2] There is an additional problem with this position in that research suggests little theoretical basis for the putative formal parallels in question (Curtiss, Yamada, and Fromkin 1979).

proponents of the second view (Greenfield 1978; Greenfield *et al.* 1972) correspond to this third view as well. (For example, formal parallels may exist as a reflection of a shared cognitive basis.) The question of general purpose versus domain-specific learning mechanisms is not specifically addressed in this model; but the implication of the position is that since language and related nonlanguage developments both depend on a third, shared principle, then the mechanism responsible for the acquisition of the shared principle could not be domain-specific.

Our findings support and refute different aspects of this view. The specific ties which have been proposed between language and nonlanguage developments include the nonlanguage sensorimotor achievements of object permanence, means–ends relations, knowledge that others can serve as agents, and use of communicative gestures, and the language milestones of acquisition and use of first words and word combinations. In all of our cases the individuals involved have, at the time we studied them, displayed both the language and the hypothesized related nonlanguage sensorimotor abilities. To this extent our findings are consistent with the claim that sensorimotor achievements may co-occur in normal development with specific language milestones because they depend on shared cognitive principles. The three cases discussed previously suggest nevertheless, that there was a possible dissociation in time between their acquisition of first words and first word combinations and their achievement of the sensorimotor knowledge found to correlate with these linguistic developments (i.e., those previously listed). However, since in two of the three cases we did not work with the children during language acquisition, and in the third case the delay in language acquisition was socially imposed, this potential refutation of the claim cannot be demonstrated by our data. What can be refuted by our data are claims of ties between these same sensorimotor abilities and syntax; claims of links between other nonlanguage abilities (e.g., drawing, symbolic play, classification skills, and general representational ability) and the acquisition of syntax; and claims of ties between action abilities such as nesting and hierarchical construction and syntax. In all three of our cases there are clear dissociations between development in these nonlanguage areas and syntax ability. And the dissociations are manifest in both directions.[3]

---

[3] It might be argued that the cases I've described are simply individuals with "blockage" in one domain, not children with truly independent development of language or nonlanguage function. If so, none of these cases would provide evidence against the hypothesis that there is a common cognitive basis for grammar and nonlanguage abilities. But if two areas are governed by the same cognitive principles, blockage must involve not

Our findings can be viewed as partial support for this third position. Our findings can also be viewed as refuting it in part, and irrelevant to other aspects of the position. In either summation, our findings suggest that the ties between linguistic and nonlinguistic development are principally those tying certain aspects of semantics to nonlinguistic cognitive development. The proposed ties, supported or not, leave the acquisition of syntax unexplained.

This conclusion is, in general, consistent with still another model of language acquisition—the "autonomous linguistic" position (Wexler & Culicover 1980; Roeper 1972; Chomsky 1975; 1980). This position holds that correlations in development between language and nonlanguage acquisitions do not preclude the possibility that language may be learned by principles unique to it. Correlations may be artificats of cortical maturation; i.e., both sensorimotor intelligence and first words and word combinations may reflect a certain state of brain maturation without one system being dependent on the other or otherwise nontrivially related to the other.

The anecdotal reports of the acquisition of first words by six months and first word combinations by 9–12 months in American Sign Language (McIntire 1977; Mindel & Vernon 1971; Schlessinger & Meadow 1972), if supported by systematic investigation, support a view in which language acquisition is tied to brain maturation rather than to sensorimotor developments; i.e., earlier maturation of visual cortex (Bay 1975) permits the earlier onset of language development in a visual modality. The only other explanation for these data would be if the proposed prerequisite or linked sensorimotor abilities are actually attained at a considerably earlier point in development than is widely assumed. Some recent findings (Bower 1974) suggest that this latter explanation may be correct. If this is so, however, none of the current formulations of cognitive models of language acquisition can be correct.

Regardless, our data cannot decide between the third cognitive model and the Autonomous Linguistic model. Our data fall somewhere between the two. While consistent with the autonomous linguistic

---

underlying capacity or cognitive knowledge, but domain or channel-specific factors or emotional factors affecting performance in only one of the areas. In each area examined, however, our subjects demonstrated an ability to perform up to a certain level of difficulty and not beyond. It seems unlikely that channel-specific or emotional factors could affect performance involving only a certain degree of complexity. Coupled with the fact that none of the subjects evidenced any central or peripheral impairments such as blindness, hearing loss, vocal musculature problems, apraxis, or obvious neuromotor impairments, it appears that the critical element affecting their performance in each area was cognitive complexity.

position regarding the potential independence of syntax in development, our data suggest that not all aspects of language are autonomous or independent from nonlanguage development. Certain aspects of semantics at least, in particular, the acquisition of lexical semantics and case relations, appear to be conceptually based and fundamentally tied to nonlinguistic cognitive development.

Our data, therefore, suggest language-specific learning mechanisms limited to and specialized for the acquisition of syntax and perhaps phonology and some complex aspects of semantics. Additional data from our work taken together with other recent findings suggest two additional features to these mechanisms: (a) they are tied to the left cerebral hemisphere in most individuals, and (b) they are operative only during a "critical period" in development—before 10 years of age.

In our work with Genie, we have found from experimental neurolinguistic testing, that Genie, a right-hander, appears to be using her right hemisphere for both language and nonlanguage cognitive functioning (Curtiss 1977; Curtiss, Fromkin & Krashen 1978; Fromkin et al. 1974). Behavioral measures have bolstered these experimental findings (Curtiss 1979). In direction and degree of asymmetry, in level of performance as well as style of performance (including error types), and in receptive linguistic abilities, Genie closely resembles the disconnected adult right hemispheres of split-brain subjects (Curtiss 1979; Zaidel 1973; 1976; 1978; Zaidel & Sperry 1974). Since Genie has two otherwise functioning cerebral hemispheres, and since she has developed intellectually and linguistically to a considerable degree since her discovery, we hypothesize that those aspects of language that Genie has not acquired are learned by mechanisms tied to the left hemisphere (in right-handers), while other cognitive abilities are not. This hypothesis tying language-specific (or syntax-specific) learning mechanisms to the left hemisphere but not other learning mechanisms is consistent with data from childhood hemidecorticates.

Dennis and her colleagues (Dennis 1980a; 1980b; Dennis & Kohn 1975; Dennis & Whitaker 1976; 1977) as well as others (Day & Ulatowska 1979; Rankin, Aram & Horwitz 1980) have demonstrated that the two cerebral hemispheres are not equipotential for language; even in cases of infant hemidecortication or hemispherectomy, the two hemispheres are equivalent in linguistic ability only with regard to phonological knowledge and the comprehension and production of lexical semantics and semantic relations (Dennis 1980a; 1980b). In all other semantic and syntactic abilities tested, the left hemisphere outperforms the right hemisphere. This is so despite the fact that the two hemispheres are equivalent in both verbal and nonverbal intelligence and cognitive stage. Other recent work (Grossman 1978; Kraft, Mitchell, Languis & Wheatley 1980; Read, personal communication; Risse 1978) also indicates that general intelligence and Piagetian cognitive abilities are bihemispheric or interhemispheric in nature, and not the special attribute of either individual hemisphere.

The differences between Genie's linguistic abilities and the considerably greater linguistic abilities of the left-hemidecorticates may be partially explained by the presence of Genie's left hemisphere, which while it may be nonfunctional for the acquisition of language, may still be exerting inhibitory control over the right hemisphere. Cases of infantile hemiplegia, where the diseased hemisphere is not surgically removed early in life show lasting effects of the influence of that hemisphere over the healthy one. An additional explanation for Genie's more limited language ability than the childhood left hemidecorticates may lie in the notion that there is a critical period for language acquisition. Genie may have been beyond a critical period for language acquisition when she began learning language, whereas the childhood hemidecorticates were not.

The evidence that language-specific learning mechanisms may be functional only during a "critical period," a period tied to childhood before about 10, comes again primarily but not solely from Genie. Genie is the only extensively studied case of first language acquisition beyond 10. In her case we have strong evidence that despite a decade of language-learning, Genie is limited to grammatically unelaborated or grammatically uninflected word strings—what Givon (1979) describes as a "presyntactic" mode or a "pragmatic mode of discourse." Given her continually increasing level of intellectual functioning, we may hypothesize that the acquisition of those aspects of language she has not mastered are critically dependent on age, somewhat as Lenneberg (1967) hypothesized. Such an interpretation is supported by data on language development in cases of pre or perinatal unilateral lesions (Rankin *et al.* 1980) or recovery from aphasia (Hécaen 1976; Woods & Teuber 1978), anecdotal data from cases of first language acquisition of American Sign Language past puberty, and data from other cases of feral and isolated children (Curtiss 1981a; 1981b).

The hypothesis that language-specific or syntax-specific learning mechanisms operate only in childhood also provides a possible explanation for an unrelated body of data—the differences between a pidgin (a simplified linguistic system which is created from contact between two or more mutually unintelligible languages—a sort of hybrid, a reduced linguistic system which closely resembles Givon's "pragmatic mode of discourse") and a creole (a full-blown linguistic system descended from a pidgin). (See Bickerton, this volume.)

A major difference between the two is that a pidgin has no native speakers, whereas a creole is (at least by many definitions) a native language for some community of speakers. A second major difference is the fact that a pidgin has greatly reduced morphology and limited syntactic devices, whereas in a creole such grammatical elements are richly exploited, although in a fairly invariant fashion, in contrast to establishment languages. Some prominent researchers on pidgins and creoles, for example, Bickerton (1977) and Naro (1973; 1979) have hypothesized that the source of difference between a pidgin and its corresponding creole is the involvement of a LANGUAGE FACULTY by the child acquiring the creole as a first language, and its unavailability for use by the adult pidgin-learner. What Naro and Bickerton refer to as the language faculty corresponds in part to what I am calling language-specific learning mechanisms. In its greatly reduced structural properties, pidgins look much like the simplified language systems produced by feral and isolated children older than 10 and Genie. Naro (1979) in fact has recently pointed out the substantial overlap between grammatical characteristics of pidgins and Genie's grammatical abilities. The implication is that the development of pidgins and "presyntactic" speech in general does not involve or require the utilization of language-specific learning mechanisms, or a separate language faculty.

Conclusion

All of these data converge to suggest that if there are multipurpose learning mechanisms such as those which might underlie the development of general intelligence, they cannot learn language, at least not certain aspects of language. Language acquisition does not appear to be simply one instance of the general cognitive development of the child. Certain early developing semantic knowledge may be correlated with specific cognitive developments because they are based on common cognitive principles, but syntactic development does not seem to be tied to nonlanguage cognition in this fashion. There appear to be language-specific learning mechanisms, and a separate human faculty of language of which these play a major part in development. This separate faculty of mind can be impaired selectively in childhood or adulthood, and can develop selectively in childhood or be left selectively intact in adulthood. Given an intact language faculty, with intact language-learning mechanisms and intact social and cognitive functioning, the human mind can do what so far no other form of intelligence can do: not only learn language but create language.

References

Bates, E., Benigni, L., Bretherton, I., Camaioni, L., & Volterra, V. (1977) From gesture to the first word: On cognitive and social prerequisites. In M. Lewis & L. Rosenblum (Eds.), *Interaction, conversation and the development of language*. New York: John Wiley and Sons.

Bates, E., Benigni, L., Bretherton, I., Camaioni, L., & Volterra, V. (1979) Cognition and communication from 9–13 months: Correlational findings. In E. Bates *et al.* (Eds.), *The emergence of symbols: Cognition and communication in infancy*. New York: Academic Press.

Bates, E., Bretherton, I., Beeghly-Smith, M. & McNew, S. (In press.) Social bases of language development: A reassessment. In H.W. Reese & L.P. Lipsott (Eds.), *Advances in Child Development and Behavior: 16,* New York: Academic Press.

Bay, E. (1975) Ontogeny of stable speech areas in the human brain. In E. Lenneberg & E. Lenneberg (Eds.), *Foundations of language development: A multi-disciplinary approach,* Vol. 2, 21–30.

Beard, R.M. (1963) The order of concept development studies in two fields. *Educational review, 15:*3, 228–237.

Bennett, T.L. (1978) A developmental pragmatic and psycholinguistic study of repetition in the speech of Genie. Unpublished doctoral dissertation. University of Southern California.

Bickerton, D. (1977) Pidginization, creolization: Language acquisition and language universals. In A. Valdman (Ed.), *Pidgin and creole linguistics*. Bloomington: Indiana University Press. Pp. 49–69.

Bloom, L. (1973) *One word at a time*. The Hague: Mouton.

Bower, T.G.R. (1974) *Development in infancy*. San Francisco: W.H. Freeman and Co.

Brown, R. (1973) *A first language: The early stages*. Cambridge: Harvard University Press.

Bruner, J.S. (1975) From communication to language: A psychological perspective. *Cognition, 3,* 255–287.

Bruner, J.S. (1977) Early social interaction and language acquisition. In H.R. Schaffer (Ed.), *Studies in mother–infant interaction*. New York: Academic Press.

Chomsky, N. (1975) *Reflections on language*. New York: Pantheon Books.

Chomsky, N. (1980). The linguistic approach. In M. Piattelli-Palmarini (Eds.), *Language and learning: The debate between Jean Piaget and Noam Chomsky*. Cambridge: Harvard University Press.

Clark, E. (1975) "Knowledge, context, and strategy in the acquisition of meaning." In D.P. Dato (Ed.), *Georgetown University Round Table on Languages and Linguistics*. Washington, D.C.: Georgetown University Press.

Clark, E. (1973) What's in a word? On the child's acquisition of semantics in his first language. In T. Moore (Ed.), *Cognitive development and the acquisition of language*. New York: Academic Press.

Clark, E. (1977) First language acquisition. In J. Morton (Ed.), *Psycholinguistics: Developmental and pathological*. New York: Cornell University Press. Pp. 33–72.

Corrigan, R. (1978) Language development as related to stage VI object permanence development. *Journal of child language 5:2*, 173–190.

Corrigan, R. (1979) Cognitive correlates of language: Differential criteria yield differential results. *Child development, 50*, 617–631.

Cromer, R. (1976) The cognitive hypothesis of language acquisition and its implications for child language deficiency. In D.M. Morehead & A.E. Morehead (Eds.), *Normal and deficient child language*. Baltimore: University Park Press.

Curtiss, S. (1977) *Genie: A psycholinguistic study of a modern-day " wild child"*. New York: Academic Press.

Curtiss, S. (1979) GENIE: Language and Cognition. *UCLA working papers in cognitive linguistics, 1*, 16–62.

Curtiss, S. (1981a) Feral Children. *Mental retardation and developmental disabilities, 12*, 129–161.

Curtiss, S. (1981b) Dissociations between language and cognition: Cases and implications. *Journal of autism and developmental disorders, 2*, 15–30.

Curtiss, S., Fromkin, W., & Krashen, S. (1978) Language development in the mature (minor) right hemisphere. *ITL: Journal of applied linguistics, 39–40*, 23–27.

Curtiss, S., Fromkin, V., Krashen, S., Rigler, D., & Rigler, M. (1974) The linguistic development of Genie. *Language 50:3*, 528–554.

Curtiss, S., Kempler, D., & Yamada, J. (1981) Language and cognition in development. Paper presented at the 1981 meeting of the Society for Research in Child Development, Boston, Massachusetts.

Curtiss, S. & Yamada, J. (1981) Selectively intact grammatical development in a retarded child. *UCLA working papers in cognitive linguistics, 3*, 61–91.

Curtiss, S., Yamada, J., & Fromkin, V. (1979) How independent is language? On the question of formal parallels between grammar and action. *UCLA working papers in cognitive linguistics, 1*, 131–157.

Davis, L., Soldi, N.S., Gardner, H., & Zurif, E.B. (1978) Repetition in the transcortical aphasias. *Brain and language, 6*, 226–238.

Day, P. & Ulatowska, H. (1979) Perceptual, cognitive, and linguistic development after early hemispherectomy: Two case studies. *Brain and language, 7*, 17–33.

Dennis, M. (1980a) Language acquisition in a single hemisphere: Semantic organization. In D. Caplan (Ed.), *Biological studies of mental processes*. Cambridge: MIT Press.

Dennis, M. (1980b) Capacity and strategy for syntactic comprehension after left or right hemidecortication. *Brain and language, 10*, 287–317.

Dennis, M. & Kohn, B. (1975) Comprehension of syntax in infantile hemiplegics after cerebral hemidecortication: Left hemisphere superiority. *Brain and language, 2*, 475–486.

Dennis, M. & Whitaker, H. (1976) Language acquisition following hemidecortication: Linguistic superiority of the left over the right hemisphere. *Brain and language, 3:3*, 404–433.

Dennis, M. & Whitaker, H.A. (1977) Hemispheric equipotentiality and language acquisition. In S. Segalowitz & F. Gruber (Eds.), *Language development and neurological theory*. New York: Academic Press. Pp. 93–106.

Edwards, D. (1973) Sensory-motor intelligence and semantic relations in early child grammar. *Cognition, 2*, 395–434.

Elkind, D. (1961) Children's discovery of the conservation of mass, weight, and volume: Piaget replication study II. *Journal of genetic psychology 98:2*, 219–227.

Elkind, D. (1966) Conservation across illusory transformations in young children. *Acta psychologia, 25:4*, 389–400.

Ervin-Tripp, S. & Mitchell-Kernan, C. (Eds.) (1977) *Child discourse.* New York: Academic Press.

Fromkin, V.A., Krashen, S., Curtiss, S., Rigler, D., & Rigler, M. (1974) The development of language in Genie: A case of language acquisition beyond the "critical period." *Brain and language, 1,* 81–107.

Gesell, A. (1940) *The first five years of life: A guide to the study of the preschool child.* New York: Harper & Brothers.

Givon, T. (1979) *On understanding grammar.* New York: Academic Press.

Goldschmid, M.L. & Bentler, P. (1968) *Concept assessment kit—Conservation, educational and industrial testing service.* San Francisco.

Goodenough, F. (1926) *Measurement of intelligence by drawing.* New York: Harcourt, Brace, and World.

Goodnow, J. (1977) *Children drawing.* Cambridge: Harvard University Press.

Greenfield, P. (1976) The grammar of action in cognitive development. In C.O. Walter, L. Rogers, & J. Finzinred (Eds.), *Conference on human brain function.* Los Angeles: BRI Publications Office.

Greenfield, P. (1978) Structural parallels between language and action in development. In A. Lock (Ed.), *Action, symbol and gesture: The emergence of language.* London: Academic Press.

Greenfield, P., Nelson, K., & Saltzman, F. (1972) The development of rulebound strategies for manipulating seriated cups: A parallel between action and grammar. *Cognitive psychology, 3,* 291–310.

Greenfield, P. & Schneider, L. (1977) Building a tree structure: The development of hierarchical complexity and interrupted strategies in children's construction activity. *Developmental psychology, 13:4,* 299–313.

Greenfield, P. & Smith, J. (1976) *Communication and the beginnings of language: The development of semantic structures in one-word speech and beyond.* New York: Academic Press.

Grossman, M. (1978) Grammatical and cognitive factors in processing linguistic reversals. Paper presented at the International Neuropsychology Society, Minneapolis, Minnesota, February.

Harris, D.B. (1963) *Children's drawings as measures of intellectual maturity: A revision and extension of the Goodenough Draw-a-man test.* New York: Harcourt, Brace, and World.

Hécaen, H. (1976) Acquired aphasia in children and the ontogenesis of hemispheric functional specialization. *Brain and language, 3,* 114–134.

Hulme, I. & Lunzer, E.A. (1966) Play, language, and reasoning in subnormal children. *Journal of child psychology and psychiatry, 7,* 107–123.

Ingram, D. (1978) Sensorimotor intelligence and language development. In A. Lock (Ed.), *Action, gesture and symbol: The emergence of language.* New York: Academic Press.

Inhelder, B., Lezine, I., Sinclair, H. & Stamback, M. (1972) Les débuts de la fonction symbolique. *Archives de Psychologie, 41,* 187–243.

Kellogg, R. (1969) *Analyzing children's art.* Palo Alto, California: Mayfield Publishing Co.

Kraft, R.H., Mitchell, O.R., Languis, M. & Wheatley, G. (1980) Hemispheric asymmetries during six- to eight-year-olds performance of Piagetian conservation and reading tasks. *Neuropsychologia, 18:6,* 637–644.

Laurendeau, M. & Pinard, A. (1970) *The development of the concept of space in the child.* New York: International Universities Press.

Lenneberg, E.H. (1967) *Biological foundations of language.* New York: John Wiley and Sons.

Lovell, K., Healey, D., & Rowland, A.D. (1962) Growth of some geometrical concepts. *Child development, 33:4,* 751–767.

Lovell, K., Hoyle, H., & Siddall, M. (1968) A study of some aspects of the play and language of young children with delayed speech. *Journal of child psychology and psychiatry, 9,* 41–50.

McIntire, M. (1977) The acquisition of American Sign Language hand configurations. *Sign language studies, 16,* 247–266.

Mindel, F. D., & Vernon, M. (1971) *They grow in silence: The deaf child and his family.* Silver Springs, Maryland: National Association of the Deaf.

Naro, A. (1973) The origin of West African pidgin. *Papers from the ninth regional meeting, Chicago Linguistic Society.* Pp. 442–449.

Naro, A. (1979) A review of pidgin and creole linguistics. *Language, 55:*4, 886–893.

Nelson, K. (1977) Facilitating children's syntax acquisition. *Developmental psychology, 13,* 101–107.

Newson, J. (1978) Dialogue and development. In A. Lock (Ed.), *Action, gesture and symbol: The emergence of language.* New York: Academic Press.

Nicolich, L.M. (1977) Beyond sensorimotor intelligence: Assessment of symbolic maturity through analysis of pretend play. *Merrill-Palmer Quarterly, 23,* 89–99.

Piaget, J. (1967) *Play, dreams and imitation in childhood.* London: Routledge and Kegan Paul.

Piaget, J. (1980) Schemes of action and language learning. In M. Piattelli-Palmarini (Ed.), *Language and learning: The debate between Jean Piaget and Noam Chomsky.* Cambridge: Harvard University Press.

Rankin, J., Aram, D., & Horwitz, S. (1980) A comparison of right and left hemiplegic children's language ability. Paper presented at the eighth annual meeting of the International Neuropsychological Society.

Reich, P. (1976) The early acquisition of word meaning. *Journal of child language, 3:*1, 117–123.

Risse, G.L. (1978) The performance of aphasic patients on developmental conceptual tasks of Piaget. Paper presented at the meeting of the International Neuropsychological Society, Minneapolis, Minnesota, February.

Roeper, T. (1972) Approaches to a theory of language acquisition. Unpublished doctoral dissertation. Harvard University.

Rosch, E., Mervis, C.B., Gray, W., Johnson, D., & Boyes-Braim, P. (1976) Basic objects in natural categories. *Cognitive psychology, 8,* 382–439.

Saltz, E., Dixon, D., Klein, S. & Becker, G. (1977). Studies of natural language concepts. III. Concept overdiscrimination in comprehension between two and four years of age. *Child Development, 48,* 1682–1685.

Saltz, E., Soller, E. & Sigel, I. (1972) The development of natural language concepts. *Child Development, 43,* 1191–1202.

Schlesinger, I.M. (1974) Relational concepts underlying language. In Schiefelbusch, & L.L. Loyd (Eds.), *Language perspectives—Acquisition, retardation, and intervention.* Baltimore: University Park Press.

Schlessinger, H.S. & Meadow, K.P. (1972) *Sound and sign.* Berkeley: University of California Press.

Sinclair, H. (1970) The transition from sensory motor behavior to symbolic activity. *Interchange, 1,* 119–126.

Sinclair, H.J. (1975) The role of cognitive structures in language acquisition. In Lenneberg and Lenneberg (Eds.), *Foundations of language development: A multidisciplinary approach.* New York: Academic Press.

Snow, C.E. (1972) Mother's speech to children learning language. *Child development, 43,* 549–565.

Snow, C.E. (1977) Mother's speech research: From input to interaction. In C. Snow & C. Ferguson (Eds.), *Talking to children*. Cambridge: Cambridge University Press.

Snow, C. & Ferguson, C. (Eds.) (1977) *Talking to children: Language input and acquisition*. Cambridge: Cambridge University Press.

Snyder, L. (1978) Communicative and cognitive abilities and disabilities in the sensori-motor period. *Merrill-Palmer quarterly, 24*, 161–180.

Trevarthen, C., & Hubley, P. (1978) Secondary intersubjectivity: Confidence, confiding, and acts of meaning in the first year. In A. Lock (Ed.), *Action, gesture and symbol: The emergence of language*. New York: Academic Press.

Wallach, L., Wall, A.J., & Anderson, L. (1967) Number conservation: The roles of reversibility, addition, subtraction and misleading perceptual cues. *Child development, 38:2*, 425–442.

Weisenburger, J. (1976) A choice of words: Two-year-old speech from a situational point of view. *Journal of child language, 3:2*, 275–281.

Wexler, K. & Culicover, P. (1980) *Formal principles of language acquisition*. Cambridge: MIT Press.

Whitaker, H. (1976) A case of isolation of the language function. In H. Whitaker & H. Whitaker (Eds.) *Studies in neurolinguistics,* Vol. 2. New York: Academic Press.

Wohlwill, J.F. & Lowe, R.C. (1962) Experimental analysis of the development of the conservation of number. *Child development, 33:1*, 153–167.

Woods, B. & Teuber, H. (1978) Changing patterns of childhood aphasia. *Annals of neurology, 3:3*, 273–280.

Yamada, J. (1981) Evidence for the independence of language and cognition: Case study of a "hyperlinguistic" retarded adolescent. *UCLA working papers in cognitive linguistics, 3*, 120–160.

Yamada, J. (forthcoming) Evidence for the independence of language and cognition: Case study of a "hyperlinguistic" retarded adolescent. Unpublished doctoral dissertation. University of California, Los Angeles.

Zaidel, D. & Sperry, R. (1974) Memory impairment after commissurotomy in man. *Brain, 97*, 263–272.

Zaidel, E. (1973) Linguistic compentence and related functions in the right cerebral hemisphere of man following commissurotomy and hemispherectomy. Unpublished doctoral dissertation. California Institute of Technology.

Zaidel, E. (1976) Auditory vocabulary of the right hemisphere following brain bisection of hemidecortication. *Cortex, 12*, 191–211.

Zaidel, E. (1978) Concepts of cerebral dominance in the split brain. In F. Buser & A. Rougeul-Buser (Eds.), *Cerebral correlates of conscious experience*, Proceedings of the Senanque Symposium, August 1977. Amsterdam: Elsevier.

Zukow, P., Reilly, J. & Greenfield, P. (In press) Making the absent present: Facilitating the transition from sensorimotor to linguistic communication. To appear in K. Nelson (Ed.), *Children's language*, Vol. 3. New York: Gardner Press.

18 PATRICIA SIPLE

Signed Language and Linguistic Theory

Current linguistic theory has been derived exclusively from the study
of spoken languages. Signed languages[1] are exceptional in that they are
visual–gestural, differing from spoken languages in their modes of
perception and production. Only within the last decade have signed
languages become acceptable to linguists and psycholinguists as
legitimate areas of study. Prior to that time, "signed languages" were
viewed as primitive communication systems lacking the special
properties required for classification as languages. It is not surprising,
then, that much of the early linguistic research focused on
demonstrating that signed languages should not automatically be
excluded from study, and that one signed language, American Sign
Language (ASL), was indeed a language. Fischer (1974), for example,
concluded from her study of language universals that, "By virtually all
criteria except those concerned with speech and hearing, the sign
language used by the deaf among themselves is indeed a language [p.
188]." Today, few would disagree. ASL satisfies all proposed language
universals except those requiring a vocal-auditory channel. More
importantly, when these channel specific universals are rewritten at
a more abstract level, both signed and spoken languages pass the test. To
the extent that universal language criteria are taken as a definition of
language, acceptance of ASL as a language is changing our very
definition of language as I will demonstrate in this chapter.

[1] Although the term "signed language" is not so commonly used as "sign language," it
will be used consistently throughout this paper since the point is to contrast SIGNED
language with SPOKEN language.

313

EXCEPTIONAL LANGUAGE AND LINGUISTICS

Once ASL had generally acquired the status of language, researchers set out to look for differences between signed and spoken language. Surely, the thinking went, such a drastic change as a change in modality must alter some of the basic characteristics of language structure and processing. Some of us (e.g., Siple 1978a) argued that there might well be modality specific language universals—characteristics of language that hold for all languages within a particular modality, but not across modalities.

An argument can be made that the vocal-auditory system is particularly adapted for language (see, for example, Studdert-Kennedy 1980). Through years of evolution, the vocal–auditory system and the structure of spoken language have become quite congruent. No such evolution has taken place for visual–gestural communication, at least not in recent history.[2] It can easily be seen that signed languages, like spoken languages, are constrained both by the anatomy and physiology of the production system (Mandel 1979) and perception system (Siple 1978b), and that an understanding of these constraints can further our understanding of the specific linguistic patterns that have evolved. The more interesting question for linguistic theory, though, concerns the possibility that within the range of producible and visually perceptible gestures, the visual–gestural language channel may require different underlying language structures than those of spoken languages.

Two issues have dominated the search for differences between signed and spoken languages. Both are related to a major purported difference between the auditory and visual sensory systems: The auditory system is said to be specialized for temporal information whereas the visual system is specialized for spatial information. Many psychologists (e.g., Kosslyn & Pomerantz 1977; Paivio 1971) have argued that spatial–pictorial information is processed differently from temporal–linguistic information. The strongest form of this argument claims that while the internal representation of auditory temporal–linguistic information is discrete and featural, visual spatial–pictorial information is represented in an analog, or picture-like format. Given this generalization, the structures and rules of signed languages should be continuous, or analog, in nature to be congruent with the visual–gestural communication channel (See DeMatteo 1977, for an expansion of this position). The often apparent transparency, or iconicity, found in signed languages lends intuitive support to this conclusion. Thus a major issue in sign language research has been to

---

[2] There are those, of course, who argue persuasively that the origin of spoken language lies in prehistoric gestural communication systems. See, for example, Hewes (1973).

determine whether analog or featural theories best describe signed language structures and processing, or more generally, whether the processing of signed language is more like that of pictures or of spoken language.

A second proposed area of difference between signed and spoken languages involves the co-occurrence of linguistic units. Because signs occur in space, the potential exists for higher-order language units to occur simultaneously. At some levels, of course, all language must be sequential, but the level at which a language becomes sequential may depend on modality. Klima (1975) for example, has argued that, in general, signed languages are simultaneous at the phonological level whereas spoken languages are sequential.

In the sections to follow we will examine these two potential areas of difference between signed and spoken languages, first at the sublexical, or phonological, level, and then at the lexical level. Despite the great potential for modality-based differences between signed and spoken languages, we will be surprised to discover that the similarities far outweigh the differences. Those differences between signed and spoken language which are purported to occur, will be seen to be more quantitative than qualitative. The broad range of underlying similarities between signed and spoken language, I will demonstrate, have great bearing on linguistic theory. Modality–bound characteristics will be seen to be peripheral to the two language systems, and it will be proposed that the study of the similarities between the two language systems can serve to enrich and strengthen our notion of abstract linguistic constructs.

For our purposes it will be important to review sets of experimental studies of processing signed languages, ASL in particular. Interestingly, in research involving signed language, the traditional psycholinguistic method referred to elsewhere in this volume has often been reversed; instead of attempting to ascertain the psychological reality of proposed linguistic structures, sign language researchers have tended to use results from conventional experimental paradigms to infer linguistic structure.

Visual–pictorial or discrete featural?

Sublexical Structure and Processing

Although it is possible for human speech sounds to vary continuously, all lexical units, morphemes or words, for all known spoken languages can be described with reference to a small set of speech sounds, or phonemes. Only a subset of these occur in any one language. Within a particular language, meaningful lexical units are formed from concatenations of a few of these arbitrary sounds with the allowable arrangements described by a finite set of rules. Prior to 1960, this duality of patterning was not thought to exist for signs. In that year, Stokoe published the first serious linguistic description of the structure of signs of American Sign Language. Stokoe (1960) presented linguistic evidence that ASL signs could be described with a finite set of visual–gestural units, or sign phonemes. Three categories of sign phonemes were necessary to describe signs: handshapes, locations, and movements. Each sign is articulated as one or more handshapes, performing one or more distinct movements at a location, or locations, described relative to the signers' body. Using this descriptive system, Stokoe and his colleagues have characterized over 2,000 signs (Stokoe, Casterline, & Croneberg 1965; 1976). Although it may be necessary either to add information about palm orientation as a separate phenome category or as additional hand-shape information to distinguish minimal pairs of signs like SHORT and TRAIN, Stokoe's work demonstrated that the sublexical structure of signs can be described by a finite set of discrete, arbitrary units.

In a spoken language, not all combinations of the language specific set of phonemes are found in the language. Phoneme combinations are constrained by a set of rules particular to the language. In signed languages, too, not all possible combinations of sign phonemes occur; there are definite constraints on sign formation. In spoken languages, specific phonological rules vary from language to language, but only a few types of rules occur for all languages. While a description of phonological rules is far from complete for any signed language, the types of phonological mechanisms that have been described for ASL are the same types described for spoken languages. These include assimilation, dissimilation, deletion, and insertion (Battison 1974; Battison, Markowicz, & Woodward 1973; Frishberg 1975; 1976).

If the same set of sign phonemes were used in all signed languages, and if sign formation for all signed languages were governed by the same set of formation constraints, the fact that these constraints exist would not be very interesting. It could be argued that the constraints were determined solely by the anatomy and physiology of the production and perception systems. Ease of articulation and perception is an important factor for phonological constraints in both spoken and signed languages. However, it is important for linguistic theory that spoken language structure is more tightly constrained within a particular language. In English, only a subset of possible phonemes are used and not all possible pronounceable sequences of these phonemes are permitted. Preliminary analyses of signed languages other than ASL suggest that the same statement can be made for signed languages. A comparison of Chinese Sign Language and ASL has shown that an overlapping but not identical set of sign phonemes exists for the two languages and the mechanisms governing morpheme, or sign, formation are not the same (Bellugi, Siple, & Klima 1979).

Given these parallels between signed and spoken language structure, we might want to revise our definition of phonology. Perhaps phonology should not be defined as ". . . the study of the sound patterns found in human language [Fromkin & Rodman 1978, p. 101]," but as the study of the sublexical patterns found in human language. Yet, before we take this step, we may want more evidence that the discrete units (sign phonemes) and the constraints on their combinations are a part of the user's knowledge of the language and play a role in the processing of signed language.

Even though a discrete featural discription of sign morphemes is possible, the processing of signs might take an entirely different form. Visual information can be represented adequately in discrete formats as well as analog ones (Hinton 1979; Palmer 1977); and it is a matter of current debate whether the nature of mental representation of visual–pictorial information (whether it is analog or discrete) can be determined experimentally (Anderson 1978; Pylyshyn 1979). However, there is some evidence that pictures are processed differently from language material, at least for early levels of processing (see, for example, Anderson 1976, and Nelson, Brooks & Borden 1974). Given this state of affairs in the psychological literature, questions about the nature of sign language processing need to be restated. Instead of asking whether representation is analog or discrete, a more interesting question is "Are signs processed more like pictures or more like words in those situations where we have reason to believe that there are differences between the processing of pictures and words?" Because signed language serves the same functions as spoken language, we might expect processing to become identical at some level. Depending on one's theoretical orientation, the question may be, "At what level of processing does processing of these two language types become indistinguishable?" Certainly, the frequency, intensity, and temporal characteristics of speech are "analog." It is the processing system that unitizes, categorizes, labels this information—that transforms it into a discrete representation. Do the same kinds of processing occur for signed linguistic information?

That native users of ASL possess a knowledge of the discrete sublexical structure of sign morphemes has been verified in many domains (See Bellugi & Klima 1979, and, especially, Klima & Bellugi 1979, for reviews of this work). Slips of the hand, like slips of the tongue, occur in signed language. These slips of the hand more often involve the transposition of phonological elements than of the whole signs. Signs often originated as iconic or mimetic forms. An analysis of historical changes in sign formation by Frishberg (1976) clearly indicates that signs have, over time, become more arbitrary and constrained, with phoneme components changing so that the resulting sign more closely agrees with the phonological rules of the language. When new signs are created, as they often are in jokes and in poetry, the new sign is frequently formed by substituting one sign phoneme for another in an existing sign.

Strong evidence for the signer's use of discrete sublexical structure of signs in language processing is provided by experimental studies of short term memory for sets of signs. These studies were modeled after studies of the short term processing of English syllables and words by hearing speakers of English. Results of studies of spoken languages indicate that speech is decomposed into phonological linguistic components and maintained for immediate recall. In fact, even when the items to be remembered are presented as written English words, the visual information is recoded into a phonological code. For spoken language, two general results implicate the use of a speech code for short term memory. The first is based on the analysis of errors in ordered recall. Intrusion errors (items substituted in recall for presented items) have been shown to be auditorily similar to presented items (e.g., Conrad 1964). In a second type of study, similarity of the lists themselves is manipulated and ordered recall of these sequences varying in similarity is compared. In general, auditory similarity decreases recall while visual and semantic similarity show no effect (see, for example, Baddeley 1966). While maintenance of an auditory (analog?) image of speech can account for some of these results, the preponderance of evidence suggests that speech is recoded into a discrete phonological linguistic code. Both error patterns and overall recall are best predicted by a linguistic featural analysis of the material presented (Hintzman 1967; Wickelgren 1965). Other evidence that the speech-based code is related to articulation and linguistic structure rather than auditory imagery comes from studies of cogenitally deaf individuals. In studies of short term memory for English letters and words, some deaf individuals appear to recode the information into a speech-based linguistic code and maintain the information in that form (Conrad 1972; 1979). There is, then, good evidence for speech-based, sublexical encoding of English words. Our studies of memory for signs parallel the studies of spoken/written language.

When signs are presented for immediate recall, several coding alternatives are possible: Semantic interpretations could be derived immediately and maintained; the signs could be translated into English words and maintained in a speech code; visual pictorial images of the signs could be maintained; or the signs could be decomposed into their phonological linguistic components and maintained in a sign-based linguistic code. Both intrusion error analyses and studies manipulating similarity suggest that, analogous to the findings for spoken language, signs are recoded into a discrete phonological linguistic format and are maintained in that form for recall.

Analyses of intrusion errors have been reported by Bellugi, Klima, & Siple (1975). Common intrusion errors made by deaf, native signers during the ordered, written recall of sign lists were compared with the signs that had actually been presented in the position of the intrusion, but were not recalled. Common errors, those that occurred more than once throughout the study, were paried with the list items for which they had been substituted. Independent judges, hearing-individuals who did not know ASL, rated the English translations of the pairs for semantic and auditory similarity and the signed forms of the pairs for visual similarity. These ratings were compared with similar ratings of common errors made by hearing individuals recalling spoken English words. Nearly all intrusion error–list item pairs were judged low in semantic similarity. Intrusion errors for signed lists were shown to be highly visually similar to the list items for which they were substituted, but low in auditory similarity to those list items. Intrusion errors for hearing individuals recalling spoken words were high in auditory similarity when compared with presented items.

These intrusion error results, while eliminating the semantic encoding and auditory recoding hypotheses, are compatible with either of the latter two coding alternatives for signs. Signs that have phonemes in common and are articulated similarly also look similar. Thus, signs similar in formation are pictorially similar. High visual similarity would be predicted for phonemic encoding and for imagery encoding. A closer look at list item–error pairs provides some support for the phonemic code hypothesis. First, the majority of common intrusion errors differed from the list items by only one sign phoneme; and in many cases, the resulting pairs differing in handshape were minimally different pairs according to a distinctive feature system proposed by Lane, Boyes-Braem, & Bellugi (1976). Given that signs had to be translated into written English words for recall, this result is striking. Second, in an earlier study (Bellugi & Siple 1974) requiring signed recall as well as in this study, a few intrusion errors showed a difference of only one sign phoneme, but a clear difference in visual similarity. An example of this type of pair is shown in Figure 18.1. The sign NEWSPAPER was given as an error for the list sign BIRD. The gross difference in location of articulation makes the two signs visually–pictorially quite different: yet, formationally, they differ by only the one sign phoneme, handshape and movement are the same.

Further support for the discrete phonemic code hypothesis comes from studies where list structure was directly manipulated. Signs vary in their degree of iconicity, the extent to which the sign itself depicts the thing or event it represents. A strong form of the imagery hypothesis would predict that highly iconic signs would be better remembered because of their stronger connections with already available visual representations. However, Klima & Bellugi (1979) report that a study comparing recall of lists of signs low in iconicity with lists of highly iconic signs showed no difference in recall as a function of iconicity.

When within-list sign similarity is manipulated, results support and extend the conclusions drawn from intrusion error data (Bellugi, Klima, & Siple 1979). In one study, recall of phonologically similar but semantically dissimilar sets of four signs was compared with recall of random, unrelated sets of signs. All signs had been used in previous studies and were matched for recall difficulty based on recall when the

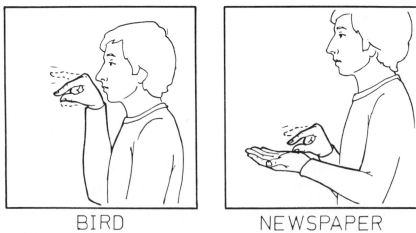

BIRD   NEWSPAPER

Figure 18.1. Illustrations of the ASL signs BIRD and NEWSPAPER which differ only in location of articulation. (Siple, P., Fischer, S.D. & Bellugi, U. Memory for nonsemantic attributes of American Sign Language Signs and English Words. *Journal of Verbal Learning and Verbal Behavior*, 1977, *16*, 561–574.)

signs occurred in random lists. Just as auditory similarity decreases recall for hearing individuals, sign formational similarity was shown to decrease recall for deaf individuals, fluent in sign language. On the average, 69% of the random lists were recalled correctly whereas only 52% of the formationally similar lists were correctly recalled. In this study, signs in similar lists were identical in location and were made with highly similar handshapes. They differed primarily in movement.

In a second study, the different categories of sign phonemes (handshape, location, and motion) were examined separately for their effect on recall. Recall of lists of five signs with one phoneme in common was compared with recall of random lists of the same signs used in similar lists in the same serial positions. Signs similar in location produced the expected decrement in recall. Similar handshape, on the other hand, actually increased recall. Movement similarity produced no recall difference; however, this may be a result of the classification system used for movement. These differential effects on recall suggest that an analysis of the signs based on these phoneme categories is carried out when signs are processed for maintenance in short term memory. Handshape phonemes seem, in this study, to serve a higher-order organizational function for sets of signs whereas location and movement phonemes do not. The extent to which these effects can be attributed to visual–pictorial list similarity can be evaluated by examining the average visual similarity ratings assigned to each list for each similarity type by hearing individuals who did not know ASL. Lists similar in handshape and in location were rated about equally similar visually, and more visually similar, on the average, than lists similar in movement; yet handshape and location similarity produced different effects on recall. Something about the phoneme categories themselves produced the differential effects observed; they cannot be entirely accounted for by visual–pictorial similarity as an imagery hypothesis would suggest.

Siple, Caccamise, & Brewer (forthcoming), provide much needed evidence for the use of a discrete phonological code in signed language processing outside the domain of short term memory. In this study, hearing and deaf individuals, varying in their sign language skills from completely unskilled to fluent, were asked to learn the English translations of 22 new, "foreign language," vocabulary items. Actually, these new signs were signs which were invented to include certain properties while following the rules of ASL sign formation. The 22 invented signs included 11 pairs of signs, each pair differing in only one sign phoneme. Subjects viewed all sign-word pairs and were then asked to select from four words the English word that had been paired with each sign. The four alternatives included the correct word, the word paired with the sign similar in formation, and two other distractor words. Sign similarity interfered greatly with learning; over 83% of all errors involved the choice of the word paired with the similar sign.

Formational errors (choice of the word paired with the similar sign) for the two members of each sign pair were combined to form an index of discrimination difficulty for the phonemes contrasted. A major question in the study concerned the possibility of qualitative differences in the patterns of discrimination difficulty as a function of the sign language skill level of the learner. It was argued that unskilled individuals would use general visual–pictorial processing operations to encode the signs. To the extent that skilled signers were using discrete phonological linguistic codes that differed from visual pictorial codes, qualitative differences were expected. The order of difficulty of the 11 sign pairs is shown in Table 18.1 for skilled and unskilled signers. Significant differences in order of difficulty were found for these two groups, reflecting differences in encoding strategies. The most difficult pairs for unskilled signers to discriminate were those that were most

TABLE 18.1
Percentage of Formational Errors and Ranked Difficulty of the 11 Sign Pairs
for Skilled and Unskilled Signers

	Skilled		Unskilled	
Sign pair[a]	Rank	Percentage of all formational errors	Rank	Percentage of all formational errors
Movement: Down/to right	1	5.1	3	6.3
Location: Temple/cheek	2	5.2	5	7.7
Location: Forehead/chin	3.5	5.9	2	6.1
Orientation: Palm left/palm in	3.5	5.9	1	5.8
Handshape: 3/K	5	8.1	10	12.3
Handshape: A/O	6	8.2	9	11.3
Location: Upper body/neck	7	8.8	4	7.6
Handshape: R/H	8	9.8	8	10.9
Movement: Inward/outward	9	12.0	7	8.7
Movement: Counter clockwise/clockwise	10	12.6	6	8.4
Orientation: Palm up/palm down	11	18.3	11	14.9

[a] Pairs are identified by the parameter differentiating them and a rough description of the difference between the two signs. Alphabetic letters refer to the closest manual alphabet letter for the handshape used. (Siple, P., Caccamise, F., & Brewer, L. Signs as pictures and signs as words: The effect of language knowledge on memory for new vocabulary. To appear in *Journal of Experimental Psychology: Learning, Memory* and *Cognition*. Copyright by the American Psychological Association. Reprinted by permission of the publisher and author.)

similar in terms of overlapping visual–pictorial information. This visual–pictorial similarity was not so detrimental to the skilled signers who could apply their knowledge of sublexical sign structure to decode and maintain the signs. An example of two sign pairs from this study shown in Figure 18.2 illustrates this point. The first pair, contrasting the handshape 3 with the handshape K, is very similar pictorially. That pair was among the hardest for unskilled signers, ranking tenth, while it was among the easiest for skilled signers, holding the rank of 5 in difficulty. The second pair, contrasting two facial locations, the temple and the cheek, is intermediate in pictorial similarity and was of intermediate difficulty for the unskilled group. These data provide evidence for the use of phonological linguistic knowledge when encoding new signs; and, additionally, suggest that this linguistic code differs qualitatively from a code derived from general visual–pictorial processing.

The linguistic and psycholinguistic data concerning the sublexical structure and processing of signed language lead to strikingly similar conclusions. Linguistic description of the discrete elements and rules governing their combination is analogous to that for spoken language. Modality affects the articulation of the language, but not the abstract, systematic linguistic structure. In the same way, the processing of signs is analagous to the processing of words from spoken language. Whether, in general, visual–pictorial processing is analog or discrete seems of little importance for the study of signed language processing. Very early in the language processing sequence, signed information is recoded in a discrete, language-based format in the same way that speech is recoded. The demands of the visual system have not been found to change the underlying formal language structure.

The words "phoneme" and "phonological" have been used throughout this discussion even though most textbook definitions would automatically rule out their use when describing signed languages. Stokoe and his colleagues (Stokoe, Casterline, & Croneberg 1965, 1976) initially developed a completely new vocabulary to describe the sublexical structure of ASL. They used words like "chereme" and "cheremic" to emphasize the difference in language modality. Yet, the accumulated linguistic and psycholinguistic data demonstrate the striking similarities at the sublexical level for signed and spoken language. It is confusing to use different terms to describe the same phenomena. Given the extent to which sign phonology mirrors that of spoken language, it can be argued that the meaning of the term itself should be made more abstract, or modality free; that the definitions of the terms used should reflect the abstract nature of the language phenomena being described.

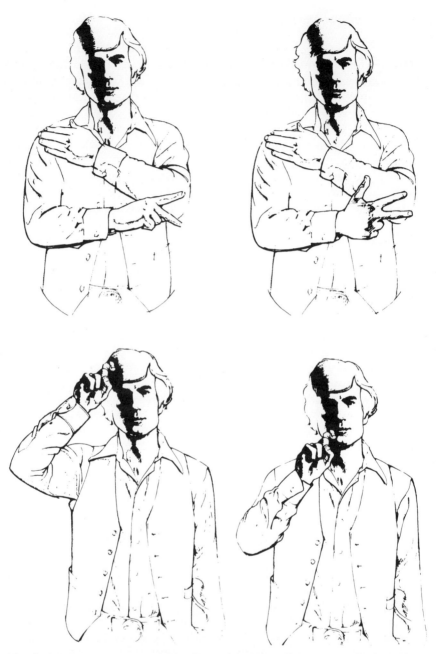

Figure 18.2. Line drawings of two invented sign pairs. The upper pair differ only in handshape; the lower pair, in location. (Siple, P., Caccamise, F., & Brewer, L. Signs as pictures and signs as words: The effect of language knowledge on memory for new vocabulary. To appear in *Journal of Experimental Psychology: Learning, Memory* and *Cognition*. Copyright by the American Psychological Association. Reprinted by permission of the publisher and author.)

Morphological Structure and Processing

Spoken languages differ in the types of mechanisms used to put together the meaningful units of the language, morphemes, to form ideas, or sentences. Some languages indicate case relations, tense, number, and many other semantic concepts primarily through the addition of inflectional morphemes to existing sentence elements. For languages in which these morphemes mark case relations, word order need not be used for that purpose and is, therefore, less constrained than in languages like English, which rely more heavily on word order structure to indicate case relations. Initial investigations of ASL confirmed a long held belief that sign order was relatively free in ASL (Fischer 1974, 1975). While subject–verb–object order is most common in modern ASL, there are many situations in which signs can freely occur in any sentence position. Generally, as sentence structure becomes more complex, sign order is more constrained. Given the relative freedom of word order, it should come as no surprise that ASL is a highly inflected language.

Studies of ASL morphology over the past 10 years have begun to uncover the mysteries of lexical and syntactic structure in signed language. For American linguists, somewhat biased toward looking for mechanisms and structures similar to those of English and other well-studied languages, the task of describing ASL at this level was particularly difficult. The productive use of bound morphemes to add to existing vocabulary was not seen in ASL. Instead, it seemed that the iconic nature of signs and their visual–spatial nature made them infinitely modifiable. This, along with the difficulty in being able to separate mimetic gestures from actual signs, led many to agree with DeMatteo (1977) that if an underlying structure existed at all, it must, in part at least, involve analog structures and processes. Now, with the work of Supalla & Newport (1978) and Klima & Bellugi (1979) and their collaborators, it has become clear that both derivational and inflectional morphological processes occur in ASL, and that these processes can be described by a discrete morphological structure analagous, at an abstract level, to the morphological structure of spoken language.

Evidence for a discrete, featural analysis for the derivation of ASL nouns and verbs has been elegantly presented by Supalla & Newport (1978). A distinction between nouns and verbs has been posited as universal to spoken languages (Hockett 1963). Thus, the Stokoe *et al.* (1965, 1976) claim that related ASL nouns and verbs were identical suggested that the noun–verb distinction was modality specific. Detailing the noun–verb distinction in ASL required a reanalysis of the nature of movement in signs since the distinction seemed to occur in that part of the sign. After providing a discrete abstract featural discription of movement in signs, Supalla and Newport show that ASL nouns and verbs related in form and meaning ". . . share handshape, place of articulation, and shape of movement but differ from one another by systematic changes in directionality, manner, and frequency of movement [p. 94]." They postulate an abstract underlying phonological form from which nouns and verbs are derived through the application of morphophonemic rules. This postulated abstract system, like that proposed for other derivational processes (Klima & Bellugi 1979), is, once again, analogous to that hypothesized for spoken languages.

Inflectional morphology takes a very advanced form in American Sign Language. As with derived forms, inflection is accomplished through the modification of one of the sign's parameters, or phoneme categories. Handshapes are used productively as classifiers to indicate characteristics of the referent of an associated noun, while changes in movement are used to express case relations, aspect, manner and other semantic distinctions.

The number of types of derived and inflected forms described for ASL is large. Bellugi (1980) says that as many as 50 different forms have been identified and that number is sure to increase. Changes in movement provide the mechanisms for most of these. Early descriptions of morphological processes in ASL (e.g., Fischer 1973; Fischer & Gough, 1978; Friedman 1975) demonstrated that these changes were not specific to the sign in question. Instead, the use of distinct changes in movement were shown to apply to a particular form class, or classes, and to be determined by syntactic considerations. Slow reduplication was shown, for example, to inflect verbs for continuous aspect; fast reduplication, for habitual aspect.

Once a number of inflected forms based in movement had been described, further analysis of these movement changes showed that these changes, while possibly iconic in orgin, could be analyzed into a set of component dimensions, each with two or three discrete values (Bellugi 1980; Klima & Bellugi 1979; Supalla & Newport 1978). It now appears that a finite set of spatial–temporal movement dimensions; including planar locus (vertical, horizontal), direction (upward, downward, sideways), manner (continuous, hold, restrained), and rate (fast, slow); will be sufficient to describe the large number of morphological processes in ASL involving movement. As Bellugi (1980) notes, "At this level of analysis, the system of features underlying ASL morphology exhibits a striking similarity to the system of phonemic features in spoken languages [p. 127]."

Finally, the processes by which these complex forms are determined also appear to be analogous to those hypothesized for spoken languages (again, see Bellugi 1980; Klima & Bellugi 1979; and Supalla & Newport 1978). Surface forms are hypothesized to be derived through the application of posited morphophonemic rules operating on abstract underlying forms of the signs. These abstract forms may never themselves appear as surface forms. Rules can be applied recursively to produce complex expressions. The order in which rules are applied is important. Different orders yield surface forms differing in meaning. While these forms may have an iconic origin, when the iconic nature of the inflected form runs counter to the meaning achieved by the systematic application of morphological processes, "iconic" meaning is overridden by rule governed meaning.

Classifiers are also used productively in American Sign Language (Kantor 1980; Kegl & Wilbur 1976). ASL classifiers consist of a set of handshapes which can be substituted for the handshape parameter of the underlying form of a verb or noun. As with classifiers in spoken languages, classifiers in ASL are used to indicate the size, shape, and other physical characteristics of an associated object. For example, the 3 handshape can be substituted for the underlying handshape of some verbs to indicate that a vehicle (e.g., car, train, bus) is performing the action. The use of classifiers is determined by syntax as well as by sign formational structure (Forman & McDonald 1978; 1979; Kegl & Wilbur 1976). While it is possible, given the spatial nature of signs, to vary some characteristics analogically through an infinite array, only a small set of classifiers are actually used in ASL. Both the discrete semantic categories for which these classifiers are used and the rule system governing their use are analogous to those for spoken languages.

As was shown for simple signs, the processing of morphologically complex signs appears to make use of the discrete, underlying units hypothesized in the linguistic description for initial encoding. Two studies, one a study of short term memory encoding (Poizner, Newkirk, Bellugi, & Klima 1980) and the other a study of the similarity of movements in signs (reported in Bellugi 1980), implicate the use of discrete movement features in the processing of signs.

In the Poizner, *et al.* study, four-item lists of signs were presented for immediate, signed, ordered recall by native signers. Lists contained from two to four inflected signs, the remaining ones being uninflected, basic signs. Both accuracy and error analyses suggest that inflected signs were encoded as a basic sign plus inflection. Accuracy of recall decreased as the number of inflected signs in the list increased; the easiest lists to recall were those with only two inflected signs. While some errors involved the misordering of entire items, many more involved the rearrangement of sign components and/or the deletion or addition of inflectional morphemes. Specific errors included recalling the basic sign components in the correct order, but transposing the inflections; and adding an additional inflection to an already inflected list item.

A second study reported by Bellugi (1980), argues persuasively that the movement features of inflected forms are processed independently of other sign features. Using a technique developed to study the perception of motion, small lights were placed at important locations on a signer's hands and arms. Sets of three signs (basic and inflected) were then videotaped in a darkened room so that all that appeared to the viewer were moving patterns of light against a black background. Scaling and cluster analyses of similarity judgments made by deaf individuals indicated that the movement patterns were perceived and encoded in terms of a finite set of postulated underlying linguistic dimensions of movement. Interestingly, similarity judgements by hearing individuals did not yield the same scaling and cluster analysis results as those for deaf individuals. This result supports the conclusion from our vocabulary learning study (Siple *et al.* forthcoming) that the discrete linguistic structure of signs is not based on general visual–pictorial processing.

Once again, linguistic properties are reflected in psychological processing. A finite number of derivational and inflectional morphemes in ASL make possible indefinite variety in ASL sentences. To the extent that it has been examined, the linguistic structure of these morphemes, and of the underlying forms to which they are applied, is discrete and featural. A system of rules analogous to those for spoken languages govern the application and interpretation of these morphological forms. Processing of linguistically complex signs involves a decoding based on the discrete linguistic structure rather than on general visual–pictorial processing. At this level, too, the spatial nature of the visual system has not seemed to affect language structure.

Klima & Bellugi (1979) have argued that there is one way in which the discrete featural discription of ASL structure differs from that of spoken languages. For spoken languages, the underlying structural units from which derivational and inflectional morphemes are formed are the same units making up the underlying structure of basic words, or free morphemes. For ASL, Klima and Bellugi argue that the dimensions of movement that describe movement-based inflected forms differ from those that describe basic lexical items. Bellugi (1980), following a suggestion by Lane, proposes that this difference exists because the two types of information (basic lexical and inflectional) co-occur. We will take up the issue of simultaneity in the next section. However, whether there are separate layers of information is still an open question.

Studdert-Kennedy (1980), referring to the work of Supalla & Newport (1978), suggests that the evidence for ". . . this separation into layers may be more apparent than real [p. 105]." A resolution awaits a more complete analysis of the underlying structure of signed forms. However, even if a separation into layers of information is shown to exist for some types of ASL inflections, such a separation seems not to be a general requirement of the signed modality. If it were, one would expect to find such a separation for handshape-based inflections as well, but that is not the case. Handshapes used in basic signs are also used as classifiers. In fact, Kantor (1980) has shown that the morphologically more complex usage of these handshapes is acquired later by children learning ASL as a native language.

Simultaneous and Parallel, or Sequential?

The strongest claims about differences between signed and spoken languages have centered around the issue of simultaneity. Nearly all investigators of signed language structure point out that the phonological units of spoken languages combine sequentially to form higher-order units while the phonological components of signs (handshapes, locations, and movements) occur simultaneously. Klima (1975) suggested that this difference may be a true modality difference, reflecting the visual–spatial nature of signs. All languages, spoken and signed, have both sequential and simultaneous structure. Klima says, though, that, "The sequential aspect goes one level lower in the hierarchy of unit types for spoken language [p. 250]." Spoken languages become sequential at the level of the phoneme, while signed languages become sequential at the level of individual signs. A modality-based explanation for this difference in level of simultaneity was presented by Bellugi & Fischer (1972). In a comparison of the rate of signing and rate of speaking, these authors concluded that signs take longer to produce than words, but simple signed sentences or propositions take about the same amount of time to express in both signed and spoken languages. If, as this suggests, there is an underlying cognitive constraint on the rate at which language must be transmitted in order to be processed efficiently, then signed languages must compensate for the additional time necessary to produce individual signs. One obvious compensating mechanism is to produce more of the information at the same time.

With the discovery of the productive derivational and inflectional systems in ASL, the issue of simultaneity has become more important. Within a complex sign, two or more levels of information co-occur; the derivational or inflectional information is embedded within the sign. This new evidence of simultaneity has led to even stronger claims of difference between signed and spoken languages. Klima & Bellugi (1979), alluding to the "simultaneous multidimensional changes in movement imposed on signs," say that the morphological processes of ASL ". . . are in form totally unlike such processes in spoken language [p. 109]."

Simultaneity, as it has been described by these authors, cannot be denied. However, we can question the extent to which this simultaneity constitutes a true difference from spoken language. To what extent is the information truly simultaneous? No still photograph really captures the essence of a sign. A sign occurs in time, and signs flow together through smooth transitions in handshape, location, and movement. At what point in time in the execution of a sign is the handshape of a sign determined? Its orientation? Its location? Its movement? Are the phonemes of a sign processed in parallel while those of spoken words are processed sequentially, or is processing similar for both signed and spoken language? Finally, is it true that simultaneity like that found in ASL is never found in spoken language? Is it possible that this difference is a quantitative rather than qualitative one? Information regarding these questions is scant. What does exist though, would indicate that differences related to simultaneity of production may be more quantitative than qualitative and that the processing of signed and spoken languages may proceed along very similar paths.

Some theorists (O'Connor & Hermelin 1978, for example) have suggested that the visual system is specialized for processing spatial information while the auditory system is specialized for processing temporal information. Even if this is the case, it cannot automatically be assumed that the processing of visual information proceeds in parallel, and the processing of auditory information proceeds sequentially. It has proven extremely difficult to find experimental situations which determine whether visual information from two spatially distinct locations is processed at the same time. Recently, some investigators (e.g., Shiffrin & Schneider 1977) have argued that parallel processing does occur, but only for very well practiced tasks in which the component processing operations have become automatized. Even this claim has not, however, gone unchallenged. In general, data can often be accounted for by either parallel or sequential processing models and it may not be possible to separate these models experimentally. If the nature of processing is unclear for spatially presented visual information, it is equally unclear for temporally presented auditory information. When modeling both auditory and visual processing, it has been necessary to propose that very short term sensory memories hold relatively unprocessed incoming information so that chunks of it are available simultaneously for further processing.

When signs are considered the processing issue is even more complicated since the visual information is in some sense simultaneous, yet it occurs over time. Two studies shed some light on the processing of ASL signs. Tweney, Heiman, & Hoemann (1977) report a study of the comprehension of lists of common signs by fluent deaf signers under various conditions of temporal disruption. Comprehension of signs was compared with comprehension of spoken words by hearing speakers of English under the same disruption conditions. While sign identification varied as a function of both frequency and duration of interruption of the visual signal, signs were identified correctly more often than spoken words in all combinations tested. It is impossible to determine, however, whether this resistance to disruption shown by signs is due to the co-occurrence of information in the signs, a greater predictability of signs given partial information, the fact that signs take longer to produce than words, or some combination of these or other possibilities. Another study, reported by Grosjean, Teuber, & Lane (1979) and summarized by Grosjean (1980) suggests that the different types of information in a sign are not identified simultaneously. Individual signs were presented repeatedly for increasingly longer durations and native signers were asked first to copy what they had seen and then to guess what sign had been presented. Orientation and location were the first sign characteristics to be copied correctly, quickly followed by handshape. The movement of the sign was identified last, and correct identification of movement was usually necessary for correct identification of the sign. These results suggest that the identification of sign phonemes is ordered in processing.

On-line processing studies of morphologically complex signs have not yet been reported. The Poizner et al. (1980) data suggest that inflectional information is encoded separately from the information in the basic sign. However, it is not known whether one of these types of information is identified before the other or whether they are processed in parallel with either part having the possibility of being identified first. Given what we know about the processing of speech, it might not be surprising to find that these two types of information are processed concurrently. Marslen-Wilson (1975) and others, have suggested that the processing of speech is parallel and interactive in the sense that phonetic, lexical, syntactic and semantic analyses take place concurrently, rather than serially. While there is a sense in which such processing is parallel, it is still possible that processing is not truly parallel in that a processing system could be switching rapidly from one level to the other. In support of his parallel interactive model, Marslen-Wilson reports data from a shadowing task with disrupted stimuli in which errors made by subjects are syntactic and semantic as well as phonetic. Interestingly, for similar studies of shadowing of ASL, Mayberry (1979) and McIntire & Yamada (1976) report errors related to these same levels of processing.

When compared with signed language, the sequential nature of spoken language is always emphasized, but just how sequential is spoken language in reality? Syllables and words are described as sequences of concatenated consonant and vowel phonemes. Yet acoustic analysis of spoken syllables and words has shown that this strict sequencing is often more in the linguistic representation than in the articulation. Within a syllable, co-articulation of consonant and vowel is the rule rather than the exception. Liberman, Cooper, Shankweiler, & Studdert-Kennedy (1967) have argued that this parallel articulation may be a requirement of the auditory processing modality. If phoneme segments were presented discretely at a typical speaking rate,the auditory system might be unable to resolve them.

Consideration of ASL phonology has led many to speculate on the structure of the possible analog to the syllable in ASL (e.g., Chinchor 1978; Kegl & Wilbur 1976). Chinchor (1978) has taken the position that handshape together with location and orientation, is analogous to the spoken consonant; and movement is analogous to the vowel. Using this formulation, she has reconsidered somewhat disparate phonological phenomena described for ASL. Whatever the status of this particular formulation, it seems clear that the issue of simultaneity at the sublexical level is far from resolved. Both production and perception of signed and spoken languages may be more similar than their present descriptions would have us believe. Observed quantitative differences in the use of simultaneity at this level may reflect no fundamental differences in language structure and processing.

As was indicated earlier, simultaneity on the morphological level occurs frequently in ASL, and it has been suggested that simultaneity at this level clearly distinguishes ASL from spoken languages. Such a conclusion may be premature. Forman & McDonald (1978; 1979) have argued that it is important to compare ASL with other types of spoken languages (especially non–Indo-European ones) before attributing this clear difference between ASL and English-like languages to modality. Navaho is a highly synthetic language with a well-developed predicate classifier system. When Forman and McDonald compared the Navaho classifier system to that of ASL, striking similarities emerged. Moreover, they point out that such a comparison may often result in a reanalysis of the spoken language system. In the tradition of analysis of language into sequential meaningful units, the Navaho verb system has been described as composed of a verb stem preceded by a number of prefixes. Among these prefixes is a small set of adverbial ones. Yet, according to Forman and McDonald, the Navaho "verb stem" carries meaning about the shape of the related object rather than the verbal meaning. This function of the Navaho verb stem is analogous to the function of certain handshape classifiers in ASL. The verbal meaning is carried, Forman and McDonald argue, by the prefixes in Navaho and by the path of movement in ASL. We have already seen that handshape and movement information are not simultaneously available in ASL signs. Given this high degree of similarity between Navaho and ASL, it would seem that if ASL is considered to be simultaneous in these situations, then Navaho must also be considered simultaneous; if the analysis of Navaho is presented as sequential, then ASL description should be presented as sequential.

Comparisons of other ASL derivational and inflectional systems with spoken language systems other than English have not been carried out; nor do we have anything like a complete description of the structure and processing of the complex movement phenomena found in ASL. Several questions about simultaneity remain: Do other signed languages show the same kinds of "simultaneity" found in ASL? Are there spoken languages which show similar phenomena? To what extent are the descriptions of similar signed and spoken languages analogous? A strong case for modality differences cannot be made until these questions are answered. The possibility clearly exists that even on the morphological level purported differences between signed and spoken languages due to simultaneity may be more quantiative than qualitative.

Summary and Conclusions

Comparison of the structure and processing of signed and spoken languages at the sublexical and lexical levels leads to a surprising conclusion. For the broad range of linguistic structures examined, changing language modality seems to have little, if any, effect on either language structure or processing. Given the arguments of some psychologists about possible differences in visual and auditory processing, this similarity is all the more striking. Researchers like O'Connor and Hermelin (1978) leave the impression that the visual processing system is unfit for processing temporal, linguistic information. They argue that, for written forms of spoken languages, the visual information is rapidly recoded into an auditory-based format and processing proceeds as if the information had been presented auditorily. I have shown that, for the structures examined here, language processing and structure transcend these supposed modality differences. This result is important for linguistic theory to incorporate. The structure and processing of language seem to be determined by abstract cognitive principles related to communication rather than modality specific ones.

Two issues important in the comparison of signed and spoken language—discreteness and simultaneity—have been considered here in detail. Analyses of both the sublexical and lexical structure have demonstrated that discrete featural systems analogous to those described for spoken languages best describe ASL structure. Furthermore, both linguistic and psycholinguistic evidence suggest that featural systems are a part of the signers' knowledge of the language and play a role in language processing. Very early in the processing sequence, signed language processing seems to be determined by language structure rather than by general visual processing mechanisms. "Evidently," as Studdert-Kennedy (1980, p. 102) suggests, "duality of patterning did not evolve . . . merely to circumvent limits on speaking and hearing, but . . . has a more general linguistic function that must be fulfilled in both spoken and signed languages."

Simultaneity does seem to be an important feature of signed languages. However, we must be careful to describe what is and is not meant by "simultaneity." To say that information occurs simultaneously in a sign is not to say that temporal characteristics are unimportant for linguistic description, nor does it imply that all information in a sign is available for identification at the same time. When simultaneity is examined more closely, it appears that similar kinds of simultaneity occur in spoken languages. It has been suggested that simultaneity as it occurs in the spoken syllable may be a product of demands of the language processing system—that the rate at which information should arrive for efficient comprehension would be beyond the resolving power of the auditory system if production were in the form of discrete units. Since the time necessary to produce sign units is even greater than that for spoken language units, it is reasonable that a greater amount of simultaneity should exist in signed languages. This expected quantitative difference does not necessarily imply any underlying structural difference or processing difference, however, beyond some very early peripheral sensory processing stage.

While there is a bias in the scientific community toward the demonstration of differences, the high degree of similarity between signed and spoken languages is of central importance to linguistic theory. This similarity suggests that, for the most part, the structure of language is not a product of the language production and perception systems, but is determined by more abstract cognitive activities related to communication. Given this generalization, the study of signed language can play at least two important roles in the formulation of linguistic theory. First, it has become clear that many definitions of linguistic constructs and specifications of linguistic systems have explicit or implicit reference to the spoken modality. With the specification of analogous phenomena in signed languages, it will be necessary to reformulate these definitions and structural systems in a way that is abstract, or modality free. Such a reformulation should lead to more rigorous theory when implicit intuitions about language as speech must be avoided. Second, as Forman & McDonald (1979) have suggested, finding similar phenomena in both signed and spoken languages may lead to a reanalysis of the spoken language data which better captures the systematicity of the human language system.

The conclusions presented here are based on a small amount of data from only one signed language, ASL. They must, of course, be accepted as preliminary. Comparative data are needed from other signed languages and more complete analyses of ASL at all levels will be necessary before the contributions of the study of signed language to linguistic theory can be fully realized. However, we may safely conclude that sophisticated cross-modality studies are necessary for our understanding of human language universals.

References

Anderson, J.R. (1978) Arguments concerning representations for mental imagery. *Psychological review, 85,* 249–277.

Anderson, R.E. (1976) Short term memory of the where and when of pictures and words. *Journal of experimental psychology: General, 105,* 378–402.

Baddeley, A.D. (1966) Short term memory for word sequences as a function of acoustic, semantic, and formal similarity. *Quarterly journal of experimental psychology, 18,* 362–365.

Battison, R. (1974) Phonological deletion in American Sign Language. *Sign language studies, 5,* 1–19.

Battison, R.M., Markowicz, H. & Woodward, J.C. (1973) A good rule of thumb: Variable phonology in American Sign Language. In R. Shuy & R. Fasold (Eds.), *New ways of analyzing variation in English* (Vol. 2). Washington, D.C.: Georgetown University Press.

Bellugi, U. (1980) The structuring of language: Clues from the similarities between signed and spoken language. In U. Bellugi & M. Studdert-Kennedy (Eds.), *Signed and spoken*

language: Biological constraints on linguistic form. Dahlem Konferanzen Winheim/
Deerfield Beach, FL/Basel: Verlog Chemie.

Bellugi, U. & Fischer, S. (1972) A comparison of sign language and spoken language. *Cognition: International journal of cognitive psychology, 1,* 173–200.

Bellugi, U., & Klima, E.S. (1979) Language: Perspectives from another modality. In Ciba Foundation Series 69 (new Series), *Brain and mind.* Amsterdam: Excerpta Medica; New York: Elsevier/North Holland.

Bellugi, U., Klima, E.S., & Siple, P. (1975) Remembering in signs. *Cognition, 3,* 93–125.

Bellugi, U., & Siple, P. (1974) Remembering with and without words. In *Current problems in psycholinguistics.* Paris: Centre National de la Recherche Scientifique.

Bellugi, U., Siple, P., & Klima, E.S. (1979) A comparison of Chinese and American signs. In E.S. Klima & U. Bellugi, *The signs of language.* Cambridge, Massachusetts: Harvard University Press.

Bellugi, U., Siple, P., & Klima, E.S. (1979) Remembering without words: Manual memory. In E.S. Klima and U. Bellugi, *The signs of language.* Cambridge, Massachustts: Harvard University Press.

Chinchor, N. (1978) The syllable in American Sign Language: Sequential and simultaneous phonology. Paper presented at the MIT Sign Language Symposium, Boston, April, 1978.

Conrad, R. (1964) Acoustic confusions in immediate recall. *British journal of psychology, 55,* 75–84.

Conrad, R. (1972) Speech and reading. In J.F. Kavanagh & I.G. Mattingly (Eds.), *Language by eye and by ear: The relationships between speech and reading.* Cambridge, Massachusetts: MIT Press.

Conard, R. (1979) *The deaf school child: Language and cognitive function.* New York: Harper & Row.

DeMatteo, A. (1977) Visual imagery and visual analogues in American Sign Language. In L.A. Friedman (Ed.), *On the other hand: New perspectives on the American Sign Language.* New York: Academic Press.

Fischer, S.D. (1973) Two processes of reduplication in the American sign language. *Foundations of language, 9,* 469–480.

Fischer, S.D. (1974) Sign language and linguistic universals. In C. Rohrer & N. Ruwet (Eds.), *Actes du colloque Franco-Allemand de grammaire transformationelle* (Vol. 2). Tubingen: Niemeyer.

Fischer, S.D. (1975) Influences on word-order change in American Sign Language. In C. Li (Ed.), *Word order and word order change.* Austin: University of Texas Press.

Fischer, S. & Gough, B. (1978) Verbs in American Sign Language. *Sign language studies, 18,* 17–48.

Forman, J.D., & McDonald, B.M. (1978) Investigations into the NP and the VP in ASL. Paper presented at the MIT Sign Language Symposium, Boston, April, 1978.

Forman, J.D., & McDonald, B.M. (1979) Constructing a phrase-structure grammar of ASL: Arguments for a noun-phrase and some cross-linguistic evidence. Paper presented at the NATO Conference on Recent Developments in Language and Cognition: Sign Language Research, Copenhagen, August, 1979.

Friedman, L.A. (1975) Space, time, and person reference in American Sign Language. *Language, 51,* 940–961.

Frishberg, N. (1975) Arbitrariness and iconicity: Historical change in American Sign Language, *Language, 51,* 696–719.

Frishberg, N. (1976) Some aspects of the historical development of signs in American Sign Language. Doctoral Dissertation, University of California, San Diego, 1976.

Fromkin, V., & Rodman, R. (1978) *An introduction to language.* New York: Holt, Rinehart and Winston.

Grosjean, F. (1980) Psycholinguistics of sign language. In H. Lane & F. Grosjean (Eds.), *Recent perspectives on American Sign Language.* Hillsdale, NJ: L. Earlbaum Associates.

Grosjean, F., Teuber, H., & Lane, H. (1979) When is a sign a sign? The on-line processing of gated signs in American Sign Language. Working paper, Northeastern University, Boston, 1979

Hewes, G.W. (1973) Primate communication and the gestural origin of language. *Current anthropology, 14,* 5–24.

Hinton, G. (1979) Some demonstrations of the effects of structural descriptions in mental imagery. *Cognitive Science, 3,* 231–250.

Hintzman, D.L. (1967) Articulatory coding in short term memory. *Journal of verbal learning and verbal behavior, 6,* 312–316.

Hockett, C.F. (1963) The problem of universals in language. In J.H. Greenberg (Ed.), *Universals of language.* Cambridge, Massachusetts: MIT Press.

Kantor, R. (1980) The acquisition of classifiers in American Sign Language. *Sign language studies, 28,* 193–208.

Kegl, J., & Wilbur, R. (1976) Where does structure stop and style begin? Syntax, morphology and phonology versus stylistic variations in American Sign Language. In *Papers from the 12th regional meeting of the Chicago Linguistic Society.* Chicago: The University of Chicago Press.

Klima, E.S. (1975) Sound and its absence in the linguistic symbol. In J.F. Kavanagh & J.E. Cutting (Eds.), *The role of speech in language.* Cambridge, Massachusetts: The MIT Press.

Klima, E.S., & Bellugi, U. (1979) *The signs of language.* Cambridge, Massachusetts: Harvard University Press.

Kosslyn, S.M., & Pomerantz, J.R. (1977) Imagery, propositions, and the form of internal representations. *Cognitive psychology, 9,* 52–76.

Lane, H., Boyes-Braem, P., & Bellugi, U. (1976) Preliminaries to a distinctive feature analysis of handshapes in American Sign Language. *Cognitive psychology, 8,* 263–289.

Liberman, A.M., Cooper, F.S., Shankweiler, D.P., & Studdert-Kennedy, M. (1967) Perception of the speech code. *Psychological review, 74,* 431–461.

Mandel, M.A. (1979) Natural constraints in sign language phonology: Data from anatomy. *Sign language studies, 24,* 215–229.

Marslen-Wilson, W. (1975) Sentence perception as an interactive parallel process. *Science, 189,* 226–228.

Mayberry, R. (1979) Facial expression and redundancy in American Sign Language. Unpublished doctoral dissertation, McGill University.

McIntire, M., & Yamada, J. (1976) Visual shadowing: An experiment in American Sign Language. Paper presented to the Linguistic Society of America, Philadelphia, PA.

Nelson, D.L., Brooks, D.H., & Borden, R.C. (1974) The effects of formal similarity: Phonemic, graphic, or both? *Journal of experimental psychology, 103,* 91–96.

O'Connor, N., & Hermelin, B. (1978) *Seeing and hearing and space and time.* New York: Academic Press.

Paivio, A. (1971) *Imagery and verbal processes.* New York: Holt, Rinehart and Winston.

Palmer, S.E. (1979) Hierarchical structure in perceptual representation. *Cognitive psychology, 9,* 441–474.

Poizner, H., Newkirk, D., Bellugi, U., & Klima, E.S. (1980) Short-term encoding of inflected signs from American Sign Language. In F. Caccamise & D. Hicks (Eds.), *Pro-*

ceedings of the second national symposium on sign language research and teaching. Silver Spring, MD.: National Association of the Deaf.

Pylyshyn, Z.W. (1979) Validating computational models: A critique of Anderson's indeterminacy of representation claim. *Psychological review, 86,* 383–394.

Shiffrin, R.M., & Schneider, W. (1977) Controlled and automatic human information processing: II. Perceptual learning, automatic reading, and a general theory. *Psychological review, 84,* 127–190.

Siple, P. (1978a) Linguistic and psychological properties of American Sign Language: An overview. In P. Siple (Ed.), *Understanding language through sign language research.* New York: Academic Press.

Siple, P. (1978b) Visual constraints for sign language communication. *Sign language studies, 19,* 95–110.

Siple, P., Caccamise, F., & Brewer, L. (forthcoming) Signs as pictures and signs as words: The effect of language knowledge on memory for new vocabulary. *Journal of experimental psychology: Human learning and memory.*

Stokoe, W.C. (1960) Sign language structure: An outline of the visual communication systems of the American deaf. *Studies in Linguistics, Occasional Papers,* No. 8. Buffalo, New York: University of Buffalo Press.

Stokoe, W., Casterline, D., & Croneberg, G.G. (1965, 1976) *A dictionary of American Sign Language on linguistic principles.* Washington, D.C.: Gallaudet College Press.

Studdert-Kennedy, M. (1980) Language by hand and by eye. (Review of *The signs of language* by E.S. Klima & U. Bellugi). *Cognition, 8,* 93–108.

Supalla, T., & Newport, E.L. (1978) How many seats in a chair? The derivation of nouns and verbs in American Sign Language. In P. Siple (Ed.), *Understanding language through sign language research.* New York: Academic Press.

Tweney, R., Heiman, G., & Hoemann, H. (1977) Psychological processing of sign language: Effect of visual disruption on sign intelligibility. *Journal of experimental psychology: General, 106,* 255–268.

Wickelgren, W.A. (1965) Distinctive features and errors in short term memory for English vowels. *Journal of the acoustical society of America, 38,* 583–588.

19 LORAINE OBLER

The Parsimonious Bilingual

What is having an accent in a foreign language, if not respect for parsimony? To the extent that learners perceive phonemes in the second language (L_2) to correspond to phonemes in their own language, it makes sense to convert the foreign phonemes to the corresponding L_1 phonemes which are more familiar and thus easier to produce. This phenomenon in the language learner is related to the monolingual phenomenon whereby if asked to repeat meaningful words or sentences, one produces them in one's own dialect. Even the severely demented monolingual patient reported by Haiganoosh Whitaker (1976) to produce no speech except in compulsive echo to speech around her, would transform what she heard into her own phonology. Of course, for L_2 learners there are countervailing forces, pushing them to master the "native" accent of the L_2. Thus a more sophisticated respect for parsimony might be reflected in construction of two distinct systems. Leopold (1939–1949) reports that his daughter, exposed to both German and English from birth, initially maintained a single lexicon, which included words with both English /r/ and German /R/, as if these were two separate phonemes. Her single system parsimony evolved to a dual system parsimony, with /r/ given its proper allophonic realization in the appropriate language context. Yet imperfect bilinguals among us will recognize that occasionally having recently switched (within a few words) from one language to the other, the wrong /r/ will be expressed even in one's first language. Moreover, certain bilinguals will evidence L_2 accents on their more proficient L_1 for an extended period during, and after, a period of speaking predominantly L_2. So the two drives toward parsimony (single system

339

Copyright © 1982 by Academic Press, Inc.
All rights of reproduction in any form reserved.
ISBN 0-12-523680-8

versus dual system) may be at odds in the nonfluent bilingual. One of my unconscious compromises has been the espousal of a single gutteral /r/ which suffices for Hebrew, French, and the nonflap Spanish /r/. A parallel behavior at the lexical level is reported by polyglots for languages learned after childhood; in searching for a word in one of those languages, words from the other post-childhood languages may come to mind, but words from the childhood languages, (even if a childhood language may be genetically closer to the language in question) do so relatively rarely. We infer that a storage system has been set up in which "foreign" words are indiscriminately mixed and kept separate from "native" words.

Consider the data from a bilingual Stroop test with regard to the notions of combined or independent language organization. As Stroop (1935) conceived this test, a monolingual first labels the color of 100 blocks of ink on a card. Five different colors are used, and the blocks are randomly ordered. After recording the baseline time to label this card, a second card is given to the subject, with the same instructions: The subject is to label the ink colors of 100 items. The items on the second card are color names, none of which corresponds to the ink color in which it is written. Subjects quickly catch on to the idea behind the trick, and start off at a fairly good pace, but soon find themselves making errors by reading the word aloud instead of labelling the color of ink in which it is written. Even if a subject is able to inhibit actually producing errors, the time taken to label the second card is invariably longer than the time for the first card, thus providing a metric for degree of interference.

In the bilingual version (Preston & Lambert 1969; Obler & Albert 1978) subjects are shown three cards, each of which is to be labelled twice, once in each of the two languages. With balanced bilinguals, the rise over baseline times is greatest when the language of labelling and the language in which the words are written are the same. However even in the conditions where the bilingual is to label in L_A and the words are written in L_B, the time to label is significantly greater than baseline time. We must assume that one cannot "turn off" perception of the language which is not being used for production, any more than the monolingual can "turn off" the reading interference on this task, a point we will return to in the second half of this chapter, when we focus on the bilingual perceptive system. For our purposes in discussing the production system, the phenomenon of interest is the error analysis. The only errors ever spoken in the crossed language conditions (words are written in L_A; the subject labels in L_B) are translations of the written word. Thus the subject is to say "black" upon seeing the word "vert" written in black ink; rather, she says "green". Even nonbalanced bilinguals labelling in their less proficient language do not break language production set on this task, thus indicating that at some level a switch has been "set" to produce only the appropriate language.

Thus a dual production system may be set up for bilinguals at the lexical level, whereas, we have argued, bilinguals with accents evidence a single system at the phonological level. Are we to assume that the balanced bilingual, who sounds like a native speaker in both languages, has mastered two phonological systems?

The evidence against dual phonological systems in the balanced bilinguals comes from a series of voice-onset time (VOT) studies administered to French–English (Caramazza *et al.* 1973), Spanish–English (Williams 1977 and 1980) and Hebrew–English (Obler 1978) bilinguals. In each study, balanced bilinguals were tested; that they were balanced was determined by a combination of self report, linguists' judgment as to no accent in either language, and language skill tests. In this paradigm, subjects are tested on two different days, one for each language. On each day instructions are in the language of that day, conversation is in that language, and all written materials are in that language. For the production task, subjects are recorded reading three lists of 30 words, one for each stop pair, *p-b, t-d, k-g.* For each pair, words beginning with each of the two sounds are intermixed, and each consonant precedes /i/, /a/, and /u/ equal numbers of times. Spectrographic measures are then made of the VOT, the number of milliseconds by which the voicing precedes or comes after the stop plosion, for each initial stop consonant, and the scores of the bilingual group are compared to scores of monolingual controls. As Table 19.1 indicates, our ten balanced bilinguals do shift set predictably between the two conditions, in the direction of the monolingual control groups. However, in no case do they perform like the monolingual controls ($p < .01$). Moreover, a strategy emerges across the three VOT continua whereby the bilinguals are closer to the Hebrew monolinguals for the voiced consonants, and closer to the English monolinguals for the voiceless consonants. Effectively, then, the bilinguals are tending toward the extremes, i.e., the earlier voiced consonant, and the later voiceless consonant. This is reflected in Table 19.2: in every instance the bilinguals' discrepancy between the mean VOT for the voiced member of a pair and the mean VOT for the voiceless member is greater than the respective discrepancy for the monolinguals. For production then, it would appear that these balanced bilinguals have a dual system governed by unitary principles which encourage maximal differentiation between the contrasting phonemes across languages.

TABLE 19.1
Group Voice Onset Time Means for Production
Measurement of milliseconds before (negative numbers)
of after (positive numbers) the stop burst.

	Unilinguals		Bilinguals	
	Hebrew group	English group	Hebrew condition	English condition
/p/	+25.6	+77.6	+58.0	+68.8
/b/	−110.8	−8.5	−96.8	−64.8
/t/	+33.9	+77.0	+73.8	+89.6
/d/	−95.8	−6.8	−85.5	−55.8
/k/	+63.7	+89.4	+93.2	+99.4
/g/	−101.0	+15.1	−92.2	−58.3

For perception, on the other hand, these balanced bilinguals presented a more unified system, intermediate to those of the monolingual groups. Anecdotal evidence which suggested that this would be the case came from my own experience with Arabic. Carefully, and well-drilled to distinguish the phonemes /x/, /ḥ/, and /h/ for production, I was also able to differentially discriminate among the three phonemes when tested on that task. However, to this day, I find I treat the three phonemes as allophones when specifically trying to look up a word remembered orally (rather than orthographically); the word has been enregistered as containing a metaphone /H/, which has for me three possible orthographic representations.

TABLE 19.2
VOT Differential between Group Averages for Voiced and for Voiceless
Stop Consonants, in milliseconds.

	Unilinguals		Bilinguals	
	Hebrew group	English group	Hebrew condition	English condition
p/b	136.4	86.1	154.8	133.6
t/d	129.7	83.8	159.3	145.4
k/g	164.7	74.3	185.4	157.7

In the perception component of the VOT study, subjects listened to a series of synthetic sounds ranging along one of the three voiceless–voiced stop continua (*p-b, t-d,* and *k-g*), and are asked to label each sound as being more like one or the other pole of the continuum. In the *pa-ba* series for our study, the subjects heard 37 different syllables, ranging from a VOT of -150 msec to +150 msec. The order of presentation was randomized at the Haskins Laboratory where the tapes were produced, and each syllable was heard 5 different times, in order to get a measure of consistency of labelling.

Analyses of the data from the perception labelling proceed by looking at the cross-over range where items are not consistently labelled either *pa,* or *ba,* for example. In Table 19.3 one sees that for English monolinguals, all items up to 5 msec post burst are labelled *b*, whereas items after 30 msec post burst are labelled *p*. For monolingual Hebrew subjects, there is a broader spread and an earlier crossover; all items up to −30 msec prior to burst are labelled *b*, while all items post 30 msec post burst are labelled *p*. For the bilinguals, the data are for the most part intermediate as the graph shows (Figure 19.1); and the same under both language conditions. That is to say in the interval where stimuli will not be consistently labelled *b* or *p* by both Hebrew and English monolinguals, the bilinguals will label items *b* more often than the Hebrew monolinguals, and less often than the English monolinguals. More important for the analysis I now propose is to look at the end points—the point after which subjects will no longer label all items *b* and the point before which not all items will be labelled *p*. These are displayed in Table 19.3, and discrepancies between voiced and voiceless members

TABLE 19.3
Voice Onset Time Perception Data 100% Labelling Boundaries

| | Monolinguals | | Bilinguals | |
	Hebrew group	English group	Hebrew condition	English condition
(p)	−30	+5	−20	−30
(b)	+30	+30	+45	+35
(t)	−5	+10	−20	−20
(d)	+35	+40	+35	+45
(k)	−10	+5	+5	−10
(g)	+35	+50	+45	+45

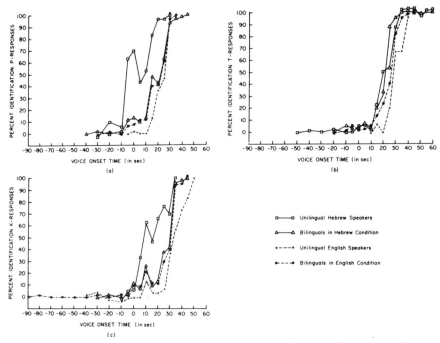

Figure 19.1. Percentage of voiceless stop responses as a function of voice onset time.

are presented in Table 19.4. Thus, Table 19.4 demonstrates that the bilingual subjects show a broader range on all six instances between the voiceless and the voiced stops than do the monolinguals. That is to say there is a broader range of perceptual uncertainty for the bilinguals than for either group of monolinguals, a broader range of acoustic stimuli

TABLE 19.4
VOT Differential between Perception Boundaries for Voiceless and Voiced Consonants, in milliseconds

	Unilinguals		Bilinguals	
	Hebrew group	English group	Hebrew condition	English condition
p/b	60	25	65	65
t/d	40	30	55	65
k/g	45	45	50	55

which they may label either p or b, depending on context, one would presume. The bilinguals, then, are maximizing the extremes of the two languages.

Further confirmation of a unitary perception system comes from these same subjects' comments on a dichotic test we gave them. In this test paradigm, different words are presented simultaneously to each ear and subjects are instructed to write down all the words they hear. In certain instances our balanced bilinguals heard words which shared phonemes across the two languages, for example, English *bite* and Hebrew /bayt/ ('house'), but our production task with monolinguals had demonstrated that the individual consonants and vowels were pronounced differently. To a trained linguist these differences were perceptible but our well-educated, balanced bilingual subjects would ask us which language we wanted them to write a stimulus word in. For perception then, it would appear strategic to set up a broad unitary system. This would additionally explain our Stroop results in which subjects could not meaningfully "turn off" or ignore the language not in use, for all it was in their interest to do so.

It would appear, then, that for the bilingual, optimal processing is achieved by a primarily dual system for production, which exaggerates the discrepancies between the two languages, and by a broad, primarily unitary system for perception, incorporating the extremes of the monolingual systems. Finding this distinction between the way the bilingual handles production and perception of two languages, and examining the different contingencies of the two processes, enhances the likelihood that separate process grammars are appropriate for production and perception of language in the monolingual.

Acknowledgements

The voice-onset time study reported here was carried out with the help of Edgar Zurif, and with Alfonso Caramazza in whose laboratory the statistics were carried out. Both studies reported here were performed in the course of long term collaboration with Martin Albert. Ursula Goldstein performed the VOT measurements.

References

Albert, M. & Obler, L. (1978) *The bilingual brain: Neuropsychological and neurolinguistic aspects of bilingualism*, New York: Academic Press.

Caramazza, A., Yeni-Komshian, G., Zurif, E., & Carbone, E. (1973) The acquisition of a new phonological contrast: The case of stop consonants in French–English bilinguals. *Journal of the Acoustical Society of America, 54*, 421–428.

Leopold, W. 1939–1949. *Speech development of a bilingual child* (4 vols.). Evanston, Ill.: Northwestern Press.

Obler, L., & Albert, M.L. (1978) A monitor system for bilingual language processing. In M. Paradis, (Ed.), *Aspects of bilingualism.* Columbia, S.C.: Hornbeam Press. Pp. 156–164.

Obler, L. (1978) A unitary phonological production system in balanced bilinguals. Paper presented at the Linguistic Society of America Meeting, Champaign-Urbana, Ill.

Preston, M. & Lambert, W. (1969) Interlingual interference in a bilingual version of the Stroop Color-Word Task, *Journal of verbal learning and verbal behavior, 8,* 295–301.

Stroop, J. (1935) Studies of interference in serial verbal reactions. *Journal of experimental psychology, 18,* 643–662.

Whitaker, Hai. (1976) A case of the isolation of the language function. In H. & H. Whitaker (Eds.), *Studies in neurolinguistics,* Vol. 2. New York: Academic Press, Pp. 1–58.

Williams, L. (1977) The perceptions of stop consonant voicing by Spanish–English bilinguals. *Perception and psychophysics, 21,* 289–297.

Williams, L. (1980) Phonetic variation as a function of second-language learning. In G. Yeni-Komshian, J. Kavanagh, & C. Ferguson (Eds.), *Child phonology,* Vol. 2, *Perception.* New York: Academic Press. Pp. 185–216.

20 JEAN BERKO GLEASON

Converging Evidence for Linguistic Theory from the Study of Aphasia and Child Language

By now we know that human beings are never ideal, whether as lovers, or, more to the point for this volume, as speakers and hearers. Linguistic theorists have generally avoided worrying about this lack of perfection by basing their theories on what should be the language of a mythical unflawed adult, someone who is beyond the stage of learning the language, but not so far gone as to be the least bit schizophrenic, senile, or aphasic. And, of course, the ideal speaker–hearer never makes jokes or waxes metaphorical, has not been to law school or cluttered up his or her brain with a second or third language. Moreover, the language spoken by the ideal speaker–hearer is truly spoken, not signed or written, and it is a durable established language, not one in the throes of birth like a pidgin-turning-creole or one that is dying on the lips of a few last speakers. Ideal speaker–hearers never make Freudian slips or play games.

With all of these exclusions and restrictions, one would hope that a great deal of progress had been made, both in the description of the core form of individual languages and in the elaboration of linguistic theory based on such descriptions. While this may well be the case, we are still left with a rather unsettled feeling about all the exceptional kinds of language discussed in the chapters of this volume. We want to know how we can account for them, and what contribution their study can make to linguistics. Ultimately, we must ask what a linguistic model should contain, whether it should include these exceptional languages,

EXCEPTIONAL LANGUAGE AND LINGUISTICS

and whether the exceptions themselves can provide any insight into general linguistic theory.

Obligatory Exceptions and Variations

The exceptional languages included in this volume can be (and have been) categorized in diverse ways. They fall into two very different broad divisions. The first kind are produced as it were obligatorily by their speakers as a result of atypical or noncanonical internal or external conditions. Thus, children or aphasic patients have no choice but to speak child language or aphasic language because of the very nature of their current state of linguistic ability. These are internally determined obligatory exceptional languages. Speakers of creolizing or dying languages also have little choice over the way they speak, but the exceptional conditions here are external and derive from an interaction of complex sociolinguistic forces. In the one instance the deviating conditions are in the speaker, and in the other, they are in the society. American sign language represents rather a combination of the two, since it is usually spoken by an exceptional population, but is a socially codified language that can be learned by anyone as a first or second language. By contrast, it is not possible for someone who is not aphasic or a child to speak more than a limited subset of aphasic or child language.

The second broad group of exceptional languages that has been presented includes such forms as bureaucratic and legal language, play languages, literary language, and other manifestations that fall under the umbrella of registral or stylistic variation. Speakers typically have voluntary control over a number of these kinds of language. It is important to remember that the first group of speakers may also produce the second kind of language: Children exhibit registral variation at every stage of language development, for instance. Very young children may use a whining tone with their parents on occasion, but not with strangers; and in their earliest games they may vary their speech to produce whispers, animal noises, or environmental sounds. By the time they reach nursery school, they have a clear but stereotypic idea about the features of various role-related registers, and speak differently when they pretend they are doctors, mothers, or babies. (Cf. Andersen 1977). Schizophrenic people can, and frequently do, produce legal documents; speakers of pidgins may tell jokes, and so forth.

While it is undoubtedly true that speakers of every one of the "obligatory" exceptional languages have control of a variety of different registers or styles within the language, research on these populations and subsequent theories have not typically taken this into account. For example, almost all theoretically oriented research on child language development has been based on only one variety of the child's speech; typically, samples recorded of the child talking to her or his mother at home. Research on aphasia has been based for the most part on "free" speech directed at hospital personnel in a hospital setting, typically a structured interview in which the examiner says something like "Tell me how you happen to have come to the hospital," or on the patient's speech in an experimental or testing situation. Only in recent times have researchers come to realize that variation exists in every kind of language, including the kinds that are thought of as exceptional to begin with. (See, for example Peters, 1977.) Ultimately, we will have to become sensitive to this point, and attempt to include in our descriptions of "child language" or "aphasic language" information about the variation that occurs in these languages. In this way, the study of one group of exceptional languages informs research on the other.

Beyond the enlightenment that this kind of study can bring about, there are many other reasons for studying exceptional languages, only some of which might be repeated here. No attempt will be made to discuss the sociological significance of the languages; nor is this the place to consider such things as the personality or intellectual characteristics associated with the use of any exceptional language.

Reasons for Studying Exceptional Languages

Perhaps the least complicated reason for studying these languages is that they represent unique and interesting linguistic systems and are legitimate areas of linguistic inquiry. In other words, they are worth studying per se.

While they are almost by definition marginal, they can or should provide information about the central language upon which each is based. Description of the core language can then be expanded to account for how the marginal system is possible. This does not mean that every marginal feature must spring in an orderly way from the core system or be totally predictable from it. In fact, as Ferguson points out, the existence of unpredictable features should alert us to the possibility of widespread phenomena of this type. Regularly occurring features in the marginal systems might also cause us to want to reconsider our linguistic analyses of the language; for instance, if essentially all competent speakers of English produce velar fricatives (*ugh!*), glottal stops (*uh uh*) and other nonEnglish phones in some varieties of their speech, phonological description might at least indicate this permeability of phonological boundaries.

The study of exceptional languages may provide insight into which parts of the core system are most basic and which are, so to speak, more expendable. Presumably, features that are always retained in exceptional languages represent the former, whereas those that never are belong to the latter category.

Exceptional languages can also illuminate the ways in which language is represented in the human brain; how it is stored, accessed, and retrieved. The processes of acquisition in childhood and dissolution in aphasia provide particularly valuable perspectives on the separable and separately represented parts of language. Converging evidence from these disciplines is beginning to provide some answers, both of a negative and a positive nature. One might begin with two instances where the evidence leans toward the negative:

Exceptional Languages are not Necessarily Simple

Exceptional languages are generally thought to be simpler than the languages from which they derive, but it is impossible to state what constitutes overall simplicity in a language. We can only point to some subsystems which MAY be hierarchically ordered and agree that within those subsystems, basic units are simpler than less basic units. This has been attempted for some parts of child language acquisition, notably the traditional areas of phonology, morphology, and syntax. Jakobson (1971), for one, has postulated a set of universal principles for the acquisition of phonological contrasts. According to this view, sounds like /u/ are more basic than the corresponding /ü/; they are acquired earlier by children and appear also to be more fundamental because a language does not exhibit /ü/ unless it has /u/, although many languages have /u/ but not /ü/. There are several other kinds of phonological simplicity that have been described (see chapters by Ferguson and Menn in this volume); single consonants are simpler than clusters, etc. But as Menn so carefully demonstrates, there is nothing simple about the phonology of child language; the actual relationship between child phonology and adult phonology is not easily derived, and different children at the same stage of development may choose very different phonological strategies, even though they may all labor under the same set of output constraints.

Within morphological systems there also seems to be some hierarchical ordering, at least in child language acquisition. In production at least, children learn the broadest, most regular forms first. Because it appears earlier in acquisition, the English plural /-z/ can be considered simpler than the plural /-əz/, which appears much later as a productive form. Subjects with Broca's aphasia, however, apparently do not find /-z/ simpler, or easier, since they are much more likely to produce plurals of words like *rose* than of words like *shoe*. Evidence from acquisition also suggests a syntactic hierarchy, in which simple active accusative sentences are simpler than, for instance, negative forms of the same sentences. (See Brown & Hanlon 1970 for a discussion of this.) Again, what is 'simple' for children may not be so for aphasic subjects. In fact, aphasic subjects may find it much easier to produce sentences like *Don't birds fly?* than sentences like *Do birds fly?* which is quite contrary to what the acquisition literature would predict. Goodglass, Fodor & Shulhoff (1967) have shown that in aphasia sentences that begin with stressed words are more likely to be produced than syntactically simpler sentences that begin with unstressed words. Children find it easier to produce utterances with few syntactic transformations, while aphasic subjects are more affected by the prosody of the utterances. In either event, the judgment that what they produce is simpler becomes a *post hoc* rationale.

Once we get beyond these traditional linguistic domains, the picture becomes even more clouded. If simplifying processes are involved in some of the exceptional languages, they cannot be specified because no postulated ordering exists in a number of domains. The pragmatic realm is a case in point: once we get beyond the earliest functions expressed by children learning language, such as DEMANDING or REFUSING, we find no real pragmatic hierarchy, either in theory or in child language itself, that would enable us to say what is pragmatically simple and what is not; one might observe, for example that OFFERING CONDOLENCES appears quite late in acquisition, but there is no reason to believe that complexity rather than life circumstances occasions this. What has become clear through the study of exceptional language is that some previous ideas about simplicity were in themselves simplistic.

Dissolution does not Mirror Acquisition

Numerous attempts have been made to investigate the speech of aphasic subjects using the same kinds of questions and techniques that have been employed in child language research in an effort to find some universals or at least commonalities in the acquisition and dissolution processes. As early as the nineteenth century, theorists had postulated, in for instance the Rule of Ribot, that acquisition in children and loss in aphasic subjects would mirror one another. Freud, in 1891, writing in his early work *On Aphasia*, used the term REGRESSION to refer to this presumed phenomenon; only much later did the term take on the psychiatric significance it carries today. Roman Jakobson (1971), although referring particularly to phonological patterning, expressed the same view when he said, "Aphasic losses reproduce in inverse order the sequence of acquisition in child language."

This idea has a great deal of intellectual appeal, and we are tempted to think that if both children and aphasic subjects perform in a particular way we have discovered something basic about language; but when we set about to test these two subject populations with comparable materials we find that in a number of ways their performance is different (Gleason 1978). Children, for instance, have more trouble than aphasic subjects with the morphophonemic variants of a given inflection, while aphasic subjects may be able to produce all of the variants of one inflection and none of another. Some aphasic speakers can produce all of the regular plurals but none of the possessives, which have the same phonological shape. While children have great difficulty with the syllabic /-əd/ and /-əz/ endings of the English inflections, the typical patient suffering from Broca's aphasia, as I mentioned earlier, finds these endings easier to produce than the /-s/ /-z/ and /-t/ /-d/ endings. Moreover, except in rare cases of degenerative disease, aphasia is not typically a condition that grows progressively worse. Usually aphasia has a sudden onset as the result of a cerebral accident, after which the patient gets progressively better, sometimes even recovering completely.

Thus, acquisition and dissolution do not represent the same process simply reversed. When people become aphasic their language does not peel back to earlier layers. If this were the case, we might expect those aphasic subjects with only a minimum of free speech to be restricted in their lexicon to words like *mommy* and *kitty* and *juice*, when in reality they are more likely to be left with a handful of ear-blistering swear words.

These are only two examples of questions about language where interesting but equivocal if not negative data exist. The study of aphasia and child language do, however, provide more positive contributions to our efforts to build a comprehensive linguistic theory. Again, let me sketch just a few general principles that one might derive from these data.

Speakers May Produce the Same Forms Without Having the Same Underlying Systems

Even if children and patients with Broca's aphasia produce the same forms, as they sometimes do, it would be a mistake to think that they have the same underlying linguistic organization, or the same competence. In the matter of metalinguistic awareness, for instance, children appear to be quite content with what they say, even when their utterances are ill formed so far as the adult language is concerned. A person with aphasia, by contrast, who repeatedly says *Baby cry* when the target is 'The baby cries', tends to express dissatisfaction with this production, often by rejecting it and trying the phrase again and again. Such a subject is thus clearly possessed of a linguistic system that allows for judgments about the speaker's own speech, while the child is not similarly endowed. Children's linguistic performance may be a more direct reflection of their linguistic knowledge, while aphasic speech may be flawed more as a result of performance constraints. There are a number of similarities between child speech and aphasic speech, but these formal similarities may stem from different functional bases.

Exceptional Languages May Reveal What is Most Productive in the Core Language

Certain forms of the core language may be more robust than others. The progressive -*ing* ending in English may have this kind of status, since it is learned very early by children and is the most likely to be retained in aphasic language. In terms of comparable data, it would be instructive to know what the status of the progressive is in the other kinds of exceptional language that have been discussed in this volume. If the progressive is the tense that we see most commonly in the other English-based exceptional languages, we have good reason to postulate that it is the most robust of the marked tense forms. One might ask the same sorts of questions of other languages; in German, for instance, it appears that the infinitive, rather than an inflected tense, is the verb of choice of aphasic individuals. One might ask which verb forms are learned early on by German children, which are likely candidates for major roles in creolized languages, and so on. Presumably such information would help to illuminate the essential structure of the language.

Exceptional Languages Confirm the Psychological Validity of Linguistic Descriptions

In building models of language, it is comforting to find that the units we have postulated are indeed separate units, and can be demonstrated to be so because aphasic patients can lose them differentially, and because children learn them separately. In this sense, the study of exceptional languages has upheld some traditional linguistic postulations. The existence of a variety of aphasia known as ANOMIA in which the patient suffers from a circumscribed loss of nouns, argues for the separate existence of nouns in linguistic systems. The fact that children learn inflections separately from substantives and that aphasic subjects can lose them separately, as they do in AGRAMMATISM, argues for the separate representation and storage of units that are also recognized in linguistic descriptions, thus revealing an isomorphism between formal linguistic analyses and the way the human brain itself has analyzed language.

Individuals Have Separate Productive and Receptive Systems

This is obviously true in a number of special linguistic situations. (see, for instance, the chapter by Nancy Dorian in this volume.) The semispeakers of a dying language understand but do not speak; they have excellent receptive systems and good sociolinguistic skills, but very little productive ability. Both child phonology and adult aphasic grammar also provide strong evidence for the existence of separate productive and receptive systems. This means that we cannot rely solely on production data, because they do not reveal what the subject actually either understands or could produce except for performance constraints. The free speech of Broca's aphasics, for example, is singularly devoid of grammatical variety; yet when presented with a structured elicitation task, even severely impaired Broca's aphasics are able to produce a variety of grammatical forms like questions, imperatives, negatives. They are not, however, able to produce complex embeddings (e.g., *She wanted them to be quiet*), or for reasons we do not understand, the future tense with *will*, even though they can understand these forms. What these subjects say does not represent what they know and what they can understand.

Exceptional Languages Reveal Important Components That Linguistic Models Lack

Differential impairment of processes not usually included in linguistic models reveals the models to be incomplete. One principle that we might propose is that anything that can go wrong separately in an exceptional language must be assumed to be separate in normal speakers as well. This means that such processes as initiating speech, continuing, stopping, recognizing foreign accents, choosing appropriate lexical variants, control over the pragmatic system, and countless others, are all part of normal speakers' linguistic repertoires, since they can all be isolated in one or another exceptional system. With regard to the lexicon itself, data from aphasic speakers who can recall elements of a word— but not the complete word (Goodglass, Kaplan, Weintraub & Ackerman 1976)—confirm phonological theory, while suggesting a processing hierarchy that must indicate something about the way that language is organized in the human brain. For instance, even when the word itself cannot be recalled, aphasic subjects may remember initial phonemes or clusters and such things as the number of syllables in the word. Any linguistic model of the lexicon must make place for some sort of listing with lexical items of an abstract representation of the shape of the word in terms of its initial sound, number of syllables, and other sublexical components.

Language May be Stored in
Larger Than Minimal Units

Finally, these studies reveal that memory plays an important role in linguistic systems. We have in recent years become so enthralled with the admitted power of generative systems, that memory, as an important process, and the possibly vast store of memorized units we each call upon every day, have somehow fallen into disrepute. Papers like Vihman's (this volume), and other work on second language acquisition, indicate that second language learners begin not so much with generative systems as with chunks, prefabricated routines, or unopened packages, as they have been called. Aphasic subjects frequently speak almost exclusively in what is called AUTOMATIC SPEECH in the aphasia literature, but would be called PREFABRICATED ROUTINES if they were children. The importance of routines in language acquisition, in second language learning, and in the everyday use of nonexceptional speakers has yet to be recognized. It is probably safe to say that we are not as endlessly creative as we are wont to think, and that we rely heavily on memory and routinized phrases in our ordinary production of speech. Linguistic models need to make room for memory, and take into account that in retrieving language the size of the units we deal with is variable: There are times when language is produced generatively, one word or one morpheme at a time, and there are times when much larger units, too large for the individual to analyze, are produced. It is thus possible to learn to use language appropriately months or even years before understanding all of the underlying units. While the extreme example of this might be the case of young Indian scholars who memorize pages of Sanskrit years before they learn what it means, it is also true of American children who learn to say *Trick or treat* on Halloween years before they know what tricks or treats are in other circumstances.

References

Andersen, E.S. (1977) Young children's knowledge of role-related speech differences: A mummy is not a daddy is not a baby: *Papers and Reports on Child Language Development.* Department of Linguistics, Stanford University, August. Pp. 83–91.

Brown, R. & Hanlon, C. (1970) Derivational complexity and order of acquisition in child speech. In J.R. Hayes (Ed.), *Cognition and the development of language.* New York: Wiley. Pp. 11–53.

Freud, S. (1953) *On Aphasia.* Translated by E. Stengel. New York: International Universities Press. [First published in German in 1891.]

Gleason, J.B. (1978) The acquisition and dissolution of the English inflectional system. In A. Caramazza and E. Zurif (Eds.) *Language acquisition and language breakdown,* Baltimore: Johns Hopkins University Press. Pp. 109–120.

Goodglass, H., Fodor, I. & Schulhoff, C. (1967) Prosodic factors in grammar—evidence from aphasia. *J. of Speech & Hearing Research, 10,* Pp. 5–20.

Goodglass, H., Kaplan, E., Weintraub, S., & Ackerman, N. (1976) The tip-of-the-tongue phenomenon in aphasia. *Cortex, 12,* Pp. 145–153.

Jakobson, R. (1971) The sound laws of child language and their place in general phonology. [Reprinted in A. Bar-Adon & W. Leopold (Eds.)], *Child language: A book of readings,* Englewood Cliffs, N.J.: Prentice Hall. Pp. 75–82.

Peters, A. (1977) Language learning strategies. *Language, 53,* 560–573.

Author Index

Subject Index

A

Abi dabi (English, play language), 187
Abstractness, in phonology, 251–252
Accent, foreign, 339
Acquisition, *see also* Language acquisition
　order of, 35, 53–54
Age, 33, 37, 45
Agrammatism, 204–205, 207, 211, 354
Akkadian, 157
Alliteration, 179
American sign language, 304, 313–335,
　348
Amerindian, 148, 153
Anomia, 354
Antony, 294–298
Aphasia, 31, 35, 36, 203–214, 218, 239,
　241, 348
　Broca's, *see* Broca's aphasia
　and schizophrenic language, 240, 244
　data collection, 349
　perseveration in, 234
Apraxia, in schizophrenia, 242
Arabic, 50–51, 53, 152
　as ritual language, 195
Argot, 84
Articles, 19–20, 182, 192
Arvanitika, 36
ASL, 304, 313–335, 348
Aspect, 19–22, 230

B

Baby talk, 49–50, 52–53, 57–58, 61, 153
Back slang (English, play language), 186–
　187
Bantu languages, 18
Bible, allusions to formulas from, 163
　poetic structures in, 152
Bilingualism, 31–32, 37, 44, 103, 158, 339–
　345
Bilinguals, French-English, 341
　Hebrew-English, 341
　Spanish-English, 341
Bioprogram, 27–28
Broca's aphasia, 204–208, 210, 351
Bureaucratic language, 7, 81–99

C

Canonical form, 178
Case grammar, 93
Cases, 44
Child language, 31, 35, 154, 159, 247–258,
　348–349

(Column 2, top)

Associations, in schizophrenic language,
　224, 236
Attention span, 297, 300
Autistic tendencies, 228
Automatic speech, 355

PERSPECTIVES IN
NEUROLINGUISTICS, NEUROPSYCHOLOGY, AND
PSYCHOLINGUISTICS: A Series of Monographs and Treatises

Harry A. Whitaker, Series Editor
DEPARTMENT OF HEARING AND SPEECH SCIENCES
UNIVERSITY OF MARYLAND
COLLEGE PARK, MARYLAND 20742

HAIGANOOSH WHITAKER and HARRY A. WHITAKER (Eds.).
Studies in Neurolinguistics, Volumes 1, 2, 3, and 4

NORMAN J. LASS (Ed.). Contemporary Issues in Experimental Phonetics

JASON W. BROWN. Mind, Brain, and Consciousness: The Neuropsychology
of Cognition

SIDNEY J. SEGALOWITZ and FREDERIC A. GRUBER (Eds.). Language Development and Neurological Theory

SUSAN CURTISS. Genie: A Psycholinguistic Study of a Modern-Day "Wild
Child"

JOHN MACNAMARA (Ed.). Language Learning and Thought

I. M. SCHLESINGER and LILA NAMIR (Eds.). Sign Language of the Deaf:
Psychological, Linguistic, and Sociological Perspectives

WILLIAM C. RITCHIE (Ed.). Second Language Acquisition Research: Issues
and Implications

PATRICIA SIPLE (Ed.). Understanding Language through Sign Language
Research

MARTIN L. ALBERT and LORAINE K. OBLER. The Bilingual Brain: Neuropsychological and Neurolinguistic Aspects of Bilingualism

TALMY GIVÓN. On Understanding Grammar

CHARLES J. FILLMORE, DANIEL KEMPLER, and WILLIAM S-Y. WANG
(Eds.). Individual Differences in Language Ability and Language Behavior

JEANNINE HERRON (Ed.). Neuropsychology of Left-Handedness

FRANÇOIS BOLLER and MAUREEN DENNIS (Eds.). Auditory Comprehension: Clinical and Experimental Studies with the Token Test

R. W. RIEBER (Ed.). Language Development and Aphasia in Children:
New Essays and a Translation of "Kindersprache und Aphasie" by
Emil Fröschels

GRACE H. YENI-KOMSHIAN, JAMES F. KAVANAGH, and CHARLES A.
FERGUSON (Eds.). Child Phonology, Volume 1: Production and Volume 2: Perception